ST. JOSEPH'S
INSTITUTE ORIENTAL
LIBRARY

D1499008

HD
8390.
D37
A5

TRADE UNION
LEADERSHIP

By the same author
POWER IN TRADE UNIONS

ARTHUR DEAKIN

TRADE UNION LEADERSHIP

Based on a study of
Arthur Deakin

V. L. ALLEN

ST. JOSEPH'S UNIVERSITY   STX
HD8390.D37A5
Trade union leadership;

3 9353 00105 6074

HD
8390.
D37A5
c.1

HD
8390
.D37
A5

ST. JOSEPH'S COLLEGE
INSTITUTE OF INDUSTRIAL RELATIONS
LIBRARY

HARVARD UNIVERSITY PRESS
CAMBRIDGE, MASSACHUSETTS
1957

ST. JOSEPH'S COLLEGE
INSTITUTE OF INDUSTRIAL RELATIONS
LIBRARY
195987

© V. L. ALLEN 1957

MADE AND PRINTED IN GREAT BRITAIN BY
WILLIAM CLOWES AND SONS, LIMITED, LONDON AND BECCLES

PREFACE

THIS book was planned and partly written while Arthur Deakin was alive and active as the general secretary of the Transport and General Workers' Union. Without his collaboration the book as it stands could not have been written. It is not a biography; it is a study of trade union leadership based primarily, but not solely, on an examination of one trade union leader, Arthur Deakin. At every stage support from him was necessary, and he gave it willingly. He agreed to have himself and his work scrutinized. Though he was a very busy man, at regular intervals for more than twelve months he discussed with me the theme of the book and the special problems which faced him. He gave me the opportunity to see him at work and he allowed me to examine the records of his Union. He did not try to exercise any influence over the formation of my opinions, and in some cases, when it was obvious that we were reasoning from different assumptions, we agreed to differ. The conclusions on all matters dealt with in the book are mine alone.

When Arthur Deakin unexpectedly collapsed and died on May Day 1955, while he was speaking at a Labour gathering, he had not seen what I had written. It would be sheer conjecture to say what his reactions to the book would have been. In many ways he disliked criticism but he was a truthful man and did not blink at indisputable evidence. Moreover, he knew that I was writing an analytical study. Had he lived to see the book completed, we would no doubt have had many more differences than we had; but I am equally sure that it would have been published in its present form. I owe Arthur Deakin a profound debt; and though this book was not written in any sense to repay it, I hope that in a small measure it will do so.

I wish to record my thanks to the Nuffield Foundation and to the Committee of the University of London Central Research Fund for the generous grants they gave me to finance the research on which the book is based.

To many people outside the trade union movement, a trade union appears as a large, impersonal, self-seeking body. In fact it is a collection of individuals bound, in the main, by a common belief, but influenced by most of the frailties of which human nature is capable. As a member of a trade union for just over seventeen years I have witnessed these weaknesses, but I have also seen in operation the powerful force of goodwill which dominates trade union activity in times of need. My need on this occasion was for information; one which, it is often said, is brusquely rejected by trade unions. This was not my experience. My knowledge of the Transport and General Workers' Union has been built up with the help of hundreds of its members whom I have had the pleasure to meet. I count scores of these members as my friends. Union officials at all levels, lay and full-time, have given freely of their time and knowledge. I am grateful to them all. In particular I would like to thank Mr. A. J. Chandler who read my typescript and discussed many matters with me; Miss Ivy Saunders who was Arthur Deakin's secretary; and all those members of the Union head office who by their goodwill made a difficult task easier and who tolerated my presence at most inconvenient times and places. Miss Ellen McCullough unfailingly encouraged me from the time when the book existed only as a germ of an idea, and I was diffident about its development, until its completion. She also read my typescript stage by stage. Mr. A. J. Corfield kindly read part of the typescript.

Among those outside the Transport and General Workers' Union I would like to thank Sir Lincoln Evans, Sir Frederick Leggett, Sir Walter Monckton, and Dr. Harold Clay, each of whom discussed Arthur Deakin's activities with me; my wife, who read through the typescript, and Mr. D. G. Macrae who criticized an early draft of the book and helped me to eliminate much that was extraneous. I am grateful to B. H. Blackwell Ltd. for allowing me to quote from *Labour Relations in London Transport* by H. A. Clegg; to the editors of the *British Journal of Sociology* for permission to reproduce as Chapter II an article by me which they published in December 1956; and to Methuen and Co., Ltd., for leave to use a quotation from *Up and Down Stream* by Harry Gosling.

My debts to others are legion but I wish to emphasize that the responsibility for everything in this book is mine.

V. L. ALLEN

LONDON
January 1957

CONTENTS

*The frontispiece is reproduced by permission of Picture
Post Library*

TABLES

NOTES ON TERMINOLOGY

1. The Strike called by the General Council of the Trades Union Congress on 3 May 1926 in support of the Miners' Federation is in this text termed the General Strike. Sticklers for nomenclature may hold that the Strike was not a General one but was a National Strike; and they may summon to their support the authority of the General Council of the Trades Union Congress itself, which refers to the National Strike in its official documents. Common usage, however, calls it the General Strike for good reasons unassociated with Syndicalist theory. It was as general in its scope as any strike could afford to be in this country. And any trade union can call a National Strike, but only a body with the full authority of the Trade Union Movement can call a General Strike such as occurred on 3 May 1926.

2. At the Rules Conference of the Transport and General Workers' Union in 1950 all references to 'Areas' in the organization and administration of the Union were deleted, and instead of 'Area' the word 'Region' was substituted. Throughout this text the word 'Region' is used even when the references are to the Union before 1950; thus, one will read of Regional Committees, Regional Secretaries, Regional Trade Group Committees, etc., in the Union for the whole of the period covered. The reasons for this are clear: it provides consistency and it is in line with current usage. There is, however, one important exception. All quotations remain as they were made, so that for the period up to 1950 'Areas' are referred to in some quotations. It is hoped that the reader will bear this in mind, and will not regard it either as a reference to a form of organization in the Union not hitherto mentioned or as an inconsistency.

Chapter One

INTRODUCTION

THERE are few people in Britain with more obvious facilities for exercising power than the general secretaries and full-time presidents of large trade unions. They are not the constitutional leaders of their unions, for in every case the authority to take final decisions rests with an executive committee or a union conference; and often their duties and rights are prescribed by their union constitutions purposely to make them the servants and not the masters of the ordinary members. Nevertheless they are the *de facto* leaders of trade unions. They are the chief executives of their organizations and they act at the most vital of the trade union decision-making stages with the confidence and authority which knowledge, understanding, and skill create. By comparison, even the most skilful of the lay members, whether as individuals or collectively, are as amateurs. The power of trade union leaders in relation to the lay members of their unions has already been examined.[1] Without doubt they make the most important individual contributions to the determination of trade union policy decisions.

The full use of power in trade unions involves implementing decisions as well as making them. It is difficult to isolate and observe the part which trade union leaders play in this process, for to get things done they depend on union organizations and administrations which are subject to many influences and which develop their own responses and momentum.

In recognition of their positions of authority, trade union leaders are drawn into the spheres of high-level decision-making in industry and politics. Their impact in these spheres, and therefore their ability to influence the course of events with which trade unions are directly concerned, is the measure of their real power. Trade union leaders may take and implement decisions within their own organizations, but such power counts for little unless it can be exerted outside trade unions in the interests of their members. The full effect of this power is hidden from view by the interactions of the many variable factors which operate in the society to which trade unions belong.

Neither the part which trade union leaders have played in implementing decisions nor their influence over industrial and political

[1] See *Power in Trade Unions* by V. L. Allen, Part II.

events has previously been examined in detail, yet both have been the subject of much concern and speculation by people inside and outside the trade union movement. In the light of this it seems desirable to discover the functional importance of trade union leaders. This book is intended as a contribution towards that end. There were three possible ways in which the task could be tackled:

(a) *By attempting to give an overall picture.* An assessment of the power of trade union leaders would involve an examination of the complex factors which make up the situations in which they operate, including the quality of the men themselves. But such is the variation between the situations that a general examination of the power of trade union leaders would not be meaningful.

(b) *By executing a number of separate studies of trade union leaders showing the relative strengths of the many factors involved and enabling the power exercised by each trade union leader to be evaluated.* This would be a long and difficult course to pursue. Trade union leaders are busy men, not easily accessible and not readily willing to be the subject of close scrutiny by outside investigators. The activities of some of them, moreover, would not justify detailed studies even if they were permitted.

(c) *By making a close study of a powerful trade union leader and using the study as a base for an examination of some wider implications of trade union leadership.* The evidence in this case would not permit generalizations to be made from it, but if a man of sufficient standing in the trade union movement could be studied it would be permissible to draw some conclusions about the power of lesser trade union leaders.

I chose to use the third method. The first step was to select a trade union leader of sufficient stature and to obtain his permission to study his activities. The most obvious choice when I considered the matter early in 1954 was Arthur Deakin, the General Secretary of the Transport and General Workers' Union. His Union had about 1,300,000 members and was by far the largest in Britain. He was a dominant member of the General Council of the Trades Union Congress, prominent in international trade union circles, and he showed a determination to exercise his power. Arthur Deakin possessed all the qualifications for the study I had in mind. He agreed to co-operate with me in examining his activities from 1940 until his scheduled retirement in November 1955. I was allowed to meet him at regular intervals, to accompany him on official Union business, and to examine Union documents and records.[1]

---

[1] A factor which eased my approach to Deakin, and which influenced his attitude towards me, was that I came from the small north Welsh community where Deakin worked for more than twenty years and which he regarded as his home. He had been a governor of my former school. This common tie profoundly affected our relationship and undoubtedly simplified my task.

I intended to base the study on the assumption that Arthur Deakin exercised power both inside and outside his Union. This assumption was derived from the public portrayal of Deakin and appeared to be valid. The study was to start with a short description of Deakin's background, including some mention of the development of the Transport and General Workers' Union and of the activities of his predecessor, Ernest Bevin. The remainder of the study was to examine Deakin at work, so as to reveal the manner in which he reached decisions, exercised control, used his influence, and generally imposed his will on men and events; and to enable inferences to be drawn which would be of value in assessing the power of other trade union leaders. The execution of the plan depended on the amount and nature of the information I could secure. There was sufficient information but its nature was such as to require substantial changes in the initial plan.

I began with information about Arthur Deakin's background. He was born at Sutton Coldfield, Warwickshire, on 11 November 1890. His father was a village cobbler and it was in the atmosphere of a cobbler's shop that Arthur Deakin spent the first ten years of his life. In 1900 he moved with his parents to Dowlais, south Wales, and it was there that he took his first job and joined a trade union. He became a roll turner in the tin plate trade and enrolled as a member of the National Union of Gas Workers and General Labourers. Shortly afterwards, in 1910, Deakin took a job as a roll turner in a steel plant in Shotton, north Wales. He relinquished his membership of the Gasworkers' Union and for a brief period belonged to the Amalgamated Society of Engineers. At the same time he joined the British Roll Turners' Trade Society. In 1911 he transferred from the Amalgamated Society of Engineers to the Dock, Wharf, Riverside and General Workers' Union but retained his membership of the Roll Turners' Trade Society until 1919, and for a time during that year he was the acting general secretary of that Society.

The expanding Dockers' Union at Shotton provided Arthur Deakin with ample scope to express himself. He became an active lay member after 1914 and a full-time organizer of the Union in 1919. In 1922, when the Dockers' Union became a part of the Transport and General Workers' Union, Deakin was appointed assistant district secretary for the north Wales area of the new Union and remained in that position until 1932, when he transferred to London to take up the post of National Secretary of the General Workers' trade group of the Transport and General Workers' Union. After three years Deakin was appointed Assistant General Secretary of the Union. Then in May 1940 the General Secretary of the Union,

Ernest Bevin, was invited by Mr. Winston Churchill to become the Minister of Labour in the war-time Coalition Government. Bevin accepted and Deakin became the Acting General Secretary of the Union. Thus began the phase with which this study is primarily concerned.

There arose out of an examination of Deakin's background four points which needed to be borne in mind when considering his later activities. First, he had been a trade unionist of long standing by 1940 and was deeply influenced by whatever ethical principles guided trade union behaviour. Secondly, his Union in 1940 was a large and well-established organization. Thirdly, Deakin was following a trade union leader of remarkable ability, and lastly he was taking over under industrial and political conditions radically different from those which existed during his formative years as a trade union official. The importance of these points became more and more obvious as the study progressed, until it became clear that unless they were examined and related to Deakin's activities the study would be incomplete and misleading and any assessments made from it about the power of a trade union leader would be inaccurate.

The decision to give more weight to the factors which made up the situation in which Deakin found himself in 1940 altered the original plan considerably. The introduction was enlarged into five chapters and occupied about a third of the completed study; and, what is more important, the section devoted to Deakin showed him less as an individual sitting on the pinnacle of trade union affairs and much more as a trade union leader operating within a live situation, with its competing demands and wide ramifications.

It became apparent that the points which were noted in Deakin's background were factors which set limits to the way in which he exercised power. To some extent they operate in the case of other trade union leaders too. Very briefly, the manner in which the factors are dealt with in the following chapters is described below.

(*i*) The first and most general limiting factor is the code of trade union ethics which brings the influence of traditions and loyalties to bear on trade union decision-making. The way in which this operates is described in Chapter II. A trade union leader cannot in every case use his own judgment, nor can he always be rational in his decisions without contravening the ethical basis of trade union activity. Chapter II shows how this basis has developed and how it has changed at its weakest spots. Arthur Deakin broke away from some traditions, such as those relating to wages demands and productivity, but he was profoundly influenced by others, particularly the tradition of loyalty. This is clearly shown in Part II of the book.

(*ii*) Restrictions were imposed on Deakin by the organization within which he worked. These were created by the interaction of a number of influences: the type of Union constitution, the composition of the members and their group behaviour, the methods of administration developed within the Union, and the quality of officials. The speed of communications within the Union, the administrative responses, and even, to some extent, the nature of decisions were determined in part by these influences, and the more firmly the Union was established the more significant they became.

In 1940 the Transport and General Workers' Union had been in existence for eighteen years. This is not long in the life of a trade union, but as the Union had started at a relatively high stage of union development it was quite long enough for it to become settled in its ways. Arthur Deakin took over the leadership of an organization which was in effective running order but which had its problems. The most difficult problem was that of integrating the behaviour of the different groups in the Union into a consistent pattern. The origin of this problem is described in Chapter III. Its development and the way in which it created trouble for Ernest Bevin are dealt with in Chapter IV. The groups which caused the trouble in the inter-war years were the London busmen and the dockers, in that order. They continued to be the dissident groups during Arthur Deakin's tenure as a leader but they reversed their order of significance. The dockers provided Deakin with a problem which he was unable to solve; which, indeed, was at its worst when he died. It is described at some length in Chapters XI and XII. The activities of the London busmen after the war are described in Chapter X.

Because the Union administration was functioning in well-laid grooves in 1940 there was relatively little freedom for the exercise of administrative leadership. Administration was not one of Arthur Deakin's strong points but, even so, he was constrained by the mechanism which Bevin and others had created and which had developed an existence which was separate from the people who operated it. This is illustrated in Chapters XIII, XIV, XV, and XVI.

(*iii*) The third factor concerns Deakin's predecessor, Ernest Bevin. It was he who set the pattern of leadership in the Union, and to some extent in the trade union movement during the inter-war years, and this influenced Arthur Deakin in two main ways. First, for eight years Deakin worked in the central office of the Union and for five of these he was Bevin's immediate subordinate. In those years Bevin was Deakin's model of a trade union leader. Deakin was, moreover, trained in Bevin's ways. He would have been a strange man if he had not reflected the influence of those formative years in his subsequent activities. Secondly, Deakin succeeded to a distribution of authority in the Union which was largely set by his predecessor, and to an administrative machine which was geared at its centre to meet Bevin's requirements. So at the outset Deakin worked under conditions in the Union which were not at all of his own making, and though he was able to effect changes to suit himself the process took time and was never complete.

The pattern of leadership set by Bevin is described in Chapter V. There he is shown as the prime architect of the Transport and General Workers' Union, devising leadership methods to satisfy the requirements of a large trade union, extending his influence into the wider trade union movement and then into politics, and all the time being willing to experiment and adapt to meet changing conditions and fresh needs. This was the kind of man Deakin followed. How Deakin was affected is not described in any one chapter; it belongs to all which describe his activities.

(*iv*) Lastly, Arthur Deakin's début as a trade union leader coincided with a reversal of the economic, industrial, and political conditions which had stunted the growth of trade unions, weakened their influence and restricted their activities during the inter-war years. The change was important for Arthur Deakin. As was mentioned earlier, Deakin had spent his formative years as a trade union official under conditions of unemployment, opposed by aggressive employers, and, in the main, watched by unsympathetic Governments. He reacted almost instinctively to those conditions and he had learned how to make the most of them. Such conditions, however, through reducing the influence of trade unions had increased their freedom to act within the community. Trade union leaders were not exhorted to include the welfare of the community in their calculations, nor was it necessary that they should.

War-time conditions increased the power of trade unions. Their help was needed to prosecute the war; they had friends in the Government, and mainly through the high level of employment they increased their size and strength. The scope of trade union action correspondingly widened. But with the extra power, trade union leaders were given responsibilities which they had never previously shouldered. At every move they were exhorted by the Government, by the press, and by prominent members of the public to consider the effect of trade union action on the community. This was for good reasons, since the war effort, and then full employment and Britain's national economic solvency, depended to a large extent upon the behaviour of the unions. The extra power that trade unions carried was in a sense conditional upon their responsible behaviour, for so important were they in the nation's economy that irresponsibility would surely have evoked Government counter-action.

So Arthur Deakin in 1940 entered a situation which was unfamiliar and which was much more exacting in its requirements than any previous one had been. It added a loyalty to the community to his already complex set of loyalties. How he responded is described and examined in Chapters VII and VIII. But throughout the chapters in Part II Deakin's response to the demands which the state of economy made on trade unions can be seen in a number of ways.

At the beginning of the present chapter it was stated that few people in Britain have more obvious facilities for exercising power than trade union leaders. In the period after the Second World War until his death in 1955 Arthur Deakin had more obvious facilities for exercising power than any other trade union leader. He belonged to a small exclusive but mixed group of powerful men in British society. His stature in this respect remains undiminished by a close examination of his activities. What the examination reveals is that his apparent power was greater than the actual power he wielded, but it is quite likely that the same could be said of the other apparently powerful men in society.

Arthur Deakin's power was many-sided and varied. It was greatest in relation to men, and it was for this reason that it appeared to be so formidable. When he was confronted by his members as individuals, in conference, in committee, or in the mass, his strategic position, specialist skills, and dominant personality enabled him to control them on most occasions and over all important issues. When he was confronted by other trade union leaders, by industrialists, or by politicians, these same qualities plus the substantial backing of his Union enabled him to achieve similar though less positive results.

At the other sides of his activities Arthur Deakin was less influential, owing mainly to the restrictions mentioned above and described in the text. To some extent he was able to influence the behaviour of his Union, but often his influence became blurred, sometimes lost, in its transmission through institutional channels. In the trade union movement his power was derived from his position on the General Council of the Trades Union Congress, which is only an advisory body, and from his advocacy; so that, apart from other factors, the autonomy of individual unions restricted his influence. His power in relation to the Government, as distinct from the individuals who comprised it, was derived from that of his Union and was dependent in the last resort upon the resoluteness of the workers he represented to act in unison. He may already have had

a significant say in the determination of the workers' decision, but
its application would be decided by events and moods and tradition
more than by exhortation.   In any case neither his Union nor the
Movement as a whole could rival the power at the disposal of the
Government.

A new and significant use of power by a trade union leader was
Deakin's attempt to alter the economic circumstances of the country
by trade union action.   Until his time trade union decisions and
behaviour had always been defensive reactions against changing
economic conditions.   Instead of accepting the economic situation
as given and concentrating purely on restrictive actions to protect
the interests of his members, Deakin endeavoured to defend them
by changing the economic situation through adopting measures to
counter inflation, raise production, and maintain full employment.
It is not a reflection on Deakin that this was the weakest part of his
power; indeed, it reflects the limitations of trade union activity.
Such has been the intensity and nature of post-war economic problems in Britain that trade unions by their actions could have worsened
them at any time, but were unable to make a clearly distinguishable
contribution towards their solution.   Trade unions, to a large
extent, were at the mercy of changing economic circumstances:
reacting, defending, responding, but rarely initiating, creating, or
even anticipating.

One might be inclined to conclude from the brief glance at Bevin
in Part I that he was more in control of his affairs than was Deakin.
In some respects he was, but this was due more to differences in
circumstances than innate differences in ability.   Bevin became a
trade union leader when there was much scope for creative work in
the Movement.   It is to his credit that he took advantage of the
scope, but he was not faced with all the formidable restrictions
which confronted Deakin.   Though he had to conform to the ethics
of trade unionism, this was easier when trade union action was
purely restrictive and aggressive than when such action came to be
deemed unpatriotic.   As the creator of an organization he was not
hampered by institutional restrictions as was Deakin.   Nor did he
have to compete with the reputation of his predecessor and contend
with established leadership practices.   Bevin had destroyed the
authority of his predecessor, Ben Tillett, before he assumed the
leadership of the new Transport and General Workers' Union.

In other respects Bevin's control was less effective than Deakin's.
He held no influence in the Governments of the inter-war years and
was never able to influence the economic circumstances one way or
the other.   To some extent he commanded an illusory power because
it was based on the relatively weak position of trade unions in his

time. There was a wider divergence between utterance and the ability to take effective action in the inter-war years than when Deakin was a trade union leader. Whatever else may be said of Arthur Deakin, this much must be admitted: he commanded a position of undoubted authority in the trade union movement at the most influential stage in its history to date; he used his authority with a wide understanding of national economic welfare; and he put sectional interests into their national context.

PART I

Chapter Two

THE ETHICS OF TRADE UNION LEADERS

HAVING stated the problems associated with the study of a trade union leader, I can now begin to describe the development of the situation in which Arthur Deakin found himself when he became the General Secretary of the Transport and General Workers' Union. The first step is to examine the loyalties and traditions which form the ethical basis of so many trade union decisions and which thereby impose limits on the freedom with which a trade union leader can act.

Trade union traditions and loyalties belong to the Movement and cannot be explained in terms of a single trade union or an individual person. They are, in a sense, the instinctive and protective creations of a class of underprivileged people in a competitive society. Consequently I have approached the subject of their examination in a broad and general way. In most sections, too, my approach has been an historical one. Without reference to history all traditions and most loyalties are meaningless.

AIMS AND OBJECTIVES

It is doubtful whether many trade union leaders regard their task as being the fulfilment of the formal aims which preface the written constitutions of their unions, and which are mainly couched in the terminology of the early Socialists. The National Union of Boot and Shoe Operatives, for example, aims at 'the socialization of the means of production to be controlled by a democratic State in the interests of the entire community, and the complete emancipation of labour from the domination of capital and land-lordism . . .'. Most trade unions consist of voluntary members who need to be provided with frequent material evidence to show why they should be in trade unions at all. Consequently the protection of workers' living standards and their gradual improvement in piecemeal fashion have taken precedence over more grandiose intentions.

Union leaders usually have no long-term aims which are precise and clearly definable and which form a pattern for present and

14   *The Ethics of Trade Union Leaders*

future activity. This is because there is no such thing as a trade
union ideology or trade union philosophy. The ideas and principles
of trade union activity over long periods cannot be fitted into a
consistent pattern; trade unions are products of the society in which
they operate and cannot have an existence which is separate from
that society. The long-term aims of many trade union leaders are
vague expressions such as 'fair shares for the workers' and are, in a
sense, figments of their social consciences. It may be said that the
few trade union leaders who are members of the Communist Party
have specific long-term aims which influence their behaviour as trade
unionists. This is so only to a limited extent, for they have to work
within the structure of a capitalist society and their day-to-day
activities are determined by the wants of their members, just as are
the activities of non-Communist union leaders. Marx did not provide trade unionists with an ideology which was separate from his
general theory of society.

There has not been a comparable vagueness about the short-term
aims of many trade union leaders. Some of them set themselves or
found themselves pursuing specific tasks that gave them an ultimate
purpose. The five men whom the Webbs called the Junta—William
Allan, Robert Applegarth, Edwin Coulson, George Odger, and
Daniel Guile,[1] methodically set about obtaining social and legal
recognition for trade unions at a time when, through the consternation caused by the Sheffield outrages in 1866, it was more than likely
that repressive legislation after the pattern of the Combination Acts
would be introduced.

The 'New Unionists' who formed the next trade union generation
of prominence had a purpose foisted on them, but they accepted it
readily. Until the spontaneous strike on the London docks in 1889,
Ben Tillett, John Burns, Tom Mann, and Will Thorne were small-
time agitators, with a social purpose no doubt, but with a minute
hearing. Then, through no design of their own, they found themselves extending trade unionism to the underprivileged groups in
society, the unskilled, semi-skilled—and, to some extent, women.

When the leadership of the Unions they had created required the
skill and patience of administrators, they handed over to men of
quite different calibre, such as Arthur Pugh, Ernest Bevin, and Walter
Citrine,[2] who aimed to knit together the large numbers of unions in

[1] All except Odger were general secretaries—Allan in the Amalgamated Society of
Engineers, 1851-1874; Applegarth in the Amalgamated Society of Carpenters and
Joiners, 1862-1871; Coulson in the Operative Bricklayers' Society (London Order),
1860-1891; and Guile in the Friendly Society of Ironfounders, 1863-1881. Odger,
a shoemaker, remained at his trade and was secretary of the London Trades Council,
1862-1872.
[2] Each was a general secretary—Pugh in the British Iron, Steel and Kindred Trades
Association, 1917-1936; Bevin in the Transport and General Workers' Union,
1922-1946; Citrine in the Trades Union Congress, 1925-1946.

the various industrial groups into compact centralized organizations and into a movement of national and international significance. These leaders worked through years of mass unemployment, of bad relations with employers, and, consequently, of restricted trade union activity.

By 1940 this period had come to a close with trade unions as secure and expanding organizations. Thereafter it became the task of men of Arthur Deakin's generation to extend the influence of trade unions and to establish their right to be consulted on all matters that came within their sphere of influence. These men believed that it was a union's job to be concerned with every aspect of a worker's life, and that therefore they should not take the general economic conditions of the country as given and work within the limitations these imposed, but should do all within their power to determine those conditions.

In each case these short-term aims have been specific and in-flexible and have been driving forces in the lives of the leaders concerned; but they formed only a part of their patterns of be-haviour.

TRADE UNION MORALITY

There is an ethical basis for decision-making in all trade unions, for the decisions taken in them must in some way be related to the objectives and traditions of trade unions. The objectives of a trade union indicate what the union is hoping to achieve, while the tradi-tions stipulate the kind of action and behaviour to be adopted in pursuit of those objectives.

Throughout the greater part of the nineteenth century a code of conduct was formed which had no theoretical basis but which gave workers unity and purpose. To provide themselves with economic protection organized workers devised practices consistent with the economic principles of the time, which prolonged work, shared work, and restricted work to their respective groups. They did not con-sider such practices to be anti-social, rather did they deem it to be unethical for workers to refuse to accept them. To maintain the cohesion of the organizations they had created, and to ensure the success of the industrial methods they employed to protect them-selves, they imposed sanctions on those members who refused to accept majority decisions.

They insisted first on the acceptance of the rules of their organiza-tions by all their members. Many early unions admitted members through initiation ceremonies, on oath and in secrecy. Now that unions are legally and socially recognized institutions, the paramount need for doing this has, of course, disappeared. But the need to see that members accept and agree to abide by the rules has remained. It was necessary to have initiation ceremonies because, apart from other factors, a high proportion of workers were illiterate. Workers nowadays can be expected to read a rule book and understand its contents; many unions, therefore, refuse to accept ignorance of the rules as an excuse for violating them.

Trade union sanctions, except where membership of a trade union is a condition of employment or where fines are imposed, are moral ones and they are applied whenever a member violates the union rules. As non-membership of a trade union is a threat to its cohesion, non-members too are often treated in the same way. Any worker who refuses to join a trade union strike, regardless of whether or not he is a trade unionist, is a blackleg, and this is a moral stigma from which it is difficult to escape. The emotion aroused in strikes has carried the stigma attached to black-legging beyond the bounds of official trade union action, and it is applied to all workers who ignore strike calls from the majority of workers in their group, in a department, a firm, a craft, or an industry.

Trade union morality has not been restricted to behaviour within trade unions. No doubt some workers felt they belonged to a distinct class before the publication of the *Communist Manifesto* and Karl Marx's *Das Kapital*, but there had been no concerted move to create a 'class consciousness' before that time. From Marx came the impulse not only to regard what classes other than the working class did as morally wrong, but also to regard the other classes themselves as evil-doers. During this phase, from the 1880s, the terminology of trade unionists changed just as a nation's terminology changes when it goes to war; the term 'brother', used as a form of trade union address, was superseded in many quarters by the term 'comrade'; the words 'profit' and 'capitalism' were given an evil connotation; wage labour was called wage-slavery; the proletariat was the only important class in society and the bourgeoisie the class to whom it was opposed; their differences were epitomized in the 'class-struggle'; the aim of the proletariat was the control of the 'means of production' and 'militancy' became synonymous with good trade union action. The new terminology meant more than just the use of words. It was in its effect on the behaviour of trade unionists in practical matters that Marxism contributed most to trade union activity. It did not create new methods or new habits for trade unionists, it codified the existing ones and related them to a purpose—the supremacy of the working class. Marx has long since been forgotten by most ordinary trade unionists, but in some respects his standards are still accepted by them; they form part of the traditions of the movement, along with those standards of morality which economic necessity caused trade unionists to establish from the first days of permanent trade union activity.

The combination of traditions and objectives as the ethical basis of trade union decision-making raises many problems for the trade union leader. His aims must always coincide with those of his union; they do not have to be identical, for he may have ambitions for his union that are in addition to its accepted aims. It is not so easy for him to do his job nowadays without breaking some of the traditions of the movement. And because the traditions are derived from the antipathy of the working class to other classes in society, the keepers of the traditions are those trade unionists who believe in aggressive industrial action. From these people come the protests at any unorthodox conduct by union leaders.

Trade union leaders are in a most vulnerable position; their behaviour is constantly under scrutiny and they are frequently called upon in their representative capacities to perform tasks which are subject to misinterpretation and provide sources of temptation. For instance, a leader who gets on easily with employers is often accused of acting contrary to trade union standards, as if it were a quality of leadership to be able to deal regularly with others whilst maintaining an antipathy towards them. Even if this quality were desirable it could only be achieved if union leaders and employers were antipathetic types. Self-made employers or managers and union leaders possess many similar qualities and may differ only in their social purposes. Both types are individualists, determined and to some extent ruthless in their determination, who have overcome obstacles placed by birth or environment. They understand each other's principles and methods and find it easy to agree upon modes of behaviour in their official connections whilst adopting radically different modes in their private capacities.

If a union leader blatantly accepts the material standards of industrialists and permits them to cloud his social purpose he is criticized by his members; if he leaves his union post to work for an industrialist on the managerial side then he is accused by them of committing grave misconduct. There are relatively few examples of the latter conduct. The trade union officials who do move into industry occasionally are usually those who have tried and failed to obtain general secretaryships and who see no reasonable opportunity of advancement. Those officials who defect because they change their social purposes usually do so before they achieve prominence.

A union leader's sense of purpose can be checked clearly if he leaves his job and moves to more lucrative employment; it cannot be checked so easily if he stays in his union, and it would be wrong to presume that one who stays is unaffected by his contact with industrialists. But it is to the credit of those who stay in their unions that they have resisted the lure of much higher salaries and living standards. Men who seek financial remuneration commensurate with ability or responsibility should not seek trade union posts. The *Sunday Times*, commenting on Mr. Deakin's impending retirement, stated that his job 'offers more real industrial and political power for lower pay than any other in the country'.[1] Much the same could be said of the chief executive posts in other unions. On the whole the union leaders' behaviour with employers, and the effects of meeting them frequently, are hidden from the view of ordinary trade unionists, and the member who dislikes his general secretary is left with much scope for imaginative creation. The public activities of the general secretaries, however, can be assessed more accurately by ordinary members because they are more easily observed.

A trade union leader by virtue of his position is a public figure. He is drawn into public activities through the State apparatus and through political parties. If he is the general secretary of a small union then usually he has only local prominence; the larger or more powerful the union the greater is the extension of his prominence.

The public stature of union leaders has been determined by the place of trade unions in the State. This in turn has depended on the numerical strength of unions and the use to which workers have put universal suffrage. Thus, when unions are strong their leading members are asked to take up public duties out of respect for their power; and when workers vote they can elect their own representatives into public positions. The two factors began to operate during the seventh decade of the last century.

The appointment or election of a working man on to a public body before 1871 was a rarity. When, in 1866, Robert Applegarth asked one of Mr. Gladstone's advisers for the appointment of two experienced trade unionists to the Royal Commission on Trade Unions which was to be set up, he was told, as if nothing could be more preposterous: 'They would be inquiring into themselves.'[2] The idea of a working-man Royal Commissioner was inconsistent with official traditions.[3] Although there were many elections for Improvement Boards, Burial Boards, Vestries, and Municipal Corporations at that time it was virtually impossible for working men to contest them because of the financial qualifications candidates had to possess. John Normansell, the secretary of the South Yorkshire Miners' Association from 1864 till 1875, who was reputed to be the

[1] 30 January 1955.
[2] *Robert Applegarth*, by A. W. Humphrey, p. 144.
[3] *History of Trade Unionism*, by S. and B. Webb, p. 265 (1920 edition).

first working-man town councillor, had to have £1,000 lodged in the bank in his name by his union before he possessed the financial qualification to stand for election in Barnsley in November 1872.[1] The separately elected school-boards which existed between the 1870 and 1902 Education Acts provided trade unionists with an opportunity of performing public service, but they had to wait for the Local Government Acts of 1888 and 1894 before they could secure election as local government representatives.

The first significant public recognition of a trade union leader was Robert Applegarth's appointment as a member of the Royal Commission on the Contagious Diseases Acts in September 1870. Applegarth's executive was a local one elected by the London branches, and about seven of these branches took exception to his appointment. They sent wordy resolutions to the executive complaining that Applegarth was using his position as general secretary 'as a mere medium to other and more lucrative engagements'.[2] The opinion of these London branches was not held by any provincial branch which deliberated the matter, and in general the feeling of the members was reflected in a resolution from Islington, moved by John Prior, who succeeded Applegarth as general secretary. It stated:

> Whatever may be the result of the deliberations of the Commission . . . it is enough for us to know that the Government have at last recognized that working men have a right to be fairly and directly represented on boards which are instituted to inquire into questions which affect their interests and those of the community at large. What would we not have given for a precedent which we could have cited when we vainly tried to induce the Home Secretary to appoint a working man on the Trades Union Commission. But the precedent which we needed has been created at last. . . .[3]

The union executive vacillated in its attitude. At first it agreed that Applegarth should sit on the Commission; then under pressure from the London branches it said it would 'not sanction the G.S. sitting on any Commission in the day-time'. By March 1871 it was looking 'upon the appointment . . . as an honour to our Society . . .'. The following month the executive composition was changed and, led by Randal Cremer,[4] it stated that it had no objection to Applegarth's sitting on the Commission

> so long as he discharged his duties on such Commission after office hours . . . nor shall we allow our vanity to be tickled by the mere sentiment which has been imparted into the question, such as the

1 *Ibid.*, p. 305.
2 Monthly Report, Amalgamated Society of Carpenters and Joiners, October 1870.
3 *Ibid.*, March 1871.
4 See below, pp. 31–32.

'honour reflected on the Society by the General Secretary having been selected as a member of the Royal Commission', &c., as we have yet to learn that any honour can be reflected on any body by an inquiry into such a loathsome subject. . . .[1]

Whereupon on 29 April 1871 Applegarth resigned from the Society. For many years after 1870 the Government relied on the 'New Model' unions and the County Mining Associations as their main sources for workers' representatives. A post was offered to Applegarth in the Board of Trade but he refused it, thus forfeiting 'the dubious distinction of being the first man to step from leadership in the Labour movement to a position under the Government'.[2] That distinction was claimed by his successor, John Prior, who became a Factory Inspector in 1881.[3] The Webbs report that there was great jubilation at this appointment.[4] Prior and the members of his union were certainly flattered.

'After mature consideration,' he wrote, 'I determined to accept the responsibility thus entrusted to me, feeling that the offer was a compliment, not only to myself but to the Society . . .'.[5] His executive did not vacillate this time. They thanked the Home Secretary 'for appointing Mr. Prior to such an important position'. Members and branches sent their congratulations and suggested that a fund be set up for him 'to give expression to our unfeigned pleasure at the great honour done to our esteemed chief officer'.[6]

Afterwards the number of Government openings for trade union leaders slowly increased. A. J. Mundella, the President of the Board of Trade, started a Labour Bureau with a Labour Correspondent in 1886. The post was given to John Burnett, the general secretary of the Amalgamated Society of Engineers, who in earlier days had led the rank-and-file campaign for the nine-hour day but who later had mellowed into a campaigner for Gladstone and the Liberal Party. A deputation from the Trades Union Congress in January 1893 was informed by Mr. Mundella—still President of the Board of Trade but in a new Government, Gladstone's fourth—that

[1] Monthly Report, A.S.C. & J., May 1871.
[2] *Robert Applegarth*, by A. W. Humphrey, p. 264.
[3] After the enactment of the Factory and Workshop Act, 1878, the Trades Union Congress pressed for the appointment of a number of practical working men as sub-inspectors of factories. In January 1881 the Home Secretary agreed, as an experiment, to appoint a working-class representative to the position of inspector and offered the job to Henry Broadhurst, the stonemason who was then secretary of the Parliamentary Committee of the Trades Union Congress. Broadhurst declined to leave his trade union work and suggested Prior as a suitable candidate. This is Broadhurst's version (quoted by the Webbs, *History of Trade Unionism*, p. 372n). Prior in a letter to his executive wrote: 'I had been recommended by . . . some gentlemen who, although not trade unionists, have rendered invaluable services to the cause of labour. . . .' (A.S.C. & J. Monthly Report, March 1881.)
[4] *History of Trade Unionism*, p. 372.
[5] A.S.C. & J. Monthly Report, March 1881.
[6] *Ibid.*, April 1881.

the Bureau was being expanded into a department with a Commissioner of Labour, a Chief Labour Correspondent and three additional Labour Correspondents, a staff of clerks, and local correspondents in large provincial towns, and that it was to issue a monthly Gazette.[1] Burnett was promoted to Chief Labour Correspondent; C. J. Drummond, who had resigned the general secretaryship of the London Society of Compositors over policy differences in 1892, was given a post and Robert Knight, the leader of the United Society of Boilermakers, was offered a post but refused.

The miners' leaders had forced themselves into prominence through their electoral successes after the 1867 Reform Act. William McDonald, the university-educated miners' leader,[2] along with Thomas Burt, the leader of the Northumberland Miners' Confident Association for almost fifty years from 1865, became the two first working-men Members of Parliament in 1874. In the General Election of 1885 eleven trade union leaders were elected to Parliament and six of them were miners. The achievements were crowned by the appointment of Henry Broadhurst in 1885 as Under-Secretary of State for the Home Department. Then in 1892 Thomas Burt became the second ex-working man to hold a Government post when he was appointed Parliamentary Secretary to the Board of Trade. The trade union officials who, as recently as 1867, were regarded as 'pothouse agitators, "unscrupulous men, leading a half idle life, fattening on the contributions of their dupes", and maintaining, by violence and murder, a system of terrorism which was destructive, not only of the industry of the nation, but also of the prosperity and independence of character of the unfortunate working men who were their victims',[3] were now respectable members of the Liberal Party, fit to be given subordinate Ministerial positions (where, incidentally, they had very little influence), to sit on Royal Commissions, and to become civil servants. What is more, social barriers were being penetrated, for trade union leaders were being fêted by the Prince of Wales and his family.[4]

Trade union leaders of this period were not rebels against society; they worked to alter it, no doubt, and with a zeal that compares well with that of any other generation of trade unionists, but they had no intention of substituting a completely different system for the one in which they were achieving recognition. Nor can it be assumed that these leaders were, in the main, acting contrary to the

[1] *History of the United Society of Boilermakers*, by D. C. Cummings, pp. 131–132.
[2] 'Born in Airdrie (in 1821) he went to work at the pit at the age of eight. In his twenty-fifth year he entered Glasgow University, supporting himself there by his savings and by his work as a miner during the summer months.' (*The Miners*, by R. Page Arnot, p. 44.)
[3] *The History of Trade Unionism*, by S. and B. Webb, p. 325.
[4] Both Henry Broadhurst and the complete executive of the London Trades Council were entertained at different times at Sandringham in the 1880s.

wishes of their members.   Having a mason, miners, and carpenters
in Parliament, on Royal Commissions, and the rest, must have made
a profound impression on ordinary trade unionists.   And even over
such a contentious matter as mixing with Royalty, most trade
unionists would have accepted the view of Keir Hardie, who was by
no means an orthodox man, that 'if I am fit to represent the working
classes of Merthyr, I am fit to attend a garden party at Windsor'.[1]

At the height of the success of the Liberal trade union leaders in
the 1880s a new code of behaviour for trade unionists was being
advocated.

> During the years 1887–89 [the Webbs wrote] the conscientious adhesion
> to the Liberal Party of most of the Parliamentary Committee was made
> the occasion for gross charges of personal corruption.   The General
> Secretaries of the great Unions, men who had for a lifetime diligently
> served their constituents, found their influence undermined, their
> character attacked, and themselves denounced, by the circulation all
> over the country of insidious accusations of treachery to the working
> classes.[2]

It was at this stage that a standard of behaviour was being derived
from Marxism which had 'class-consciousness' as its basis.   The
new expanding group of trade unionists consisting of Keir Hardie,
John Burns, and Tom Mann, in their dress and behaviour epitomized
the changes that were advocated.

> The 'old' delegates [John Burns said] differed from the 'new' not only
> physically but in dress.   A great number of them looked like respectable
> city gentlemen; wore very good coats, large watch chains and high hats
> —and in many cases were of such splendid build and proportions that
> they presented an aldermanic, not to say a magisterial form and
> dignity. . . . Amongst the 'new' delegates not a single one wore a tall
> hat.   They looked workmen.   They were workmen.   They were not
> such sticklers for formality or Court procedure, but were guided more
> by common sense.[3]

But common sense rarely emerges intact after a conflict with formality; it is weakened in its vulnerable spots—where it touches
personal behaviour and concerns a man's ego.

When new leaders took on the role of their predecessors as public
figures they were met at every move by formality.   It needed only
time to perform the change.   The paths that were cut by McDonald,
Applegarth, Burt, and Broadhurst were those trodden by the New

---

[1] *J. Keir Hardie*, by William Stewart (published by the I.L.P.), p. 283.   Hardie had
criticized the visit of King Edward VII to Russia in 1908 and consequently was excluded from one of the King's garden parties.
[2] *History of Trade Unionism*, p. 400.
[3] Reporting on the 1890 Trades Union Congress.   Quoted by Raymond Postgate
in *The Builders History*, p. 343.

Unionists who, despite the workers' dress and Socialist ideas, eventually accepted the traditions of society which initially they had professed to despise. The new leaders found that the trade unionists' code of honour which they had propagated was more effective as a gauge for criticism than as a standard to be followed. John Burns, more quickly than most, changed his direction and, in December 1905, became the first ex-working man Cabinet Minister as President of the Local Government Board in Sir Henry Campbell-Bannerman's Liberal Government. Many of the early Socialist agitators who held high trade union positions, such as Ben Tillett, Will Thorne, and George Barnes, decided eventually that since they had to work in a particular form of society they would accept its standards. They continued to support Labour Party policies in public, but considered that such policies demanded no change in behaviour from those which were based on social values of a completely different kind. This inconsistency was not confined to trade union leaders.

In addition to the impact of ordinary formalities on the behaviour of Socialist trade union leaders came the impact of war in 1914. This was felt in three ways. First, it severely tested some of the principles to which many leaders had publicly attached themselves, for it foisted on them a real situation which had only previously received theoretical consideration. Many of the trade union leaders who were not pacifists had expressed opposition to imperialist wars, and the declaration of war strained the emotions of these as well as of the pacifists. This was resolved for some by the declaration of support for the war policy of the Liberal Government made by the Parliamentary Committee of the Trades Union Congress in September 1914. Secondly came a decision by the Labour Party Executive and Labour M.P.s to collaborate with a Liberal, then a Coalition, Government and to accept Government posts which, the Webbs stated, 'was in flagrant violation of the very principles' of the existence of the Labour Movement.[1] Never before had trade unionists decided to sink political as well as class differences in the wider interests of the nation. Thirdly, they were asked to suspend some of their most coveted industrial rights for the duration of the war and this they did through the Treasury Agreement of 1915.

The temper of the rank and file was in favour of collaboration, and at the Trades Union Congress in September 1915, the first to be held after the declaration of war, only seven delegates out of three

[1] *The History of Trade Unionism*, by S. and B. Webb, p. 693. Arthur Henderson (Friendly Society of Ironfounders), William Brace (Miners' Federation), G. A. Roberts (Typographical Association), G. J. Wardle (National Union of Railwaymen), James Parker (N.U. of General Workers), John Hodge (British Steel Smelters), J. R. Clynes (N. U. of General Workers), and G. N. Barnes (formerly A.S.E.) all accepted Government posts during the course of the war.

hundred voted against the patriotic motion proposed by the Parliamentary Committee.[1] Successive Labour Party Conferences and Trades Union Congresses endorsed this decision. Tom Shaw of the United Textile Factory Workers' Association asserted that the 'answer as to what the Labour Movement wanted at the beginning of the War was given by the workers when they voluntarily enlisted to fight for a cause they thought was the cause of freedom'.[2] The opinion of the leaders was far from being unanimous. Mrs. Webb stated that at a joint meeting of the Executive of the Labour Party and the Labour M.P.s the voting was eighteen votes to twelve in favour of taking office. There was some confusion about the motives of those who voted to collaborate with the Government. Mrs. Webb did not think that those in favour of collaboration were influenced unduly by the prospect of receiving the high incomes attached to Government posts or by the desire to give the Germans a thorough beating. She considered their main motive to be 'the illusion that the mere presence of Labour men in the Government, apart from anything they may do or prevent being done, is in itself a sign of democratic progress . . .'. On this she commented that 'Neither as individuals nor as a class do Labour men realize that they are mere office-mongers when they serve with men of trained intelligence or even with experienced middle-class administrators.'[3] But what some of these men lacked in intellectual ability they made up in stubbornness and this was a quality Mrs. Webb neglected to consider. Not so J. R. Clynes. At the Labour Party Conference in January 1917 he said he 'knew there were people who thought that men like Mr. Henderson, in comparison with their greater capabilities, could be shaped and moulded in any way. The same thing was said about a man like Mr. Hodge. Of all the men in the Labour Movement those were two of the most stubborn kind, and once they took their stand on any question they were immovable.'[4] It was at the 1917 Labour Party Conference that the essential issue was discussed.

A few trade union leaders who were prepared to count the cost of waging a war in terms of the sacrifice of trade union principle thought it was too great. They were, as J. H. Thomas pointed out, opposed not to Labour joining the Government but to the terms on which Labour went in. One delegate maintained that 'Mr. Henderson and the others were simply held as hostages for the good behaviour of Labour.'[5] Fred Bramley, the general secretary of the Trades Union Congress, 1923–1925, Ben Tillett, and David Kirk-

[1] Beatrice Webb's *Diaries, 1912–1924*, p. 43.
[2] Labour Party Conference Report, 1917, p. 97. Shaw became the Minister of Labour in 1924 and Minister for War in 1929.
[3] Beatrice Webb's *Diaries, 1912–1924*, p. 73.
[4] Labour Party Conference Report, 1917, p. 96.
[5] C. G. Ammon (became Lord Ammon in 1944).

wood[1] expressed their opposition. Ernest Bevin, making his first appearance at a Labour Party Conference, said that the Labour leaders ought to have considered the character of the men with whom they had decided to collaborate. He recited some of the offences against Labour alleged to have been committed by Lloyd George and Lords Rhondda, Devonport, Derby, and Milner, and said that these men were undesirable colleagues for Labour leaders.[2]

Neither the delegates who agreed on collaboration by 1,849,000 votes to 307,000 nor Arthur Henderson accepted these sentiments. 'They had been told many times', Arthur Henderson said, 'in the days before ever there was a war that they had been guilty of selling the Movement without getting anything in return.' But he had never viewed the matter from that standpoint. He thought that in a national crisis if they had to associate with any form of Government they ought to concern themselves more with what they were going to give than what they were likely to get.[3]

The First World War affected the attitude of the public and Government towards trade unions as institutions in society, and fears that unions were working to bring about widespread ruin of trade and capital were largely dissipated by the responsible approach of unions to the war. Trade unions became a part of the recognized scene. Some were still to wage bitter strikes for almost eight years, but sufficient was known about them to make it clear that their motives were not subversive. Union leaders were brought into frequent and widespread contact with employers and Government representatives on Government committees. They learned how to work on joint committees, to iron out differences and reach compromise solutions. What is more, the rank and file were more prepared to allow them to do this without labelling them as saboteurs. Class differences in society had not changed but they were beginning to be treated differently. The united efforts in the war had worn through in places the Marxist interpretation of the class struggle; class patriotism at least had taken a blow from which it never recovered.

LOYALTY

It has already been mentioned that the task of decision-making for a trade union leader is complicated by the existence of trade union traditions. An added difficulty is created by the interaction of contending loyalties such as the needs of the union, the majority

---

[1] Kirkwood was the militant leader of the Clyde Workers' Committee; at that time defying his union, the Amalgamated Society of Engineers, and the Government; later Lord Kirkwood.
[2] Labour Party Conference Report, 1917, pp. 96–97.
[3] *Ibid.*, p. 87.

opinion in it, the prestige and strength of the Trade Union Movement, the maintenance of effective union/employer relationships,
the stability of the Labour Party, and the welfare of the community.

It needs little imagination to see what mental contortions a man
would have to perform in order to take cognizance of all these
factors.   Furthermore, he would not always be dealing with quanti-
tative problems but with political abstractions such as justice,
liberty, and rights.   This situation has tended to discount reason,
and problems have been confined to black and white categories.
Some factors, of course, may be deliberately neglected, indicating
that some loyalties are more intense than others.   Also a decision
may be taken that is based on only part of the considerations,
because the requisite knowledge of the situation is not available
to the individual, or because he has not fully appreciated the sense of
the situation, or because he lacks the intellectual tools necessary for
a full appraisal of the problem.   Moreover, there may not be time
to think out a problem, and speed of action may be more important
than a balanced decision.

The trade union leaders of the last century established the tradition
of absolute loyalty to majority decisions which present-day leaders
have inherited.   This loyalty formed the basis of that unified action
which was the strength of their unions.   Most of them refused even
to accept that they had obligations to workers outside the precincts
of their respective groups.   This left not only semi-skilled and unskilled workers to form their own unions, but also craftsmen in new
trades such as electrical engineering and heating and domestic
engineering.   Then gradually the ground for a wider-based loyalty
was prepared, not at first as one would have expected, through the
Trades Union Congress, but through federations of trade unions,
such as the National Transport Workers' Federation, which were
formed to present a united industrial front to employers.   The
president of the National Transport Workers' Federation, Harry
Gosling, has described what was entailed for leaders working in the
new industry-wide federations:

> Once an individual trade union is well organized and has secured the
> principle of recognition from the employers with whom it is connected
> it is a comparatively easy matter to make and keep agreements involved.
> Readjustment also, after a sectional dispute, is fairly simple under such
> conditions.   But once federation exists an entirely new set of circum-
> stances is created.   Federation means co-operation and that means the
> stronger must help the weaker.   No longer are employers able to make
> their bargains with those whom they cannot afford to ignore at the
> expense of others; at the same time the stronger sections of the men can
> no longer go gaily and inconsiderately ahead with the weaker ones left

far behind. A new and wider loyalty comes into play; a federation must be dealt with as a whole both in attack and defence. But if these new conditions make far higher demands on the loyalty of the men, they also beget new and heavy responsibilities for those in charge. The leaders' business, never even in early days an easy one, becomes onerous indeed.[1]

Until 1926 other attempts at unified action broke down in the main over the inability of union leaders to meet the still more exacting demands of a movement-wide collective responsibility. The Parliamentary Committee of the Trades Union Congress carried little authority in the Movement and rarely initiated policy. For the purpose of united action unions endeavoured to form extra bodies such as the Triple Alliance; and even after the reorganization of Congress and the formation of the General Council in 1920 the unions still looked to sectional alliances to add to their strength. Then from 1927 the moral status, and therefore authority, of the General Council was gradually increased, though the constitutional authority of the Council remained virtually unchanged.

With its enhanced status the General Council called increasingly for a new leadership quality from its members. They were required to submerge their identities as leaders of autonomous unions and to act as trade unionists in the widest sense. In this role they sometimes collectively advocated policies which were contrary to the immediate interests of some of their unions, and on occasions they became parties to policy statements which their own unions rejected. An incident of the latter kind occurred over the General Council Circular No. 17, *Communist and Other Bodies*, composed in October 1934, which asked each executive of affiliated unions to 'give consideration to the possibility of drawing up regulations or amending rules of your organizations so as to empower them to reject the nominations of members of disruptive bodies for any official position within your organization . . .'. The 'Black Circular', as it was called, was discussed heatedly at the 1935 Trades Union Congress and six members of the General Council had to speak against it in the names of their respective unions. Such a dilemma was bound to be faced as long as the General Council possessed no powers of direction over affiliated unions. But its significance depended also on the willingness of the General Council to take the initiative in policy formulation which in turn was related to its status in the Movement and the extent to which it was accepted as the voice of the Movement by the Government and other institutions.

The basic loyalties of trade union leaders were strained further after the Second World War, when trade union co-operation

[1] *Up and Down Stream*, by Harry Gosling, p. 157.

influenced the outcome of national problems; and when the community interest required solutions to labour problems which were unpalatable to sections of the trade union movement. Such action sometimes threatened the unity of the organizations of those members of the General Council who had supported the solutions.

The employer/union relationships before the First World War were simplified by their straightforwardness. There were few industries with negotiating procedures for settling disputes and claims; therefore, though the maintenance of an agreement with an employer was an ethical matter for a union leader who had put his signature to it, it was not a matter on which depended the continued use of established negotiating machinery. The latter factor has become increasingly important. The effectiveness of permanent negotiating procedure depends on the willingness of the participants to follow it through without resorting to lock-outs or strike action. Consequently the rules of each joint negotiating body usually contain a clause to this effect. Of all the single factors that influence internal union relations, and sometimes inter-union relations, this type of clause has been of the utmost importance in recent years. Ordinary members, impatient of the delays that procedural settlement of disputes entails, on occasion take matters into their own hands and strike. Union leaders, even though they may sympathize with their members, cannot side with them without threatening the existence of the negotiating machinery. Not only do employers refuse to negotiate under duress; they also tend to lose faith in the usefulness of agreements and may even be tempted to employ similar disruptive tactics. Once the leaders refuse to recognize the actions of their members, and sometimes even feel it necessary to condemn them, they are placed in the invidious position of involuntarily strengthening the hand of employers and straining their own primary loyalties. On the whole, union leaders have supported the use of the machinery they have assisted in creating, whatever the consequences. Indeed one has gone so far as to state that 'an employer who conceded a wage claim under a strike threat performed a criminal act which was both immoral and bad business'.[1]

It is important, once collective bargaining machinery has been created, that participants should be prepared to accept its findings. That is just as necessary when a wage claim is rejected as when it is granted, for over a long period the terms of settlements vacillate between giving satisfaction and giving dissatisfaction to both employers and unions, and if a union rejected settlements it disliked

---

[1] Harry Douglass, General Secretary of the Iron and Steel Trades Confederation. Reported in the *Manchester Guardian*, 6 January 1955.

then employers would be entitled to act likewise. The machinery would rarely be operated.

Another problem, imposing a formidable strain on union leaders, has been created by the rejection of signed national agreements by ordinary members. The leaders become intimate with the conditions under which the negotiations are carried on: they know, for instance, what the lay members often do not know, how obdurate the employers are and what alternatives to the accepted terms are offered. The final terms ought to be related to these alternatives as well as to the original demand in order to assess their worth. Yet this is not always attempted by the members. They frequently judge an agreement by its absolute value to them, or in relation to what they wanted, without inquiring whether their wants were obtainable under the conditions then existing. Nevertheless, the onus for rejecting an agreement cannot always be placed on the members. Union leaders have a responsibility to see that the initial demand is within the bounds of possibility, and they are not always correct in their calculations. They should also see that they know what the members would accept and that the position is fairly and clearly explained to their members when the terms are announced. There may be real differences of understanding about the factors involved in a union claim. To the ordinary member a claim for a wage increase always means the possibility of maintaining or increasing his standard of living: to a leader with a grasp of the economic situation it may mean possible adverse national economic consequences.

The range of possible correct explanations of the rejection of a national agreement places the union leader in a dilemma and increases the risk to his organization of adopting an inviolable rule of sanctifying agreements. Quite possibly he could be at fault by placing an inadequate agreement before his members. Ought he to acknowledge his faults and reject the agreement, almost before the ink of his signature is dry? If he did, employers would certainly consider him an unreliable person with whom to negotiate and would be hesitant about negotiating a second agreement. Moreover he would be a strange leader who so readily admitted his faults. Most union leaders have stood firm and have refused to countenance in any circumstances the unconstitutional rejection of an agreement. Their views were expressed by Arthur Deakin when he told a Court of Inquiry into a dock dispute that 'having entered into an agreement it is an obligation to see that it is carried out, not merely in the spirit but in the letter, until such time as adjustments are made by negotiation around the Conference table'.[1] Few union leaders, however, would argue that an agreement should never be terminated

[1] 21 October 1954.

before its date of expiry, or that the strike weapon should never be used to force an issue once the agreement is no longer valid.   They insist, though, that an agreement shall be terminated in accordance with the correct procedure.

One can sympathize with those leaders who have misjudged the temper of their members and who, in consequence, have been faced with unofficial strike action.   But ought this to be rectified through the leader's relinquishing leadership and following the call of his members at the expense of both employers and the public?   It does not mean that an action is right because it is supported by masses of men; solidarity can be achieved without reference to the merits of a case.   The relationship between the leader of a union and the members is an internal matter which ought to be resolved within the union, but the price of an internal solution is often high.   After the refusal of the leaders of the National Union of Railwaymen to strike with the locomotive men in 1924 a breakaway union for signalmen was formed[1]; the year before, Ernest Bevin had refused to break an agreement with the port employers and he lost members to the newly named National Amalgamated Stevedores and Dockers' Union; and in 1954 Arthur Deakin lost dock members to the same union in part because he believed in the sanctity of agreements.

It has been assumed so far that the maintenance of collective bargaining machinery is of the utmost importance.   An individual trade union leader, however, has his own scale of values, and if he rates solidarity within his organization higher than the worth of bargaining machinery then he will disregard agreements when he considers it necessary.

THE ACCEPTANCE OF STATE HONOURS

Once trade unions had become not only legally recognized but socially accepted institutions, there seemed to be no logical reason why its leaders should not be accorded the same social status by the State as that received by leaders of other established institutions, such as political parties.   There were reasons, of course, why union leaders ought to have refused to be fitted neatly into the social structure of society.   In the first place, trade unions were instruments for achieving social as well as economic equality.   Secondly, it was inconsistent with good leadership for a trade union general secretary to mark himself off from his members by accepting social distinctions.   And thirdly, because the true relationship between a leader who accepts an Honour and the members of the Government who are responsible for having it conferred is rarely known to the

---

[1] *The Lighted Flame*, by Norman McKillop, p. 141.

rank and file, the suspicion of patronage can easily be created. The suspicion may have no foundation in fact, but once it is suggested no amount of denial is able to remove its effect completely. In that last connection it was not to the advantage of the first Trade Union leaders who accepted Honours that they received them from Lloyd George, who unashamedly practised patronage. Of the Birthday Honours List that gave the former trade unionist David Shackleton[1] a knighthood, James Sexton[2] a C.B.E., and Ben Turner[3] and Robert Young[4] each an O.B.E., *The Times* wrote: 'If honours must be bestowed for no ostensible public service, let the real reason for their bestowal be frankly stated in every case . . . in a dreary waste of baronets . . . the old atmosphere of party bargaining hangs heavy over the List.'[5]

The dispute about Honours mainly concerns the limit above which Labour leaders ought not to go. Mr. Arthur Henderson, who was made a Privy Councillor in January 1915, described this later as 'an honour, and may I say I hope it is the only honour that any Labour man will ever accept. In my opinion, it is the only honour that is pure in the whole of the honours given in this country.'[6] And the criticisms in the main have been levied against those who have accepted knighthoods and peerages. A distinction can however be made between these. A knighthood is a mark of social grading that involves no obligation. This is not the case with a peerage. Given that a House of Lords exists with political and judicial functions, and that considerable unbalance exists between the representatives of the Conservative and Labour parties, then a trade union leader who accepted a peerage could at least do useful work there. But he would still be a party to anachronistic social distinctions.

Knighthoods

Since 1914 trade union leaders have increasingly given tacit support to the social fabric of the State. Neither by their speeches nor by their actions have the majority rebelled against it; and by their acceptance of Honours they have accepted the implicit obligation to perpetuate the system. The first former working man with trade union connections to receive a knighthood was Randal Cremer in

[1] Shackleton was then Permanent Secretary to the Ministry of Labour. He had been the president of the Weavers' Amalgamation, a member of the Parliamentary Committee of the Trades Union Congress, 1904–1910, and its chairman in 1908 and 1909.

[2] General Secretary of the National Union of Dock, Riverside and General Workers, 1893–1922.

[3] General President of the National Union of Textile Workers.

[4] General Secretary of the Amalgamated Society of Engineers, 1913–1919.

[5] *The Times*, 4 June 1917. There were three viscounties, five baronies, twenty-five baronetcies, and fifty knighthoods.

[6] *Arthur Henderson. A biography*, by Mary Agnes Hamilton, p. 104. He said this in a speech at Edinburgh in 1922.

1907. He was not knighted, of course, for his trade union work, which received no mention even in *Who's Who*, but for his work for international arbitration. Cremer had been one of the founders of the Amalgamated Society of Carpenters and Joiners in 1860 and for two and a half years from 1864 he acted as the secretary of the First International Workingmen's Association of which Karl Marx was a prominent executive member. After Cremer came Shackleton in 1917.

Though with the advent of a Labour Government in 1924 a number of trade union leaders assumed high government office, no attempt was made to break with social tradition and convention in such matters as Court dress and functions. The Labour Prime Minister, Mrs. Hamilton records, 'was all for continuity and for ritual'.[1] One former union leader emerged with a knighthood from that Government. He was James O'Grady, who on the dissolution was appointed to the post of Governor of Tasmania. In 'strict accordance with precedent he was created a K.C.M.G.'.[2] The times were not propitious for the conferment of knighthoods on practising trade union leaders. The Movement was displaying a renewed surge of militancy which resulted in some antipathy between the industrial and political wings of the Labour Movement.

The next stage occurred in 1931 when James Sexton, Ben Turner, and Robert Young, the three who had received lesser honours from Lloyd George, were created knights. These were more in the nature of political honours than anything else and they aroused little comment.[3] If it had been a shocking thing for trade unionists to be knighted one would have expected *The Times* to be shocked, but it made no comment. This was an indication of the change that had taken place in the attitude of conservative minds towards trade union leaders. The change was confirmed by its remarks on the Birthday Honours List in 1935. 'As for our national affairs,' *The Times* remarked, 'the great part played in them by the Trade Unions is recognized by the fact that two members at the next meeting of the

[1] Op. cit., p. 237.
[2] *The Times* (obituary notice), 11 December 1934. O'Grady had been an organizer for the National Amalgamated Furnishing Trades Association, the general secretary of the National Federation of General Workers, and in 1898 the president of the Trades Union Congress. The appointment of a member of the Labour Party to a Colonial Governorship created a precedent and was criticized. O'Grady, however, proved a complete success. The *Yorkshire Post* commented (24 February 1925) that 'his remarks showed that he is indeed a great Imperialist'.
[3] Sexton had combined his trade union work as a national supervisor of the Docks Section of the T. & G.W.U. with a Parliamentary career. He retired from full-time trade union work in 1928 and was near the end of his political career as well. Turner was the president of the National Union of Textile Workers at the time of the investiture, but he too was a politician and from June 1929 till June 1930 he was the Secretary for Mines in the Second Labour Government. The third recipient of a knighthood, Robert Young, was solely a politician at the time, having relinquished the general secretaryship of the A.S.E. in 1919.

T.U.C. will be Sir Arthur Pugh and Sir Walter Citrine.'[1] Never
before had trade union service been recognized in such a fashion.
Neither of the men had undertaken political activities, and though
Pugh had only eighteen months to remain in office as general
secretary of the Iron and Steel Trades Confederation, Citrine had
many years of active union work ahead of him.   And the recognition
had come from a 'National' Government, dominated by Conservatives and bitterly opposed by the Labour Party.   No further trade
unionists accepted knighthoods until after the Labour Government
had been formed in 1945; then it became a commonplace occurrence.[2]

Peerages

The selection of trade unionists for elevation to the House of
Lords has been undertaken much more moderately.   Sir Walter
Citrine in reply to a critic in 1935 who stated that the path he had
taken when he accepted a knighthood led up to a coronet, said:
'Your Secretary could have had a Coronet long ago if he had wanted
it—and from the hands of a Labour Government . . .'.[3]   The first
trade union peer, however, was created by Mr. Winston Churchill
in January 1944.   He was William Westwood, the general secretary
of the Shipconstructors' and Shipwrights' Association, who was the
Chief Industrial Adviser to the Board of Admiralty, 1942–1945, on
leave of absence from his union.   Westwood had received an O.B.E.
in 1920.[4]   Amongst the peers created by the Labour Government
after 1945 were a number of men with varying degrees of trade union
prominence.   Most of these were primarily politicians who had
started out as union officials[5] and only one, Reginald Crook who

[1] *The Times*, 3 June 1935.
[2] The following general secretaries received knighthoods during and after 1945;
Mark Hodgson, United Society of Boilermakers (1945); John Hallsworth, National
Union of Distributive and Allied Workers (1946); Luke Fawcett, Amalgamated Union
of Building Trade Workers (1948); George Chester, National Union of Boot and Shoe
Operatives (1948); John Stephenson, Plumbing Trades Union (1948); Will Lawther,
President, National Union of Mineworkers (1949); Vincent Tewson, Trades Union
Congress (1950); Richard Coppock, National Federation of Building Trade Operatives
(1951); Lincoln Evans, Iron and Steel Trades Confederation (1953); Andrew Naesmith,
Amalgamated Weavers' Association (1953); Alfred Roberts, Card, Blowing and Ring
Room Operatives (1955); Tom O'Brien, National Association of Theatrical and Kine
Employees (1956); Tom Williamson, National Union of General and Municipal
Workers (1956).
[3] T.U.C. Report, 1935, p. 429.
[4] Charles Latham, who became a peer in December 1941, had been a member of the
executive of the National Union of Clerks from 1915 and its president in 1917, but he
ceased his union work (part-time) on starting in business on his own as an accountant
in 1927.   Subsequently he became the Leader of the London County Council.   On
his creation, an announcement was made from 10 Downing Street that his and three
others were 'not made as political honours or rewards but as a special measure of
State Policy'.   They were designed to strengthen the Labour Party in the Upper
House during the Wartime Coalition Government (Labour Party Report, 1942, p. 56).
[5] Joseph Henderson was president of the National Union of Railwaymen from 1933–
1936, but both before and after those dates he was a Member of Parliament.   He
became Lord Henderson in 1950 but died before taking his seat in the House of Lords.
David Kirkwood, noted as a leader of shop-stewards during the First World War,

2+T.U.L.

became a peer in 1947, continued in office afterwards. He was the general secretary of the Ministry of Labour Staff Association from 1925 to 1951. Sir Walter Citrine was given a peerage on relinquishing his union office to join the National Coal Board; A. G. Walkden received his nine years after retiring from office[1] and Charles Dukes became Lord Dukeston shortly after retiring from the position of general secretary of the National Union of General and Municipal Workers. Dukes was Chairman of the Trades Union Congress in 1946 and its vice-Chairman in 1947, during which year he was a peer.

Explanations of Behaviour

If there are trade union ethical reasons for allowing the Honours system to disappear by default, what explanations have been given to justify the actual behaviour of trade unionists in accepting Honours?

First, it is said that the matter is unimportant; Arthur Henderson took this view. When the first Labour Government was criticized for its ready acceptance of tradition and convention Mrs. Hamilton wrote that 'Henderson took small interest [in the issue]. He would have been glad to see panoply dropped, as a sign that a Labour Government was not going in for "continuity". But fuss over secondary matters was altogether alien to his temper. Let those who liked functions go to them. As for clothes, what did they matter, anyway?'[2] Arthur Deakin adopted a similar attitude. When his Union delegate conference debated a motion in 1953 that deplored 'the acceptance of titles and honours by leaders of the Labour Movement bestowed by Tory Governments . . .', he asked the delegates not to waste the time of the conference on a triviality, as they had much more important matters to discuss. 'I do not regard a title', he said, 'as an honour. I regard it as a costly luxury to the recipient.' On another occasion Deakin said that people in the Movement regarded the matter lightly; that even those who objected soon forgot about it and that it in no way affected the relationship between leaders and their members.[3] In the main this was a correct interpretation. When the principle involved in Walter Citrine's acceptance of a knighthood was questioned in 1935, Citrine said that

---

became Lord Kirkwood in 1951. Lords Hall, Lawson, and Macdonald had been active in the Miners' Federation relatively early in their careers.

[1] Citrine did not resign from his post as general secretary of the Trades Union Congress—he was given 'leave of absence for an indefinite period, on the understanding that he would be free to return to the service of the Congress in a position of equal status to the one he [had] so long held . . .' (T.U.C. Report, 1946, p. 24). Walkden had been the general secretary of the Railway Clerks' Association, 1906–1936. He had been a Member of Parliament from 1935 till 1945, when he went to the House of Lords.

[2] *Arthur Henderson. A biography*, p. 237.

[3] In a discussion with the writer in January 1955.

he had looked in vain for a statement of policy covering it from either
the Trades Union Congress or the Labour Party. He asked:
'. . . has Congress laid down any such principle? Honours are not
new. Honours have been accepted by very important persons in
our Movement, not only in the last few years, but ranging over many
years. . . .'[1]

In most cases, as with Applegarth and Prior, the reaction of the
ordinary members has been eulogistic rather than critical. Arthur
Pugh, knighted at the same time as Citrine, expressed in his union
journal 'his keen appreciation for the large number of messages of
congratulations . . . received from members, branches, and branch
officers'.[2] The members of the Ministry of Labour Staff Association
reacted similarly when their general secretary was created a peer in
June 1947.[3]

The question of honours had been raised formally at the Labour
Party Conference in 1933 in a motion which stated that this 'Conference declares that no member of the Labour Party shall accept
Honours for political activities'. It was moved incompetently,
aroused no interest, and was passed over for other business. When
in 1935 Citrine's acceptance of a knighthood focussed attention
on honours, the Trades Union Congress meted out similar treatment
to a motion 'regretting that active leaders of the Trade Union
Movement should accept honours at the hands of a Government
which is not established in the interests of the workers'. As Arthur
Deakin suggested, the criticisms contained no sustaining force.

This was amply illustrated by the Labour Party's handling of the
subject in 1935 and 1936. In 1935 the Labour Party Conference
placed 'on record its conviction that Socialist participation in such
functions and honours can be justified only in exceptional circumstances for the express purpose of frustrating the propaganda of the
capitalist parties . . .'[4]; it asked for a clearer definition of the
Socialist attitude towards 'ceremonial functions and so-called
honours' and for a National Executive Committee Report on the
acceptance of Honours, to be presented to the next year's conference.
On the Constitutional Sub-Committee of the National Executive,
which was given the task of producing the report, sat J. R. Clynes,
chairman; Sir Walter Citrine and A. G. Walkden (later Lord

---

[1] T.U.C. Report, 1935, p. 429.
[2] *Man and Metal*, June 1935.
[3] Crook had been ill and was convalescing when he received the news. In the
following issue of his union journal the union president wrote: 'I imagine that his
recovery to full health is going to be accelerated, not only by the news of the great
Honour, but by the hundreds of wires and letters of congratulations from members
of our rank and file—to senior officers of the Ministry of Labour and other Government Departments, members of the Cabinet and ordinary citizens.' (*Civil Service
Argus*, July 1947.)
[4] Labour Party Conference Report, 1935, p. 238.

Walkden) as trade union representatives; the Rt. Hon. F. O. Roberts of the Typographical Association as a Labour Party Executive representative, and seven others.[1]

The Report stated that hitherto the Party had not laid down any policy on the questions of participation in ceremonial functions or the conferment and acceptance of Honours. It explained the purpose of peerages—'so long as the House of Lords continues to exist, the Labour case must be competently presented there. . . . Further the creation of Peers in large numbers may prove to be the only possible way to abolish the House of Lords'; of membership of the Privy Council—it 'marks the status of a Cabinet Minister under the Constitution as it exists today'; of 'the Order of Merit, Honorary University Degrees, and the Freedom of Cities and Boroughs'— they 'are conferred on persons of distinction, and as a recognition of merit and service'. It significantly omitted reference to the honours that were causing consternation, except by implication. 'In the Civil Service', it stated, 'the conferment of Honours is a method of establishing status.' It concluded that it 'would be impossible for the Labour Movement to lay down a binding rule which would bar individuals from accepting Honours. A ruling of this kind could only be enforced by expulsion from the Party, and if any Honours are to be recognized at all, the Movement would be called upon to differentiate between the Honours which could be and could not be accepted—a task which would not be without serious difficulties.'[2] A delegate called the report an 'exhibition of tight-rope walking' and a majority of the delegates agreed with him. On a show of hands they agreed by 185 votes to 174 to refer the report back to the National Executive.[3] The subject inspired hardly any debate, and if it had been considered at all important by the National Executive they would have called for a card vote. No mention was made of it at any subsequent Labour Party Conference or Trades Union Congress.

Secondly, the acceptance of Honours has been considered by some in the trade union movement to be the prerogative of individuals. This follows, of course, from the attitude described above. The consequence of this practice is that one cannot generally apply the attitude of the movement to the individual union leaders. It is wrong to assume that because a union leader carries no Honour he has not been offered one. Those who have refused Honours cannot be listed, because refusals are normally secret, but it is known that some leaders have refused to bind the movement to the principle of

---

[1] They were George Dallas, Hugh Dalton, C. R. Attlee, H. J. Laski, H. B. Lees-Smith, H. Scott Lindsay, and Lord Snell.
[2] Labour Party Report, 1936, Appendix VII, p. 293.
[3] Labour Party Conference Report, 1936, p. 257.

not accepting certain Honours though they follow that course themselves. Arthur Deakin was one of these. Although he had accepted certain Honours,[1] he had on two occasions declined a knighthood.

Those who have accepted knighthoods and peerages have done so for reasons which are mainly personal. A man may have been flattered, or, as has been said on more than one occasion, his wife may have been the deciding influence. Emotion has probably been more important than logic in most cases. The right of a trade union leader to take independent action in the matter was supported by Deakin. 'It would be a very mistaken policy', he said, 'for this Union to turn its back on that traditional freedom of a person to use his own judgment and make his decision as I have done in regard to a matter of this character.'[2] Though a union general secretary or president would normally consult his executive before accepting an Honour, it is likely that the executive would decline to intervene, as did the General Council of the Trades Union Congress in 1935 when Citrine approached it. At the Congress Citrine said: 'I do not know whether other individuals in this Congress may have been approached on this subject and perhaps have accepted something, but I anticipate like myself they acted on their own responsibility. They acted as they thought right. I am not at the moment concerned with giving my reasons why I acted as I did.'[3] Nor at any other moment did he give his reasons. Others have been just as silent.

What justification is there for a trade union leader to treat the receipt of an Honour, particularly a knighthood or a peerage, as an individual matter? Can he lay claim to the same civic rights and individual liberty of an ordinary citizen as Sir Walter Citrine did?[4] It is sometimes said that a union leader gets his Honour for performing public duties which lie outside the field of his trade union work. The journal of the National Federation of Building Trade Operatives, for example, stated that its general secretary got a knighthood as 'a recognition of a life-long public service, both in municipal and other spheres'.[5] A trade union leader, however, is a public figure by virtue of the office he holds and his public offices depend mainly on his official union status. To remove the status is to reduce his influence considerably. A Government when it is recommending the award of the highest State Honours is acknowledging power and influence, and those Governments most keenly aware of the power

[1] C.B.E., C.H., and membership of the Privy Council.
[2] T. & G.W.U. Biennial Delegate Conference (B.D.C.), June 1953.
[3] T.U.C. Report, 1935, p. 431.
[4] Cf. T.U.C. Report, 1935, p. 431.
[5] *The Operative Builder*, March–April, 1951, p. 42.

of trade unions recommend most Honours for their leaders.   Hence
the high proportion of union leaders who receive Honours during
war-time and when there are Labour Governments.[1]   In 1938 three
General Council members were Commanders of the Order of the
British Empire (C.B.E.) and one an Officer of the Order (O.B.E.).
By 1946 thirteen possessed one or other of these honours, one was
a Companion of Honour, and two held knighthoods.

An official compiler of Honours Lists must, moreover, be conscious
of the distribution of power within the trade union movement, and
the Honour handed out must bear some relation to this.[2]   Charles
Bowerman was made a Privy Councillor in 1916 when he was the
general secretary of the Trades Union Congress[3] and the last two
men to hold this office have been knighted.   All except two of the
practising trade unionists to receive knighthoods have been members
of the General Council of the Trades Union Congress and the two
exceptions were prominent in their own field.[4]   Even within the
General Council the relative positions of power are recognized.
Such has been the change in the trade union attitude towards
Honours that now a knighthood (or the offer of one) is taken to
indicate leadership ability.   This was acknowledged by the General
Council when it wrote that the 'knighthood [Sir George Chester]
was awarded in 1948 attested the place he had won in the front rank
of Trade Union leadership'.[5]   As in the Civil Service the conferment
of Honours is a method of establishing status, so in the trade union
movement is it tending to become a recognition of status.   Lesser
leaders than those mentioned above have received correspondingly
less important Honours.   The recognition, however, is not of the
status of general secretaries as individuals but as leaders of unions
and this is determined by the relative amount of power the various
unions hold.

Lastly, the attitude of some union executives is to treat an Honour
to a general secretary as an honour to the union.   For example,
when the general secretary of the Iron and Steel Trades Confederation was knighted in 1935, the union journal recorded that 'we feel

[1] This is not the whole reason.   There is a belief amongst many trade unionists
that there is nothing inherently wrong with the Honours system so long as the Honours
are distributed by a Labour Government.   Sir Walter Citrine scored a debating point
in 1935 when he said: 'if the Honours system is wrong . . . it cannot be right for the
Labour Government to distribute Honours, can it?'   (T.U.C. Report, 1935, p. 431.)
[2] The principal determinants of this position are its absolute size and its industrial
strength.   Some unions are powerful simply because they are big, others because they
are highly organized in vital industries.   Prestige is derived from either of these
factors plus good leadership.
[3] He was general secretary from 1911 till 1923.
[4] They were Richard Coppock and John Stephenson, the general secretary and
president of the National Federation of Building Trade Operatives.
[5] T.U.C. Report, 1949, p. 87.   Sir George Chester was the general secretary of the
National Union of Boot and Shoe Operatives, 1930–1949, and a member of the T.U.C.
General Council, 1937–1948.

that our Chief Administrative Officer has enhanced the prestige of our great organization'.[1]   This assumes that there is an identity between the ethical basis of the trade union movement and the Society in which it operates; that the same conception of Honour holds for both.   One accepts or rejects this assumption according to one's conception of the purpose of trade unions.   If trade unions have as a purpose the elimination of social privilege then surely values based on social inequality should be unacceptable to them. Moreover, if the argument in the previous paragraph is valid, it is mistaken to think that an Honour enhances the prestige of a union; it merely accords recognition to prestige already secured.

[1] *Man and Metal*, June 1935.

Chapter Three

THE FORMATION OF THE TRANSPORT AND GENERAL WORKERS' UNION

THE behaviour and activities of a trade union leader are influenced by the organization he leads as well as by the traditions and loyalties which were described in the preceding chapter. He has to work within the procedures of the organization at a pace determined by constitutional practice and by the fact that the organization is operated by fallible human beings. And he has to meet whatever problems are created by the peculiarities of the organization. In order to understand the problems of organizing and administering a union it is necessary to know something about its origin and development. In this study we are concerned with Arthur Deakin's leadership of the Transport and General Workers' Union, and this chapter aims to describe how this Union was formed and developed.

THE AMALGAMATION

Trade unions throughout the greater part of the nineteenth century were formed on a craft basis. There was little collusion between unions, even in industries such as the building industry where a number of craft unions experienced similar industrial conditions. The amalgamations of that period were between local unions catering for workers in the same craft. There were no multi-craft amalgamations.[1]

The difficulties in the way of multi-craft amalgamations and the success of the development of single-craft unions, such as the boilermakers and carpenters, led Sidney and Beatrice Webb to definite conclusions about trade union organization which have been invalidated by subsequent experience. They believed that effective trade union action depended on the members of a union being interchangeable in their jobs, and that if this were not so the organization would be unstable. 'The very aim of uniformity of conditions,' they wrote, 'the very fact that uniformity of trade policy

---

[1] When, for example, William Newton and William Allan formed the Amalgamated Society of Engineers in 1851 they failed to persuade the patternmakers, foundry-workers, metal-mechanics and smiths to relinquish their autonomy and craft identity.

is indispensable to efficiency, makes it almost impossible to combine in a single organization, with a common purse, a common executive, and a common staff of salaried officials, men of widely different occupations and grades of skill, widely different Standards of Life and industrial needs, or widely different numerical strengths and strategic opportunities.'[1] They could not foresee that under the exigencies of changed industrial conditions men would overcome their prejudices and construct organizations to meet their needs.

The unions which were established after the London Dock Strike in 1889 catered for semi-skilled and unskilled workers. Dockers, transport workers, gas workers, general labourers, and many other types combined in permanent organizations which possessed few of the conditions the Webbs believed necessary for an effective trade union organization. Nevertheless, these unions expanded. But because they found that excessive competition for members and unco-ordinated trade union action reduced their effectiveness *vis-à-vis* employers and the government, they formed their own federations for joint action.

On the initiative of the Dock, Wharf, Riverside and General Workers' Union a National Transport Workers' Federation was formed in 1910. It comprised about thirty-six unions concerned with organizing seamen, dockers, carters, and others engaged in waterside transport work. The general labour unions had already formed a consultative body, the General Labourers' National Council,[2] in 1908. The latter body concerned itself with arranging for the mutual recognition of the cards of its affiliated unions, with the elimination of demarcation disputes and with encouraging amalgamation. Both federations simplified and improved negotiations in some of the industries they covered by raising industrial issues to a national level and by concluding agreements with the national representatives of employers. But, like cartels, they suffered from an inherent instability and were threatened with disintegration whenever matters arose on which uniform policy could not be achieved without a disproportionate sacrifice by some unions in the Federation; or whenever a union thought it could benefit from unilateral action. The autonomy of the unions in the federations prevented effective co-ordinated industrial action. After the First World War it became increasingly clear to the leaders of the Dock, Wharf, Riverside, and General Workers' Union and the National Union of Dock, Riverside and General Workers, that they needed the advantages of a federation for satisfying separate trade interests and the benefits of a highly centralized administrative machine for

[1] *Industrial Democracy*, pp. 138–139.
[2] Called the National Federation of General Workers in 1917.

2*

issues requiring common action. These could only be secured
through the kind of amalgamation which satisfied sectional trade
interests without permitting the constituent unions to retain their
full autonomy.

Successful amalgamations require the removal of several points of
friction. There is the reluctance to relinquish trade identity and
autonomy. Unions interested in amalgamating are often of different
sizes and the smallest unions fear being absorbed, with the loss of
traditions and rights and without adequate representation. Unions
often have different degrees of solvency: financially weak unions are
usually keener to amalgamate than are larger, wealthier organizations
or small organizations with a high *per capita* valuation. An amalgamation may involve wealthy unions' subsidizing other unions and,
perhaps, taking over their liabilities. How to pool the resources of
a number of unions raises a major difficulty. Before 1948, when
unions carried out Friendly Society functions, they frequently had
different scales of contributions and benefits and members were
reluctant either to forgo relatively high benefits or to agree to pay
higher contributions if amalgamation involved either of these. The
greater the differences in size and wealth of the organizations
concerned the bigger the sacrifices that might be involved.

Yet despite these and other difficulties there was a strengthening
of trade union forces by amalgamation from 1918 to 1924. During
the war the Government, through its control of the coal mines and
the railways and through the arbitration tribunals it had established,
became an important regulator of wage rates. National rates in
some industries were substituted for local rates and trade union
officials in particular industries had to work together more closely
than they had done hitherto. Their war-time experiences showed
them the advantages of closer unity, and soon after the war a number
of amalgamations were formed.[1] It was not unusual then for the
leaders of the two dockers' unions to discuss amalgamation; the
nature of their task, however, was exceptional.[2]

The Annual General Council Meeting of the National Transport
Workers' Federation in June 1920 passed a resolution favouring an
amalgamation of transport unions. Resulting from this, on 14 July
1920, a Joint Sub-Committee consisting of seven representatives from
the Dock, Wharf, Riverside and General Workers' Union and six
representatives from the National Union of Dock, Riverside and

[1] For example, the Amalgamated Engineering Union, Amalgamated Society of
Woodworkers, Amalgamated Union of Building Trade Workers, National Union of
Foundry Workers, National Union of Vehicle Builders, and the National Union of
Sheet Metal Workers.
[2] The leaders of other non-craft unions were discussing amalgamation during this
period. See *General Union*, by H. A. Clegg, Ch. I, for a description of the activities
which led to the formation of the National Union of General and Municipal Workers.

General Workers[1] met to examine the difficulties of amalgamation, under the chairmanship of Harry Gosling who was not a member of either union but was the president of the National Transport Workers' Federation.[2] The committee decided to invite fourteen unions[3] to form a new organization with a new title 'and to be developed on a departmental basis with National Trade Groups to prevent loss of identity'. The latter decision was the kernel of the proposed organization and was destined to overcome the problems of conflicting trade interests which Sidney and Beatrice Webb thought were insuperable in a single unit of government. The idea is attributed to Ernest Bevin who was then the Assistant General Secretary of the Dockers' Union. It may have been derived from the system of trade departments in the American Federation of Labour which Bevin inspected when he visited the U.S.A. as a fraternal delegate from the Trades Union Congress in 1915.[4] Nevertheless its application to the problem in hand was a piece of constitutional ingenuity.

At this stage the sub-committee did not envisage one big union for general workers. Bevin had intended to invite the National Union of General Workers and other similar unions to take part in the original amalgamation but he had been opposed by representatives from the transport unions. Most of those who had objected to issuing invitations on a wider scale did not join the amalgamation.[5] The success of subsequent amalgamation discussions and ballots, however, lent support to the advocates of one big union.

The Conference of representatives of the unions met on 18 August 1920 and decided unanimously in favour of amalgamation.[6] An Amalgamation Committee consisting of one representative from each union was established with Bevin as its secretary and Gosling as chairman. After selecting a title for the new Union they decided

[1] They were: Ben Tillett, Ernest Bevin, D. W. Milford, H. W. Kay, R. O'Grady, F. Semark, W. Batt, and James Sexton, G. Milligan, P. McQuaide, P. McKibbins, H. O. Pugh, M. Reid for the two unions respectively. The latter union was commonly known as the Liverpool Union.
[2] He was also the general secretary of the Amalgamated Society of Watermen, Lightermen and Bargemen.
[3] National Union of Dock, Riverside and General Workers; Dock, Wharf, Riverside and General Workers' Union; Scottish Union of Dock Labourers; National Amalgamated Labourers' Union of Great Britain and Ireland; National Shipping Clerks' Guild; National Union of Docks, Wharves and Shipping Staffs; Amalgamated Stevedores Labour Protection League; North of England Trimmers' and Teemers' Association; Labour Protection League (South Side); Cardiff, Penarth and Barry Coal Trimmers' Union; Amalgamated Society of Watermen, Lightermen and Bargemen; Weaver Watermen's Association; Mersey Watermen; National Union of Ships Clerks, Grain Weighers and Coalmeters.
[4] Harry Gosling visited the U.S.A. as a fraternal delegate the following year. He, too, could have been impressed by the A.F. of L. organization.
[5] Stated by Bevin at a joint amalgamation conference with the National Union of General and Municipal Workers in January 1926.
[6] The Weaver Watermen's Association was not represented but it asked to be informed of any decisions reached.

to extend its scope to cover road transport workers and they invited seven further unions to join in the discussions.[1] Between August and December 1920 a complete amalgamation scheme was drafted, and was accepted by representatives from nineteen unions at a conference on 1 December 1920. The Conference pledged itself to do everything in its power to get it adopted by the members of the unions concerned.

The first stage of a difficult amalgamation process had been completed. It was not easy to convince the established leaders of many trade unions that their members would benefit if they would relinquish their independent authority and take up subordinate posts in a large organization.[2] Many of the unions competed for membership and, in London particularly, the relations between full-time officers were strained. The amalgamation scheme had to unite widely different types of workers together into a permanent organization without initially disturbing the traditions and methods of organization of the different unions. Three years after the Union had been formed Bevin, when talking about branch administration, said: 'I want to say that if we had attempted at the beginning to work out a uniform system we should never have had the amalgamation. We found so many systems in operation that we had to carry on what was then being paid and we find that no one system will work. . . . You cannot, right away, impose a uniform system on 1,870 branches.'[3] He had warned his provisional executive council: 'We have not got to be upset by anomalies, we have got to tolerate them and you must give me five years in which to work out a uniform system.' In addition to different methods of organization the rates of contributions and the rates and types of benefit payment varied between unions. When trouble arose in 1925 over funeral benefits

[1] These unions were: the United Vehicle Workers; National Union of Vehicle Workers; Liverpool and District Carters' and Motormen's Union; Amalgamated Association of Carters and Motormen; North of Scotland Horse and Motormen's Association; United Road Transport Workers' Association; and Scottish Horse and Motormen.
[2] It is often thought that the main obstacle to amalgamation lies in the vested interests of full-time officials. Francis Williams expressed this opinion when he wrote about the formation of the T. & G.W.U. 'Presidents and General Secretaries', he wrote, 'who had grown accustomed to being the undisputed monarchs of all they surveyed, even if what they surveyed was small, did not take kindly to proposals which meant the disappearance of their offices and the merging of their authority in that of a vast new organization in which they would be at best but minor territorial chieftains.' (*Ernest Bevin*, p. 101.) The President of the new Union, Harry Gosling, did not take this view. He wrote: 'Often I have heard it said by "left wingers" that the officials of a trade union are usually anti-amalgamation, but the events in our own union entirely confound that statement. Twenty general secretaries (by 1927), a number of assistant secretaries, treasurers, and other chief officials willingly gave up their old status and gladly undertook the new duties to which they were allocated.' (*Up and Down Stream*, by Harry Gosling, p. 186.) Gosling's opinion is supported by the evidence. Some of the union leaders were more eager to belong to a large amalgamated union than were their ordinary members. James Sexton was one such man. See his autobiography, *Sir James Sexton, Agitator*, p. 268.
[3] 1925 Biennial Delegate Conference.

Bevin said: 'I have often said that when you are trying to bring about amalgamation there is more trouble about Funeral Benefit than anything else.'[1]

The Amalgamation Scheme which is reproduced in Appendix I shows, as far as a written constitution can show, how it was proposed to surmount these difficulties. Each member was given dual representation throughout the union. His trade interests were looked after by a regional[2] and national trade group committee in one of five trade groups which covered the whole of the membership. Each national trade group committee was allowed one representative on the General Executive Council. For administrative purposes the Union was divided into eleven regions with one representative for each on the General Executive Council. Transferring officials were to suffer no decrease in salary and all of them were to be given the right to retain their jobs or to receive compensation in lieu of their jobs. Members of amalgamating unions could either continue to pay contributions and receive benefits on their pre-amalgamation scales or they could pay the new rates and accept the new scale of benefits set for the Union. New members had to accept the new rates.

Ballots were held in twenty unions, and, in some cases after second ballots, fourteen of them met the requirements of the Trade Union (Amalgamation) Act.[3] Eleven of these unions met in conference on 11 May 1921 and decided that the new Union would officially function from 1 January 1922.[4] They replaced the Amalgamation Committee by a Provisional Executive Council and elected provisional Executive officers. Harry Gosling was unanimously elected President; Bevin, in competition with Stanley Hirst, general secretary of the United Vehicle Workers' Union, was elected Provisional Secretary; and H. W. Kay of Bevin's union became the Provisional Treasurer.

The officials and executive members then set about creating the administrative machinery of the Transport and General Workers' Union. The first task was to draw up a constitution in preparation for a Special Rules Conference in September 1921. The Rules Drafting Committee circulated copies of a constitution to a thousand branches with a request to send only 'such amendments as they sincerely desired and as would challenge principles'. One hundred

1 Ibid.
2 Here and hereafter areas in the Union are referred to as regions. See note at the beginning of the book.
3 The Trade Union (Amalgamation) Act of 1917 required that in each trade union the votes of 50 per cent. of the members entitled to vote should be recorded and that the majority in favour of amalgamation should be at least 20 per cent. of those voting before an amalgamation could be brought about.
4 Three unions that voted to amalgamate had not received the results of their ballots when this conference was held.

and eighty-nine branches forwarded amendments for examination
but none aimed to alter the basic structure of the organization, and
despite the Executive's request, few amendments were concerned
with principles.

The construction of a suitable framework for the organization of
the new Union was only one task, and perhaps not the most important, confronting the Provisional Executive.   Uniting approximately
297,500 workers,[1] belonging to fourteen distinct and competitive
unions, was a human relations problem of some complexity, and
until the allegiance of the many thousands of voluntary officials had
been obtained little progress could be made with the administrative
reorganization of the unions.   Local committees were set up throughout the country to obtain unity of action, and conferences of full-
time officers were held in each region to arrange for them to work
together harmoniously.   Altogether 245 officials, excluding clerical
staffs, were taken over by the new union.   The salaries and conditions of employment of the officials varied widely between the unions,
and though under the amalgamation scheme the new union was
under obligation to employ them at the same salary rates and
conditions, it was clear that inequitable differentials would have to
be removed; and as their functions were shuffled and regional
hierarchies were created, rewards had to bear some relation to
functions.

Bevin knew that whilst care had to be taken not to arouse resentment against the new union, the ordinary members, and potential
members, would judge it on its achievements; and with that touch
of ruthlessness which is an essential quality of leadership he
endeavoured to weed out inefficient officials.   Provisionally all
present general secretaries were employed as assistant secretaries and
national organizers were attached to the head office.   Few of the
unions involved in the amalgamation had regional organizations (as
distinct from organizers working in the field) and much time was
spent in procuring premises in the regions and in staffing them.

Ernest Bevin was most anxious to establish the machinery of the
National Trade Groups and to appoint the National Group Officials.
At the December 1921 meeting of the Provisional Executive Harry
Gosling was entrusted with the Inland Waterways Section; Alfred
Short with the Administrative, Clerical and Supervisory Section[2];
W. Devenay was made responsible for the General Workers'[Section;
and Ben Tillett was given the direction of the International and
Political section.   Bevin assumed the responsibility for convening

[1] The paper membership of the Union was given as 350,000.
[2] Alfred Short, M.P., had been general secretary of the National Union of Docks,
Wharves and Shipping Staffs, a union, as its name indicates, concerned with the
organization of administrative workers.

the Docks, Wharves and Quays, the Road Commercial and Road Passenger Transport sections. These people had to convene provisional trade group committees at regional and national levels, arrange for elections to these committees, and advise on the selection of specialist officials for their groups. A few weeks after the new Union had been launched officially, full-time permanent officials were appointed to the Trade Groups who were to help carry the Union through its growing pains. All the National Trade Group Secretaries were selected on Bevin's recommendation; he kept the Docks Group for himself and Harry Gosling, the President, supervised the Waterways Group.

Membership and finance returns were obtained from the branches so that the Union's resources could be calculated; following this the branches were allocated to their respective regions and steps were taken to shape the regional administrative machinery. So that the opinions of the members as expressed in their branches could be communicated through the different levels of the new hierarchy with as little delay as possible, Bevin drew up a procedure for holding committee meetings which he communicated to the group and regional secretaries.

There was a limit, however, to the instruction that Bevin could give to his subordinates, particularly regional secretaries who were out of London for most of their time. Necessarily they had to be left to build up their local administrations, and they did so in a manner that made it difficult to impose uniformity of method later when more thought could be given to such matters.

Getting the support of the rank-and-file members for the amalgamation involved much field and propaganda work. Though the number of members opposed to the amalgamation was relatively small, they could have damaged the amalgamation by working against it in their branches or by encouraging their branches to secede from it. It is remarkable that there was so little activity of this kind. Bevin and his Executive had decided that whereas tolerance should be shown to peculiar practices, traditions, and conflicting opinions within the amalgamation, there could be no tolerance shown to those who threatened to break the amalgamation by secession.

The last point to be made in this section concerns the actual work of the Union during the process of the amalgamation. Though the amalgamation task was exacting and absorbed much of the attention of officials, there could be no break in the continuity of service which the unions were formed to provide. The new Union was under an obligation to take over all the agreements with employers contracted by the amalgamating unions and to maintain the representation of these unions on industrial and trade boards.

The methods of negotiation were in a process of simplification and this had a direct bearing on the ability to amalgamate heterogeneous groups of workers. Federations were being formed to represent employers at a national level after the war; national Joint Industrial Councils were being established, and negotiations on issues of wages and vital conditions of employment were tending to be settled nationally. The Shaw Award for dockers in 1920, in which Bevin played so prominent a part, encouraged the development of national negotiations in the dock industry. The movement of industrial activity to the centre gave national officials much greater control over the affairs of unions than they had had hitherto when intricate local negotiations were undertaken. Without this added control the amalgamation would have been more difficult to achieve.

Difficulties arose, however, from factors outside the trade union movement. The initiation of the amalgamation discussions in 1920 almost coincided with the end of the post-war boom period and the most critical stages in the creation of the Transport and General Workers' Union occurred during a state of relatively high unemployment. During slump periods trade unions lose members and are weak in relation to employers; this at the very time when their members need them most. It could be said, then, that the time was unpropitious for creating a new trade union. The unions actually lost members during the eight months between the ballot and when the amalgamation took effect. On the other hand the general realization among active trade unionists that the unions were weak at the wrong time might have stimulated them to desire and work for a bigger, stronger union. In one sense, however, the time was unsuitable. Nothing impresses members more than results and during high unemployment trade union gains are negligible; the unions become essentially protective societies concerned with resisting wage reductions. The benefits of this function are not easily seen nor readily appreciated. There was unrest among London omnibus workers, and before the Union officially existed a conference had to be convened in London to review the whole situation. Bevin reported at the beginning of May 1922 that 'Applications had been received for reductions in wages, and revision of working conditions in connection with practically all the members the Union represents . . . consequently this had led to the handling of a large number of actual strikes, and continuous negotiations of a national, local and individual character, and it had also resulted in a heavy expenditure.'

Whatever the intentions of Bevin and his Provisional Executive concerning the centralization of union control, the events of these early years forced them to leave much authority in the hands of local officials and even when industrial disputes of some magnitude occurred they gave the officials directly concerned plenary powers in negotiations.

AN AMALGAMATION POLICY

There was no stage during the 1920s or the 1930s when it could have been said that the amalgamation process was complete and that the Union had become settled into a rigid institutional form. As can be seen from Appendix II there were only three years between 1922 and 1940 during which an amalgamation did not take place. Each of these years was marked by special circumstances that turned the attention of unions to other things. In 1927 unions were struggling to overcome the effects of the General Strike, and in 1931 and 1932 they were suffering from the impact of severe unemployment. Bevin said in 1925: 'We are continually amalgamating . . . we cannot, therefore, make the Union too rigid.' It was possible for unions to amalgamate for specific services and retain autonomy in their internal government.[1] In September 1922 negotiations were held between representatives of the Transport and General Workers' Union and the North Wales Quarrymen to determine amalgamation proposals. The Quarrymen would not accept complete amalgamation so it was agreed that autonomy should be granted to their Union in its internal affairs, that the existing legal benefits of the Quarrymen's Union should remain unaltered, that it should continue its separate affiliation to the T.U.C., but that its financial obligations should be taken over by the parent union.[2] The North Wales Craftsmen and General Workers' Union and the National Amalgamated Union of Enginemen, Firemen, Motormen, Mechanics and Electrical Workers amalgamated on similar terms.[3]

At the 1933 Biennial Delegate Conference of the Union Bevin was questioned about the agreements the Transport and General Workers' Union had with some of these unions, which were due for renewal. He said that ballots were costly and could not be

[1] This had been done by the United Vehicle Workers before the amalgamation. An organization previously known as the Amalgamated Carters, Lorrymen and Motormen's Union had drawn up an agreement with the United Vehicle Workers under which they retained autonomy in organizing, administration, and selection of officers, and became known as the North of England Commercial Section of that union. The Transport and General Workers' Union took over this arrangement and has continued it to the present day.

[2] At this stage an additional region in the union was constituted in North Wales. It was divided into three sections—the Quarrymen's Section, Craftsmen's Section, and General Workers' Section, and each Section had its own district committee. Arthur Deakin was one of the full-time officials allocated to the region. This is the first mention of him in the Executive minutes.

[3] When the latter union amalgamated in 1926, after an unsuccessful attempt to join with the Electrical Trades Union, it formed a complete and new trade group for Power Workers with its general secretary as the national secretary of the group.

undertaken in the case of every union which wished to amalgamate. Instead, the unions concerned agreed to merge certain of their functions for a specified period. That, he said, satisfied the Registrar. When a number of unions had concluded such agreements they could be included in the same ballot for amalgamation at a greatly reduced cost to the parent union.

The merger overcame a difficulty concerning Transport and General Workers' Union representation on the General Council of the Trades Union Congress. After the reorganization of the Trades Union Congress in 1920 seats on the General Council were allocated to trade groups and only unions within each group could nominate candidates for the seats allocated to that group. The whole Congress, however, cast votes to determine who sat on the General Council. This meant that a small union which became absorbed in another union in a different T.U.C. trade group, lost its right to nominate for the General Council. This, Bevin claimed, was unfair to unions wishing to amalgamate.[1] By leaving the amalgamating unions the right to affiliate to the T.U.C. as a separate entity it was possible to enlarge the union representation on the General Council. The general secretary of the North Wales Quarrymen's Union sits on the General Council as a representative of the Mining and Quarrying Group though the Transport and General Workers' Union can nominate only in the Transport (other than Railways) Group.

Ernest Bevin, on his own initiative during 1922, had extended invitations to many unions to amalgamate with the Transport and General Workers' Union. He was no longer thinking in terms of a union for dock and allied workers and transport workers as the names of the unions he made contact with indicate, and undoubtedly he could see one big union for general workers as a practical possibility. In a methodical fashion he aimed to draw these workers into a single permanent organization which would rival any employer or group of employers in economic power.[2] Requests to

---

[1] Amalgamation can, of course, favour a union unduly. When the unions in the general workers trade group amalgamated, the parent union claimed all the seats on the General Council allocated to that group. This was the case of the National Union of General and Municipal Workers.

[2] Not long after Bevin joined the Movement he became possessed by this idea. When he addressed the 1915 Convention of the American Federation of Labor as a fraternal delegate he said: 'What was the position prior to this outbreak [1914–1918 War]? I want to say . . . that we were coolly and deliberately planning for the perfection of a large organization in order that we could come to death grips with the great social problems of the old country.' (Report of Proceedings of the Thirty-Fifth Annual Convention of the American Federation of Labor, 8–22 November 1915, pp. 216–219.) J. R. Clynes referred to the attempt to form this 'large organization' during amalgamation discussions between the Transport and General Workers' Union and the National Union of General and Municipal Workers in 1926. He said, 'I think it was in another part of this building [Central Hall, Westminster] on the eve of the war that we had a most comprehensive representation of delegates considering the question of that scheme.'

amalgamate were made to the Street Masons, Paviers and Road-
makers' Society, the Operative Bakers, Confectioners and Allied
Workers, the National Union of Agricultural Workers, the National
Sailors' and Firemen's Union, the Liverpool and District Carters' and
Motormen's Union, and other unions. Bevin received the whole-
hearted backing of his Executive Council in his aim to widen the
basis of the Union and in May 1923 they resolved 'That the policy
of this Executive Council be to invite unions to amalgamate wherever
possible, and that during periods between the meetings of the Council
the General Secretary be authorised to approach any union deemed
advisable on the question of amalgamation.'

At a later stage, just prior to the General Strike, negotiations were
being held to bring together the Transport and General Workers'
Union, the National Union of General and Municipal Workers, the
Electrical Trades Union, and six smaller unions. Bevin was extremely enthusiastic about this when he reported to his Executive:

> I would also just call to your mind the enormous value to the movement
> such an amalgamation would be. For instance, the Prime Minister is
> proposing to introduce an Electricity Bill, which, if passed, virtually
> means a national organism for the distribution of electricity and a
> great controlling factor in connection with production. Now, if the
> National Union of General and Municipal Workers, the Electrical
> Trades Union and this Union—including the Power Group—are within
> one organization, it practically gives to us the control of this great new
> development on the Labour side. Amalgamation would mean the
> completion of the organization of the Dock Industry. It virtually
> means that the Gas Industry would be organized within one Group.
> The great Municipal Services and a large number of other Industries
> would be organized within one Group. . . .

An amalgamation between the Transport and General Workers'
Union and the National Union of General Workers had been
suggested at the end of 1922, but it had been put aside because of the
formation of the National Union of General and Municipal Workers
of which the latter Union was a part. During 1925 correspondence
passed between Ernest Bevin and Will Thorne, general secretary of
the National Union of General and Municipal Workers, which
resulted in a meeting of representatives of the two unions on 18
November 1925. Then on 6 January 1926 an amalgamation joint
conference agreed to the principle of amalgamation and appointed
a committee to pursue it. The executives of the two unions
endorsed this agreement. On 14 April 1926 an amalgamation sub-
committee was appointed with instructions to collate information
about the organization of the unions by 5 May 1926. Negotiations
lapsed because of the General Strike, but correspondence concerning

the proposed amalgamation was renewed on 17 May 1926 and continued until October. Then Bevin went to America for three months and Thorne found it inconvenient to attend meetings, so the matter was allowed to drop and was never again renewed. If an amalgamation had materialized a union with about 658,000 members would have resulted, and much duplication of effort and useless competition for members would have been avoided. The union would have had a clear field in many industries—Bevin envisaged a membership of a million and a half in a short time. The thought of this evoked excitement from some of the representatives participating in the discussion. They all liked the idea of one large union. But beyond this desire for bigness there were no powerful motives to draw the representatives together, and they argued over minor matters such as the ability of union officials to carry out their union duties whilst in Parliament. If either union had been in financial difficulties the story would have had a different ending.

The impetus which unsettled industrial conditions had given to amalgamations in most industries in Britain after the First World War had lost none of its force by 1926. In fact it was becoming more and more apparent that a greater unity was necessary if trade unions were to withstand the impact of unemployment, antagonistic employers, and an unsympathetic government. Some unions, however, were seeking unity through a strengthening of the Trades Union Congress and through industrial alliances. They saw no reason why they should lose themselves in the expanding Transport and General Workers' Union empire. The leaders of these unions did not share Bevin's conception of union strength through one large union. In fact at the 1924 Hull Trades Union Congress it was resolved: '(*a*) That the time has arrived when the number of trade unions should be reduced to an absolute minimum. (*b*) That the aim should be as far as possible organisation by industry with every worker a member of the appropriate organisation.' The General Council was instructed to draw up a scheme for organization by industry and a scheme to secure unity of action, 'without the definite merging of existing unions, by a scientific linking up of same to present a united front'. It was three years before the General Council was able to present its report on the resolution. In the interim the General Strike brought amalgamation discussions to a close, revealed the ineffectiveness of industrial alliances, and strengthened Ernest Bevin and his Executive in their belief that unity of action could best be obtained through amalgamations. Up till 1926, the Transport and General Workers' Union, though concentrating on the expansion of its own direct control, was more willing, perhaps, than any other large union in the country to co-operate with other unions in industrial struggles. It was the practical experience of alliances which caused Bevin's disillusionment.

THE INDUSTRIAL ALLIANCE AND AFTER

During 1924 Bevin became increasingly suspicious of the action taken by employers' organizations and he warned his regional officials to be ready for action. He planned joint action with the National Union of Railwaymen, and early in 1925 agreed to establish a joint committee with the Amalgamated Engineering Union for the same purpose. In April 1925 the Miners' Federation suggested to a number of trade unions, including the Transport and General Workers' Union, that they should form an Industrial Alliance to support each other in times of need.[1] Bevin's Executive agreed to participate in the scheme, but significantly added the rider 'that the most effective way of securing the desired unity was by the process of amalgamation'. Realistically, they saw that in the circumstances an alliance was a more practical proposition than an amalgamation, but felt that an alliance would bring nearer the day when complete amalgamation would be possible.

The Joint Conference of the executives concerned set up a sub-committee to construct a draft constitution for the Alliance and Bevin was chosen to act as its secretary.[2] The Draft Constitution which was presented to a second Joint Conference in July 1925 was a real attempt to overcome the defects of the Triple Alliance, which Bevin had called 'a paper alliance'; it bore the marks of his belief in central control.

The membership of the Transport and General Workers' Union voted in favour of the Alliance, by 44,898 to 3,492 votes. Then in July 1925 the Union changed its rules to enable it

> to join with other Trade Unions or Organizations in the formation of or to become a member of such Industrial Alliance or any other body having for its objects the furthering of the interests of labour, trade unionism or trade unionists notwithstanding that such alterations authorize in certain events (*a*) the imposition of a general levy, (*b*) the sanctioning of a general strike, (*c*) the pooling of the Union's funds, and (*d*) placing the conduct of a movement under the sole control of the Executive of such Industrial Alliance or other body without taking a vote on any such matter by ballot of all the members of the Union. . . .

[1] The other unions were the National Union of Railwaymen; the Associated Society of Locomotive Engineers and Firemen; the Amalgamated Engineering Union. The National Transport Workers' Federation and the Federation of Shipbuilding and Engineering Trades were also invited to participate.
[2] Also on the sub-committee were A. J. Cook, P. Dickenson, F. Smith, A. G. Walkden, and Herbert Smith.

Although the constitution of the Alliance had been agreed upon by the interested unions in November 1925, it was not until 23 April 1926 that the Alliance committee was able to report the results of union ballots on the question; even then the Railway Clerks and the Heating Engineers were not able to report a result. This delay destroyed the value of the Alliance, for the General Strike came too soon. A full conference of the unions in the Alliance had been arranged for 1 July 1926—almost two months after the General Strike. During the Strike the Alliance was forgotten, though Sir Arthur Pugh, Chairman of the Trades Union Congress in 1926, stated that its programme formed the basis on which the General Strike was conducted.[1]

Ernest Bevin, after his experiences in the General Strike, recommended to the Biennial Delegate Conference of his Union in 1927 that the rule relating to the Industrial Alliance should be rescinded. He said that with the Movement in its present state of development the Executive was not prepared to hand over any of its power to a central authority. His recommendation was adopted and the Union rules reverted to their pre-1925 form.

Thereafter Ernest Bevin, through his General Executive Council, proceeded methodically to add to his already large Union by amalgamation, by merger, and by special agreements. It was clear that there was only one course of deliberate policy for the Union: it was to get bigger; it could not, by design, get smaller. Moving from strength to strength, there was never at any time cause to doubt the wisdom of the policy Bevin was pursuing. Radical structural changes arise out of weakness and fear. Neither of these elements was present in the leadership of the Transport and General Workers' Union.

After the impact of the Great Depression it was the small unions which were taking the initiative and approaching Bevin about mergers. In 1933 the Union was approached by the National Union of Blastfurnacemen, the National Union of Co-operative Insurance Society Employees, and the Scottish Busmen's Union; in 1935 the Electrical Trades Union asked for a renewal of amalgamation discussions initiated in 1926 and discontinued because of the General Strike. The advantages of large trade union organizations under the conditions of the rationalization of British industry in the 1930s were unmistakably clear and desirable.

The mergers and amalgamations of the 1930s did not add appreciably to the size of the Union—the size was increased mainly by normal recruitment of non-unionists—but they did add to the complexity of its membership. The original amalgamation was

[1] *Men of Steel*, by Sir Arthur Pugh, p. 389.

mainly a fusion of dockers and transport workers with a smattering of workers from other industries. It was not a general union in the same sense as was the Workers' Union. Even in 1926 from 60 to 65 per cent. of the members were transport workers. The membership in 1940 was distributed among a range of industries that are too numerous to mention here. The Union had approximately 150,000 members in the metal, engineering, and chemical industries; 63,000 members in Government and public services; about 32,000 members in the building trades; 171,000 general workers, and 9,000 administrative, clerical, and supervisory workers, as well as quarrymen, agricultural workers, and flour-milling workers; it was the most important union in the docks, road passenger transport, and road commercial transport.[1]

[1] The last two figures are for 1938.

Chapter Four

THE AFTERMATH OF THE AMALGAMATION

WE now know sufficient about the formation and development of the Transport and General Workers' Union to be able to deal with the source of some of the major internal problems which faced Arthur Deakin.   They were rooted in the past and had been as troublesome to Bevin as they were to Deakin.   In this chapter they are examined and described.

THE PROBLEM OF INTEGRATION

A union which consists of men with a variety of clearly defined skills and occupations and dissimilar social backgrounds and traditions starts off with an administrative problem of some magnitude, for there is no principal criterion to determine which things are to be done nor how they are to be done.   To make an organization possible and meaningful it is necessary that the objectives of its members should be capable of being integrated.[1]   The bigger the union the more difficult this becomes.   And when a union includes a number of small unions within its organization it has the additional problem of reconciling the different aims of those unions.

This problem of integration does not beset all 'general unions', for few of them in the past or the present have possessed the conditions which gave rise to it.   The Workers' Union, for example, contained workers of no particular skill; its members were adaptable semi-skilled and unskilled workers in engineering and allied industries.   The diversity of their trade interests was enormous but they were not fixed trade interests; the men were interchangeable and recognized this by their willingness to move from job to job. These groups were always in a state of flux; never able to develop traditions; never feeling that they were different from other groups of workers.   It was possible to integrate the pattern of behaviour of its members without recourse to special constitutional devices.

The National Union of General and Municipal Workers has a membership pattern similar in some ways to that which the Workers' Union possessed; admittedly it possesses some clearly definable groups such as gas workers, and municipal workers, but they are not

[1] Cf. *Administrative Behaviour*, by Herbert A. Simon, p. 4.

workers with distinctive skills or group traditions of militancy or independence. Consequently it can proceed with apparently few administrative upsets and without any special provisions for group interests.

The Transport and General Workers' Union is different in these respects from other unions concerned with organizing general labour, for in addition to the general workers who form the bulk of the membership it has two important and distinctive groups. One is formed by the dockers and waterside workers. They are pertinaciously group-conscious with a tradition of militancy and possessing, in many cases, special skills. In this respect they are comparable only with the miners. The other group consists of the London road passenger transport workers. This group is enigmatic. From the beginning of its association with the Union in 1922 it has possessed constitutional machinery over and above that possessed by other sections of the Union, and it has developed a tradition of militancy which is not to be found amongst other groups of busmen. London busmen together are excitable, volatile, and, like the dockers, group-conscious. Their conditions of work bring them together in garage and depot canteens where they can discuss grievances; the garage as a unit of organization is compact and manageable; and there is easy and rapid communication between garages. Their closely-knit organization has made them susceptible to pressure group activities.

Amongst the general membership of the Union there are workers with distinguishable characteristics, such as metal trade workers, building workers, agricultural labourers, and government workers, but without militant traditions. Within the general membership the workers in the mass-production motor car industry show signs of developing a group consciousness which may make them difficult to control in the future; at present, however, the composition of the group is too fluid for it to have distinctive characteristics. Commercial road transport workers too, on occasions, can display a unity of industrial action.

In the Transport and General Workers' Union there has always existed a major problem of integrating the pattern of behaviour of these groups, and this has involved influencing their behaviour to make integration, and therefore administration, possible. The dockers and London busmen have needed more guidance than other groups on fundamental trade union matters and continually they have had to be reminded of the benefits of amalgamation—that is, their existence together in one large union has had to be justified. Once in an amalgamation it is not always easy to see what advantages are derived from it; the benefits are taken for granted and the disadvantages are magnified disproportionately. Their behaviour has included periodic attempts to form breakaway unions. These moves against the unity of the organization bear no relation to the size of the Union. Bevin found the problem troublesome, recurring, and incapable of complete solution.

THE DOCKERS

Ernest Bevin had a special interest in the dockers. He acted as the national secretary of the Dock Trade Group and thereby was able to be fully informed on all dock matters and to deal personally with their problems and negotiations. Even so they were troublesome. This is illustrated by three prominent examples of their behaviour.

1. Not long after the Union had been formed, the employers in the dock industry presented a memorandum to the dockers' representatives asking for an extension of the working day and an alteration of overtime rates and conditions of employment. Then on 3 July 1922 they demanded a reduction of 2s. per day in day wages but they offered to refrain from pressing for the wage reduction if the Union would discard some of the restrictions on working conditions which it had successfully imposed in the past. Bevin refused to consider this for the reason that it was easier to recover a wage loss than to improve working conditions. His point of view was carried. Both parties agreed to a staggered reduction in wages. There was to be a reduction of 1s. per day on 2 October 1922 and a further reduction of 1s. eight months later, if by that time the cost of living index had fallen to an agreed level. In the circumstances the agreement reflected an astute piece of negotiating by Bevin for which the dockers had cause to be grateful.

Before the agreement was signed it was explained to the dockers in all the main ports and in most ports there were majorities in favour of accepting it. It was discussed and endorsed by a national delegate conference of dock workers and by the General Executive Council of the Union. There was no indication that the dockers felt strongly about it one way or the other. Yet during the last week of June 1923, just after the second wage reduction had been implemented, about 40,000 dockers struck work against the agreement. The strike threatened the unity of the amalgamation for it was a large-scale repudiation of Executive authority—the first of its kind—and an expression of no confidence in the Union constitutional procedures.

The strike lasted for seven weeks. During that time it was discussed by the national delegate conference of the Union. The matter was one of great delicacy: an uncompromising reprimand of

the dockers' action might have severed them from the Union; on the
other hand, approval of the strike might have destroyed the newly
established collective bargaining machinery in the dock industry and
weakened the Union's ability to conduct its own business.   Eventually the delegates agreed to sympathize with the dockers' grievance,
remind them of the need to use constitutional machinery, and
appeal to their sense of solidarity.   The strikers were not criticized,
nor were they instructed to return to work.   The officials were
quickly learning that the future of the Union depended largely on its
ability to be tolerant towards unconstitutional acts without creating
a lack of confidence in constitutional procedures.

A few thousand of the strikers in London left the Transport and
General Workers' Union and joined a small London union called
the Stevedores' Labour Protection League which was then reorganized and renamed the National Amalgamated Stevedores,
Lightermen, Watermen and Dockers' Union.[1]   This resulted in the
expulsion of that Union from the Trades Union Congress.   The
secession was on a relatively small scale and was confined to London
but it was a significant symptom of group restlessness.

2. The second incident started when a docks official named Potter
acted unconstitutionally and was suspended from his job.   The
secretary of the Docks Group in Region 1, F. Thompson, informed
the Assistant General Secretary that the suspension had dislocated
the work of the Group and that it was impossible to fill Potter's
place.   Thereafter the case became magnified and set in motion a
train of events which had little connection with the initial incident.

The London members of the lay Region I Dock Committee
resolved that unless Potter were reinstated by a given date, all
London dock officials, committee members, and branch officers
would cease acting for the Union.   This was a threat to strike and
not to form a breakaway, though there was talk that attempts were
being made to form a new union.   The Finance and Emergency
Committee and the General Executive Council held a spate of
meetings, including some with Potter and Thompson, at the end of
which Potter was dismissed.   Then Thompson and four other full-
time officials went on strike.   The Executive acted with restraint and
respected the right of its officials to strike.

The situation was most unusual.   The general atmosphere prevailing in the port areas indicated that some efforts were being made
to form a new union but no material evidence could be found; there
were no circulars or instructions to branches relating to it.   The
five officials resigned and the Executive, interpreting this as a sign of

[1] The activities of this union were to disturb the T. & G.W.U. again in 1954.   In
1927 its section catering for lightermen and watermen separated to form the Watermen,
Lightermen, Tugmen and Bargemen's Union.

development, took positive action on the London Docks to campaign against the creation of a breakaway union. It is not known how far the five officials went towards forming their own union, nor is it known what rank-and-file support they had, except that it was insufficient to launch a union.

On 21 October 1926, not much more than a month after the suspension of Potter, the Assistant General Secretary received a circular from Thompson headed "The National Union of Transport and Allied Workers" which stated that there was insufficient support for a new union and advised all members who had allied themselves with it to re-unite with the Transport and General Workers' Union. It added:

> In taking this action we realize that we cannot immediately control conditions through the new organization nor can they be preserved by partial organization in two or more Unions, with a probable dead weight of non-unionism in addition, but at the same time we urge all Dock workers to carry out that policy which has been repeatedly challenged. . . . We express no regrets for the action we have taken, actuated as we have been to assert our Trade Union principles, and our desire to form an organization standing solidly for Trade Union ideals and action, and untrammelled by bureaucracy.

As a special measure the Executive decided to allow the dock membership in London to elect officials to fill the vacancies caused by the resignations. Nothing more was heard of Thompson, but the other four who resigned with him were allowed to stand for election and were elected.

3. The last secessionist movement on the docks during Ernest Bevin's tenure as general secretary occurred in Glasgow in 1931. The trouble started over a misunderstanding about the terms of the amalgamation in 1923 and throughout it was based on a desire for greater self-determination by the Glasgow dockers. The Glasgow Docks Branch had been the major part of the Scottish Union of Dock Labourers before 1923. This Union was invited to join the amalgamation in 1922 and it took part in the ballot. An overwhelming majority of those voting were in favour of the amalgamation, but the Union failed to secure the necessary 50 per cent. quota of votes. Two other ballot votes were held with the same result, because of the refusal of most of the members of the Glasgow branch to vote. In the April 1922 vote only 877 Glasgow members voted out of about 3,000. The general secretary of the Scottish union, however, was keen to bring his Union into the amalgamation and he persisted in his efforts to bring it about. It was achieved eventually through a special agreement which was accepted by slightly over 50 per cent. of the total membership of the Scottish union on 15

December 1922. A small number accepted the result of the ballot under protest, and acted as a focal point for disaffection among the Glasgow dock workers until 1931.

The Glasgow branch had eight officials who worked full-time on Union business. These men were branch officials whom the branch claimed it had been given the right to elect annually when it had transferred to the Transport and General Workers' Union. The rules of the Union stated clearly that full-time officials were to be appointed and that branch officials were to be elected; but they did not provide for the selection of full-time branch officials. No written evidence could be produced to substantiate the claim of the Glasgow branch, so, in view of the vagueness of the rule, the Executive gave its own interpretation, which was that the Glasgow branch did not have the right to elect its own officials annually.

In June 1930 the branch instructed solicitors to seek an interpretation in a court of law of the rule which stated: 'Branch officers shall be elected at the annual branch meeting by show of hands, or by ballot if so decided by the meeting.' Bevin was asked if he would accede to the branch's demand, to prevent an expensive litigation, but he refused.

The judgment went in favour of the Glasgow branch, first in the Lower Court in Scotland and later in the Higher Court on appeal by the Union. The decision of the Scottish Court, Bevin was advised, applied equally to England. As there were a number of full-time branch officials in the Union who had not been elected by their branches, there was a possibility of widespread changes in the terms of employment of these men, unless the Executive were prepared to engage in further litigation or take steps to change the disputed rule. The latter course was taken. The Biennial Delegate Conference in 1931 passed a resolution confirming 'the action of the Council in the appointments of Permanent Branch Officers which it has made'. Bevin told the Conference that he was not concerned with the Court decision as it affected Glasgow, but only with its wide implications. 'We, therefore, proceeded', he said, 'in precisely the same way as Parliament does when it passes a Bill of Indemnity and amends the Law when an unexpected decision is given upsetting the whole of a particular form of administration.'

The Glasgow dockers were indignant that their Court victory should be nullified by a change in the rules, and became more determined than ever in their opposition. The Executive was faced with three possible courses of action: (1) It could force the acceptance of the revised constitution on the Glasgow members and expel those who rejected it. As the Glasgow members were solidly behind their branch committee this would have caused the secession of the branch

from the Union.   (2) It could refuse to appoint at all and allow a
sufficient percentage of the income of the branch to cover administrative costs and the salaries of full-time branch officials.   A number
of branches of the Union were financing full-time branch secretaries
in this way.   The branch, however, would have to agree not to ask
for permanent officials.   (3) As a temporary measure the officers of
the branch could be treated as working branch officers, elected by the
branch and employed on a day-to-day basis by the General Executive
Council.

The Finance and Emergency Committee was prepared to adopt
the last method until the Biennial Delegate Conference in 1933,
provided the Glasgow branch would accept a Conference decision
on the matter as final.   This the branch would not do unless the
Executive would make a joint recommendation with it to the
Conference to ensure success for the branch.   An impasse was
reached and all further efforts to find a settlement were unsuccessful.

The former general secretary of the Scottish Union of Dock
Labourers believed that a settlement was frustrated by branch
members who from the start had not wanted an amalgamation; that
they had interfered with Regional and Central Office directives since
1923; and that they were intent on forming a breakaway union.
The branch secretary, however, stated that he did not know of any
machinery having been formed in readiness for a breakaway, except
that they had had the experience of maintaining the branch for the last
six months without control or guidance from any quarter.   He stated
that there was a psychological resistance from the members, which
had always existed in Scotland, against the contributions going to
London.   He realized that a breakaway was a serious problem 'but
the determination to elect annually was so keen and the instrument
and methods in the hands of the branch itself were such, that a
breakaway could be effected in one day'.   He was supported by the
branch which resolved, on 27 December 1931, that if the General
Executive Council did not accede to its request the branch committee
would 'take all steps necessary to form a Scottish Union as from
January 1, 1932, in which our members shall enjoy full and complete
autonomy'.

The Finance and Emergency Committee decided to expel the
officials of the branch if they attempted to put the resolution into
effect.   The Union organization was geared to prevent a breakaway
from being established; arrangements were made to continue the
Union organization on Glasgow docks, a full statement of the
dispute was prepared for circulation to the dockers, and a mass
meeting of the branch members was called to hear the Executive
case.   The Union was not successful.   There were no important

divisions in the ranks of the Glasgow dockers and they knew that they could operate as an independent unit; they had done so before 1923 and might still have been independent had it not been for the determination of their general secretary to join the amalgamation.

The Scottish Transport and General Workers' Union was formed and remains in existence to this day. A month after its formation the Glasgow Shipowners' and Dock Labour Employers' Organization granted it recognition, though not until 28 April 1944 was it admitted to the National Joint Council for Dock Labour, and then only on the understanding that it limited its activity to the Glasgow and Campbeltown Docks.

LONDON BUSMEN

These formed the other group which gave Bevin and his Executive most trouble. Until 1920 they possessed their own small Union, the London and Provincial Licensed Vehicle Workers' Union. Then they amalgamated with the United Vehicle Workers which became a part of the Transport and General Workers' Union. Because of this quick transition from complete autonomy to being a section of a large centralized organization, the London busmen fitted uneasily into the trade group system of the new Union. Moreover, they did not consider themselves as a part of a national passenger transport industry.

All the passenger transport workers in the Union belonged to a single trade group. They elected regional trade group committees which in turn elected a national trade group committee. This Committee was responsible for transacting and overlooking all union business relating to the pay, hours, and working conditions of the road passenger transport workers. The group had its own full-time national secretary and specialized regional and district officials. Within it the London busmen formed a large but not preponderant part. They had representation on the Region I trade group committee, but they had to sit with representatives from the Home Counties which were in that region. This was a long step from the autonomy they possessed prior to 1920, and at the outset they pressed successfully for a greater measure of self-determination. They were allowed to elect a Central London Area Bus Committee of lay members which was to act with the functions of a national trade group committee and possessed the right of direct access to the General Executive Council. It did not have to work through the normal trade group machinery.

Passenger transport within the area of Greater London was carried on by a group of companies generally known as the London Traffic

Combine.   The most important of these companies was the London General Omnibus Company, Limited.   There were four stages in the hierarchy of this company: the garages; fifteen districts, each including a certain number of garages; three divisions composed of districts; and the headquarters of the company.[1]   The Union organization corresponded with the Company hierarchy.   A branch was based on each garage and all the branches were grouped into three districts which coincided with the Company's divisions.   The members in each district elected a district committee which in turn elected the Central London Area Bus Committee.[2]   Each branch elected a delegate to attend the conferences representing the whole section called to discuss outstanding matters relating to London bus conditions.   The General Secretary of the Union stated at the 1937 Biennial Delegate Conference that the executive had spared no expense for the operation of the London busmen's machinery: 'we have allowed more . . . Bus Committee meetings, more Delegate Conferences . . . in this section than in any other section in the Union'.

It is not easy to say whether these special provisions did or did not simplify the administration of the road passenger workers group and ease the problem of integrating the London busmen into the Union. For, whereas the desire for self-determination was partially settled, the way in which it was settled enabled a determined minority to wield disproportionate power and eased the translation of agitation into official action.

During the late 1920s and the 1930s the Transport and General Workers' Union became a target for Communist Party activities. At first these were carried on through the National Minority Movement but, owing to its lack of success, it was reorganized by the Communists in 1932 into the Rank-and-File Movement. The National Minority Movement was based on an individual membership of trade unionists; it was a body outside of the trade union movement and, as such, it could be proscribed by unions, and trade unionists who belonged to it could be disciplined.   This was not so easily done in the case of the Rank-and-File Movement, for it was based on the support of trade union branches and shop-stewards' organizations and had no individual membership.

The Communists concentrated on getting powerful lay trade union committees to affiliate to the Movement.   In the Central London Area Bus Committee they found one such committee which fairly quickly came under the control of the London Busmen's Rank-

[1] Cf. *Studies in Industrial Relations*, Series A. No. 33.   'The London Traffic Combine', I.L.O., 1930.
[2] Later, at the request of the Section, the representatives on the Central Committee were elected by a ballot vote in each district.

and-File Movement. From then onwards its policy ran counter to that of the Union Executive and there was no way in which the Executive could change it except by suspending the machinery, declaring the Movement subversive, and taking disciplinary action against its leading members. On the other hand, if the early attempt to appease the London busmen had not been made they might have tried to form a breakaway union sooner than they did and with greater success than was eventually achieved. Perhaps difficulties would have arisen in any event from the Rank-and-File Movement, though without the Central London Area Bus Committee it would have been less effective than it was amongst London busmen.

The formation of the London Busmen's Rank-and-File Movement coincided with a wage dispute in 1932; the leaders of the Movement contended that it was formed to combat a reduction of wages in the London Bus Section. The claim is supported by H. A. Clegg in his book *Labour Relations in London Transport*. He stated that it originated from a meeting of branch delegates called in August 1932 by Mr. A. F. Papworth to take action against a wage cut and a proposed dismissal of 800 men by the London General Omnibus Company, and was at first called the 'Provisional Committee of Garage Delegates'. Shortly afterwards the 'Provisional Committee' changed its name to the 'Rank and File Committee'.

> On October 5th a busmen's rank and file conference decided that their movement should continue on the basis of branch affiliations; that garage committees should be set up, each sending six representatives to the Rank and File Committee, two of whom should represent the inside staff; that a direct approach should be made to the members of branches which declined to affiliate. The policy of the committee was not to form a 'breakaway' union, but to organize within the union to oppose attacks on wages and conditions.[1]

The Finance and General Purposes Committee in its final report on the activities of the Rank-and-File Movement in 1937 did not think that this was the reason for the formation of the Movement. It stated:

> We have carefully examined this contention and cannot accept it. In point of fact, the Union put up a strong resistance to the proposed wage reduction, and was eventually successful in effecting a settlement without a reduction, and it is clearly established that this settlement was in no way influenced by the Rank-and-File Movement. In our considered view the wage problem of 1932 was made the excuse for bringing the Movement into existence; it was not, however, the real driving force behind its formation.

Two factors support the official Union view: first J. R. Campbell,

[1] Pp. 30–31.

3+T.U.L.

in a speech at the Seventh World Congress of the Communist International in 1935, attributed the formation of Rank-and-File Movements to deliberate Communist Party policy; and secondly, the steps to form a London Busmen's Movement were taken almost eight months after the claim for a wage reduction had been submitted to the Union by the employers. A movement arising spontaneously to prevent a wage reduction would surely have appeared earlier in the dispute. Moreover, the Movement should have dispersed on the successful conclusion of the negotiations. It did not do this; instead it claimed credit for preventing the wage reduction and grasped the opportunity to extend its activities.

It was formed into an organization within the Union, with a constitution, elected officers, and committees and an official journal called the *Busmen's Punch*. It maintained a constant attack on official Union Policy and blatantly interfered with the constitutional treatment of Union business. The Movement undoubtedly obtained wide support from the London busmen.[1] It claimed in 1937 that thirty-one out of fifty branches in London had affiliated to the Movement, and Arthur Deakin during a speech to the 1937 Biennial Delegate Conference said that all except one of the members of the Central Area Bus Committee supported the Rank-and-File Movement. This occurred despite the attempts of three successive Biennial Delegate Conferences to curb its activities.

The Coronation Strike

The activities of the London Busmen's Rank-and-File Movement culminated in the Coronation Strike of London busmen in 1937 which lasted from 1 May to 26 May and concerned almost 25,000 workers. Briefly, in December 1936 a special Delegate Conference of busmen in London agreed to open negotiations with the London Passenger Transport Board to improve the existing wages and conditions agreement and to negotiate for a seven-hour day. The discussions were terminated because the Board sought to impose the acceptance of two principles on the Union: (*a*) no departure from the eight-hour day, and (*b*) the grouping of schedules, as a condition for further negotiations. The Union refused to accept these and Bevin urged

---

[1] Unofficial activities among the busmen members of the Union were not confined to London. In the spring and summer of 1937 there was a series of strikes starting with the Scottish Motor Traction dispute in March which involved 8,850 workers. Bus strikes occurred in the Eastern Counties, including Norwich, Cambridge, Newmarket, and Cromer (797 workers for 16 days in April, then 560 workers for 11 days in May); West Kent and East Sussex (1,840 workers for 22 days); Essex and South Midland Counties (for 20 days); Oxford (590 workers for 8 days); Hull (309 workers for 3 days); Liverpool and District (500 workers for 3 days). The Rank-and-File Movements had much scope for their activities, and though there is no evidence to show that they were involved in all of these strikes they undoubtedly had a gay time that year.

that negotiations 'should proceed by way of examination of the proposals and counter-proposals without any commitment to principles'. The Union modified its demand, pressed for a seven-and-a-half-hour day and the discussions with the Board were renewed. This time the Board rejected the claim on the grounds that (*i*) the question of a shorter working day was a national problem, and (*ii*) the cost of meeting the claim was beyond the resources of the Board. The position was one of deadlock in March 1937, so the Central London Area Bus Committee passed a resolution to terminate the existing agreement and asked the General Executive Council to give it plenary power to withdraw labour on the expiration of the notice to terminate the agreement. The resolution was endorsed by a Special Conference of London busmen and was accepted by the General Executive Council with the proviso that Bevin should try to settle the problem by negotiations in the meantime. The Union had a further meeting with the Board on 9 April 1937 but no solution was reached.

The strike began on 1 May. It had the full support of the men and officials but was confined to London busmen. The tramwaymen, supported by the Executive, refused to take sympathetic strike action, much to the annoyance of the busmen, who considered the refusal as being 'contrary to . . . the spirit of amalgamation upon which the Union is founded'.[1] By 26 May the Executive had decided that it was time it reasserted its authority over the strikers. It withdrew the plenary powers from the Central London Area Bus Committee and instructed Bevin to enter into negotiations with the Board through the Ministry of Labour. On that same day a strike settlement was reached and the men returned to work.

The strike was marked by numerous incidents which showed a pronounced antipathy between the Central London Area Bus Committee and the General Executive Council. The Committee refused to accept the Executive document analysing the strike position on 11 May and circulated its own leaflet to prejudice the consideration of the Executive opinion. Later, when the General Secretary refused to circulate a resolution from the Committee, it was distributed by an outside agency and appeared in the *Daily Worker*. And those branches which were known to support the Executive were inundated with leaflets from the London Busmen's Rank-and-File Movement.

Questions can rightly be asked about Bevin's behaviour during the dispute. He knew that the Central London Area Bus Committee was controlled by Communists and Communist sympathizers. Why then had the Committee been given plenary powers in the first place?

---

[1] Special Delegate Conference, 25 May 1937. See *Labour Relations in London Transport*, by H. A. Clegg, Ch. IV, for an account of the strike.

and why was the strike allowed to continue so long before they were withdrawn? In the first place Bevin believed in the justice of the busmen's case and felt that the strike was necessary. He also believed in the effective use of constitutional procedures. When the Committee asked for plenary powers to conduct a strike it was making a legitimate request to do something in which Bevin believed. Moreover, not only was the Committee the correct constitutional body to handle the strike, but also from its composition it was the most suited. An early and open conflict between the Committee and the Executive would have depressed the morale of the busmen.

Once the role of the Rank-and-File Movement became clear during the strike, then the withdrawal of plenary powers from the Committee was a matter of strategy primarily in relation to the unity of the organization. Bevin, Francis Williams has stated, 'deliberately allowed the Central Bus Committee . . . to take over control of the running of the strike, gambling on his belief that the men in power on the Committee would over-reach themselves, put forward demands incapable of acceptance, and by revealing the bankruptcy of their leadership would destroy their chance to undermine union discipline in the future'.[1] He was determined to reduce the threats to the unity of his Union which arose from unofficial action assisted by people outside the Union. He had warned delegates of his Union about such action in 1933. Each time, he said, it 'is worked on precisely the same lines, the same propaganda, the same outlook, the same kind of literature and the same base treachery'.[2] He did not exclude the London Busmen's Rank-and-File Movement from these strictures.

Unofficial action based on a permanent organization in opposition to the Union Executive had a number of serious consequences. A union, like any sound organization, must be run along consistent and recognized procedures. This was not being done in London. Some branch officials used the constitutional procedures for the business of the Union, whereas others passed Union matters on to the Rank-and-File Movement. The ordinary members did not know which way to turn. Decisions to strike taken at snap meetings, carried by active nuclei, and resulting in the establishment of picket lines, could not easily be ignored or refuted by ordinary members. Even the most conscientious member was reluctant to cross an unofficial picket line, for what mattered to him in the first instance was the solidarity of his group. The instigators of unofficial strikes traded on this loyalty and made a mockery of union obligations. The mental picture of a group of strikers defying their Executive aroused

---

[1] *Ernest Bevin*, by Francis Williams, p. 115.
[2] T. & G.W.U., B.D.C., 1933.

sympathy from other members of the Union which was not expressed in strikes but by resolutions to the Executive supporting the strikers. This attitude, which Bevin thought was stupid, often occurred in London. 'Immediately unofficial disputes crop up, and the Union is faced with a difficulty,' Bevin wrote in 1934, 'resolutions are received urging the Union to make the disputes official ones, and they proceed on the assumption that the Executive and the Union are always wrong.'[1]

In the matter of planning an unofficial dispute the Communist Party was willing to give expert guidance. During the Finance and General Purposes Committee's inquiry into the activities of the Rank-and-File Movement it brought to light a statement issued by the Communist Party to Party members who were involved in the unofficial strike against the Scottish Motor Traction combine in March 1937. An unsuccessful attempt was made during the strike to extend the Rank-and-File Movement to the Scottish bus section and the statement dealt with the lessons in tactics which the Communist Party considered could be learnt from it. It described how unofficial strikes could be won. The demands of the strikers, it stated, should strictly correspond to the power they possessed; they should not immediately be too costly to the management and should preferably concern such questions as victimization, harsh disciplinary action, and schedules. The statement emphasized the need to pay more attention to the bus industry by developing a Communist Party group in every garage and by turning the branches into Communist strongholds. These lessons were not ignored by the rank-and-file leaders of the London busmen.

Some Consequences of the London Busmen's Rank-and-File Movement

At no time during the 1930s did the Executive of the Union counter unofficial activities by political discrimination, though it came near to doing so in 1937. In 1933 the Union adopted a change of rules which required members standing for office to sign a declaration to observe the constitution of the Union; the declaration, as the events showed, was not observed in every case and the Executive went to the 1937 Biennial Delegate Conference with proposals for further changes in the rules. In June 1937 Ernest Bevin had told his Executive that it would be necessary for it to give serious and detailed consideration to the whole problem of unofficial movements. 'I must ask the Council', he said, 'to deal with the matter whatever the consequences may be, as it is impossible for the officers and the regularly elected Committees to carry out their duties when there is an organization within an organization. . . .' As a result of this

[1] Report to G.E.C., June 1934.

exhortation the Finance and General Purposes Committee was instructed to conduct an inquiry into unofficial movements. This was done in two stages because of the proximity of the Biennial Delegate Conference. An Interim Report, which did not cover the Central London Area Bus dispute, was produced with general recommendations including proposals for the alteration of rules, and was presented to the Conference; later a more detailed Final Report covering the Bus dispute was presented to the Executive.

The Interim Report requested the Conference to take immediate steps to make the rules stronger and clearer so that new members could 'feel that they have the protection of the Union against interference by any unofficial body inside the Union or bodies that may seek to interfere with the business of the Union from outside'. It asked the Conference to declare:

(*a*) That a definite end must be put to Rank and File and similar organizations within the Union, or any other form of organization not authorized by the constitution.

(*b*) That any Member who takes part in any such unofficial action shall be liable to disciplinary action.

(*c*) That no branch or other section of the Union shall affiliate to, or associate itself with, any unofficial body, nor shall any literature be read at any branch meeting received from or issued by such bodies.

(*d*) That any decision arrived at by a branch contrary to the rules shall be regarded as definitely out of order, and shall not be operated by the Officers or Committeemen of the branch.

(*e*) That the practice of holding unofficial meetings and predetermining policy outside the constitution of the Union shall render the persons responsible liable to disciplinary action.

(*f*) That the practice of issuing journals or literature not authorised by the Union and utilising the machinery of the branches, or other means, for their distribution shall be abolished.

(*g*) That the practice of circulating fixed resolutions intended to attack the Union or interfere with its policy shall cease.

The Conference made the declaration as requested and amended the rules to enable the Executive to remove from office any official who disregarded the constitutional procedures of the Union, and to proscribe any organization which dealt 'with questions of wages, hours of labour, conditions of employment, or any matters affecting the Union's interest . . . which, in the opinion of the Executive Council, is contrary, detrimental, inconsistent or injurious to the policy and purpose of the Union . . .'. The General Secretary gave an undertaking to the Conference that before the Executive proscribed a body under the amended section of the rule it would first consult with the Regional Committee or Committees concerned. When in the following year Bevin explained to his Regional Secretaries the procedure for dealing with Fascist intervention in Union affairs, he said that it was the same as that relating to Communists but 'the essential point . . . is, that a person can only be dealt with on his or her individual conduct as a Member of the Union and not because of membership of any political party'.

After the strike the machinery of the Central London Area Bus Committee was suspended by the General Executive Council and eight strike leaders were either expelled from the Union or suspended from holding office. The cause of the trouble had not been removed and worse was to come in the form of a breakaway union. The Executive established temporary Union machinery to give the members and officials time to think over the problem and called a delegate meeting of the section to examine its proposals. The busmen were difficult customers. The members of a newly elected Central Area Bus Committee resigned in September 1937 in protest against its treatment by the Executive, and the busmen's delegates were no less recalcitrant. At successive delegate conferences they criticized the Executive and resolved to get the expelled members reinstated.

The Executive was obliged by the pressure of opinion among the busmen to explain its attitude towards expulsions generally. It stated in October 1937 that

> If a person is expelled and the expulsion is upheld by the Appeals Committee that decision is final and if the person desires again to become a member of the Union, it can only be dealt with on the basis of his application for admission and not on a Conference resolution or resolutions from branches. The question of whether or not a person is admitted to the Union again would depend on the conduct of the person concerned. If the occurrences which led to the expulsion are entirely removed, and time has elapsed to indicate that they have been so removed, and application is then made to be admitted again to the membership of the Union, the Executive Council will always consider such applications on their merits. The same applies to suspensions. . . .

Two who were expelled, A. F. Papworth and J. W. Jones, were allowed to rejoin the Union after they had given written assurances that they would abide by the constitution of the Union in future. Later both of them became members of the General Executive Council. The busmen were not satisfied by the Executive statement, and at delegate conferences in March and April 1938 they pressed for the reinstatement of all the expelled members.

The Executive was in an awkward position. It had to maintain discipline—a refusal to do so would have amounted to complicity in undermining its own authority—but it did not want to encourage the establishment of any breakaway union, the idea of which was being canvassed on the Central London Area Bus Committee.

Moreover, it knew that whatever happened about a breakaway some of the dissidents would remain in the Transport and General Workers' Union, so it could possibly be left with a competitive union at its flank and some of the most active leaders of the unofficial movement still within its ranks. In the discussions on the Rank-and-File Committee of Busmen, there had not been a majority in favour of forming a breakaway union, for it was Communist Party policy to gain control of the Union and not to break it. In a Communist Party statement distributed in Scotland in 1937 and quoted by Arthur Deakin at the Biennial Delegate Conference it stated:

> Our slogan must now be, strengthen the Union and change the leader-ship. We must show first that the effect of breakaway unions is weakening the power of the men. We must refer to the fact that we have had some hard knocks from the Management, and breaking away is helping Bevin to get rid from the Union of the most militant members, those who eventually hope to challenge Bevin's position. To do this we must change the Executive Council, which we have power to do. We must strengthen the Union as a fighting force so that we can win positions on the Executive.

A breakaway union called the National Passenger Workers' Union was eventually launched on 25 February 1938 by a section of the Central London Area Bus Committee, with W. J. Brown, general secretary of the Civil Service Clerical Association, as its honorary president. It gained little support in the provinces; its members came mainly from the branches of the promoters of the Union in Central London. As with other breakaway movements it was not possible to assess the support it received in the first instance, for members of the Union are not considered lost until they are thirteen weeks in arrears, and even then it is difficult to distinguish between deliberate secession and normal wastage.[1] The estimates of the support received by the breakaway differed according to their source. Ernest Bevin claimed that its progress in the Central London area was negligible. At its inception the leaders of the breakaway forecast that 'within a year we shall be 150,000 strong'.[2] It started with the support of only three of the strike leaders and eight of the 150 branch officials in the bus fleet, yet on 29 August 1938, the *Manchester Guardian* reported: 'It is claimed that in Central London 8,000 drivers and conductors employed by the board belong to the new union. . . .' The Transport and General Workers' Union, during the same month, claimed 27,000 members from the 30,000 Central London bus workers employed by the London

---

[1] Sea-going seamen are an exception to this rule. They are permitted to extend their arrears to six months (Rule 20, Clause 13).
[2] *The Times*, 24 February 1938.

Passenger Transport Board and stated that some of the remaining 3,000 were non-unionists.

The effect of the breakaway was to submerge the grievances many London busmen had against the Union and unite them behind the Union officials. On 2 March 1938 a conference of branch officials of the Bus Section affirmed their allegiance to the Union and opposed the breakaway; leading Communist busmen published a leaflet to the same effect. A newly elected Central London Area Bus Committee deprecated the move to split the Section, and many branches sent in expressions of loyalty to the Transport and General Workers' Union. In his report to his Executive in March 1938 Bevin stated that breaking away from the Union

> seems to be a recurring problem in London. . . . We have always had this element in London for ever threatening as to what they will do unless we give way to them, and it is better that the whole of this business should come to a head. It will probably result in cleaning it up once and for all. . . . In a great Union of this character, we must always expect to be attacked by someone. . . . I am not sorry in a way that this business has come to a head. We have lived under the threat for years. . . .

Although Bevin looked upon the affair as a cleansing process he took steps to restrain the activities of the breakaway union. Meetings of the divisional committees of the Central London Area Bus Section and special conferences were held; publicity was given to the Executive views and, to placate the Bus Section, Bevin told the delegates 'if they would put this unofficial business outside of their ranks altogether, and arrive at a final and irrevocable decision that there should be none of it in their Section; if they would act within the constitution as all the other Sections did, they need have no fear of this or any future Executive suspending their machinery'.

The National Passenger Workers' Union, however, continued to exist with a hard core of support for another eight years, engaging in litigation with the London Passenger Transport Board and the Transport and General Workers' Union and endeavouring to bring together for joint action other unions which, like itself, claimed to be non-political.

OTHER TRADES

In the 1920 Amalgamation Scheme provision was made for five trade groups and for subsections for numerically important trades within three of the groups. The Docks Group had a subsection for Coal Shipping; the General Workers Group had one for the Metal and Chemical Trades; and the Road Transport Group had subsections

3*

for the Passenger and Commercial transport workers. The provision of a large degree of autonomy to trades in industrial matters
was taken seriously by the members, and whenever the opportunity
arose members with common interests in the Union presented claims
for group status. The possibility of achieving group status acted as
an incentive to officials to increase the membership, for, to a large
extent, the principal criterion for group status was size; the granting
of the status, too, was regarded by the members as recognition that
they had characteristics which distinguished them from the mass of
general workers. Thus, occupational pride was given an avenue for
expression. Road passenger transport workers claimed their own
group at the beginning, so the Union started off with six groups;
the number increased to ten by 1940. Each of the new groups was
formed following an amalgamation or a merger, so that the amalgamating or merging union could preserve some of its practices and
autonomy.

As groups expanded it was the Union policy to subdivide them
into trade union sections as a step towards group status. A group
was able to have its own trade machinery and specialist officials
at all stages of the Union, whereas a section only had a specialist
national official and a national trade committee and at other stages
had to use composite trade officials. Workers in agriculture, the
fishing industry, and the government and public services had their
own sections. And a Flour Milling section existed as a result of a
pre-amalgamation agreement between the National Union of Flour
Millers and the Dockers' Union. The right to form trade groups
rested with the Biennial Delegate Conference and each time it met
there were a number of claimants to trade group status. Very few
were granted.

There was only one recorded case of the formation of a breakaway
in the general trades before 1940, and that occurred in April 1930
when a move was made by two full-time officials in London to form
a National Union of Coal Workers. Approximately 166 men were
enrolled, of whom only thirty had seceded from the Transport and
General Workers' Union. After a short time the task was given up
and the cards and documents relating to the breakaway were sent to
a Commercial Services official in Region I.

The members who belonged to relatively small unions had to
learn how to operate a federal structure in which there was a division
of functions. Not all the difficulties arose from the demands for
more self-determination in the Union: some arose because the
members did not know how to use that amount of autonomy which
the constitution gave them. For example, matters which should
have been handled within the trade groups were sometimes passed to

the Biennial Delegate Conference. But once the members had learnt how to act fully within the scope of the trade groups and saw the need for the limitations which had been imposed on them, the constitution of the Union functioned effectively. It satisfied the aspirations for self-determination of the groups within the general trade membership of the Union and it gave them the advantages which size can give in the trade union movement.

Chapter Five

A PATTERN OF LEADERSHIP

So far I have examined some of the aspects of the situation which were caused by the behaviour of men in the mass. They were either caused instinctively as were some of the loyalties and traditions described in Chapter II, or they arose out of organized activity, as Chapters III and IV show. In this chapter I attempt to complete the description of the situation by showing the manner in which it was influenced by Ernest Bevin, the most prominent man in the Union during the period. The chapter deals with Bevin's particular ability as a leader of men and with the methods he employed in the Union, in politics and in industry.

BEVIN'S METHODS OF ORGANIZATION

Establishing Authority

When the idea of an amalgamated union for dockers, transport workers, and general labourers was canvassed after 1918, there was no shortage of candidates for positions of leadership. In the main the men most intimately concerned with the amalgamation were leaders in their own right. Many of them died without leaving any means of assessing their abilities. The qualities of a few have been recorded or remembered. Harry Gosling, James Sexton, Ben Tillett, Stanley Hirst, Sam March, and Alfred Short were all relatively well-known and respected union leaders. Gosling, Sexton, and Tillett were members of the General Council of the Trades Union Congress before the amalgamation occurred. Yet the driving force behind the creation of the new Union came from none of these but from the assistant general secretary in Tillett's union, Ernest Bevin.

An assistant general secretary is normally unheard and unsung and rarely obtains for himself a position of power superior to that of his general secretary. From this one can gather the strength of Bevin's personality. He was the secretary of the amalgamation sub-committees set up in 1920 and 1921, and when on 19 May 1921 the eleven unions which had voted in favour of amalgamation held a delegate conference he was elected as the provisional secretary of the Union. When he stood for the position of permanent General Secretary he received an overwhelming majority of the votes cast. Admittedly the candidates who opposed him in this election were weak ones, but this in itself was significant. It revealed his success in the backstage struggles which resulted, for example, in the non-appearance of Ben Tillett as a candidate for any important post.[1]

Bevin's leadership qualities were apparent before the amalgamation took place. When he went to the convention of the American Federation of Labour as the fraternal delegate of the Trades Union Congress in 1915 he had been a trade union member for only five years; nevertheless he addressed the convention with the self-assurance of an established labour leader. One doubts whether Bevin ever admitted the existence of superiors; on the contrary he seemed to set out to prove they did not exist. His behaviour at the Labour Party Conference in 1917 when he made his first intervention was that of a man whose hand was at the helm, not that of a recently elected national organizer. By 1921 he was known as a controversial and powerful trade union figure, noted as the Dockers' K.C. and as the organizer of the Councils of Action established to prevent British military action against Russia.

The acceptance of Bevin as a leader by the general secretaries of the fourteen amalgamating unions indicated not only the strength of his personality but also his ability. Men cannot be coerced into an amalgamation, they have to be handled into it, and one of Bevin's chief qualities was the manner in which he handled men. He was tolerant and willing to compromise to bring unions into the amalgamation.[2] In some cases compromise is a sign of weak leadership, but it was not so with Bevin; he was an empiricist concerned with reaching solutions to problems, but once a solution had been reached he gave a clear undeviating lead. At the amalgamation conference in 1921, before he had been elected as general secretary, he told the delegates that so long as he was a leader he was going to say to members what in his judgment they should do. He was equally forthright with officials of the Union and he expected his leadership to be accepted unchallenged.

It is said that Bevin pursued his objectives relentlessly and permitted no man to stand in his way. He conceded responsible union posts to the leaders of the amalgamating unions only where it was

[1] See *Memories and Reflections*, by Ben Tillett, p. 245; also *Ernest Bevin*, by Francis Williams, pp. 106–109.

[2] When he was discussing the possibility of amalgamating with the Scottish Horse and Motormen's Association in 1939 he said with a frankness that was characteristic of him: 'There are two contributing factors to amalgamations—one is sweet temper and the other is overdrafts. Both are helpful, but if you discuss with anybody with a big stick you create the wrong kind of atmosphere to begin with. You have got to begin persuasively and you would not be in this room today as you are if I had not been congenial personally.' (T. & G.W.U., B.D.C., 1939.)

necessary for tactical reasons, and where he could bring in young men of his own choice he did so. Harry Gosling's position as President and Stanley Hirst's as Financial Secretary were concessions to help to achieve unity between the diverse groups. Ben Tillett, who was an M.P., was quietened with the secretaryship of the Union's International Department, which gave him freedom to travel abroad.[1] Three other general secretaries, James Sexton, Alfred Short, and Sam March[2] held Union posts but they were primarily Parliamentarians. March was on the verge of retiring when the amalgamation took place and was the national secretary of the Road Commercial Transport Group for a few months only; he became a Member of Parliament at the end of 1922. After convening the Administrative, Clerical and Supervisory Trade Group, Alfred Short became its national secretary, but only until February 1923. He was a Member of Parliament during and after the amalgamation. Bevin, however, contended that a man could not do the two jobs adequately, and in consequence Short resigned his Union post. Only Harry Gosling, James Sexton and Ben Tillett were allowed to combine political and union work until their retirement.[3]

Later, under the terms of separate amalgamation agreements, the general secretaries of four newly amalgamated unions became national officials.[4] By the time these amalgamations occurred Bevin's position was firmly established. In the main he preferred to look upon the leaders of the unions in the amalgamation as men of the past and upon himself as the man of the future. Even Gosling, who held a potentially powerful position as the full-time president, was placed in the category of past leaders. When he addressed the first Delegate Conference of the Union in 1923, Bevin said: 'We live not for today, we live for the future. Gosling, Tillett and Sexton and the others built the foundations of this movement under difficult circumstances. The circumstances are different now than then, they were more difficult then than now, but they have made their great contribution. We have got to carry on—you and I. . . .'

If Harry Gosling had been as much preoccupied with power as

[1] Tillett was M.P. for North Salford from 1917 till 1924. Gosling was M.P. for Whitechapel from 1923 till 1930.

[2] General Secretaries of the National Union of Dock, Riverside and General Workers, the National Union of Docks, Wharves and Shipping Staffs, and the National Union of Vehicle Workers respectively.

[3] Of the remaining general secretaries John Twomey who had belonged to the National Amalgamated Labourers' Union became a national organizer and J. W. Meggison an area secretary. J. W. Meggison, of the North of England Trimmers' and Teemers' Association, died in September 1922. E. H. Maun, general secretary of the Amalgamated Association of Carters and Motormen, became an area commercial road transport group secretary, then an area secretary. I could find no record of the positions of the remainder.

[4] These unions were the National Union of Enginemen, Firemen, Motormen, Mechanics and Electrical Workers, the North Wales Quarrymen's Union, the 'Altogether' Builders' Labourers' Society, and the Workers' Union.

Bevin there might have been damaging strife within the Union. As it was, he contented himself with the role of figurehead and accepted Bevin's leadership. But so long as the office of full-time president existed with constitutional powers greater than those of the general secretary[1] a potentially strong challenge to Bevin existed and Bevin went out of his way, with much less tact than he normally used, to abolish the position. His opportunity occurred when Harry Gosling became a Minister in the first Labour Government in 1924 and requested leave of absence from the Union. The Executive granted the request and, in Gosling's absence, added that it proposed 'to review the whole question of the Presidency of the Union with full liberty of action'.[2] When the Labour Government was defeated in October 1924 and Gosling lost his Government position, he presented himself to the Executive with the intention of being restored to the position he had held prior to his entry into the Government. Instead of his job, Gosling was told that the Executive had decided 'it would be inadvisable to reinstate the Presidential position on general grounds'. He was offered the national secretaryship of the small Waterways trade group, a job he had held before in conjunction with the presidency.

It was clear that Bevin had not sounded his fellow officers before advising his Executive, for the decision aroused a strong protest from the National officials and officials attached to Region I (London and the Home Counties). On 17 November 1924 many of them met at the Union head office and elected a deputation to see the Executive about Gosling's position. The Executive refused to meet the deputation whilst the other officials remained away from their work, but the officials were adamant and remained on the premises. Though officially the Executive ignored the deputation, it was impressed by the strength of the protest and the uniform indignation against its treatment of Gosling. Unable to support its action in the face of opposition, the Executive rescinded its previous decision and reinstated Gosling as President of the Union. Bevin was wiser for the experience and made no further effort to depose Gosling. He decided what should have been decided at the outset—that the time to take action was when Gosling retired.

Relations with Officials

It has been said that because of Bevin's desire to exercise power he tended to surround himself with men who were less able than he was himself, and to keep away from the centre of activities those who

[1] The President was chairman of the General Executive Council with a right to vote and also the chairman of all important national union conferences.
[2] February 1924.

showed signs of rising to the top rank.[1] This is not a correct interpretation of Bevin's attitude. The employment of men of relatively inferior ability need not be the outcome of a leader's intolerance of rivals. From his subordinates Bevin demanded loyalty to himself and to the decisions he made because he looked upon himself as the leader, and because he was the official mouthpiece of Executive opinions. It was not an unreasonable demand to make; indeed, it was a necessary condition for maintaining the unity of his organization.

Loyalty and high ability are not incompatible qualities and a dichotomy is created only when loyalty requires the acceptance of decisions which are either illogical or are not based on correct evidence, or both. It was true that Bevin was suspicious of intellectuals because he was never sure where their dialectics would lead them next, but he did not deliberately look for men of second-rate ability. On the contrary he sought men of high quality for responsible Union posts and brusquely ignored precedents standing in the way of such appointments. A number of the first group of men to hold national positions in the Union later achieved prominence in various fields.[2]

The loyalty expected by Bevin from his subordinates was returned in full by him. He would criticize his officials in private, but in public or before the ordinary members he gave them his complete support. Under the shield of collective responsibility he encouraged them to use their initiative. And from the outset he set an example to his officials by the manner in which he devolved authority to his immediate subordinates. He did it so that he gave scope to their initiative and judgment and eased his own burden without detracting from his authority as General Secretary of the Union. Both John Cliff and Arthur Deakin as Assistant General Secretaries covered a wide range of activities, including delicate internal matters concerning breakaway unions and unofficial activities. Bevin provided his assistant with a thorough training in leadership techniques. It was not fortuitous that Deakin was able eventually to fill the role of leader of the Union.

Whenever there was a conflict of opinion between Bevin and any

[1] Cf. *Ernest Bevin*, by Francis Williams, p. 112.
[2] John Cliff, the Union's first Assistant General Secretary, eventually became the Deputy Chairman of the London Transport Executive. Harold Clay, national secretary of the Road Passenger Transport Group, later Assistant General Secretary, became President of the Workers' Educational Association and a member of the Road Haulage Executive of the British Transport Commission. Arthur Creech-Jones, who was an assistant to a national secretary, became a national secretary after a year. He was the Secretary of State for the Colonies in the post-Second World War Labour Government and a member of its Cabinet. There were others who remained with the Union as administrators and organizers and were of a comparably high quality.

other official, the latter had to give way, for Bevin believed firmly in the validity of his own arguments. Yet in his own manner Bevin accepted criticism. An official who disagreed with him, and told him so, might find a few days later that Bevin had thought of a new idea—identical in substance with the criticism.

He had little faith in the collective opinion of officials about Union problems. From 1932 he held irregular conferences with them, but he said in 1945 that his 'experience when they had been held in the past was that they were not very helpful'.[1] He conceded, however, that the General Secretary should have some form of consultation with the officials of the Union. Bevin's belief in empiricism appeared to be emphasized more in his relationships with his own officials than with employers. Throughout his union career he struggled to achieve a regular and formal relationship with employers, yet he did not think that the same was desirable with his officials either for obtaining advice or for settling their grievances.

Both he and his Executive seemed at first sight to adopt a paradoxical attitude towards the representation of officials, because they refused to acknowledge that the Union was an employing body and that there might be a case for an association of union officials. In the early years of the amalgamation a transient Fraternity of Officers of Region I had been formed which, before it petered out, worsened rather than improved Bevin's relationship with his officials. Memories of it were revived in March 1940 when the officials of Region I submitted proposals to Bevin for the formation of an Officers' Representation Association. The Association was to have a constitution and an annual subscription and its objects were: (*i*) to promote complete co-operation and comradeship amongst the Officers in the general interests of the Union; (*ii*) to provide an avenue for free and open discussion of all matters relevant to the employment and welfare of the Officers; and (*iii*) to be the only medium for representations to the Regional Secretary, Regional Committee, the General Secretary, or the General Executive Council, on matters affecting the individual or collective interests of the Officers, within the constitution of the Union. The reply of the Union Executive was 'that the Union would not countenance the formation of any organization which was virtually a Union within a Union, or a constitution such as that proposed with subscriptions, funds, etc., [as] an arrangement of such a character was contrary to the spirit of the Union and would only result in bringing the Officers into conflict with the Union, and the vital principle of democratic control'. No objection was raised to the formation of committees of officials to discuss specific grievances.

[1] Conference of National and Regional Secretaries, 1945.

The paradox was more apparent than real. Though a union is in fact an employing body, the relationship between the ordinary members in the mass or their representatives on union lay committees on the one hand and full-time officials on the other, is not an employer/employee relationship. The officials are equivalent to subsidized lay members who, in order to be in a position to make strong representations to employers, are removed from dependence upon employers for a living. Full-time officials are given a vital role in union constitutions; the manner in which they serve with the lay committees determines in large measure the effectiveness of democratic control in a union. The existence of a union for officials would create a formal relationship between them and the lay members and would undoubtedly interfere with the spirit of serving a cause and, perhaps, make it more difficult to exercise lay control. Bevin's sense of the matter was right but it had the appearance of intolerance.

The difficulties which arose between Bevin and his officials in the early years were bound up with the state of the Union. For at least a decade after its formation the Union was saddled with too many officials, and Bevin's task was to reduce their number so that it bore some relation to the size of the Union. This, plus the task of unifying the wages and conditions of employment of officials, brought him into conflict with any collective action taken by the officials. The situation required that combination of ruthlessness and understanding which Bevin possessed. He endeavoured to reduce the number of officials mainly by wastage but there had to be dismissals and compulsory retirements. When the Workers' Union amalgamated in 1928 all its full-time officials were taken over and so inflated the Union staff that Bevin had to re-tackle the problem. Fortunately there was a high proportion of retirements in 1930 and many vacancies were not filled. Staffing problems were intensified by the large-scale unemployment of the early 1930s which left regions with officials but relatively few members. In such cases officials were made redundant after consultation with those concerned. Even at the end of 1938 Bevin thought that the Union was carrying sufficient officers to cope with a much larger membership.

The officials of the Union had to be relied upon to sink their pre-amalgamation prejudices and to collaborate in the development of the Union. Exhortations and regulations were of little use in this matter, and the most that Bevin could do was to set an example of complete devotion to the Union and the cause it represented. The actual control of the officials was effected partly by the general secretary, where national officials were concerned, and by regional secretaries in the case of local officials,[1] and in all instances by the operation of the Union constitution.

An important factor in the control of officials was Ernest Bevin's personality. Many of the officials were able men who could have commanded high salaries in other spheres of activity, but they remained with the Union. Some, who never found full expression for their abilities in the subordinate union administrative jobs they held, sacrificed their ambitions. They all, in one way or another, came under the influence of Bevin and even those who disliked him stayed with the Union. He could rightly have claimed to have been the unifying force during and after the amalgamation. With a lesser person at the head, particularly in the early years, the Union could have been split through internal dissension. The form of control which Bevin exercised over his officials was peculiarly his own.

A Conception of Union Democracy

Although Bevin fully appreciated his own capabilities, he knew that the source of his power was the support he received from the mass of his members.[2] In order to get their full backing he acted at two levels. Firstly he obtained the support and confidence of the ordinary members, and secondly he ranged the General Executive solidly behind him in his activities.

The first stage involved, as he fully realized, interpreting correctly the wishes of his members and basing his interpretation on the conviction of the ordinary members that they were the Union and were responsible for the decisions taken. It was frequently emphasized in the *Record*, the Union journal, even before the Union was officially formed, that the lay members were to control the new Union, and whenever Bevin had the opportunity he reminded his members of their power and obligations. But he was not an addict to mass action which, he said, 'very often is blind action'.[3] He explained its limitations when he said, in relation to the Industrial Alliance and the impending conflict with employers,

> When the fight does come, then in our movement under this alliance, virtually, but only for the period of dispute, the Executive Council of

[1] Bevin told a conference of National Officers and Regional Secretaries in 1938 that regional secretaries should act as general secretaries in their own regions.
[2] After he had resigned from the Wartime Coalition Government along with the other Labour Members in 1945 he told delegates from his Union: 'I have said to Arthur Deakin over and over again, "Keep that chair there, just as it is. As long as the fellows in 10 Downing Street know that I have that chair to fall into, my strength is added to." I have never been under any delusion. You can have the best brain in the world, but unless you have solid support behind you you are nothing. Do you think for one moment I could have held that office for five years if they hadn't known that if they shot me out when I differed from them there might be trouble outside?' (T. & G.W.U., B.D.C. 1945.)
[3] Biennial Delegate Conference, 1939.

the Alliance become the dictators, and conduct that movement to its logical conclusion. I do not want to mislead anybody. I hope I have made that quite clear. I have always taken this view about a fighting democracy. It is all right to shape policy and decide settlements. It is an instrument you cannot scrap with. There are too many generals.[1]

As a trade union often had to be a fighting democracy, Bevin's Executive frequently made important decisions for the members. Even so, he made sure that the decisions were backed, at one stage or another, with rank-and-file support. This was most effectively done by convening delegate conferences for the workers concerned when important decisions had to be taken. Whenever he spoke as his Union representative, whether from the rostrum at the Trades Union Congress or at a Labour Party Conference, he disclosed whether or not he was speaking with the authority of the Union. The Union card vote was used with the same fidelity to the expressed opinion of the representatives of the rank and file. Before a vote was taken on an issue at the Labour Party Conference in 1936 he appealed to have it postponed so that he and his delegates could consult together. 'Some of us are here', he said, 'with delegations and no decision. We are scattered right across the Hall and it is impossible for anybody to exercise the card vote one way or the other.'[2]

In the use of union democracy, as in some other matters, Bevin was a tactician. He was pressed by a number of branches before the 1923 Delegate Conference of the Union to distribute Executive minutes to branches; their claim was based on democratic rights but he successfully opposed it. To distribute the Executive minutes, he said, would be equivalent to broadcasting what action the Union was going to take, and on what scale. He wanted the Executive to have a free hand. Employers' organizations did not publish their minutes. In addition he thought it was unwise to show the divisions within an Executive over taking a particular course of action.

Throughout the 1930s Bevin looked more and more to union education as a democratic device. The members had to be taught their obligations and shown their limitations. He wrote in 1936: '. . . the lay members must be conscious that there are certain things they cannot do, and that they must leave the Officers to carry out the tasks in which they are employed to specialize, the lay member supplementing this work and thereby making a very happy combination'.[3] He did not want blind, emotional support from his members. 'We have got to create, in a Union like this', he said, 'a great

---

[1] Biennial Delegate Conference, 1925.
[2] Labour Party Conference Report, 1936, p. 206.
[3] Report to the General Executive Council, November 1936.

bulwark of understanding in order that at all times we will have key men who understand our principles, our policy and responsibility and duties in order to guide the rest of our fellows.'[1]

It was to assist in the creation of this understanding that a Union Education Scheme based on a correspondence course was launched in 1939. Previously he had relied upon his Union journal and the national press to convey information to the Union members, but he did not know the extent to which the journal was read, and as for the press, he wrote: 'It is becoming increasingly difficult to convey through the ordinary Press the real facts relative to any given situation. When we issue official statements the journalists seem to regard it as their duty to re-write the statements in such a manner that, very often, they no longer convey what we have attempted to issue to the members. We have, therefore, devised special plans of communication.'[2] He also experimented with issuing periodical bulletins dealing with the trade affairs of particular sections. Bevin's concern about a more effective use of the channels of communication, and his appreciation of education to improve union democracy, occurred rather late in his Union career, but he nevertheless anticipated by many years what other union leaders were to think.

Intelligent support needed to be based on loyalty to the Union, which in turn was derived from a number of factors, most of which Bevin was able to influence only indirectly. One cannot accurately list the factors that cause men to support an organization regardless of the material benefits it provides. Many of them are abstruse and all vary in their effect on individuals. But Bevin was aware that men are influenced by size and grandeur and a sense of importance, as well as by such things as tradition and spirit, and he set out to provide imposing central premises in the various regions which would act as symbols of those factors. The members of the Union Property Committee in their report to the Executive stated that they believed 'that the provision of centres of this character would give a sense of stability to the Union and a feeling of confidence amongst the membership'.[3] Transport House in London quickly became the Mecca for trade unionists, and Bevin believed that both it, and the centres provided in Cardiff, Birmingham, and Manchester, were important psychological assets.

The highest constitutional committee in the Union is the General Executive Council, and Bevin made sure that whenever he spoke or acted on behalf of the Union he did so with the backing of that committee. This was his second stage in ensuring that solid union support lay behind him. He rarely deviated from this policy; when

[1] Biennial Delegate Conference, 1939.
[2] Report to the General Executive Council, 1936.
[3] General Executive Council Minute, 2 March 1939.

it was not possible to summon the Executive members to a meeting he would sound their opinions and obtain their decision by a postal ballot. By referring most matters to the Executive before taking action Bevin did not reduce his powers as a leader; he was still able to take the initiative, but whether or not he retained it depended on his ability to convince the Executive members with his arguments. He could have acted and then reported back to his Executive to justify the course he had taken. His method, however, possessed two main advantages. Firstly it considerably strengthened his position as a Union representative. In the face of criticism from inside or outside of the Union he was able to show that he was speaking and acting on Executive instructions; moreover, there was no likelihood of his action being repudiated by his Union. Secondly it had a profound psychological effect on the Executive members, for it was they who were determining policy even though it was under his astute guidance. Though sometimes the Executive rebuffed Bevin, in the main and on important Union issues his superior ability and specialist knowledge enabled him to persuade them to accept his proposals as their own.

BEVIN'S ROLE IN POLITICS

Ernest Bevin had little faith in political action of any kind until the General Strike revealed to him the utmost limit of industrial action. Then he viewed it with greater discrimination and saw more value in legislation as a means of improving wages and working conditions in some of the industries in which his Union had members. Because, throughout his trade union career, Bevin believed that working-class power lay in the trade unions and not in the Labour Party, he preferred to make direct contact with the Government whenever he wanted to take political action for the benefit of his members. Nevertheless he was drawn into Labour Party activities through his stature as a trade union leader.

The emergence of Bevin as a Labour Party policy-maker was dependent on, and coincident with, the departure of J. Ramsay MacDonald and Philip Snowden from the leadership of the Labour Party. He disliked both men intensely. Whilst this attitude towards the Party leadership prevailed he played no part in the inner councils of the Labour Party and his role was confined mainly to that of an advocate at conferences, of a spokesman for organized labour, and as the leader of a union with, in 1930, the fourth largest card vote.[1] This role was far from being an insignificant one, but he had

[1] The Miners' Federation, the National Union of Railwaymen, and the National Union of General and Municipal Workers each carried more votes.

no constitutional position in the Party; he was never a member of its National Executive, nor was he a representative of the Trades Union Congress on the National Council of Labour[1] until after MacDonald had left the Party.

As Bevin became more active in the determination of national Labour Party policy, he saw more clearly the field of activity in which political action by the Labour Party was necessary. The change in his attitude occurred principally in connection with foreign affairs. When he aimed to change the Government's policy towards Russia in 1920 he did so through industrial action by assisting in the formation of the Council of Action and by encouraging his own Union and others to refuse to handle either in manufacture or in transport, munitions to be used against Russia. Such action would not have been countenanced by him in the 1930s. When the Labour Party debated the use of the General Strike to prevent war, in 1934, Bevin spoke strongly against it. He preferred to use his ability and power within the Labour Party to align its foreign policy with his own conception of it, rather than to undertake separate industrial action.

It so happened that the Labour Party devoted much time to foreign affairs after its devastating electoral defeat in 1931. Its major debates were about disarmament, the use of sanctions, and then re-armament. This preoccupation suited Bevin not only because he considered the Labour Party to be the custodian of foreign affairs for the Labour Movement but also because he had developed an absorbing interest in foreign affairs. He displayed a breadth of knowledge about them and an aptitude for interpreting them that enabled him to give an undeviating lead to the Movement at a time when consciences were disturbed and attitudes were vacillating. He adopted an unpopular attitude over war and peace, but the policy of collective security he advocated ultimately became the policy of the Labour Party. In those vital years of the mid-1930s when the Labour Party foreign policy was being crystallized, Bevin's power as a policy-maker in the Labour Movement was most probably greater than at any other period of the inter-war years.

The body on which Bevin found his political niche was the National Council of Labour. It consisted of representatives of the Trades Union Congress General Council, the Labour Party Executive, and the Parliamentary Labour Party. To this body the Trades Union Congress was able to remit matters which required political action. It had been formed in 1921, following the success of the Council of Action in the previous year, to enable Labour to speak with one voice on all of its common ends. It met infrequently

[1] Until 1934 it was called the National Joint Council.

during the 1920s and was of little consequence in the Labour Movement. During the Labour Party troubles of 1931 it was discarded; then resuscitated and reconstituted in December of that year. As a sign of its serious intent it arranged to have regular monthly meetings.

Bevin claimed a hand in the reconstitution of the National Council of Labour[1] and served on it from 1932 till 1937. By the mid-1930s not only the Trades Union Congress but also the Labour Party Conference remitted motions to the National Council of Labour; it issued an important series of policy reports for the Labour Party and was an effective policy-making body. Some Constituency Labour Parties viewed it as a trade union dominated junta which had exceeded the bounds of its original function of co-ordination and had superseded the authority of the Labour Party Executive. There was no doubt that the National Council of Labour accumulated considerable power in the Labour Movement during the time Bevin served on it. He said himself that it had gone beyond being simply a co-ordinating body. 'It has done a thing which I think is of inestimable value to this Movement . . .' he told a Labour Party Conference; 'You have an immediate Programme, and that Programme is based upon preconsiderations of the facts and data relating to it . . . and in that both the Trades Union Congress and the Labour Party have had the benefit of one of the finest pieces of staff work that any Movement has been blessed with.'[2]

Ernest Bevin took part in politics as a trade union leader, not as a politician, and, foreign affairs apart, he regarded himself as the spokesman of the Trade Union view and, *ipso facto*, of the rank-and-file view. He looked upon himself as a protector of trade union interests, and whenever the Labour Party ventured into fields of activity regarded by trade unions as their own he was quick to point out that it was trespassing. On the Labour Party side, he said that he was only a labourer. He added, 'Some might think the Trade Union leaders spent their time in trying to dictate to the rest of the Movement. . . . On the Committees, on the National Council of Labour and in the other departments the Trade Union representatives were doing no more than trying to contribute the benefit of the experience and knowledge they had gained through their positions and their connections.'[3] In the sphere of high politics this is most probably what Bevin did do, though he did it in his own assertive manner. Francis Williams has stated that Bevin would often deliberately arrive late at meetings of the National Council of Labour, and 'ignoring the seat reserved for him at the main conference table

1 Cf. Labour Party Conference Report, 1935, p. 180.
2 Labour Party Conference Report, 1937, p. 174.
3 Labour Party Conference Report, 1935, pp. 243–244.

where the members of the three executives sat, would take up a position by the wall among the officials . . . with . . . a self-confident assurance that, should he decide to intervene, where Bevin sat would prove to be head of the table'.[1]

Most Labour Party Conferences in the inter-war years were concerned with formulating alternative Government policies which they had little chance of implementing. The absence of power bred an attitude of irresponsibility which, to Bevin, appeared in marked contrast to the manner in which trade unions tackled their problems. He said, 'our work is eminently practical, and it is to deliver the goods to our members, and we know, as leaders, the absolute folly of putting up programmes that are not likely to be realized, . . '.[2]

It is doubtful whether Bevin fully accepted the independence of Labour Members of Parliament from the Labour Party Conferences, and he was irked when Labour Party delegates shunned final decision-making because the application of policy rested with the Parliamentary Labour Party. When the question of the Government's armament policy was debated in 1936 and Mr. Herbert Morrison posed its treatment by the Labour Members as one of Parliamentary tactics 'to be settled in the light of the circumstances of the time by the leaders of the Parliamentary Party and the Parliamentary Party itself, after such consultation as may be necessary', Bevin replied:

> I do not cast any reflections, but we are trained in the Trade Union school, where we have to deal with delegate Conferences and we cannot pass the buck to anybody, and we would not if we could. We have to face our members honestly, because we have got to live with them again the next day and onwards; and whether they like our views or not we remain friends about it. . . . Do not let us . . . burke the issue. Take the burden of the Parliamentary Party upon our shoulders, as a Conference. . . .[3]

In the Labour Party the arguments of Ernest Bevin were backed by the weighty support of the Transport and General Workers' Union card vote.[4] It was not always cast on the side of orthodoxy, popular causes, or with the majority in the Labour Party. It was used to support some of Bevin's 'intellectual' critics as well as to oppose them; for example it assisted Sir Oswald Mosley on to the National

[1] *Ernest Bevin*, by Francis Williams, p. 180.
[2] Labour Party Conference Report, 1933, p. 161.
[3] Labour Party Conference Report, 1936, pp. 202–204.
[4] In reply to those who said that trade union leaders were dependent upon their card votes Bevin said: 'Out of curiosity I took out the names of persons for six years past who called for Card Votes, and do you know that not a single union has called for a Card Vote for six years. It was either asked for by the Executive or called for by Local Labour Parties or Socialist bodies.' (Labour Party Conference Report, 1937, p. 146.)

Executive of the Labour Party and Sir Stafford Cripps out of the
Party.[1]   But Bevin, if a labourer in politics, was a skilled labourer
and even bereft of his Union vote he was a formidable political
adversary in committee or in conference.   'I think we will agree that
a Dockers' K.C. is as good an advocate as anyone trained in the
Temple', said Mr. Attlee after Bevin had replied to a speech by Sir
Stafford Cripps in the 1933 Labour Party Conference.   His open and
forthright attitude to those who opposed him, often amounting to
rudeness, was not an alternative for substance; it supplemented it.
Bevin brought a powerful intellect to bear on those political problems
he considered to be important.[2]

ACTIVITIES IN INDUSTRY

Methods and Tactics

The Transport and General Workers' Union, and with it Bevin as
a leader, emerged on an industrial scene that contained the essential
conditions for strife.   There was a developing rate of unemployment;
a sense of frustration among workers resulting from the First World
War and the unfulfilled election promises which followed it; a
continuation of a Syndicalist belief in the 'class struggle'; an absence
of negotiating machinery in most industries and a lack, therefore, of
a negotiating state of mind among trade unionists and employers
alike; and unions, because they were bigger through amalgamation,
were more powerful.   The type of industrial leadership given by
Ernest Bevin in the first instance was then, to some extent, pre-
determined.   He would have found it difficult at the outset to have
pursued a consistent policy of conciliation and moderation.   As it
happened neither Bevin nor his Executive desired to give up the use
of the strike weapon.[3]

Along with the pursuit of a strike policy, the Union was
developing the means for a peaceful settlement of industrial disputes.
The early 1920s marked the beginning of a drive for formal relationships with employers at a national level, and Bevin, starting with his
success at the Shaw Inquiry in 1920, was involved in it.   This dual
approach went on until after the General Strike in 1926.

The emphasis of Bevin and his Union during this period was

---

[1] About Mosley, Bevin remarked: 'At least we did it quite constitutionally.'
(Labour Party Conference Report, 1937, p. 145.)

[2] How inapplicable in Bevin's case, and in the case of some other union leaders of
his period, was Beatrice Webb's scathing comment made in 1917, that 'The Trade
Union Movement has become, like the hereditary peerage, an avenue to political
power through which stupid untrained persons may pass up to the highest office if
only they have secured the suffrages of the members of a large union.' (*Diaries
1912–1924*, p. 89.)

[3] Report to Special Rules Conference, September 1921.

completely on an industrial solution to their problems which was undisturbed even by the Labour Government of 1924. Bevin reported to his Executive, 'I am of the opinion that if we rest on the industrial side for one moment it will be fatal to our progress, and even to the Labour Government. It would be too big a price to pay, and we must therefore go on with the economic war, waging it the whole time, and utilizing every available opportunity on behalf of the class we represent.' On 16 February 1924, five days after Bevin wrote his report, he led the whole of the dock section of his Union out on a strike which lasted until 14 March. He incurred the wrath of many for his action, and the Labour Government, in Bevin's words, 'rushed down to Windsor to get [the Emergency Powers Act] signed, in order to operate on me. . . . I do not like emergency powers, not even when they are operated by my friends.'[1]

The strike was justified in the Union journal by the following statement, which indicates clearly the attitude adopted by Bevin and his Executive at that time.

> The Union has had to face criticism from various quarters because it has pursued a vigorous industrial policy while its own political friends are in office in the State. We welcomed a Labour Government as keenly as anyone, and have made our contributions to the building up of a Labour political movement which has made that Government possible. We appreciate the importance of political action. Nevertheless, the industrial situation has not been altogether of our making, and to a great extent trouble has been due to the unreasonableness of the employers. They took full advantage of the slump period to drive the workers' standards down to the lowest possible level, and that created, after the war experience, a feeling of deep bitterness and resentment. Forward movements were, therefore, inevitable, and most of them began with the first indications of trade improvement and long before a Labour Government was thought possible.
>
> These movements could not have been checked, nor would it have been wise to have held them up because a Labour Government assumed office. After all, the demands made were and are perfectly legitimate . . . to check the movement would be to dispirit the workers, to weaken their faith in industrial action, and to encourage the employers to encroach still further on the present standards.[2]

The dockers had only been back at work a week when an official strike of London tramwaymen was launched which lasted until 31 March. A Court of Inquiry into the dispute was set up by the Minister of Labour and negotiations with the employers were resumed after the Court had published its findings. After eleven days the tramwaymen returned to work with a wage increase. This was a justification of the act.

[1] Labour Party Conference Report, 1933, p. 161.
[2] *The Record*, April 1924, p. 124.

Whilst he saw the need for strike action, Bevin paid much attention to tactics. To define explicitly the tactics to be employed he drew up a memorandum in November 1924 concerning *Wage Claims, Negotiations and Strike Action* which his Union Executive endorsed. It is reproduced here in full:

(1) Organisation of a new industry.—The Workpeople must be definitely informed that it is necessary for them to show their regard for the Union by bringing themselves into compliance before Wages and Conditions Claims are submitted on their behalf.

(2) Payment of Dispute Benefits.—Payment of Dispute Benefits shall be limited to members who are strictly in compliance, other than in very exceptional cases, which must be subject to a special decision by the General Executive Council, to whom all the facts must be forwarded.

(3) Negotiations.—Every effort must be made to exhaust the ordinary negotiating machinery before any consideration is given to the question of a strike or mention made thereof.

(4) Sympathetic Action.—When applications are submitted for authority to declare a strike the Officer concerned shall state clearly what action is necessary to win the strike. Where sympathetic action is necessary the position must be thoroughly examined with a view to ascertaining, prior to the strike taking place, the Section likely to be affected.

(5) Attitude of Employers.—Greater regard must be paid to the attitude of the Employers concerned and an endeavour made to ascertain the possibility of counter moves and the nature of the forces they can bring to their aid in case of necessity.

The steps necessary to meet effectively the counter moves of the Employers must be fully examined.

(6) Sectional Stoppages.—Sectional stoppages must be discouraged, especially those of the lightning character. (The experience of the Union during the past three years is that lightning strikes are the reverse of successful; that the cost associated with same is very heavy; and that, following upon their termination, they invariably result in loss of prestige to the Union and loss of membership.)

(7) Procedure in Time of Strikes.—When a strike of any character takes place, the Strike Committee is not permitted to call out sections of the membership outside the province of the particular strike in relation to which powers have been granted. If an extension of a strike is deemed necessary, the full facts must be reported to the Centre in order to afford the General Executive Council an opportunity of considering the position and of giving a decision.

All Strike Committees must consult with the local Officers concerned, and be in possession of their views before arriving at any decision. Where the official view differs from the view of the Strike Committee the facts must be reported to the Centre for decision.

Strict regard must be had to the prevention of interference with trades and sections not affected by the particular dispute.

(8) Strikes taking place without Executive Sanction.—Whilst the General Executive Council do not strictly lay it down that, under no circumstances, can a strike be supported which takes place prior to their being afforded an opportunity of considering the position, it is necessary to understand clearly that the circumstances necessitating such action must be very exceptional to warrant a support.

(9) Plenary Powers.—Where plenary powers are granted, they shall not be deemed to be valid longer than the periods elapsing between the meetings of the General Executive Council and the Finance and Emergency Committee, or vice-versa. At each meeting of the General Executive Council or the Finance and Emergency Committee a review will be taken of the cases where plenary powers have been granted and not exercised, and they will either be reaffirmed or withdrawn, according to the circumstances prevailing at the time of the review.

(10) Agreements.—Where agreements exist, strict regard must be had to the obligations of the Union in relation to such agreements, in the form of notices, etc.

The industrial policy Bevin was pursuing was strictly related to the changes in the general economic conditions of the country. In 1922 when the rate of unemployment was 14·1 per cent. in Great Britain,[1] the second highest rate for any year in the 1920s, and when in consequence employers were forcing wage cuts, Bevin used the negotiating machinery wherever possible. He realized the difficulty of preventing wage-reductions under such circumstances but he was able to slow down the application of some by exhausting the constitutional procedures of the negotiating bodies. The Union policy became aggressive in 1924 when the general unemployment rate fell to 10·2 per cent. The next year he counselled his members to entrench and not to involve themselves in any serious wage movements, for unemployment had increased. He was conscious of the weakness of his Union when there was a high rate of unemployment and resented the employers taking advantage of it. When they did he waited patiently for retribution. Some years later he stated his objection to opportunism in wage negotiations. 'The Trade Unionist', he said, 'does not want to be always fighting for increased wages or resisting reductions; he wants stability, providing that stability is based upon a proper standard of living. . . .'[2]

After 1926 Bevin continued to react to economic fluctuations whilst deploring the need to do so. In the trough of the depression in 1931 there was a move by employers to reduce wages. 'The attack is being extended over such a wide front', he wrote, 'that the position is becoming almost bewildering. . . . I am not so foolish as to suggest that at all times and under every condition there must be no

---

[1] *Full Employment in a Free Society*, by Lord Beveridge, p. 47.
[2] Labour Party Conference Report, 1929, p. 185.

adjustment of wages. As a matter of fact, these adjustments—up and down—are going on all the time, but that is something different to the general attack which is being made now. . . .'[1]   But he realized that unless the problem of unemployment could be solved there would continue to be such attacks on wages.

There had been so much unemployment after 1921 that a high rate was taken for granted and, in order to focus attention on it, Bevin, in 1930, 'was not sorry that unemployment had taken an acute turn'.[2] Indeed, he gave as one reason for wanting industrial peace the need to see 'unemployment demonstrated in all its nakedness'. Bevin quoted an American Minister of Labour who pointed out that strikes or lock-outs very often merely restricted production and created a kind of vacuum which had to be filled up afterwards and which concealed the true industrial situation.   That is what had happened in Britain, Bevin contended, from 1921 to 1926.[3]   At both the Labour Party Conferences held while there was a Labour Government during the Great Depression, Bevin spoke with emphasis about unemployment.

It was stated above that the Transport and General Workers' Union, for the first four years of its existence, used two different forms of industrial action.   Though strikes and peaceful negotiations are vitally different, they are not mutually inconsistent methods provided priority is given to negotiations.   This view of strike action is generally accepted today, and as long as the use of strikes is exercised in this way the right to strike can be safeguarded.   In the years before the General Strike, however, strike action stood as a distinct and independent method for determining issues between workers and employers, and was an alternative to formal negotiations, though indeed negotiations of some sort followed strikes except where one side or the other capitulated.   In such a manner was it used by the Transport and General Workers' Union.   In those few post-war years, only a relatively small number of trade unionists considered the strike weapon to have revolutionary significance, but the implications of the manner in which it was being used were revolutionary.   It was, in part, this realization by even the most aggressive trade union leaders during the General Strike which changed their attitude towards strike action; thereafter it became accepted as the weapon of the last resort.

The General Strike[4]

It is not intended here to describe the General Strike but only to show, briefly, the part played in it by Bevin and to give his appraisal of it.

[1] Report to General Executive Council, May 1931.
[2] Labour Party Conference Report, 1930, p. 197.
[3] Ibid., p. 198.
[4] See Notes on Terminology at the beginning of the book.

Ernest Bevin achieved no public prominence during the Strike nor during the first stage of giving national union support to the miners in their struggle with the coal-owners nine months earlier. But as he was a man with recognized organizing ability and the leader of a union whose co-operation was vital to the success of any general industrial action, he was assured of an important position behind the scenes at both times.

At the time of the coal-mining dispute in July 1925, Bevin was not yet a member of the General Council of the Trades Union Congress,[1] but he was drawn into the dispute in two ways. Firstly, with C. T. Cramp of the National Union of Railwaymen, he was the author of the scheme to place an embargo on the transport of coal from 31 July 1925 if the coal-owners did not withdraw their notices to terminate the National Wages Agreement in the mining industry.[2] Secondly, his Union was one of the four transport unions which were due to operate the scheme.[3] His Executive also decided to take action to prevent industrial concerns from using their accumulated coal stocks once the embargo was in force.

The trade union side of the dispute was in the hands of the General Council of the Trades Union Congress. On the afternoon of the day appointed for the enforcement of the embargo, the General Council was informed that the Government had decided to pay a subsidy to the coal-owners for nine months to enable the miners' wages to be maintained at their existing levels, that the coal-owners had agreed to suspend the notices terminating the Wages Agreement, and that an inquiry was to be held into the industry. The embargo was not enforced and trade unionists in general proclaimed a victory. The General Council rejoiced too, but tempered its joy with the warning that 'while there is little doubt that the conflict has been avoided, the Trade Union Movement must be alert and vigilant in case the necessity should again arise for it to act in defence of its standards'.[4]

In the General Strike Bevin was more closely involved in decision-making, though as a junior member of the General Council he did not belong to the inner group which comprised the Negotiating Committee. The General Council had not heeded its own warning. It had not been vigilant and had no plans for action in case a clash between the miners and coal-owners occurred when the subsidy expired at the end of April 1926. 'In fact', Bevin said, 'the General

[1] He was first nominated for a General Council seat in late 1924 and elected in 1925.
[2] For a description of events leading up to 31 July (Red Friday) and for details of the scheme, see *The Miners—Years of Struggle*, by R. Page Arnot, pp. 371–387.
[3] The others were the National Union of Railwaymen, the Associated Society of Locomotive Engineers and Firemen, and the Railway Clerks' Association.
[4] Concluding sentence of a letter to the affiliated unions of the Trades Union Congress sent out on 31 July 1925.

Council did not sit down to draft the plans until they were called together on April 27th, and it is better for everybody to know the task that was thrown upon us from April 27th to May 1st . . .'.[1]   It was under the tense, hurried conditions following 27 April that Bevin's talents were used effectively.   He, perhaps more than any other member of the General Council, endeavoured to organize the Strike successfully once it was evident that it would take place.   His aim for a co-ordinated and disciplined withdrawal of labour, for regulated strike behaviour, and for unity in returning to work, was an aim for efficient strike organization which was independent of the reasons for starting and ending the strike.

Not surprisingly Bevin became a member of the Strike Organization Committee of the General Council, and was the General Council spokesman on organization.   The miners' leader, A. J. Cook, singled him out for praise for making 'every effort possible to bring into being machinery to cope with the requirements'.[2]   And at the end Bevin displayed the independence of mind which marked his later activities in industry and politics.   When the Council met the Prime Minister and seven of his Ministers to state that the strike was being terminated, it was Bevin who opposed unilateral concessions and asked for assurances from the Government that there would be facilities provided for the reinstatement of workers and that there would be immediate negotiations to settle the miners' strike which was continuing.[3]   This was more than Mr. Baldwin had expected and more than he was prepared to concede.

In 1921 Bevin had criticized the Triple Alliance for being a paper alliance.[4]   He made no such complaint about the General Council during the General Strike.   Once the decision to take strike action in support of the miners had been taken by the affiliated unions, the General Council assumed executive power in the Movement, and this, in Bevin's opinion, had a significant effect on the conduct of the Strike.   It enabled the Strike Committee to plan in the belief that its plans would be implemented and thus improved the quality of the plans.   When Bevin peremptorily announced the arrangements for the distribution of essential food supplies his manner was accepted by the combined union executives as befitting the circumstances. He told them, 'You must take your orders and obey them, believing

---

[1] *The Mining Crisis and The National Strike 1926*, Official Reports, 1927.   Report of Special Conference of Executives of affiliated unions, 20 January 1927, p. 10.   The preparations would not have been so hurried had the General Council accepted a memorandum submitted by Walter Citrine, then acting secretary to the Council, who compiled it after hearing a speech made by Mr. Churchill.   Presumably the speech was the one Churchill made on 10 December 1925, in which he stated the Government's preparedness for a dispute.
[2] *The Nine Days*, by A. J. Cook.   A pamphlet quoted by Page Arnot.
[3] Page Arnot, op. cit., pp. 446–449.
[4] Ibid., p. 262.

that those of us charged with the responsibility of guiding will give the best guidance we can . . .'.[1]

Trade union criticisms of the General Council in this case were about its arbitrary use of power. It was said, for instance, 'what right had the General Council to end the Strike?' Bevin's answer was that

. . . Everybody in that conference believed that the Trade Unions affiliated to Congress became for the purposes of that dispute one union. I have been asked: did you agree to this being done or that being done? I venture to suggest that every Executive agreed simply to put their power into our hands as the members of the unions put their power into yours, and in that you trusted us come weal or woe, and agreed to accept our decisions in the conduct and settlement of that dispute. . . .[2]

The effect of the authoritative position of the General Council and the loyalty shown by the ordinary members was undermined in Bevin's opinion by the lack of unity in ending the strike and the bitter arguments about it afterwards. He resented the castigation of the General Council for doing something he felt it had a right to do.

The Triple Alliance, the abortive Industrial Alliance, and then the General Strike caused Bevin to be disillusioned about united action by trade unions. 'There is too much jealousy over personalities', he told delegates from his own Union. 'I was never in a movement in my life where it was brought out so strongly. No matter which of us may be leaders in a movement, if our personality stands in the way of arriving at a settlement, we should stand aside. . . .'[3] The lack of co-operation between the leaders, he thought, had 'demoralized the movement from one end of the country to the other'.[4] He did not forget the lessons in unity he learned in those years, and he pointed to them in 1945 when delegates from his Union were discussing the creation of a federation for transport workers. 'You can meet the railwaymen or any other Union any time you like,' he told them, 'but I suggest you keep the power of the Union in the hands of this Executive and this Delegate Conference and not go on any longer delegating it to other people. I am sure I speak with long

[1] *The Mining Crisis and the National Strike 1926*, Official Reports, T.U.C. (Report of a Special Conference, 29 April to 1 May 1926, p. 34.)
[2] Ibid. (Conference Report, 20 January 1927, p. 45.) Charles Dukes, then a delegate at the Special Conference of Executives of affiliated unions on 20 January 1927, endorsed Bevin's opinion. He said: 'My impression was when we left that conference [29 April to 1 May] that the Executives attached to this movement had pooled their responsibilities, had sunk their identity, had conceded their power, plenary power, to the General Council . . . and I believe it was the impression of the overwhelming majority. . . .' (Ibid., p. 58.)
[3] Biennial Delegate Conference of the Transport and General Workers' Union 1927.
[4] *The Mining Crisis and the National Strike 1926* (Conference Report, 20 January 1927, p. 46).

experience when I say that you will only be disappointed in the end
and that it will not produce the goods.'[1]

The General Strike had given Ernest Bevin an early opportunity
to reveal his leadership qualities on the General Council of the
Trades Union Congress.   Thereafter he became its most prominent
member, and with Walter Citrine, who had joined the Council as an
assistant secretary just before Bevin was elected to it, he helped the
Council to create and assert moral leadership over the trade union
movement.   It was in the endeavour to restore to the General
Council some of the prestige it lost after the General Strike that
Bevin and Citrine engaged in what I consider to be some remarkable
and overlooked leadership tactics.

The Mond-Turner Talks

To understand the full significance of these talks to Bevin in
particular it is necessary to have a clear picture of the post-General
Strike situation.   Firstly, the stock of the General Council had
sunk low, and much of the authority it had begun to accumulate after
its reorganization in 1920 had been lost.   Mr. Arthur Pugh, the
chairman of the General Council in 1926, wrote that the 'criticism of
the General Council varied from vituperation at the one end to a sort
of pitying scorn at the other, over what they evidently regarded as the
incapacity and cowardice of the General Council'.[2]   The Government added to the humiliation of the Council by passing the Trade
Disputes and Trade Unions Act in 1927, which declared illegal
sympathetic strikes and any strike 'designed or calculated to coerce
the Government either directly or by inflicting hardship upon the
community'.   The General Strike fell into both of these classifi-
cations.   There was every possibility that given no action to the
contrary the General Council would drift back into the ineffectual
position of the Parliamentary Committee it had replaced.

Secondly, the General Strike, for many unions, had been contrary
to the terms of their agreements with employers, and formal trade
union/employer relationships had ceased in a number of cases.   The
largest association of employers in the iron and steel industry, the
Iron and Steel Trades Employers' Association, insisted that John
Hodge, president of the Iron and Steel Trades Confederation,
should sign a document, drawn up by them, admitting his union's
guilt in striking.[3]   Hodge signed it.   Francis Williams states that
Bevin secured the reinstatement of his dock members 'only at the
cost of signing a new and to him humiliating agreement with the
Port of London employers in which he had to admit that his own and

[1] T. & G.W.U., B.D.C. 1945.
[2] *Men of Steel,* p. 403.
[3] *Workman's Cottage to Windsor Castle,* pp. 363–373.

the Stevedores' Union had wilfully broken the previous agreement'.[1] In Scotland the Scottish Daily Newspaper Society decided against employing trade unionists in future and other Scottish newspaper employers insisted that the Scottish Typographical Association should sign a pledge not to take part in a lightning strike in future.[2]   In the printing industry in England and Wales many firms refused to reinstate strike hands and went non-union, or established company unions.[3]   In those industries where formal relationships had not been established before the General Strike, the position of union officials became untenable and many of them were prevented from undertaking their work.

Thirdly, the membership of most unions declined after the strike and their incomes were reduced as a consequence, but owing to the burden of strike victimization, and, in some cases, out-of-work benefit, their financial commitments were increased.   The result was that many unions were near bankruptcy.

On the whole, the situation could hardly have been worse.   And whilst an improvement could be expected from favourable changes in the state of trade, the morale of the Movement, in terms of the confidence of its members in its leaders and its attitude towards employers, could only be restored by forthright leadership.

The second half of 1926 and most of the following year were much too full of recrimination and matters basic to the survival of individual unions to provide an opportunity for the exercise of leadership within the Movement.   Appeals came from outside the Movement, from prominent public figures, for a changed attitude from leaders within it, but there was no positive response.[4]   Some trade union leaders were invited to weekend talks and suchlike meetings to discuss the situation, but most of them refused to accept invitations extended to them in their individual capacities or to take part in discussions without the knowledge of their respective Executives.[5]

No overtures were received from employers during the period between the General Strike and the Trades Union Congress in September 1927.   This was not surprising.   The employers, after all, were in positions of strength.   The Prime Minister, Mr. Baldwin, had appealed for industrial peace, but his appeal was rejected out of hand by the Trades Union Congress in 1927.   Bevin moved the rejection at the Congress.   He placed the responsibility for industrial peace squarely in the laps of the Government and employers.   Mr.

[1] *Ernest Bevin*, p. 140.
[2] *A Hundred Years of Progress*, by Sarah Gillespie, pp. 219–223.
[3] *The Typographical Association. Origins and History up to 1949*, by A. E. Musson, pp. 420–421.
[4] Bevin stated that Lord Astor, Mr. Rowntree, and other such people had approached him (Report to G.E.C., February 1928).
[5] Stated by Bevin in his Report to G.E.C., February 1928.

Baldwin's 'facing both ways policy', he added, was responsible for
the industrial troubles of the last three or four years. There was
justification, Bevin thought, for Mr. Baldwin's resignation.[1]

At the same time as Bevin was making his rousing and defiant
speech, people concerned with industrial harmony were contemplating the remarks made earlier in the week by the chairman of the
Trades Union Congress, George Hicks. In his presidential address,
he had shown the first sign of a new lead from the General Council
to the Movement. He said:

> . . . Practically nothing has yet been done to establish effective machinery
> of joint conference between the representative organizations entitled to
> speak for industry as a whole. . . . Such a direct exchange of practical
> views . . . would be of far greater significance than the suggestion . . . for
> a spectacular national conference under Government or other auspices
> . . . and might yield useful results in showing how far and upon what
> terms co-operation is possible in a common endeavour to improve the
> efficiency of industry and to raise the workers' standard of life. . . .

He wanted negotiations between the representatives of the Trades
Union Congress on the one hand and representatives of the Federa-
tion of British Industries and the Confederation of Employers'
Organizations on the other.[2]

The speech evoked no positive response from the employers'
organizations. In October, a month later, the National Confederation of Employers' Organizations issued a statement in which the
view was expressed that discussions of the problems of industry
could be most effectively carried on in the separate industries through
the existing negotiating machinery. The Engineering Employers'
Federation expressed the same opinion shortly afterwards. This,
the General Council replied, 'showed an entire misapprehension of the
President's address, which referred . . . to those broader questions
of industrial organization, technique, finance, and management,
which are common to all industries, and with which the joint
negotiating machinery of the individual industries is not empowered
to deal'.[3] Sir Alfred Mond,[4] in a letter to the General Secretary of
the Trades Union Congress on 23 November 1927, stated that no
existing organization of employers was empowered to discuss with
the General Council the questions the General Council had in mind
and for that reason he and twenty-three other influential industrialists had agreed, as individuals, to meet the General Council.

At a special session of the General Council on 20 December 1927

[1] T.U.C. Report, 1927, pp. 314–316.
[2] Hicks stated this explicitly at the T.U.C. in 1928 (cf. T.U.C. Report, 1928, p. 425.)
[3] T.U.C. Report, 1928, p. 210.
[4] Chairman of Imperial Chemical Industries, Ltd.

it was agreed to accept Mond's invitation. A sub-committee, including Bevin amongst its members, was appointed to consider procedure for the meeting, and on 12 January 1928 a full joint conference was held between the General Council and the Employers' group. So began the Mond–Turner talks.[1]

What value could be derived from such talks? Though some of the signatories to Mond's letter held responsible positions in employers' organizations, they were acting in their individual capacities and could not commit their respective business organizations to any decisions likely to result from talks with the General Council.[2] The members of the General Council met on the same footing with no right to commit the unions. They took no more power to the discussion than the employers could give in return.[3] The members of the General Council knew that even if talks had been held with employers' organizations there would have been severe restrictions on the application of any recommendations they made. It followed that talks with a group of unrepresentative employers would be little more than an intellectual exercise.[4] The value of the talks lay in the formulation of proposals which the General Council could take to Congress and not in the implementation of the proposals.

The justification to Congress of talks with unrepresentative employers presented little difficulty. The opposition to talks of any kind came only from a relatively small left-wing section of the Trade Union Movement which accused the General Council of treachery. Nevertheless, the General Council had to frame its actions and intentions to show that they were consistent with the traditions of the Movement. Ernest Bevin looked on the talks as a means of discussing national economic problems. With whom can you meet to discuss unemployment? he asked. 'Government Departments who do nothing? No, I would rather sit down with some considered policy on a problem of that character facing the capitalists themselves across the table—not in alliance with them, for I am no more in alliance with them than I am in alliance with the dockowners or anybody else whom I have to fight every day. Is the strike the only way to fight? Cannot we fight by

---

[1] Ben Turner was the president of the T.U.C. in 1928.

[2] In the debate at the Trades Union Congress 1928, Walter Citrine said they 'represented directorships in 189 companies; they included 98 chairmen of those companies; 2 past presidents, 6 vice-presidents, and 3 other members of the Executive of the Federation of British Industries, as well as the chairman and past chairman of the National Confederation of Employers' Organizations, 2 past chairmen of the Iron and Steel Manufacturers' Association, the chairman of the Chemical Employers' Federation, the chairman of the Flour Milling Employers' Federation, and the president of the Association of Chambers of Commerce.' (Report, p. 408.)

[3] Stated by Bevin at the 1928 Congress. (Report, p. 448.)

[4] Citrine said at the 1928 Congress: 'My considered opinion [is] that there will be a great difficulty on the part of employers who have signed this report to get it accepted by their associations. . . .' (Report, p. 413.)

discussion as well as by starvation? Cannot we fight by intelligence?'[1]

Much had happened between the Congresses of 1927 and 1928, so that at the same time as the General Council was asking Congress to accept the principle of the talks it was asking it to endorse the interim report resulting from them. The report described the incidents leading up to the first joint conference with the employers; it outlined the scope of the conference and contained statements about some of the problems that had been discussed. By having the report accepted by an overwhelming majority[2] the General Council was given a vote of confidence which helped to restore it to its pre-General Strike position and acted as a base for an impressive accumulation of moral authority in later years. For Bevin, at least, a primary object of the Mond–Turner talks had been achieved.

The direct results in industry, however, were negligible. The interim report which was accepted by Congress in 1928 was rejected by the National Confederation of Employers' Organizations and the Federation of British Industries. Even the employers who signed the report could not, or would not, implement its recommendations in their own organizations. When the scope of the talks was being determined it was agreed that outside the affairs of individual industries the entire field of industrial reorganization and industrial relations should be discussed. Bevin said he was concerned that nothing should be excluded from discussion, but he pressed all along for priority to be given to vital trade union matters and, significantly, joint statements were subsequently published on trade union recognition, victimization, and the prevention of disputes,[3] which contained nothing inimical to the interests of trade unionists. Doubtless these statements assisted the endeavour of unions to re-establish formal relations with employers.

The talks with the Mond group were suspended early in 1929 while a committee of representatives of the Trades Union Congress, the National Confederation of Employers' Organizations, and the Federation of British Industries explored the possibility of a form of consultation between them. These organizations had never met formally before. A scheme of consultation was compiled and was accepted by the three bodies concerned during 1930 and 1931. These endeavours, however, were overtaken by events. Unemployment had increased to an unprecedented level and, so far as employers were concerned, whatever justification for high-level consultations had existed previously, had disappeared. The Mond–Turner talks

[1] T.U.C. Report 1928, p. 450.
[2] By 3,075,000 votes to 566,000.
[3] The only other statements issued were on the creation of a National Industrial Council, Rationalization, and the Gold Reserve and its Relations with Industry.

and the scheme for consultation had become things of the past by 1932.

A pattern of trade union leadership arose out of the turbulent events of the 1920s which was consolidated during the years up to 1940. Trade union leaders became less willing to engage in strikes and to be drawn into them by the precipitate action of their members. In large part their attitude was determined by the implications and exigencies of the General Strike. These bred tolerance. 'We on our side', Bevin said, '. . . began to apply reason for the solution of our problems, immediately we found a willingness on the part of the rest of the community to adopt reason.'[1] And though the General Council, in evidence to the Macmillan Committee on Industry and Trade, stated that any attempt by employers to reduce the living standards of workers 'would un-questionably provoke the most bitter and prolonged industrial conflict of modern times',[2] the unions, in fact, defended themselves against wage-cuts during the depression mainly by negotiation. They were on the defensive for most of this period and, until 1938, there were no significant developments in either the attitudes of leaders or the methods they employed.

A REACTION TO WAR CONDITIONS

Under the threat of war in 1938, the Government, as in 1915, had looked to the unions for their support. This generation of trade union leaders had not before been called upon to co-operate with the Government. On the contrary, the General Strike and the Trade Disputes and Trade Unions Act of 1927, had created in the minds of union leaders much ill-feeling towards the Government. So when the Government, in general terms, asked the unions to give priority to the production of armaments, to assist in increasing the mobility of labour, and to accept some dilution the response was lukewarm. The Confederation of Shipbuilding and Engineering Unions believed that the Government should state its requirements in categorical terms. Bevin, too, was dissatisfied with the indefinite-ness of the Government requests. He told the national trade group secretaries of his Union who were concerned with the requests that

it is the Government's duty to lay before the employers the volume of output they require and to ascertain from the employers whether they can give the output required. If the employers say no owing to lack of skilled or other labour, it seems to me that it is the duty of the Govern-ment to ask the employers what changes they require and then have a

[1] Report to G.E.C., February 1930.
[2] T.U.C. Report, 1931, p. 283.

Tripartite Conference. . . . [The] Government appears to be adopting a very subtle method of avoiding anything in the nature of a Treasury Circular, or the entering in as a Government with the Unions of any agreement or obligation to restore the position at the end of the period, and I can visualize the Unions being left in a very unfortunate position. The course that would be followed . . . is that the Government merely gives the order for the aeroplanes, etc., to the industry; they use their position as a Government to create, psychologically, a position to enable the employers to get concessions from the Unions, but at the end the Unions will be left to the process of Collective Bargaining without any support, to restore the conditions.[1]

These were practical trade union objections unrelated to the political complexion of the Government, except that a Government more closely related to the unions would most probably have given them the guarantees Bevin desired.

When the War Office asked the railway unions and the Transport and General Workers' Union for their co-operation in raising personnel for the Supplementary Reserve of the Royal Engineers, the executive committee of the National Union of Railwaymen decided that it could not give it in view of the record of the Government in international affairs and its failure to outline clearly its intentions in the event of further aggression by Fascist countries. On the other hand the Transport and General Workers' Union Executive pointed out the danger of making co-operation in the acceleration of the rearmament programme dependent upon the Government's changing its foreign policy—it could, the Executive thought, have possible reactions in the future in relation to entirely different problems. Arising out of this problem the Executive of the Transport and General Workers' Union decided, on 8 April 1938, 'that neither on the immediate issue, nor any other issue arising in the future, could it be party to making industrial Trade Union action dependent upon the political policy of the Government of the day'. This was not a startling admission of the industrial independence of trade unions for, in the main, independence had always been exercised. The alternative would have severely handicapped trade union action. The statement made it clear that the Union was not prepared to hang on to the coat-tails of the Labour Party whether or not the Party was in office; and for this it was important. On 27 April the General Council, in a letter to the Prime Minister, expressed a similar view.[2]

The trade union movement, in principle, was prepared to collaborate with the Government in dealing with re-armament. The

[1] Policy Memorandum addressed by the General Secretary to National Trade Group Secretaries, 6 May 1938.
[2] T.U.C. Report, 1938, pp. 228–229.

situation was not analogous to that just before the First World War. The Labour Movement had been hostile to the Nazis from 1933 onwards and was prepared to support a war against them. There was not, in 1938, as intense a class feeling among the rank and file as there had been before 1914, so that expressed moderation towards a politically antagonistic government was not considered to be heresy. The union leaders were able to act according to their bent with relatively little fear of moving out of step with their members.

The collaboration in practice was restricted to working with the employers and government representatives on committees, until the Labour Movement decided to join with Mr. Winston Churchill in forming a coalition government. It was not until then that the Government was prepared to pay the price of co-operation from trade unions. Indeed, the unwillingness of Mr. Neville Chamberlain to give specific guarantees of protection to trade unions in exchange for the relaxation of regulations and custom, caused some union leaders to become suspicious of every move of the Government towards regulation. Ernest Bevin was one who, through his suspicion, tended to become unco-operative.

> The thing we have to do [he told his Executive in March 1940] is to maintain our Union intact and to be ready to fight for liberty immediately it is challenged, and I think I can claim that the speeches I have delivered, and the attitude I have taken up, have considerably helped to check the growing demand of the Government and the bureaucracy to deprive us of our liberty of operation. We have ever to be vigilant, and I regret that in this generation there is not a greater keenness among our own people to realize how important this question of liberty of thought, freedom of the press and the right of the trade unions, really is. . . .

The job of removing the suspicion from the minds of most trade union leaders by giving them the guarantees they desired fell to Bevin when he became the Minister of Labour. In return trade unions agreed to work more closely with the Government. A new phase in trade union leadership began.

4*

PART II

Having described the development of the situation in which Arthur Deakin found himself in 1940, we can now turn to his activities as a trade union leader. In the years 1940–1955 trade unions were strong and so were the external economic and political influences acting on them. There was less scope than during any previous period for independent action by trade union leaders. Power, they discovered, carried with it responsibilities. In the following chapters we shall see what type of leadership emerges when a man with a forceful personality leads a large well-established union in such circumstances.

Chapter Six

QUALIFICATIONS FOR REPRESENTATIVE LEADERSHIP

THE effect which Arthur Deakin's leadership had on the behaviour of his Union and on the industrial and political situations with which he was concerned will become clear in the following chapters. At this stage it is sufficient to say that it resulted from a conscious and deliberate endeavour by Deakin to impose his own value judgments wherever he was able.

It is incorrect, perhaps, to talk about Deakin's 'own value judgments', for he did not view himself as a single, private individual, but as a workers' representative and, as such, as the mouthpiece of the desires and aspirations of his members. This was a bold claim to make. In this chapter the claim is briefly examined.

THE ACCEPTANCE OF A LEADER

Once a General Secretary of a trade union has been formally selected, whether by appointment or by election, he has to be informally accepted by the majority of the ordinary members. The formal stage provides him with constitutional authority and the informal one determines whether or not leadership can be exercised effectively. In an elective post the two are to some extent combined. There, all the members are asked to state a preference for a particular person and it can be assumed that the one who secures the necessary majority is informally accepted by at least those who voted for him.

The General Secretaryship of the Transport and General Workers' Union is an elective post. When Deakin was elected in 1945 he received 58·5 per cent. of the 347,523 votes that were cast; thus, at least 203,314 members were prepared to accept his leadership. For effective leadership, however, he needed the support, tacit or active, of many of the remaining 815,755 members who either voted for other candidates or abstained from voting for one reason or another. To get this he had to reflect the desires and points of view of those members on matters of practical significance. His claim to be a workers' representative had to be a substantial one.

THE RELEVANCE OF BACKGROUND AND EXPERIENCE

Until he became a full-time official of the Union at the age of twenty-nine, Deakin worked as a roll-turner in an iron and steel works situated in a relatively small north Welsh community. There, workers from Staffordshire, Lancashire, and south Wales mingled with the indigenous north Welsh to form a concentrated and over-specialized section of Britain's heavy industry, subjected to the extremes of depression and economic prosperity. In the setting of the heavy manual work that was characteristic of the iron and steel industry, of Welsh non-conformity (Deakin was a member of the Primitive Methodist Chapel), of local politics and part-time trade union activity, Arthur Deakin's interests and values were formed.

It would be incorrect to describe him as an ordinary worker, for his range of interests was wide. Yet he was not much out of the ordinary. His experiences as a manual worker gave him an understanding of the reactions and emotions of the workers he was to represent, and his activities in the community brought him into close social contact with them and widened his understanding of ordinary people. For a further thirteen years he worked and lived amongst the same people as a full-time trade union official.

The effect of Arthur Deakin's background on his later national activities was profound. He did not consider that at any stage he ceased to be a member of the working class; he spoke and acted with the conviction of one who knew what his members wanted because he was one of them, rather than as one who relied on interpretation to discover their wishes. For that reason he regarded it as an insult to be called 'out of touch' with his members.

But some members considered that his removal first to the position of a full-time trade union official and then from the intimacy of his local community to the apparent isolation of Transport House, had divorced him from the workers he represented. And so to some extent it had. He was physically removed from them and could not possibly have been acquainted with their precise reactions to given industrial situations. But this acquaintance was not necessary and in any case it would have been impossible to acquire in such a large heterogeneous organization. He, as a leader of the Union, was required to know what the general responses of the industrial sections of the membership of his Union, sometimes the whole of the membership, would be to given situations. For example, how would they respond to a policy of wage restraint, to a break with the World Federation of Trade Unions, or to a rule excluding Communists from office in the Union?

Arthur Deakin was able to gauge the responses of his members without a precise knowledge of the industries in which they worked, because his responses were so very often theirs, too, and because his intense loyalty to his members and their interests was in no way impaired by his removal to Transport House. He continued to talk the language of the ordinary members and in his attitudes and social behaviour he remained virtually unchanged. Deakin's feeling of oneness with his members was an essential element in his leadership qualities and could only have been derived from his background and experience.

It would be incorrect to assume, however, that because a trade union leader has a working-class background and experience he thereby remains unaffected by physical remoteness from his members in terms of position and of the size of the union. There is plenty of evidence to show that some men soon forgot their early experiences when they were removed to top union positions, but these cases do not belittle the importance of having shared the experiences of the ordinary members; they simply draw attention to the need for the ability to utilize them in the formulation of decisions and as guides to action. A working-class background and experience without this ability become meaningless. A trade union general secretary who had had a different background and experiences from his members could operate effectively, provided he possessed the ability of interpretation and of being able to assess the responses of his members through transposing himself into their circumstances. The possibility of miscalculation, however, would be greater, and he would exercise a different type of leadership from the working-class leader. His link with his members would be primarily a functional one.

The relationship between Arthur Deakin and his members was marked by two characteristics. First, any of his actions which were interpreted as being against the interests of his members were not considered to be a straightforward dereliction of his duty but a betrayal of his class. This was an admission by even his most severe critics in the Union of his membership of their class. Secondly, his relationship with his members was authoritarian in a way that it could not have been had he not come from the ranks of the workers he represented.

As a possible explanation of the authoritarian nature of working-class leaders, Maurice Duverger said that they concentrate on the exercise of power by virtue of the positions they hold because they realize that they possess no natural intrinsic superiority.[1] But a tendency towards authoritarianism in a voluntary society can have

[1] *Political Parties*, p. 171.

an effect which is a reversal of its intentions unless the members are willing to accept it. Why did members of the Transport and General Workers' Union accept it? Why indeed do members of most unions accept it? There are a number of explanations which possibly together answer the question.

In the first place workers who are accustomed to industrial discipline expect it in other fields, and when it is provided in a trade union they do not question its presence. The inverse is true. Workers such as dockers have a relatively undisciplined industrial existence and they are equally undisciplined in their trade unions and object most strongly to the exercise of authority by their leaders. Then there is a tendency to admire aggressiveness in a person. This may not be confined to working-class groups but it certainly applies to them. Indeed, aggressiveness is viewed by some as being synonymous with good leadership, particularly when it is imagined that it is used against employers. Arthur Deakin provided much scope for admiration in this respect. Lastly, it is characteristic of working-class people to behave openly in their relations with each other, without inhibitions and often without prejudice to future relations. This can be seen in many aspects of working-class life but it is clearly demonstrated in trade unions. Arthur Deakin was regarded as an equal by his members; free to be abused and to abuse, to be praised and to praise. He was able to be open and outspoken in all his relations with trade union members. On a number of occasions he had heated exchanges with some of them and certainly the exchanges were not always one-sided. Some members showed no lack of temerity in moving motions of no confidence in him. Undoubtedly Deakin by his aggressive attitude encouraged altercations with his members. The significance of the incidents, of which there were many, was that they revealed a way of raising and frequently of settling differences within the Union that was understood by both Deakin and his members; it was in complete harmony with their temperaments and it assisted in maintaining the cohesion of the organization. Rarely did he or his members resort to sneers, sarcasm, or subterfuge in their dealings with each other.

CONCEPTION OF PURPOSE

In general terms Arthur Deakin epitomized the aspirations of the ordinary members of his Union. He was moderate in his aims and, in most cases, tolerant in pursuit of them. On all important matters of policy his members as a whole gave him their support and approved of his methods; even his more intolerant treatment of Communists received the support of a majority of the members.

And when his loyalty and sense of responsibility to the community caused him to act more cautiously than some of his members wished, he nevertheless reflected the sentiments of most of them. Whether Arthur Deakin was right or wrong in his purpose, progressive or reactionary, is irrelevant here. The pertinent factor is that the dissenting sections of the membership were small but vocal and therefore exaggerated in importance.

After he had moved from the parochial atmosphere of north Wales to a national position in London in 1932, Deakin began to think of his Union purpose in national terms. He looked upon it then and thereafter as being the removal of the economic and social inequities which affected the semi-skilled and unskilled workers who comprised the membership of his Union. His conception broadened during his early years as a trade union leader and he frequently expressed it in political terms, but his particular purpose never became wholly subordinate.

From about 1940 Deakin talked of the 'socialization of industry'[1] as a political panacea for the ailments of society, but he was never a whole-hearted supporter of the policies which it entailed. He hedged his acceptance of it with various qualifications. He wanted no radical changes in the ownership of industry during the war nor in its method of organization.[2] He saw difficulties in the way of implementing Socialist measures and preached caution. Towards the end of the war he talked not of the 'socialization of industry' but of a 'policy of planned economy'. The change involved more than the use of different nomenclature. It was a movement away from wholesale nationalization and related controls to a belief in the use of *ad hoc* measures and a restricted application of nationalization.

During the post-war period Deakin supported all the Bills for nationalization which the Labour Government introduced and the controls they retained and initiated. But he showed no desire for further nationalization or controls, except for a form of price control. He came to believe that social and economic inequities were not inherent in the type of capitalist economy in which he lived; that they could be removed by adaptations without disturbing the framework of society.

This change in Deakin's attitude was inevitable under conditions in which the living standards of workers were improved, for he did not believe at any time in the validity of the class conflict in a

[1] 'Socialization', said Emanuel Shinwell, 'means the full application of socialist policy and indeed it goes far beyond what is usually meant by nationalization of industry.' (Labour Party Conference Report, 1942, p. 116.)

[2] At the T.U.C. in 1942 he opposed a motion calling for a greater measure of 'active participation by trade union representatives in the administration and management of all vital war industries' mainly, he said, because the idea was impracticable. (T.U.C. Report, 1942, p. 176.)

capitalist society. Like so many of his members, he disliked
injustices in society and initially accepted a ready-made political
panacea without realizing that he could not accept the premise of
the class conflict on which it was based. He did not accept the view put
by a delegate at the 1953 Biennial Delegate Conference of his Union
that 'either the Tories stink or they are all right'; or that the Labour
Movement was aiming to destroy the capitalists. 'We are not trying
to destroy anyone,' he said. 'We are trying to secure a readjust-
ment of the balance of things which will enable us to be as privileged
as the privileged class of today.'[1] On another occasion he said, 'I
do not believe, at this period of our development, that there is an
innate wickedness and spirit of perversity amongst the industrialists,
that out of sheer cussedness they will not give us the consideration
to which we regard ourselves as being entitled.'[2] Some members
criticized Deakin for saying of the Conservative Ministers when the
denationalization of road transport was taking place that they were
'not all a bad bunch'.[3] When he was asked to explain his point of
view at the Union Biennial Delegate Conference later in 1953 he
singled out Sir Walter Monckton as one from whom 'we have a
square deal and have been able to do things which were difficult to
do when our own people were at the Ministry. . . .' He did not
practise the hypocrisy of criticizing men in public for the sake of
tradition when he worked with them amicably in private. Nor for
that matter did many of his members. As they judged employers
on their merits and accorded recognition to good ones, so they
judged Governments and the policies for which they stood.

One last indication of Arthur Deakin's attitude towards the theory
of the class conflict was provided by his belief that the well-being
of the workers depended fundamentally upon the prosperity of
industry and not upon political systems. In his later years this was
indicated clearly by his association with campaigns to increase
productivity and by his acceptance of methods, such as work study,
calculated to improve industrial efficiency. His attitude was not a
post-war development, though it changed its emphasis during the
Labour Government's term of office after 1945.

One of his earliest achievements when he became a full-time trade
union official was to negotiate an agreement providing for good
working conditions, relatively high wages, and minimum wage
scales in the iron and steel works where he was previously employed.
This occurred in 1920. In November 1921 the firm closed down
because it was unable to sell its products and it did not resume
production until July 1922. He realized then how futile it was to

1 Biennial Delegate Conference, July 1953.
2 Eleventh All-Ireland Delegate Conference, October 1952.
3 Bristol Festival of the Union, 28 February 1953.

have good agreements for wages and conditions of work when there was no security of employment. This incident had a permanent effect on his interpretation of trade union problems and he frequently referred to it.

It influenced his attitude towards full employment. 'In planning the new order', he said in 1943, 'the State must accept an obligation to its citizens. This will not be met merely by the provision of social insurance. We cannot live on social insurance. After the war a high level of employment will be an economic and moral necessity. . . .'[1] Deakin considered the same end to be a trade union responsibility too.

> Trade Unions [he said] are not merely agencies solely for the fixation of wages and the regulation of working conditions. Our responsibility to our membership covers a much wider field. We must have regard to that wider economic policy, that planned relationship between the State and its citizens which will enable us to plan our industrial activity in such a way as to provide full employment and rising standards of life, building up a great measure of social security. . . .[2]

The main cause of the closure in 1921 of the iron and steel plant with which Deakin was involved was its inability to compete with foreign producers. Deakin saw then that employers and trade unions did not have a black and white relationship, and in his subsequent relations with industrial management he did not act as if it did. A good illustration of his attitude occurred in 1938. Ernest Bevin had reported that Courtaulds, the silk and rayon producers, were in a financially precarious position, due he said to 'the shortening of production and the general international situation which . . . affected nearly all classes of trade outside of armament production'. The Transport and General Workers' Union were endeavouring to negotiate a wage increase with the firm and Deakin, in the absence of Bevin who was in Australia, was in charge of the negotiations. In August 1938 Deakin reported to the Union Executive:

> There is no possibility of securing a wage increase by negotiation at the present time and to seek to secure one by strike action would, I feel, simply lead to disaster. It has, therefore, been decided in consultation with the General Secretary, that it will be better in the long run to accept the present position, maintain the good relationships and review the position periodically so that when trade improves we shall be in a position to bring about a successful result of these negotiations.

The decision was approved by a representative delegate conference of the section of the Union concerned.

Arthur Deakin's understanding of the problems facing employers

[1] T. & G.W.U., B.D.C. 1943.
[2] Eighth All-Ireland Delegate Conference, 1946.

and his willingness to make allowances for them, sometimes to assist in solving them, was extended in the post-war years to an understanding of all aspects of the nation's economic problems. The solution of these problems he related to the well-being of his members, and by doing so in his vigorous and forthright manner he injected a sense of social responsibility into industrial relations. It should not be thought that he was always altruistic in his advocacy. The policies he propounded were of direct and immediate benefit to large sections of his membership as well as indirectly beneficial through their effect on national prosperity. And to a large extent this explains the success of his advocacy.

Arthur Deakin believed that the responsibility of trade unions should be related positively to their power. What the full responsibilities were can best be described by Deakin himself. He said they were:

1. To preserve the standard of living of our people.
2. To take full part in achieving that measure of planned economy which will enable our people to enjoy the advantages that arise from modern developments in industry and benefit from the technological knowledge and resources that have been made possible during recent years.
3. To realize as a Trade Union Movement that we have got a social responsibility to the community at large.

The third responsibility weighed heavily with him.

I would say [he added] that it should not be the policy or within the grasp of any single Trade Union or group of Trade Unions having a privileged position to pursue policies to the disadvantage of the interests of the community. In other words, if the Trade Unions are to maintain that influence and that position in the economy of the country which they claim for themselves, the pattern of their policy must be related to the needs of the community at large in addition to serving the interests of the people they represent.[1]

[1] Twelfth All-Ireland Delegate Conference, August 1954.

Chapter Seven

INDUSTRIAL ACTION

THE following is an account of the manner in which Arthur Deakin handled the industrial interests of his members. It shows him performing his primary trade union function in the most complex of circumstances. Most of the chapter is about his concern for the real wages of his members, for it was this matter which revealed most clearly the quandaries of his leadership.

The first section deals with the attitude of the Trades Union Congress towards a wages policy in war-time. Arthur Deakin was involved in the determination of this attitude only in so far as the full General Council was consulted. He was not a member of the inner counsels of the trade union movement during the war but he and his Executive were prepared to follow the lead they gave. The relevance of the war-time attitude here is that it retained its significance after the war when Deakin had become prominent as a trade union policy-maker.

WAGES POLICY IN WAR-TIME

The industrial policies of trade unions between the General Strike and the outbreak of war were moderately executed. Voluntary negotiating machinery was used preponderantly and wage demands, though related only to trade union needs and unconnected with any consideration for the state of the economy, were realistic. In 1939 the Government had no immediate cause for concern over the behaviour of trade unions.

The first official suggestion that trade unions should moderate their wage demands still further was made by the Chancellor of the Exchequer, Sir John Simon, at a meeting of the National Joint Advisory Council on 6 December 1939.[1] There he described the factors which were inflationary. It would be necessary, he pointed out, for Great Britain to finance the war from its own resources; imports would be limited to essential foodstuffs and materials and there would be a

[1] The National Joint Advisory Council was formed in October 1939 and was composed of national trade union and employers' representatives, presided over by the Minister of Labour. When Bevin became Minister of Labour in May 1940 he suggested that the N.J.A.C. was too large for his purpose; as a result the smaller Joint Consultative Committee was formed. From 1941 until June 1946 the N.J.A.C. was left in abeyance. Arthur Deakin was not a member of either the N.J.A.C. or the J.C.C. during the war.

corresponding limit to the supply of commodities on the home market. Earnings, on the other hand, would increase through overtime or piecework payments. The final result would be a reduction in real wages.[1] Sir John did not suggest that there should be no demands for wage increases at all, 'but that a standard, different from the kind of standard used in peace time, should be introduced, which would effect a slowing down of wage increases. . . .'[2] He spoke in guarded terms and enunciated principles rather than specific lines of action. The representatives of the General Council said that his suggestion did not involve an equal sacrifice between members of the community, and emphasized 'that the General Council had no authority to control the activities of the unions with regard to wage applications and it would be resented were they to attempt to do so. . . .'[3] At the next meeting of the National Joint Advisory Council the trade union representatives stated that in their opinion the influencing of wage negotiations was 'impracticable and undesirable'.[4]

The discussion on the regulation of wages was taken up by the Joint Consultative Committee at its first meeting on 22 May 1940, when the new Minister of Labour, Ernest Bevin, asked for 'advice as to the best means of removing wage problems from the field of prompt controversy during the next few months.'[5] He made three suggestions: (*a*) that it might be possible to have a uniform basis of adjustment of wages to be applied to all industries by a special tribunal; (*b*) that an independent element might be introduced into the normal negotiating machinery; and (*c*) that arbitration might be made compulsory after the negotiating machinery had failed to produce a settlement.

The first two suggestions were rejected by the trade unionists on the Committee mainly for the reason that they wanted the existing wage-negotiating machinery to be disturbed as little as possible. The third suggestion was approved by the Joint Consultative Committee and recommendations were made to the Minister of Labour which he accepted. 'In this period of national emergency', the Committee stated, 'it is imperative that there should be no stoppage of work owing to trade disputes.' To fulfil this condition 'the machinery of negotiation existing in any trade or industry for dealing with questions concerning wages and conditions of employment shall continue to operate. . . . Matters in dispute which cannot be settled by means of such machinery shall be referred to arbitration for a

---

[1] T.U.C. Report, 1940, p. 169.
[2] Ibid.
[3] Ibid.
[4] Ibid.
[5] Ibid, p. 171.

decision which will be binding on all parties and no strike or lockout shall take place.'[1]   Arising from these and other recommendations and after considerable negotiation the Minister of Labour issued Order 1305 which provided that:

> When the dispute is reported to the Minister he may take steps to secure a settlement by appointing a single arbitrator, or by referring it to the Industrial Court.
>
> If all other steps to conciliate the dispute fail, he may refer the dispute to the new National Tribunal which he has set up.
>
> This Tribunal consists of a permanent Court of three, and one representative each from the trade unions and the employers. . . .[2]

Although Order 1305 represented a considerable change from the pre-war practice of settling disputes, it entailed no change in the ordinary method of wage negotiation in most cases and it did not restrict wage demands.   The Government had to take up the issue of wage demands separately with the trade union movement, and it did so through the publication of a White Paper on *Price Stabilization and Industrial Policy*[3] and through meetings between Ministers of the Government and the General Council at which the main theme of the White Paper was reiterated. The White Paper, as with all Government pronouncements on wages policy, was in guarded, non-committal terms.   In the circumstances it could not be otherwise.   The Government did not have a uniformly agreed wages policy.   The Treasury, at various times during the war, had prepared plans for the control of wages which were the subject of rows in the Government.   Bevin in particular was never prepared to accept a rigid wages policy, though when he became a member of the Government he pressed for restraint in making wage claims.

The Government White Paper showed the mark of Bevin's hand, for it asked for wage stabilization whilst stating that since 'the outbreak of war, the existing joint voluntary machinery for wage negotiations has operated successfully.   Increases in wage-rates have been reasonable; the authority of the unions in the day-to-day adjustment of wages and conditions has been maintained; the freedom of opportunity to make claims and to have them discussed has enabled industrial peace to be maintained.'   The Paper then went on to outline the Government's price stabilization policy; to ask for restraint in making wage demands; and to state the grounds on which legitimate wage increases could be conceded.

The request made in the White Paper and further similar overtures by the Government were rejected by the Trades Union Congress in

[1] Ibid.
[2] Ibid; p. 172.
[3] Cmd. 6294.

1941 on the advice of the General Council, which suspected the Government of trying to control wages. Sir Walter Citrine, when giving the reasons for the rejection of what he called 'the hoary device of trying to fix wages by regulation', said:

> If you once shatter the confidence of the workmen in the system whereby their wages and conditions of employment are regulated during war-time, I am sure you will strike a more vital blow at the fabric of unity which is necessary to carry us through this War than by any other means. . . . At the outbreak of this War . . . I said, broadly, that we were trying to do two things: we were trying to do everything to combat Nazism but we were also trying to restrain the inevitable development of bureaucracy which war would bring with it. In other words, we were going to retain our independence, we were going to retain the maximum of our liberties, irrespective of from what quarter the encroachments came. Can you imagine any greater extension of bureaucracy than that wages should be determined over the heads of the Trade Unions, over the heads of employers, by some Government authority? . . .[1]

Citrine and other members of the General Council were aware of the dangers of inflation and they advocated measures such as price control, subsidies, the control of profits, and increased saving, to combat it. They were aware, also, of the inflationary effects of unrestrained wage demands and throughout the war they acted with moderation.

The refusal of trade union leaders to accept Government interference in the determination of wages was simply a refusal to abdicate their authority in the most important field of their activity and in the main was unrelated to external factors. The rejection of planned wage stabilization, on the other hand, must be considered against the background of the Government prices policy during the war, if policy it may be called. The Government desired to peg wages to a cost of living index which was based on household budgets collected in 1904 and which bore little relation to the flow of working-class expenditure during the Second World War. The Government historian, R. J. Hammond, related that the index was retained in use largely on account of its out-of-date weighting, which underestimated the extent to which the cost of living had actually risen. He said: 'It was this fact—offering the possibility of shrinking real wages, as would undoubtedly be necessary in war-time, without appearing to do so—that was in the end to dominate price policy.'[2] And when this index, to which in 1940 about three million workers

[1] T.U.C. Report, 1941, pp. 362–363.
[2] *Food*, Vol. I, 'The Growth of Policy', by R. J. Hammond, pp. 103–104. In that book and in the volume 'Civil Industry and Trade', by E. L. Hargreaves and M. M. Gowing, appears a fascinating account of war-time price fixing. Both volumes are in the United Kingdom Civil Series of *The History of the Second World War*, published by H.M. Stationery Office and Longmans.

had their wages tied by sliding-scale agreements, did not show an
adequate price stability, it was clumsily and deliberately manipulated.

Trade union leaders were aware of these facts. But, as Deakin
and others stated, the unions were prepared to exercise restraint
through their own discretion and for this reason they found the
index useful. The rank-and-file members, while distrustful of any
index which did not show the same movements as their current
family costs, were unaware of the major deficiencies of the index in
use and in general they accepted its validity. Its stability removed
some of the impetus for wage increases which emanates from the
rank and file and, in many cases, left the union leaders to use their
own initiative in the matter.

OTHER WAR-TIME MATTERS

Arthur Deakin never went through the phase of being a militant
strike leader as did some of his contemporaries on the General
Council; indeed, not once did he lead a large-scale strike. So when
official strike action became regulated by the National Arbitration
and Conditions of Employment Order 1305 he did not have to break
with his past. The part of the Order affecting strike action was the
least important part in Deakin's opinion. He was much more
concerned about the facility the Order granted of making recalcitrant
employers face up to their obligations by compelling them to observe
fully the decisions reached by the National Arbitration Tribunal.
Whenever possible, however, Deakin preferred to establish suitable
forms of arbitration procedure within existing voluntary machinery
rather than use the National Arbitration Tribunal. Legal compulsion, he thought, could be useful but its area of application should
be restricted. In other words, he favoured it when its application
was clearly in the interests of trade unionists. When some delegates
in 1943 pressed to have the right under the Essential Work Orders
to take legal action against employers if they violated certain
conditions, Deakin replied that 'if action is taken against the employers, then action must be taken in every case against the workers.
That is something that we have sought to avoid.'[1]

A slight problem for trade unions which arose out of the effectiveness of Government war-time controls and over which Deakin was
concerned was that workers tended to attribute improvements in
working conditions and wages to the Government rather than to
trade unions. In order to meet the problem, he told his Executive,

[1] T. & G.W.U., B.D.C., 1943. In 1945 Deakin went so far as to press for a statutory
guaranteed weekly wage in all industries and for the enforcement by law of all wage
agreements negotiated between trade unions and employers. He wanted, he said, to
preserve after the war the advances secured by war-time legislation. (T.U.C. Report,
1945, pp. 256–257.) He did not persist in his demands for long after the war.

'we must adopt a new method of approach, emphasizing the fact that the reforms now being secured are primarily due to trade union organization, and, further, that any progress in the future will be conditioned entirely by the strength of trade union membership and the policy pursued by organized labour.'[1]   In reality the war-time factors which facilitated the expansion of trade unions were of greater potency than this one problem, and, regardless of the attribution of credit for achieving better working and living conditions, trade unions expanded.

IMMEDIATE POST-WAR VIEWS OF WAGE REGULATION

The end of the war did not change for the better the national economic environment within which trade unions operated.   The case for subordinating their sectional interests to the needs of the economy lost none of its force.   Through their industrial action they influenced the level of production and through their wage demands they affected the level of prices and the saleability of products in the foreign markets.   The war-time depreciation of industry, the switch from war to peace-time uses, the loss of both sources of supply of essential raw materials and export markets, the intensified inflationary conditions caused by the diversion of goods from home consumption to the export markets, and the release of the pent-up war-time demand for goods on the home market, combined to make vital the sense of purpose of trade unions.   To grasp this point one has only to imagine the effect on the post-war economy of a deliberate policy of strike action.

It was inevitable, then, that the Government of the day, whatever its political complexion, would need to work closely and harmoniously with the trade union movement.   The relief at the end of the war which reflected itself in a revulsion of ordinary people from physical controls made it necessary for the Government to seek collaboration rather than to rely on legal compulsions.   The natural, though sometimes uncomfortable, allegiance between the Labour Government and the trade union movement demanded that there should be collaboration.

Yet over the issues of wage determination and wage stabilization, trade unions remained uncompromising.   For instance, when Deakin reported on a meeting of Trade Union Executives and members of the Government on 6 March 1946, he stated:

> The question of a national wage policy, which is being so strongly urged from certain quarters, was introduced from the floor during the discussion.   There was no disagreement with our declaration—that 'wage

[1] 10 March 1941.

policy' is a term so vague and uncertain that it may not mean anything but might, in a general way, at some time be interpreted as constituting a 'wage ceiling', which the Trade Union Movement is not prepared to accept.   We took our stand on the inalienable right and record of the proved ability of trade unions to raise the standard of living of their members through the usual channels of negotiation.[1]

When in May 1947 Sir Stafford Cripps said in a public speech that wage rates should not be raised at that time and that 'we must discipline ourselves to do without them until such time as they become national economic possibilities', Deakin publicly rebuked him and said, 'there are claims in at the moment that will have to be dealt with'.[2]   The depth of feeling against wage restraint in Deakin's own Union was revealed at its Biennial Delegate Conference in 1947 when it declared that it was 'strongly opposed to any attempt to freeze wages at existing levels'.

Nevertheless Deakin's attitude at this stage was changing its emphasis.   His early trade union experiences had given him an awareness of the importance of wide economic issues, but he had been apprehensive about post-war industrial relations and had therefore proceeded with some caution in his pronouncements about the post-war behaviour of trade unions.   '. . . Trade Unions cannot commit themselves in advance', he wrote in 1944, 'to the relaxation or modification of any of their practices, nor can they give pledges as to their future action in the absence of firm undertakings about the policy of the Government and the obligations to be entered into by all other parties'.[3]

As his apprehension decreased so his sense of the wide economic issues implicit in trade union problems revealed itself in the advice he tendered to his Executive and in his exhortations to his members. 'So far as wages are concerned', he told his Executive, 'it is . . . clear that increased wages mean increased prices, subsequently leading to inflation.   In my view, we must seek to increase production, reduce prices and increase the purchasing power of money. . . .'[4] A little later in the year he added that 'to achieve the full measure of production in this country we have got to remove, as Trade Unionists, some of the restrictive practices that we have found necessary to operate for so long in our own interests.   One in particular to which I would refer is the question of payment by results.'[5]   He began increasingly to make valid but unpopular statements and to move more openly to the position he held till his death as the protagonist of trade union responsibility to the community.

[1] *The Record*, April 1946, p. 207.
[2] *Daily Herald*, 12 May 1947.
[3] Report to G.E.C., 28 February 1944.
[4] 19 May 1947.
[5] T. & G.W.U., B.D.C., July 1947.

Throughout 1946 and 1947 the Government maintained contact with the General Council through the National Joint Advisory Council and through meetings between Ministers and the General Council or its representatives. Arising from some such meetings late in 1946 two Government White Papers, *Economic Considerations affecting the Relation between Employers and Workers* (Cmd. 7018) and the *Economic Survey for 1947* (Cmd. 7046) were published in January and February 1947 respectively. Cmd. 7018, which was issued after considerable amendment by the two sides of the National Joint Advisory Council, asked for restraint in making wage demands, but only by implication. The General Council had made it clear to the Government that its approval of the White Paper 'was on the definite understanding that Unions would continue to be free to submit wages applications as formerly where this was found to be necessary. Nothing in the White Paper was to be taken as restricting the rights of Unions to make claims through the normal collective bargaining arrangements. Such claims should be considered on their merits.'[1] The General Council knew in advance of the publication of the *Economic Survey for 1947* but was not consulted about its contents. However, excellent though it was as an economic statement, it made no greater demand from the trade union movement than that, along with the other side of industry, it should adopt 'a constructive and flexible approach . . . to the problem of production'.[2]

The year 1947 was a crisis year marked by the fuel shortage in the late winter and early spring and by the abortive attempt at convertibility during the summer. The aspects of these events, and other relevant economic matters which concerned trade unionists, were examined by an 'Economic Crisis Committee' appointed by the General Council for the first time on 26 February 1947. The Committee had meetings with Ministers of the Government, including one with the Prime Minister on 7 May, at which information and views were exchanged. No joint statement was issued nor was any public reference made to the need for a wages policy.

The problem of wage regulation was raised in two separate motions at the Labour Party Conference during the last week of May. The first dealt with the recruitment of labour in undermanned industries. It added 'that further delay in the adoption of satisfactory wage standards and conditions of employment within such industries constitutes a threat to the whole economic policy of the Government'. This, in Deakin's words, 'virtually meant a declaration on wages policy'. During the debate, he said, 'At its tail end it puts forward

[1] T.U.C. Report, 1947, p. 219.
[2] Cmd. 7046, p. 32.

the idea of a wages policy. We will have none of that. Under no circumstances at all will we accept the position that the responsibility for the fixation of wages and the regulation of conditions of employment is one for the Government.' He concluded by saying, as Citrine had said in 1941, that the Government would cause disunity amongst the rank-and-file members if it destroyed their confidence in the negotiating machinery and 'this would be destructive of the economy of the country. . . .'[1] The motion was accepted by the Conference.

The second motion showed the Conference in its most equivocal mood. It urged the Government to formulate a policy on wages, hours, and the distribution of the national income in order to prevent inflation and to attract manpower to where it was most needed. The motion was long and detailed and did not neglect to suggest measures to reduce unearned incomes and profits, but it was resolutely rejected on the advice of Tom Williamson[2] who spoke for the National Executive of the Labour Party. 'I am amazed', he said, 'that we should have had . . . delegates . . . advocating that the Government should take control of wages. . . . This policy if passed by the Conference could do no more than usurp the authority of the Trade Union Movement.'

Almost the whole of 1947 on this question of wages policy was clouded with ambiguities and was marked by an absence of leadership from both the Government, because it feared to venture into heavily guarded trade union territory, and the General Council, because its members felt that the matter was not their responsibility.

THE INCEPTION OF WAGE RESTRAINT

The first significant move was made by Mr. Attlee, the Prime Minister, in the House of Commons on 6 August 1947 when, during a debate on the state of the Nation, he appealed to all workers in all industries and employment not to press for increases of wages or changes in conditions which would have had a similar effect, especially where the increases were claimed to maintain traditional differentials.[3] He said: 'there has been, undoubtedly, some failure on the part of some workers to realize that shorter hours and higher wages must be matched with higher effort . . .'. The appeal was not communicated to organized labour until September 1947, when the Minister of Labour sent letters to both sides of a number of joint bodies engaged in wage negotiations asking them to bear in mind

[1] Labour Party Conference Report, 1947, p. 144.
[2] He relinquished his seat on the Executive at that Conference on becoming the General Secretary of the National Union of General and Municipal Workers.
[3] *Hansard*, Vol. 441, p. 1508.

the Prime Minister's statement during the course of their negotiations.

From then until February 1948 events moved fairly quickly. On 1 October the General Council met the Prime Minister and the Minister of Labour 'to enquire about the purpose behind the action of the Minister of Labour in writing to both sides of joint bodies in this way'.[1] The Ministers agreed not to do such a thing again but asked the General Council to agree to discuss wage movements with the Minister of Labour and the Minister for Economic Affairs, Sir Stafford Cripps. This proposal was accepted and an informal discussion took place on 14 October during which the General Council was directly asked 'to give very serious consideration to the possibilities of securing some greater stability in wages'. The General Council agreed to do this.[2]

It kept to its word and at the end of December circulated an *Interim Report on the Economic Situation* to the affiliated unions recommending 'the responsible executive committees of Trade Unions to exercise even greater moderation and restraint than hitherto in the formulation and pursuit of claims for wage increases'. The recommendation had no immediate effect. The General Council, after all, could only advise, and no decision to accept a policy of wage restraint had been made either by Congress or by the executives of the individual unions. Moreover, although the *Interim Report* stated that the General Council 'were giving consideration to the representations to be made to the Government on the means by which more extensive and stringent control of prices and profits could be developed for the purpose of maintaining future price stability', it gave the individual unions no guarantees about prices and profits, nor did it state explicitly what it meant by 'moderation and restraint'.

Mr. Attlee's statement in August was timely. For the twelve-month period from July 1946 the general index of wage rates had remained virtually stable at between 64 and 67 per cent. over the September 1939 figure. From July until December it rose to 73 per cent. over the 1939 figure.[3] The rise in wage rates, though approximately the same as the rise in prices during the same period, coupled with a worsening of the external balance of trade, resulted in a much more determined Government intervention than had occurred previously.

On 4 February 1948 the Prime Minister read a Statement to the House of Commons about *Personal Incomes, Costs and Prices*, which was afterwards published as a White Paper. Its theme was the need 'to prevent the development of a dangerous inflationary situation'

[1] T.U.C. Report, 1948, p. 289.
[2] Ibid.
[3] *Ministry of Labour Gazette,* January 1948, p. 32.

and it suggested 'that there should be no further increase in the level of personal incomes without at least a corresponding increase in the volume of production'. The Statement added:

> It does not follow that it would be right to stabilize all incomes as they stand today. There may well be cases in which increases in wages or salaries would be justified from a national point of view, for example where it is essential in the national interest to man up a particular undermanned industry and it is clear that only an increase in wages will attract the necessary labour. It does, however, follow that each claim for an increase in wages or salaries must be considered on its national merits and not on the basis of maintaining a former relativity between different occupations and industries.[1]

Trade unions were assured that the Government did not consider it desirable to interfere directly with the incomes of individuals otherwise than by taxation, but this was dependent upon trade unions and employers observing the principles laid down by the Government in their negotiations. In the negotiations with which it was directly concerned, the Government intended to follow its own precept.

The emphasis in the Statement was on freely negotiated wages; only a passing reference was made to profits, and price control appeared in it only by implication. The Statement, then, was of direct concern to the General Council. The immediate reaction of the General Council was not favourable.

First, it had not been consulted about the details of the Statement before it was made, and this was a break with the practice of consultation which had developed since 1940. To add to this affront, when Sir Stafford Cripps, with the Minister of Labour, met the London members of the General Council to discuss the White Paper, he opened the meeting by explaining the purpose of the Paper, then pushed it across the table and departed from the meeting before any discussion could take place. Such treatment did not assist those members who wished to co-operate with the Government. Secondly, the Statement did not indicate whether other sections of the community were to be asked to make comparable sacrifices. Thirdly, it appeared to trade unionists as an incomplete attempt to fight inflation because it did not provide for a sufficient measure of price control. Fourthly, the conditions under which wage increases could be justified were not clearly stated. And lastly, no reference was made to the fate of wage claims already lodged or in course of negotiation.

On the night Mr. Attlee read the Statement to the House of Commons, Arthur Deakin and other members of the Economic

[1] Cmd. 7321.

Crisis Committee of the General Council met, in order, Deakin said, 'to create that position which would enable the Trade Unions to deal with all the wages claims then in course of negotiation . . .'.[1] Then on 11 February the Economic Crisis Committee met the Prime Minister and four of his senior Ministers and discussed the outstanding matters.[2] The intervention of the General Council had a marked effect on the Government's approach, and the obscurities and ambiguities of the White Paper were cleared up to the satisfaction of most trade union leaders.

The full fruits of the intervention were revealed by Sir Stafford Cripps in the House of Commons debate on the White Paper on 12 February. He spoke of the intention of the Government to achieve price stability, even price reductions, through a more rigorous enforcement of Government price controls and through exhortations to organizations representing manufacturers and wholesale and retail distributors. His exhortations to receivers of profit were similar to those directed at wage-earners but he mentioned, in addition, the psychological importance of imposing a limitation on dividends. If a measure of restraint by profit receivers can be exercised, there is, he said, 'indeed a good chance of persuading the wage and salary earners also to exercise restraint in the use of the pressure which the scarcity of labour enables them to apply'.[3]

To allay the fears of trade unionists that the Government policy meant a complete rigidity in the wages structure, Cripps emphasized the grounds on which wage increases could be justified. The points he made were remarkably similar to those subsequently made by the General Council in the statement quoted below.

The General Council found the principles of the White Paper acceptable to the extent that they:

(*a*) recognize the necessity of retaining unimpaired the system of collective bargaining and free negotiation;

(*b*) admit the justification for claims for increased wages where those claims are based upon the fact of increased output;

(*c*) admit the necessity of adjusting the wages of workers whose incomes are below a reasonable standard of subsistence;

(*d*) affirm that it is in the national interest to establish standards of wages and conditions in undermanned essential industries in order to attract sufficient manpower; and

(*e*) recognize the need to safeguard those wage differentials which are an essential element in the wages structure of many important industries and are required to sustain those standards of craftsmanship, training

[1] Speech to the Educational and Social Council of Region 6 of the Union, 10 April 1948.
[2] The Ministers were: Sir Stafford Cripps, Mr. Ernest Bevin, Mr. Herbert Morrison, and Mr. George Isaacs.
[3] *Hansard*, Vol. 447.

and experience that contribute directly to industrial efficiency and higher productivity.[1]

All the recommendations were endorsed at a Special Conference of Executive Committees on 24 March 1948 by a majority of 5,421,000 votes to 2,032,000 votes. Thus, conditional wage restraint became the accepted policy of the trade union movement and was re-endorsed at the Trade Union Congresses of 1948 and 1949 by large majorities.

ARTHUR DEAKIN'S CONCEPTION OF A WAGES POLICY

Throughout all these deliberations Arthur Deakin played an increasingly important part as a policy-maker. He had had an unbroken membership of the General Council since 1940, but it was not until some time after the war that he began to dominate the inner councils of the Movement; certainly it was not until after Citrine had resigned from the position of General Secretary of the Trades Union Congress in 1946 to become a member of the National Coal Board. From 1947 his view that wage claims should be assessed according to their national merits was heard more and more. Why did he respond so readily to the Government's plea in 1948 and not in 1947 or earlier when the country's economic problems were no less acute? And how did he reconcile his response with his position as the General Secretary of the Transport and General Workers' Union?

1. The answer to the first question has already been given in part. Deakin had received a firm assurance about price control from the Government. He had previously believed that there would be no wages problem if prices were controlled, and from as early as 1944 he pressed for an extension of a rigorous control of prices into the post-war period as a safeguard against inflation. But he saw in 1948 how complex the problem of inflation was.

> It is all very well [he said] for people to say: 'Tackle prices, tackle profits, first.' When you come to look closely at this delicate economic question, you have some difficulty in knowing where you are to start—which comes first. Some of the applications that we have recently made could not possibly be met out of profits. It followed that if wage increases were conceded the increased cost must be passed on to the consumer. . . .[2]

With the Government assurance he was prepared to help to break into the circle of wage-price-wage increases.[3]

---

[1] Report of Proceedings at a Special Conference of Executive Committees of Affiliated Organizations, March 1948, p. 50.
[2] Labour Party Conference Report, 1948, p. 142.
[3] Special Conference of Executive Committees, March 1948, Report, p. 31.

5+T.U.L.

Both Deakin and his members had a much clearer and truer indication of retail price movements from the Interim Index of Retail Prices than they had had from the 1914 Cost of Living Index. The Interim Index, which was based on a collection of 2,000 family budgets made in 1937–38, was introduced on 17 June 1947.[1] The more suitable weighting of items covered by the index reduced considerably the possibility of a fictitious stabilization such as occurred during the war.

The years 1946 and 1947 involved much foreign travel for Arthur Deakin. He travelled about Europe as a member of the respective Executives of the International Transport Workers' Federation and the World Federation of Trade Unions more than he had ever done before. On numerous occasions up till 1954 he referred to the effect of his experiences abroad on his attitudes. 'I have had an opportunity', he remarked, 'of seeing something of the conditions of the workers in those countries where inflationary tendencies have developed unchecked, and I know that unless a close hold is kept on the value of money the result will be disastrous to the people who have to maintain themselves out of a weekly wage packet.'[2] This was not a vital factor in causing his acceptance of the Government policy, but it substantiated his belief in the need for positive action once other factors had caused him to think that way.

To some extent the same could be said of his belief that inflation would lead to unemployment. He attached greater importance to the maintenance of full employment as a condition of the well-being of workers than to any other single economic factor, and he was not prepared to tolerate anything which was likely to destroy it. The experience of the fuel crisis early in 1947 came as an unpleasant reminder to Deakin and other trade union leaders of the ease and suddenness with which unemployment could occur. In addition, he felt that if inflation got out of hand and led to unemployment it would not only adversely affect the material living standards of the workers, it would destroy the Labour Government and set the whole Movement back more than two decades. Here the loyalty of Arthur Deakin to the Labour Movement, and to the Government in particular, emerged in full strength.

Among the assurances demanded from the Chancellor of the Exchequer was one relating to profits, but it did not materially affect Deakin's approach to wage restraint. He believed that the burden should be spread equitably—he spoke of 'the incidence of the weight upon the wage-earner . . . of undue profits'—but he never thought that a limitation on dividends would have anything

1 The 1937–38 inquiry covered manual workers in general and non-manual workers with salaries not exceeding £250 a year.
2 Labour Party Conference Report, 1948, p. 142.

but a psychological effect on the problem of inflation. Indeed his attitude towards profits was a very practical one. He warned the Special Conference of Executive Committees in 1948 that if the Government-controlled profit margins were reduced and the least efficient firms had to shut down, his members might react as the miners had done when they waged stay-down strikes in pits due to be closed. For a British trade union leader this was a novel defence of profits, but it was pertinent.

For reasons about which he himself was not clear, Arthur Deakin changed his mind in 1948 about wages policies and ceased to regard them all with the same hostility. He had changed his ground in a manner characteristic of him. Once constitutional decisions were made to which he was a party then he steadfastly accepted them. But he claimed the right to have second thoughts about matters and to express them. He found no difficulty in retracting statements he had made.[1]

He remained firmly opposed to the Government control of wages and to the introduction of a legal national minimum wage. During the discussions with the members of the Government before the publication of the Prime Minister's Statement as a White Paper, Deakin said, 'the question was put to me personally, "Do you want us to name a national minimum wage?" to which I replied "No". We said that there should be the greatest possible freedom with the existing machinery which would enable us to deal with those wages which we regarded as sub-standard.'[2] This condition, which was conceded by the Government, became the escape clause for unions which wanted wage increases, for neither the General Council nor the Government would define what a sub-standard wage was. About this Deakin said: 'I am pretty sure that if we had come here today with a proposal, say, of a £5 minimum wage we should have been criticized, for failing to apprehend and appreciate all that is involved in our intricate wage structure in this country.'[3] He believed, too, that a national minimum would soon become meaningless by becoming the common rate throughout industry and that workers would find difficulty in negotiating wage increases above that rate.

One specific matter about which Deakin did change his opinion was in relation to the problem of undermanned industries. He had consistently rejected the idea that they should be given preference in the matter of wages. He did so for two reasons. (*a*) He was not

[1] When I discussed this with a member of the Conservative Government in 1955 he remarked that there was nothing wrong about it; after all, Sir Winston Churchill has said: 'I have been eating my own words all my life and I find it a very agreeable diet.'

[2] Speech to the Educational and Social Council of Region 6 of his Union, 10 April 1948.

[3] Special Conference of Trade Union Executive Committees, March 1948, Report, p. 31.

prepared to grant any privileges to groups of workers or industries which would place his own members at a relative disadvantage.[1] If the Labour Government wanted to get men into particular industries, he considered that it could use direction of labour as a means.[2] This was not altogether inconsistent with Government policy, for shortly afterwards a Control of Engagement Order was implemented. (*b*) So far as Deakin was concerned undermanned industries were composed of sub-standard workers and he saw no reason for distinguishing between them and workers in recognized sub-standard industries. He considered that any trade union catering for sub-standard workers should determine its own position in the light of their conditions and experiences and that it should bargain from that position.

Then at the Special Conference of Executive Committees called to discuss the White Paper in 1948 Deakin mounted the rostrum and announced that he had changed his mind and would accept a proposal to give preferential treatment to the mining industry. The change was of the utmost importance to Deakin. The term 'wages policy' had been given many different meanings, including wage restraint, but in each one Deakin had seen the hand of an outside agency manipulating the system of voluntary collective bargaining and they had all been equally unacceptable to him. But once the situation justified, in Deakin's eyes, the need for wages to be manipulated in order to attract labour to the mining industry, then he had to re-appraise his whole conception of wages policies.

In his new frame of mind, Deakin looked upon wage restraint not as a negative approach to the problem of inflation as some of its critics stated it was but as a wages policy which distributed wage increases according to a pre-arranged pattern. It was a policy, however, which was to be enforced by the unions themselves and not by the Government, and Deakin felt strongly about this distinction. So did the General Council as a whole. When the Minister of Labour sent out a letter to Wages Boards and Wages Councils urging them to take cognizance of the contents of the White Paper they objected strongly and pressed for its withdrawal.[3] The General Council, whilst appreciating that the Minister of Labour had some statutory responsibilities in connection with this wage-fixing machinery, stated that the letter would give the impression 'that some duress was involved in the White Paper. . . .'[4] The letter was withdrawn.

[1] T. & G.W.U., B.D.C., 1947.
[2] Ibid.
[3] The letter is reprinted in the *Ministry of Labour Gazette*, April 1948, p. 129.
[4] Sir Vincent Tewson, Special Conference of Executive Committees, March 1948, Report, p. 11.

2. In answer to the second question: Arthur Deakin was not any the less a leader of a trade union because he saw events and problems in their national and international perspectives. There is no evidence to show that in fact the industrial policy he advocated was contrary either to the short term or long term interests of his members; or that he was unaware of the implications of his actions on his members. It so happened that many of his members did benefit in the short-run from the wage restraint policy. Whether or not he was aware of this when he took his stand on the policy is not known, but it was a factor which influenced his determination to maintain it.

The membership of the Transport and General Workers' Union can be classified into four different groups. There are: (*a*) workers in the public services; (*b*) workers, such as dockers, dependent directly upon the level of foreign trade; (*c*) unskilled workers in industry whose work cannot be measured and who cannot therefore be placed on production incentive schemes; and (*d*) productive workers in manufacturing industry. Relatively few of the members of the Union in any classification have had their wage rates deter-mined by a cost of living index sliding-scale agreement, so that the level of wage-rates and the earnings of most of the members have depended directly upon the use of collective bargaining procedures. All the factors involved in collective bargaining, such as the bargain-ing power of the workers and the profitability of the enterprise, and variations in them, have had, therefore, a direct bearing upon the level of wages of the members.

(*a*) The first group was composed mainly of transport workers and municipal employees. They worked in industries where even the greater bargaining strength derived from full-employment was ineffective because the profit margins in their industries were low or non-existent and the prices of the services they provided loomed large in the cost of living. The 1950 Trades Union Congress debated a motion submitted by the Electrical Trades Union which declared, amongst other things, 'that wage increases can be met without resulting in increased prices, for example by reducing profits, and therefore calls on the General Council to abandon any further policy of wage restraint'. The motion was carried against the wishes of the General Council. In opposing it Deakin repeated an argu-ment he had used at the Special Conference of Executive Committees earlier in the year.

In the transport industry [he said] we are providing a vital service. There is no profit in the industry at this time. We can only get wage increases by increasing the charges to the consumer. When we do that, the miners in South Wales say: 'We will strike against increased transport charges.' When it is proposed to increase the fares in London you say, 'You must oppose that'. . . . But if you deal with this issue on the basis of profits made in particular industries, then those who have will gain the advantage, and those who have not, the lower income groups, will be left in the cold.   This is not a policy of reality; this is a policy of preference.[1]

Arthur Deakin was constantly concerned about the wage levels of workers in this classification.   Wage restraint for these workers was preferable to unrestricted wage demands.

(*b*) At times Deakin found it difficult to convince workers in the second group who were dependent directly upon the level of foreign trade for the volume of their work, that the policy of wage restraint operated in their interests.   The dockers, who formed a large section of this group, were in a powerful bargaining position after the war and sometimes resented not being able to use it with official union backing.   The logic of the argument that wage increases were at that time inflationary, that export prices which were high in relation to the export prices of foreign competitors reduced the volume of trade both out of and into this country and therefore reduced not only the demand for dock workers but also the ability of the industry to finance its scheme of decasualization, was not always apparent to them in the flush of their newly acquired power.

(*c*) The third group of members would have been at a relative disadvantage in a scramble for higher wages.   They were not strategically placed in industry either through the possession of special skills or through the control of production.   They were, in the true sense of the word, general workers whose well-being was a reflection of that of the economy.   Because they did not possess the bargaining power to act as price leaders in the labour market they were not able to enjoy even temporary gains from wage increases in an inflationary spiral.   The lag between their wages and prices was greater than with other workers.   Political changes apart, a general wage stability which encouraged increases in real income was their main hope of material advancement.

(*d*) The last group consisted of those workers in manufacturing industry whose earnings could be directly related to production. With many of those the level of wage-rates was important only in so far as it acted as a base from which piecework earnings were calculated and was used as a fall-back rate when piecework was interrupted or reduced by factors defined by trade union/employer agreements.   To these workers wage restraint involved no change of practice.   Their earnings depended upon their own efforts and production methods and when, by changes in either or both of these, production was increased it was considered right by the Government

[1] T.U.C. Report, 1950, p. 471.

and trade unions that earnings should increase too. To increase the earnings of these workers, Deakin encouraged the use of work-study methods and advised his officials to co-operate with managements whenever new methods of potential value to his members were introduced. Members of the Transport and General Workers' Union whose jobs could be related to production but who were not operating any form of incentive scheme were pressed to demand such schemes as soon as wage restraint was accepted.

The manner in which the vote of the Transport and General Workers' Union was cast at the Special Conference of Executive Committees in March 1948 was decided by the Executive of the Union. It was not a unanimous decision, for there were Communist Party members on the Executive who opposed a policy of moderation and there were others who had doubts about it. 'I had a long argument', Deakin said later, 'in this room with our own Executive on the matter, when I put forward the suggestion that the policy of the Government was sound and that it was no use securing advances in wages if prices advanced the day after.'[1] When in the argument against moderation cases of hardship were quoted to illustrate that some workers were living below a reasonable subsistence level, Deakin was always able to remind the Executive of the provision in the General Council report covering sub-standard wages.

There was no serious deviation by the Executive from the policy enunciated in 1948. It was endorsed by the Union Biennial Delegate Conference in 1949. Deakin presented the case for moderation and made no attempt to sweeten the pill. He told the delegates:

it is no use our passing pious resolutions . . . it is no use our saying that we are striving to create those conditions that will enable a reduction in prices to take place, if at the same time we proceed to prosecute wage claims which must have the effect of increasing prices. . . . In point of fact I am going to be brutally frank this morning. I doubt whether at this time we can get wage increases at all.[2]

Some delegates at the 1948 Trades Union Congress accused Deakin, and by implication his Executive, of accepting wage restraint with their tongues in their cheeks. This was an unfounded accusation. National wage claims for members of the Transport and General Workers' Union were submitted by the respective National Trade Group Committees but the General Executive Council had the authority, which it exercised, of vetoing any claim it considered to be contrary to the interests of the Union as a whole. During 1949 the moderation of the Executive was challenged by the National Committees of the Road Passenger Trade Group and the Chemical and

[1] Conference of National and Regional Secretaries, 17 August 1948.
[2] T. & G.W.U., B.D.C., 1949.

Allied Trades. The latter Committee asked for a substantial increase in wages, but this was rejected by the Executive, which considered that the claim should be made only for those on the minimum rate. In September 1950 the Executive rejected a demand from passenger transport workers in London that they should submit a claim for £1 per week increase from the London Transport Executive. One could give more such examples of the practical and determined way in which the policy of wage restraint was pursued within the limits laid down by the General Council.

Both Deakin and his Executive showed a tolerance towards the Government which could only have stemmed from their loyalty to it and from their understanding of its problems. Neither prices nor profits were handled to their satisfaction: the 1949 budget, they thought, was a 'great disappointment' marked by the absence of tax reliefs and an increase in the price of basic foods; then to crown it all the pound was devalued in relation to the dollar on 18 September 1949 with a consequent increase in the cost of living. During 1949 the average level of retail prices, as measured by the Interim Index of Retail Prices, rose between 3 and 4 per cent. compared with an increase of between 1½ and 2 per cent. in weekly rates of wages.[1] It became clear towards the end of 1949 that the maintenance of stable domestic prices, which had been a condition of the wage restraint policy, was moving out of the control of the Government. The situation demanded a reappraisal.

A reappraisal was undertaken by the General Council and their conclusions and recommendations were issued on 23 November 1949 entitled *Devaluation and Wages*. They were debated at the second Special Conference of Executive Committees on Wages Policy held on 12 January 1950, and were supported by the Executive of the Transport and General Workers' Union. The General Council stated that the 'dangerous inflationary tendencies which devaluation inevitably intensifies must be counteracted by vigorous restraints upon all increases of wages, salaries and dividends'; and that even in the consideration of low-paid workers 'regard be had to the general economic problems necessitating rigorous restraint'. A positive recommendation was made to unions:

> to reconsider existing wage-claims and sliding-scale arrangements with a view to holding agreed wage rates stable whilst the Interim Index of Retail Prices remains between upper and lower limits of 118 and 106; on the express condition that if and when the Index figure reaches either the upper or lower limit both sides of industry would be entitled to resume the normal consideration of wages questions in accordance with the provisions of their agreements, and that cost-of-living agreements

---

[1] *Ministry of Labour Gazette*, January 1950.

would again operate. Should neither of these limits be reached before January 1, 1951, the above arrangements shall continue until that date and be reviewed in the light of the then existing facts.[1]

These recommendations went far beyond any previous attempts in peace or war to assist the Government of the day. The 1915 'Treasury Agreement' and the Orders of the Second World War had never made such demands on the practices and traditions of the Movement. In any case trade unions were still operating under Order 1305. Whilst depending upon an effective Government regulation of prices and profits the recommendations stipulated only unilateral trade union action.

The recommendations were accepted by 4,263,000 votes to 3,606,000 votes, a majority of only 657,000. This showed a marked swing from the opinion of the 1949 Congress, held only four months previously, when the majority in favour of the General Council's wages policy was 5,447,000. Much more concern was being shown in 1950 about the lack of equity in the projected solution to Britain's economic problems. 'The wage claim that is forgone', said one delegate, 'is forgone for ever. Dividend limitation is nothing more onerous than a deferment of benefit.' The straws were in the wind. Within a matter of weeks from the January Special Conference it became clear that the suspension, even temporarily, of sliding-scale agreements was unacceptable.

The British Iron, Steel and Kindred Trades Association was prepared to suspend its agreement with employers but most other unions declined to do likewise for one or both of two reasons. First, though part of the case for the suspension of sliding-scale agreements was to make the application of wage restraint equitable amongst unions, there was no guarantee that unions without agreements would resist claiming wage increases. Secondly, unions which had agreements providing for wage adjustments to cover cost of living changes over the previous year were not prepared to forgo the wage increases which were due to them. Such action would have been equivalent to back-dating the application of the revised and more rigid form of wage restraint. The policy, then, was inequitable in its operation within the Movement.

In addition, skilled workers resented the operation of a wages policy which, by giving preference to low-paid workers, narrowed the already relatively narrow differentials between skilled and unskilled and with which they were dissatisfied.[2] This point was mentioned by Deakin in June 1950 when he said that 'in dealing with the problem of the lower-paid workers we are in a difficulty at

[1] Trade Unions and Wages Policy; Report of the Special Conference of Trade Union Executive Committees, 12 January 1950, pp. 50–51.
[1] T.U.C. Report, 1950, p. 267.

this time, from the point of view of so narrowing the gap as, possibly, to destroy incentive and the urge to become a skilled man. To that extent a first-class problem has been created and it is not easy to find a solution.'[1]

In addition, the economic conditions were easing and, as the General Council put it, in 'the light of nine months of rising productivity, increased exports, the improvement in world economic conditions, the relaxation of national controls, and the general impression of economic buoyancy, it is easy to overlook the basic difficulties which still beset us'.[2] Even the Executive of the Transport and General Workers' Union, still in favour of wage restraint, felt constrained to prepare for a change in policy. At its June 1950 meeting it stated:

> The Council is of the opinion that it would be a major disaster to allow an indiscriminate wage scramble to develop [but it] will reserve to itself the right to deal with the problem of the wages of the Members of the Union in the light of any variation in the Policy Decision of the Trades Union Congress, or following any general departure from this policy by affiliated trade unions.

The General Council itself advised 'greater flexibility of wage movements in the future than was envisaged in the policy approved by the Conference of Executives in January', but this did not go far enough to meet the wishes of the majority of the delegates.   The General Council report was referred back by the Trades Union Congress in September 1950 and a motion asking for the rejection of wage restraint was carried by a majority of 220,000 votes.

Between the January Conference of Executives and the compilation of its report for the September Trades Union Congress the General Council had changed its approach to wage restraint mainly because it realized that such a policy could not be a permanent part of trade union policy and that the Chancellor of the Exchequer tended to take its steadfast support of wage restraint for granted in his calculations. When it was suggested at a General Council meeting that the policy should be eased, Arthur Deakin objected strongly and accused the sponsors of the suggestion of 'rocking the boat'.   He favoured the retention of the January 1950 policy. However, between that meeting and the next he changed his mind and agreed to accept the modified version.

The decision of the 1950 Trades Union Congress, Deakin considered, was a great mistake.

> But [he said] be that as it may, the decision having been taken we must accept it, just as we loyally observed the previous policy which operated

1 Tenth All-Ireland Delegate Conference.
2 T.U.C. Report, 1950, p. 267.

from 1948 up to this time. However, in accepting the decision we must also recognize that it does not mean the end of wage restraint. It simply means a shifting of the responsibility. Instead of the T.U.C. having to accept an overall responsibility it now becomes the responsibility of each individual Trade Union Executive to pursue that policy of restraint best suited to the needs of its own membership, or alternatively, just allow a policy of drift to operate with an inevitable collapse of the nation's economy.[1]

He emphasized, however, 'that in the event of there being any change in the overall policy I would be no party to standing aside and sacrificing the interests of our own members . . . if at any period of time there was a general wage movement in this country we must of necessity take our full part in that movement'. His Executive endorsed these statements.

From 1950 until his death Arthur Deakin changed his attitude towards wages in detail but remained unmoved over the desirability for a moderate wages policy. He continued to tell his members that if they demanded higher wages then they had to earn them 'by greater productivity and developing the efficiency of industry'. His work on the Anglo-American Productivity Council and later on the British Productivity Council testified to his sincerity in this matter. At all times he refused to hide from his members the real facts of economic situations and the conclusions, no matter how unpalatable, which he reasoned from them. He refused to 'be a false friend and no leader at all'. 'It is no good trying to secure an illusory advantage which lasts for a week or two, following an increase in wages', he said when he was explaining to delegates of his Union in 1953 the purpose and policy of the Union. These statements were received by his members with acclamation.

His support for the Government economic policy was not given unreservedly and he reacted sharply to changes in it away from price stabilization by controls or by budgetary policy, believing constantly that price stabilization should be an integral part of the economic policy of the Government. But he knew the danger inherent in bringing political issues into the industrial field. They can rebound to the disadvantage of the workers. For example, if wage increases can be justified by tax increases then equally wage reductions can be justified by tax reductions. It annoyed him, too, to find that sometimes the moderate wages policy his Union pursued was regarded by employers not 'as a virtue, but as a weakness'.[2] But it did not arouse him to make threats, and he remained contemptuous of the increases of up to £2 per week being currently demanded by various unions.

[1] Report to General Executive Council, 27 November 1950.
[2] Stated when making a wage claim on behalf of the Port Transport workers, before a Special Tribunal appointed by the Minister of Labour in 1952.

Behind Deakin's desire for stability was a desire for a uniformity of treatment to be accorded to different types of workers. He was by nature a leader of groups with relatively little economic power. He was conscious of the relative gains they had secured in the post-war period and he wanted to retain them. This led him during his last three or four years to be apprehensive about the usefulness of any wages policy which resulted in a re-allocation of the total wages bill of the country. He expressed his fear when he visited the Labour Party Conference as a fraternal delegate from the Trades Union Congress in 1952, remarking:

> it is said that the unskilled and semi-skilled workers are receiving too great a share of the nation's income, and that a redistribution is necessary. The Trade Unions have striven laboriously over a long period of years to secure effective minimum standards, which they will not be prepared to forgo, which have resulted in improving so substantially the lot of the less fortunate section of the community.

He thought that workers in strategically placed bargaining positions should not exploit their opportunities at the expense of the less fortunate groups of workers he represented. Arthur Deakin had no time for what he called 'the economics of bedlam'.

Chapter Eight

POLITICAL ACTION

To the extent that Arthur Deakin was a politician, he was one by inheritance rather than by choice. By virtue of his position as a trade union leader he was bequeathed political responsibilities which were independent of his political beliefs. His position was a focal one within the established relationships between trade unions and political parties. Moreover, when he succeeded Bevin in 1940 neither his manner of intervening in politics nor his political values were entirely of his own making for he had been much influenced by Bevin.

The political role to which Arthur Deakin succeeded was changed in 1940 by the emergence of new factors. Then, after Deakin had served what might be termed his war-time apprenticeship in leadership, he imprinted on it his own values and marked it by his own personality.

TRADE UNION POLITICAL ACTIVITIES BEFORE 1940

Trade union political action is intended to influence the activities of the Government wherever they impinge on trade union interests, and it can be done either by direct contact with the Government or through the medium of the Labour Party or by using Members of Parliament who are also trade unionists. The extent and form of trade union political activity depends upon the degree of convergence of trade union and Government interests.

Till 1940 the economic and industrial interests of the Government touched trade unions only during crises or at the margin of their activities. They coincided where trade unions required legislation to regulate hours of work, working conditions, and wages, but this field was limited. There was no use then for regular and direct contact between the trade union movement and the Government and little contact occurred. But even if the trade union need had been great it is unlikely that trade unions would have had a stronger link with the Government, for unions were relatively weak and the Government could afford to ignore them. By necessity rather than by choice most trade union political activity was directed through the Labour Party and trade union Members of Parliament.

There have been two types of trade union political needs. One concerned social and economic equality and required major structural alterations in society for its fulfilment and of which the Labour Party was a manifestation. The other, already mentioned, required legislation to create changes in industries where voluntary negotiations could not effectively be undertaken.

The fulfilment of the first need during the inter-war years and certainly after 1926 became, in the main, the prerogative of the Labour Party and as such it grew separate from those objectives which trade unions claimed as their own. The Labour Party itself, though dependent upon the trade union movement for financial support, became an established institution which moved under its own peculiar momentum in directions which were not always in accord with trade union intentions. It became a body with which trade union leaders had relations and of which they could be suspicious, even distrustful, as well as one with which they could co-operate. The attitude of Bevin towards the Labour Party, described in Chapter V, showed clearly how pronounced the detachment of trade union leaders from the Labour Party could be. Bevin was far from being an extreme case; a number of general secretaries, some of the prominence of Arthur Pugh, played no part in politics at all.

The cohesion which the Labour Movement derived from the combination of trade union and Parliamentary work by a number of general secretaries during the first quarter of this century lessened as new general secretaries spurned political careers for themselves. In 1937 there were only four general secretaries who were also Members of Parliament; only one of them was a member of the General Council; and the combined membership of their unions was less than 94,000. But it was not the unwillingness of trade union leaders to stand for Parliament which revealed their real attitude; it was the limited extent to which they and their executives were willing to use the Labour Party to solve their problems. The relationship of the Transport and General Workers' Union to the Labour Party was not exceptional, though perhaps Bevin was more enigmatic about politics than most trade union leaders.[1] In the main the

[1] For example, early in 1924 while ciitical negotiations were being held with the port employers over the wages of dockers, he stated that he had 'adopted the principle of keeping the whole of the National Bodies and principal National Unions fully informed of developments' (Report to G.E.C., 11 February 1924). One of the National Bodies was the Labour Party and he received the following reply from Mr. J. S. Middleton, Assistant Secretary of the Party: 'Mr. Henderson has asked me to thank you for yours of the 31st ult., with resolution passed by your recent delegate conference. This new practice of a Trade Union keeping the political side of the Movement fully informed of industrial developments is somewhat of a new departure and is appreciated accordingly. . . .' It is not clear what Bevin hoped to achieve by the action other than to show a spirit of oneness with the Labour Party—an intention not consistent with his general attitude towards politics at that time—and there is no evidence to show that the action was repeated.

Union used its political affiliation to further its ends in particular industries; that is, to satisfy the second type of need.

The Transport and General Workers' Union had been mainly concerned about legislation in the docks and road transport industries and it had used Members of Parliament who were on the Union's panel of members in Parliament,[1] and to a lesser extent the Parliamentary Labour Party, to sponsor its own Bills and to protect its interests whenever Government legislation concerning these industries was being enacted.   As early as 1923 the Union members in Parliament had joined with Members of Parliament from other transport unions to form a Transport Workers' Group.   James Sexton, explaining how the group operated, said:

> Every morning when the order papers come out we scrutinize these papers item by item and any question affecting transport, either road, railway, sea or docks, is closely scrutinized.   If any bills are introduced for Dock Boards, or Dock Companies, for railways, or for road transport, by the employers' side, we go into the matter and call a meeting of the group, and if we want a concession we make our mind up to block the bill at the first report.[2]

The introduction of a Private Member's Bill in the House of Commons to protect or further the interests of Union members was much more difficult than protesting about employers' sponsored Bills, for it depended upon a Member being successful in the ballot for Private Members' Motions; and matters were not a lot easier when the Parliamentary Labour Party in opposition supported the Union.   It was still necessary for a Labour Member of Parliament to secure an early place in the ballot for Private Members' Motions, though the chances of success in the ballot were increased.

Another body in the House of Commons to which the Union could have looked for support was the Trade Union Group which consisted of those Members of Parliament who were officially supported by their respective trade unions.   As far as can be ascertained, the Group was formed in 1924 but its formation was not associated with any significant incident.   In the inter-war years it did not meet unless matters of industrial interest arose.   It is difficult to assess the importance of the Group as a medium of trade union pressure in those days, for few references were made to it.[3]   The Group was not a constitutional committee of either the Labour Party or the Parliamentary Labour Party and, therefore, it received no official mention in the records.   Its members who were also

---

[1] Members on the panel are given a fee which acts as a retainer, and a financial contribution towards the upkeep of their constituencies.
[2] First Delegate Conference of the Union, 1923.
[3] Ernest Bevin referred to its work in 1930 and said that it did not get the credit it deserved and that it ought to be strengthened. (Labour Party Conference Report, 1930, p. 173.)

members of the Transport and General Workers' Union remember
its work in the inter-war years as possessing no special significance
apart from its concentration on industrial affairs. The significance
of the Group emerged when the composition of the Parliamentary
Labour Party so changed that trade unionists in it ceased to be
in a majority.

There was no marked difference between a trade union member of
the Parliamentary Labour Party and any other member in the way in
which they conducted themselves in the House of Commons. The
tie between a Member of Parliament and a trade union carried with
it only an implicit obligation to be interested in the matters that
affected the members of that union; it did not mean that the Member
had to have no other interests or that they should be subordinate to
industrial interests.[1]

The position, then, at the outbreak of war was that the long-term
political needs of trade unions had become the prerogative of the
Labour Party and that the short-term needs of obtaining the legal
enforcement of improvements in industry and of protecting union
members against Government legislation had become the primary
political concern of trade unions. Direct contact with the Government was preferred by trade unions, but it was limited in its effectiveness because trade unions, suffering from the effects of large-scale
unemployment, went to the Government as suppliants. Indirect
contact had severe constitutional limitations, particularly as the
Labour Party was in opposition for almost all the inter-war years.
What had started at the beginning of this century as a deliberate
attempt to translate trade union ideals into legislation developed in
the inter-war years as a special form of lobbying confined to a single
political party. Trade unions, however, remained affiliated to the
Labour Party, contributed substantially to its funds, and wielded a
massive voting strength at Party Conferences.

The approach of trade union leaders to politics was one of caution
and scepticism. They distinguished between political and industrial
matters and prescribed the former as narrowly as possible. Not in
any circumstances were they willing to concede to the House of
Commons the right to make their industrial agreements. Most of
them participated in the national affairs of the Labour Party and
loyally, though sometimes paradoxically, supported its policies.

NEW FACTORS OF POLITICAL CONSEQUENCE

Such were the situation and attitudes when Arthur Deakin moved
into national prominence. There was no reason to suppose that his

[1] A Member of Parliament who acted in the House of Commons on the express
instructions of a union would risk involving himself in a breach of privilege. For
an example see *Report from the Committee of Privileges*, 17 June 1947.

attitude would differ fundamentally from that of Bevin, Citrine, or Pugh. He had been nurtured within the confines of trade union experience and his primary loyalties were trade union ones. He had been active in the politics of local government before he became a national union official, and possessed that deep but simple affection for the Labour Movement which is derived from local experiences. But he had never been a Member of Parliament, nor had he aspired to be one, and unlike some of his contemporaries he had not at any time sat on the National Executive of the Labour Party as a trade union representative. Thus equipped, he was confronted at the outset of his career as a General Secretary by three new factors which had important political consequences for trade unions.

1. The first factor concerned the role of the Government. During and after the Second World War the Government developed into the most influential single participant in the economic and industrial affairs of the nation. The Government intervened directly in matters which were of immediate concern to trade unionists: through its responsibility for maintaining full employment;[1] through its physical controls over labour; through its budgetary policy which influenced investment, therefore employment and the general level of prices, therefore real wages; through its endeavour to combat inflation by stabilizing wage levels and increasing production; and through nationalization of major industries. Trade unions could no longer look upon the Government primarily as a legislating authority. As well as being a large employer of labour it became, in a sense, a third participant in industrial negotiations, rarely represented at the negotiating table but always able to influence the economic factors around which the negotiators argued.

2. The influence of the trade union movement expanded because of the power it derived from its greatly increased membership and from the indispensable nature of its co-operation in prosecuting the war and in solving post-war economic problems. This was the second new factor. Government activities and trade union interests converged for the first time at many points and increased the need for political action by trade unions.

3. The third new factor was the entry of Labour Members of Parliament into the Government in 1940 and particularly the appointment of Ernest Bevin as Minister of Labour. Given the extreme conditions of war which existed from 1940 to 1945 and the vastly increased size of trade unions, any Government would have been compelled to seek the collaboration of trade unions. Ernest Bevin made sure that this was done in a manner commensurate with the new status of trade unions.

[1] Acknowledged by the Government in 1944. See Cmd. 6527.

The channels of communication between the Government and trade unions remained unchanged in the main, but the manner in which they were used altered radically. Bevin pursued a policy of full consultation that was applied to all Government departments. The presence of Labour Members in the Government drew from trade union leaders, especially from Deakin, a loyalty to Government decisions which supplemented the sense of loyalty created by the war conditions. This did not mean that trade unionists were uncritical of Government actions; on the contrary, as the description of the General Council's attitude to a war-time wages policy shows, on certain matters they were prepared to make no concessions to the Government. But they had less reason to suspect the motives of the Government because Bevin and his Labour colleagues were in it. Arthur Deakin was, perhaps, affected more than most because of his personal loyalty to Bevin.

THE POLITICAL BEHAVIOUR OF ARTHUR DEAKIN

'Arthur Deakin', said one of his colleagues on the General Council of the Trades Union Congress, 'was much more of a politician than most trade union leaders.' It is true that Deakin considered the political implications of all the decisions with which he was concerned in making. During the war and more so during the tenure of the Labour Government he wanted to know in what way trade union decisions would affect the policy of the Government. But it would be wrong to infer from this that he viewed political action in relation to trade union activity radically differently from the way Bevin and others viewed it in the inter-war years.

On the contrary, Deakin repeatedly emphasized the futility and even the danger of dealing with industrial problems in the House of Commons. As examples, three statements he made covering a period of eight years are quoted below.

The first statement was made shortly after the close of a national unofficial dock strike in November 1945. The dockers' unofficial strike committee had persuaded Mrs. Braddock, M.P., to present a copy of sealed orders to the Minister of Labour, Mr. George Isaacs. The Minister had refused to accept it on the ground 'that it would be contrary to Government policy to accept any representations on this matter save through the normal Trade Union Channels'. Deakin, commenting on the action of the unofficial strike committee, wrote: 'A further disservice to the dockers, and to the Trade Union Movement generally, was their demand for Government intervention, and their seeking the aid of politicians. This was a most irresponsible and mischievous attempt to destroy the authority of the Union. . . .'[1]

[1] *Sunday Dispatch*, 2 December 1945.

Then he told the Labour Party delegates in 1947 during the heat of discussions over wages and production that the 'question of incentives, the question of wages and conditions of employment are questions for the trade unions, and the sooner some of our people on the political side appreciate that and leave the job to the unions the better for the battle of production'.[1]

Thirdly, he gave the following advice to the members of his own Union at their Biennial Delegate Conference in 1953. He said:

> ... never be led into the mistake of supposing you are going to get an advantage by people asking questions in Parliament affecting your collective agreement, conditions of employment and those things which are more properly dealt with by the Union on the industrial level and through the joint negotiating machinery that you have at your disposal. As far as our members in the House are concerned ... they have done a good job of work. .... They will continue to do those things which we regard as essential, but don't you throw a spanner in the industrial relationships and into our collective agreements, into arrangements like the dock labour scheme at a time when we are dealing with these matters on an industrial plane. Let that be perfectly clear.

Arthur Deakin was as intransigent over the treatment of industrial relations by Parliament as any pre-war trade union leader, but with much more effect, for he held the confidence of successive post-war Governments which heeded his advice. Moreover, he took the precaution of impressing his attitude on those trade union Members of Parliament with whom he carried most influence. Before the debate in the House of Commons on the Government White Paper on *Personal Income, Costs and Prices* in February 1948, Deakin met the members of the Parliamentary Group of his Union and 'advised them, in view of the discussions going on between the T.U.C. and the Government, not to take precipitate action ...'. Then, at a much reported meeting with the Trade Union Group of the Parliamentary Labour Party on 16 March 1954, Deakin belligerently stated that there were certain industrial matters which could not be dealt with in Parliament.[2]

Briefly, Deakin's objections to the use of party political methods for industrial ends were as follows. Primarily, as his statement in 1945 showed, he believed that the intervention of Parliament would undermine the authority of trade unions. Therein lay his resistance to the Government regulation of wages described in the previous chapter. He was opposed to any action by Parliament which cut into

[1] Labour Party Conference Report, 1947, p. 144. He adopted the same attitude in 1950. Deakin was of course not alone in expressing this view. At the 1955 Labour Party Conference, Mr. Sam Watson said that the question of legislation to regulate strike action was one for the Trades Union Congress to decide. Mr. Watson, it should be noted, was the spokesman for the Executive of the Labour Party.
[2] T. & G.W.U. Report to G.E.C., 14 June 1954.

the basic function of trade unions, namely wage negotiation. He was not simply concerned about the preservation of trade unions because he had a vested interest in them; indeed, he rarely thought in terms of himself though he was conscious of the power he derived from his position. He believed inherently that trade unions were the most effective means yet devised for protecting the interests of workers. He thought that politicians were altogether incapable of handling the narrower interests of trade unionists and unable to mind their wider interests single-handed. He did not think that the House of Commons was a suitable place in which to negotiate.

Deakin realized, as Bevin realized after 1926, that there were fields of activity in which political action alone was effective and he was prepared to leave such matters to be determined by the mechanism of Parliament. But he was not prepared to leave them in the hands of politicians as such. Trade unions, Deakin believed, should have the right to assist in determining policy on all matters they considered vital to the interests of their members but which were not regarded as trade union prerogatives. 'We are not prepared to accept the view', he said, 'that all the sense and judgment rests in the political movement of this country. . . . We have had experience; we are not mere theorists. We have got to face the hard, matter of fact, day to day problems that confront this country at this time and if, in face of that, we have not got some contribution to make, I do not understand logic and reason. . . .'[1] On wider and more general political issues he adopted a similar attitude. 'Nor', he said, 'do we accept the position that all the wisdom resides in the politician in shaping those policies which are most likely to command the support of the electors of this country, and it would be grossly improper if we did not make our position perfectly clear in that respect. . . .'[2] He was aware of the diverse views in the Parliamentary Labour Party, some of which conflicted with the trade union view and which sometimes carried more weight.[3]

The objection to using the House of Commons as a negotiating medium was deep-seated. Deakin believed that neither understanding nor effective agreement could be reached there to the advantage of trade unionists.[4] There is, indeed, little similarity between the methods of politicians and those used in negotiations with employers. Mainly because the political party with a Parlia-

[1] T. & G.W.U., B.D.C., 1953.
[2] Ibid.
[3] He had an example of this when the Transport Bill was going through Parliament in 1947. The Transport and General Workers' Union wanted 'C' licence holders to be brought within the scheme of nationalization, but the Act omitted them. In a report to his Executive Deakin wrote that 'there was a great deal of opposition from amongst those Labour Members who are not associated with the Trade Unions, in regard to this particular feature of the Bill'. (19 May 1947.)
[4] T. & G.W.U. Report to G.E.C., 14 June 1954.

mentary majority alone possesses the power to determine policy, there is neither the tact and patience nor the willingness to compromise in the House of Commons which are necessary in industrial relations. Irresponsible statements which are a feature of politics would do irreparable damage in the negotiating room. Trade unionists are not permanently in opposition to employers as one political party is to another; therefore they have had to evolve methods of working together amicably and to practice loyalty to each other. Voluntary agreements would be valueless if this were not so. When an employer or a trade union official gives his word to the other side in negotiations it is accepted in the belief that it will not be broken for the sake of expediency. This is different from the political field where each party is looking for opportunities for political gain.

The difference of approach was revealed over the acceptance by trade union leaders of posts on the Steel Board of the denationalized iron and steel industry in 1953. The opposition to the men who took the posts came, in the main, from politicians, whereas the General Council of the Trades Union Congress endorsed the action of the men by a large majority. Arthur Deakin stated:

> I feel that having stipulated during discussions with our own Party in opposition that they should strive to secure amendments to the Act [of denationalization] in order to provide for full-time representation . . . it is a piece of humbug to suggest now that people who have accepted nomination on to the Steel Board are sacrificing the interests of the Party. The tendency in this respect would appear to be to try and subordinate the interests of the trade unions to political expediency. Whether we like denationalization or not, the fact remains that it has happened and the job of the trade unions is to see that the interests of their members are properly looked after. . . . If our policy as a Movement is to be that we shall have no part in anything that does not completely conform to our own political theories then, in my view, we are going to have a pretty thin time.[1]

Deakin and the General Council, of course, were right in their attitude. Conformity to a political theory never could be a prerequisite of trade union action, nor had it ever been so.[2] Therefore, when a Conservative Government was formed in 1951 it should not have been surprising to read the following General Council statement: 'It is our long-standing practice to seek to work amicably with whatever Government is in power, and, through consultation jointly

---

[1] T. & G.W.U. Report to G.E.C., 8 June 1953.
[2] In a letter to Neville Chamberlain, when he was Prime Minister, Walter Citrine had written that 'the General Council have always acted on the principle that its conduct in dealing with any Government on behalf of the Trade Union Movement must be regulated by industrial and not political considerations . . .'. (T.U.C. Report, 1938, p. 228.)

with Ministers and with the other side of industry, to find practical
solutions to the social and economic problems facing this country.
There need be no doubt, therefore, of the attitude of the T.U.C.
towards the new Government.'[1] Yet some trade unionists were
surprised, and Deakin felt obliged to explain the statement in speeches
to his members. At Bristol he said: 'It was specifically and clearly
stated that our relationship with the Government must continue
regardless of the colour of the Government. . . . We shall not be
guilty of fractious opposition to the Government merely for the sake
of playing politics. That would be suicidal. It would be contrary
to the best interests of the masses of people in this country. . . .'[2]
Moreover, no sensible trade unionist, least of all Arthur Deakin,
wanted to sever the relationship which the General Council had
established with the Government since 1940.

The Government policy in wartime of consulting with the General
Council on labour matters was extended and intensified when the
Labour Party was elected to power in 1945. 'We have an open
door', Deakin said in 1946, 'in relation to all State Departments and
are thus able to get our difficulties examined in such a way as would
not have been possible with any other Party in Government.'[3] The
familiarity which he and other trade union leaders had with members
of the Government enabled informal contacts to be established to
supplement formal communications. Because of the informal
nature of contacts it became evident during the post-war period that
healthy relations between trade union leaders and the Government
were significantly influenced by the personalities of the Ministers,
particularly the Minister of Labour. This factor was amply
illustrated by the satisfactory way in which Sir Walter Monckton
handled industrial relations after the Conservatives took office in
1951. If Deakin wanted to speak to the Minister of Labour he
simply telephoned or called in at his room in St. James's Square.
Consequently it was no longer possible to talk of a pattern of relations between trade unions and the Government. An intolerant
Minister of Labour who was unaware of the importance of protocol
would, regardless of his political party, receive short shrift from
trade union leaders.

The improved quality of communications with the Government
lessened the need of trade unions for their own Members of Parliament. As a consequence the Transport and General Workers'
Union tended to use the Members of Parliament on its panel less
for dealing with Union political problems and more for handling the
problems of individual members of the Union. The value of these

1 *Manchester Guardian,* 1 November 1951.
2 18th Annual Festival of the Union, Bristol, 23 February 1952.
3 National and Regional Secretaries' Conference, 16 July 1946.

Members of Parliament to the whole of the Union lay in their ability to press a trade union point of view within the Parliamentary Labour Party; to act, in a way, as a protection against non-trade union elements in the Parliamentary Labour Party. For this reason Deakin thought it 'necessary to have a vigorous and effective Trade Union Group in the House', though he viewed with some concern the efforts to revitalize the Group early in 1954 because he thought it might cause further dissension in the Labour Movement.[1]

The Union deliberately tried to discourage its officials from going to Parliament. Many factors may have been responsible for causing trade union leaders to decline seats in Parliament and, of them, the increased arduousness of both occupations was not un-important. Bevin, as mentioned earlier, did not agree to permit Members of Parliament to retain their Union posts[2] and when Deakin became a National Secretary in 1932 it had become a condi-tion of employment in his job to give up 'any Prospective Parlia-mentary Candidature for a number of years, it being required that the person appointed shall devote the whole of his time to the duties of his office'.[3] During Deakin's time as General Secretary the emphasis on straightforward trade union work increased so much in relation to political activities that the matter was raised at the 1951 Biennial Delegate Conference. A delegate said: 'We have been informed that members of the Parliamentary panel having official positions in the Union have been removed from the panel and full-time officers are being discouraged from being members of the Parliamentary panel. . . . Can we have an assurance that this will cease?' Deakin replied:

No, you cannot have an assurance. The position is perfectly clear. When a man is appointed an officer of this Union he is asked a specific question—whether or not he proposes to devote his life's work to the industrial side or whether he has any ambition to enter the political field and that is a consideration that must be borne in mind. In each case, any application that is made for inclusion in the Parliamentary panel is always related to that consideration and must of necessity be.

The paradox of trade union political action was in no way better illustrated than by Arthur Deakin in the post-war years. One would have thought that his scepticism of the usefulness of party political action would have permeated his whole attitude towards politics. In fact it left untouched the tremendous fund of loyalty he possessed to the Labour Movement, which from 1945 to 1951 was epitomized by the Labour Government. His loyalty at times was

[1] T. & G.W.U. Report to G.E.C., 1 March 1954.
[2] Harry Gosling, Ben Tillett and James Sexton were the exceptions.
[3] General Executive Council Minutes, 22 February 1932.

so intense that he stifled legitimate criticisms which could have been levied against the Labour Government, and so prevented the General Council from acting, as some of its members would have wished, as a constructive critic of the Government.   There were occasions when Deakin opposed Government proposals outright—for example when he rejected a proposal made by Mr. Herbert Morrison to examine the structure of pensions in this country—but such incidents were few.

The Labour Government he thought of as 'our' Government, elected by the efforts of the workers and therefore to be given every opportunity to prove its worth.   His support was not given superficially nor without cost to himself.   From many quarters he suffered criticism: from his own members as well as from political opponents.   When the Conservative Government was in power he reminded his members about his loyalty and said: 'I wonder whether you have forgotten the gibes that I had to accept from the Tory Press during the days of Labour Government, when it was said that Deakin was sabotaging every Trade Union consideration in his determination to maintain the Labour Party in office, that I was forgetting my duty as a Trade Unionist. . . .'[1]

Arthur Deakin's loyalty encompassed the Labour Party, but he was loyal to it as an institution which was an integral part of the Labour Movement rather than as a political instrument in its own right.   In this way was his steadfast support of the Labour Party reconcilable with his scepticism about its use by trade unions for their own political ends—though one should be reminded that his scepticism did not extend to all aspects of political activity and that he looked upon the Labour Party as the only Party through which a Government could be formed to act in the interests of the working class.

A threat to the unity of the Labour Party had wide implications in Deakin's opinion and this explains his unsparing condemnation of anyone who indulged in such a threat either explicitly or implicitly. For instance in 1953 he poured scorn on Mr. Tom O'Brien[2] after O'Brien had told a *Manchester Guardian* correspondent 'that the time has come to alter the constitutional structure of the Labour Movement so as to separate the activities of the T.U.C. from those of the Labour Party without destroying the underlying unity of the movement'.   Mr. O'Brien envisaged that the Trades Union Congress 'would divest itself of its present political activities and concentrate entirely on industrial affairs.   It would be free . . . to deal with the

---

[1] T. & G.W.U., B.D.C., 1953.

[2] General Secretary of the National Association of Theatrical and Kine Employees; a member of the General Council of the T.U.C. and, in 1953, the immediate past president of the T.U.C.

Government of the day, and would, therefore, be less embarrassed
. . . in its dealing with a Tory Government and also with industrialists'.[1] O'Brien was talking, Deakin said:

> without any consideration of the relationship that exists between the
> Trades Union Congress and the Labour Party. There is no constitu-
> tional relationship between the two. There is merely a formal arrange-
> ment which, operating through the National Council of Labour, allows
> and makes provision for both parties to consult together. The relation-
> ship between the trade unions and the Labour Party is by individual
> affiliation. . . . I am certain there is no trade union affiliated to the
> Party which would for one moment consider any disaffiliation or divorce-
> ment from this Party.[2]

The political utterances of Arthur Deakin to the press and in
speeches which referred to group action within the Labour Party and
which were directed against Mr. Aneurin Bevan and those associated
with the weekly publication, *Tribune*, are relevant here in so far as
they illustrated the temper of Deakin when the unity of the Labour
Party was threatened by dissension from within. His issue with
these people was not primarily over policy, though he differed from
them over the extent of nationalization and aspects of foreign policy;
the issue was about minority rights. With his fundamental trade
union belief in rule by the majority he objected strenuously to
factious activities. Within the Labour Party there are, he said,
'differences of opinion, mainly centred around the activities and
aspirations of individuals. This problem has always been with
political parties. There are always up-and-coming leaders who
fight for position. Presumably there always will be but it must not
be allowed to get out of perspective.'[3] Mostly his tone was less
moderate than this. He spoke of 'the antics of disruptionists within
the Labour Movement'; of those 'within the Party who have set
up a caucus'; and he asked them 'to realize that the ordinary rank-
and-file party member or trade unionist has no time . . . for their
disregard of those principles and loyalties to which our Movement
has held so strongly throughout the whole course of its existence'.[4]

Arthur Deakin took part in politics when and where he considered it to be necessary; at annual Labour Party Conferences, on
the platforms of public meetings, as a member of the National
Council of Labour, as the spokesman of his Union Executive on
political matters, and as an influential member of the General
Council of the Trades Union Congress whenever its decisions had a
political significance. He, more than any Members of Parliament,

1 *Manchester Guardian*, 2 October 1953.
2 Labour Party Conference Report, 1953, p. 194.
3 T. & G.W.U. Report to G.E.C., 2 March 1953.
4 Fraternal Address, Labour Party Conference Report, 1952, p. 127.

took cognizance of the political interests of his members and when these were affected the full and overwhelming voting power of the Union was applied. It was applied over matters of policy, so that whilst the Union did not formulate policy it very often determined the fate of policy. It was applied over what trade unionists considered to be matters of honour, such as the observance of democratically determined decisions and the related matter, the unity of the Movement.

Yet, like Bevin before him,[1] Deakin was only a labourer in politics; interested in political issues but not much concerned about party political methods. It might seem that to have had a man carrying so much political power yet caring so little for party politics would have been an inherent danger to the unity of the Movement. Yet it was not the case. The danger lay with men preoccupied with party politics. Deakin and his like have given the Labour Party a broad base from which to operate. They have characterized its federal composition, its different shades of political opinion, and have given it its resilience.

[1] See Ch. V, pp. 88–90.

Chapter Nine

THE CONSOLIDATION OF
THE TRADE GROUP SYSTEM

THE initial difficulties involved in uniting the diverse groups of workers which made up the Transport and General Workers' Union were described in Chapters III and IV. There it was shown that the trade group system in the main satisfied the aspirations for self-determination of the heterogeneous general workers. This continued to be the case after 1940, even though the Union experienced an increase in the complexity of the trades it represented.

In two ways the problem of integrating the diverse groups in the Union changed after 1940. In the first place the trade union practice of officially settling industrial disputes by conciliatory methods instead of by strike action became firm and uniform both during and after the war. Therefore whenever a group of workers within the Transport and General Workers' Union went on strike it was not easy for the Union Executive to steal the initiative from the hands of the unofficial strike leaders by taking over its control. Nor was it likely that the Executive would endeavour to satisfy disgruntled members by leading them out on strike. Secondly, as a result of the rapid growth of the membership of the Union in the general workers and engineering groups the balance of power between the Trade Groups had shifted away from the dockers and London busmen. These may have remained the most vocal groups in the Union, but the sheer weight of numbers in other groups frequently stood as an obstacle between them and achievement whenever matters that concerned dockers or busmen were discussed at the Biennial Delegate Conferences. These changes mainly concerned the groups of dockers and London busmen, whose behaviour is discussed in later chapters.

The amalgamation and merger process continued after Deakin became Acting General Secretary. But in the midst of a rapid expansion of the membership, the initiative for amalgamation and merger discussions was left for other unions to take, particularly as the unions desirous of becoming a part of the Transport and General Workers' Union were relatively small. In any case Deakin moved cautiously because, as he once said, 'very often by precipitate approach one is prevented from reaching the end in view and the task of unifying our forces is made more difficult'.[1]   Altogether, eleven unions merged or amalgamated with the Transport and General Workers' Union between the beginning of 1940 and 1955, but they were small unions and formed an insignificant percentage of the new membership of the Union during each of the years they joined with it.[2]

The complexity of the membership, and therefore the trade group structure, was virtually unaffected by the additional unions.   Six of the unions catered for river pilots, two for glass workers, and the remainder for government workers, boilermen, and transport workers respectively.   Some mention was made in 1944 about the prospects of amalgamating with the National Union of General and Municipal Workers, but Deakin was emphatic about its impracticability.   'I can say very clearly', he said, 'that amalgamation with the N.U.G.M.W. will never happen.   Their constitution is totally different [from ours].'[3]   Perhaps this was as well, for the competition between the two large general unions acted as a healthy restraint upon the activities of both.   The National Union of Vehicle Builders, the Constructional Engineering Union, and the Ulster Transport and Allied Operatives' Union all approached the Transport and General Workers' Union about the possibility of amalgamating with it, but in each case obstacles arose to prevent the amalgamation taking place.[4]   Deakin had no new problems to face arising out of amalgamations or mergers, nor were any of the difficulties of integration he inherited from Bevin affected in any way by them.

The demands for separate trade groups which were made regularly at the Biennial Delegate Conferences of the Union in the inter-war years were maintained at a high level for a number of years afterwards.   Workers in the fishing industry, agriculture, municipal work, Government work, textile industry, oil trade, dairy trade, chemical industry, and in Co-operative Societies each at various times demanded to have their own respective trade groups.   That the demands were made regularly and vociferously illustrates the value that workers placed on the trade group system.   'If an industry

[1] B.D.C. Report, 1941.
[2] The list of these unions is given in Appendix II.   The last and the largest union to become part of the Transport and General Workers' Union in this period was the Liverpool and District Carters and Motormen's Union with about 8,000 members. This union failed to amalgamate in 1922 and had a rather chequered relationship with the larger Union in the inter-war years.   The amalgamation, for which discussions had started early in 1944, took effect on 1 January 1947, when the Union became the Region No. 12 (Liverpool and District) Commercial Services Group.
[3] National and Regional Secretaries' Conference, January 1944.
[4] Arrangements were made for the transfer of members of the Ulster Transport and Allied Operatives Union but they did not materialize.   Eventually in 1954 some members went to the National Union of General and Municipal Workers and others to the Transport and General Workers' Union.

has its own Group', a delegate said, 'it gives the membership in the industry poise and dignity . . .'.[1] The membership of the Union, through its delegates in conference, acceded to the formation of only four new trade groups and, of these, three had had National Section Committees as a prelude to being given group status.

As with most others who worked in the Union, Deakin believed in the effectiveness of the trade group system and on many occasions he eulogized it. But he believed that the extent of its application was limited and that there were in 1940 almost enough groups to satisfy the requirements of the Union. He stated his attitude clearly in 1943 in reply to a motion calling for a trade group for the textile industry in which the Union had 10,000 members.

> The Organization [he said] has been built on sound lines, but . . . if this fetish of establishing Trade Groups in every section of industry is not examined and related to every known fact, then . . . you will create an organization that you cannot work, and that nobody can administer. You can carry a principle of this description to such an extent that your organization becomes hopelessly clogged. . . .[2]

The administrative factors which limited the extension of the group system were numerous, and varied from one demand to another. Some of the demands came from sections of workers that were too small to warrant separate union machinery. Deakin was not prepared to state, however, what numbers the Executive regarded as being necessary to establish a national trade group, because it depended to a large extent on the circumstances surrounding the industry or section of workers concerned.[3] He felt that if an industrial group was self-contained and distinct from other groups then, irrespective of its size, it would justify group machinery. It was becoming difficult to find new groups of workers which could be easily and clearly distinguished from the established groups and which could be formed without lopping off substantial portions of existing trade groups.

An important consideration in the formation of new groups was the relationship of the Union with other unions. On two occasions when unions which had hitherto been craft unions entered the organizing fields of the Transport and General Workers' Union it was suggested by some members that the union should establish craft sections. From January 1943 the Amalgamated Engineering Union admitted into its ranks women engineering workers who had previously been organized by only the two general unions, and the suggestion to organize engineering craftsmen was made to counter

[1] T. & G.W.U., B.D.C., 1953.
[2] T. & G.W.U., B.D.C., 1943.
[3] T. & G.W.U., B.D.C., 1945.

this act. Deakin thought it would be unwise for reasons he had stated in 1941 when dilution in the industry had raised a difficult problem of inter-union relations in the industry. He had said then that his Union was a part of a Movement and, therefore, had to submit to ordered relationships. This entailed observing the rights of other unions. His Union accepted the right of other unions to organize the craft side of the Engineering industry.[1]   At the Biennial Delegate Conference in 1953 a request was made to set up a craft section in the Building Trade Group. The Union at that time was competing for building trade labourers with the Amalgamated Union of Building Trade Workers which had widened its craft basis by amalgamating with the National Builders Labourers and Constructional Workers' Society. To accede to the request, Deakin believed, would not only be contrary to the Bridlington Agreement but would bring his Union into conflict with other unions in the building industry. 'If we walk into that one,' he said, 'we shall soon . . . perhaps, find ourselves outside the N.F.B.T.O. faced with a refusal of the craft unions to work with us. . . .'[2]

It was a different matter when the conflicting union was not considered to be a bona-fide trade union. Such was the case with the Chemical Workers' Union. This union was formed when a small Union called the Retail Chemists Association with about 500 members enrolled a section of about 3,000 members which had seceded from the Shop Assistants' Union shortly after the First World War. Though the issue was disputed, the Chemical Workers' Union was regarded by the general unions as a breakaway organization. Nevertheless it was admitted to membership of the Trades Union Congress in 1923 but lost it nine months later and remained out of Congress until 1943. The Transport and General Workers' Union had organized chemical workers in its Metal, Engineering and Chemical group and, therefore, competed for members with the Chemical Workers' Union. After this union's re-affiliation to Congress it undertook a vigorous recruiting campaign with such success that Deakin advised his Executive to form a Chemical Workers' Section. He stated that 'it was necessary to give the chemical workers' membership a sense of being a national entitity within this Union, with a National Officer specifically charged with the responsibility of dealing with the affairs of the Section and of developing organization'.[3]   A section was formed and in the quarter ending 31 December 1954 it became a fully constituted trade group.

[1] T. & G.W.U., B.D.C., 1941.
[2] Ibid., 1953. The N.F.B.T.O. is the National Federation of Building Trade Operatives, to which the T. & G.W.U. is affiliated.
[3] Minutes of the Finance and General Purposes Committee, T. & G.W.U., 19 November 1943.

A further argument against forming trade groups was that it was costly. New national officials were appointed, though occasionally where the work of two groups, such as municipal workers and government workers, was closely related, one national officer covered both groups. Separate national lay committees were still set up, however. The responsibility for creating regional trade group machinery rested with the regions themselves. A region could, if it wished, refuse to have any trade group machinery if it considered that its existing machinery was satisfactory. For instance, although the Building Trades Group was formed in 1938 there was Regional Building Trade Group machinery in only six of the thirteen regions in 1953. The precedent for leaving the initiative with the regions dated back to 1922 when 'it was found that the group system did not function in the South Wales Area owing to the fact that each trade already had its form of organization for dealing with the question of wages, conditions, etc.'.[1] In practice, then, the cost of constituting trade group machinery depended upon the size and needs of the trade concerned and the custom of the regions.

Occasionally members of trade groups or trade sections sought permission to add to their constitutional machinery to obtain an extra means of expression. National trade conferences were the most commonly sought means. The Building Trade Group was most persistent in asking for one of these to assist it to organize more of the approximate 500,000 workers in the industry who were eligible for union membership. Each time the Group was given a similar reply from Deakin: 'There appears to be in the minds of the delegates the idea that if they can only get a National Conference they can solve the problem of getting membership but that does not follow at all. The job of organizing is done on the job.'[2] Later he counselled, 'Talk, talk, talk, does not produce a single member.'[3]

Unless the Transport and General Workers' Union expands in an unexpected direction it is unlikely that its trade groups will increase in number. The Union, then, will settle roughly in its present form. The problem of integration will not be altered by changes in the complexity of membership. It may be changed, however, by the emergence of a different behaviour pattern from some groups. As groups become settled they tend to develop their own practices and create their own traditions. How these changes affect the problem of integration depends on the form they take; whether or not they are aggressive. One cannot foretell what will happen, for the behaviour of newly settled groups is unpredictable.

[1] T. & G.W.U. Annual Report, 1922, p. x.
[2] T. & G.W.U., B.D.C., 1945.
[3] T. & G.W.U. Report to G.E.C., 7 December 1953.

Chapter Ten

LONDON ROAD PASSENGER TRANSPORT WORKERS

THE London busmen, in the 1930s, were a turbulent, dissident group in the Union. In 1938 some of them had formed a breakaway union and when Arthur Deakin took over from Bevin this union was active; a thorn in the flesh of the large parent body. Thus much was described in Chapter IV.

What happened afterwards is the subject of this chapter. The breakaway union was suppressed; the group behaviour was changed by economic factors which neither the Union nor the employing body could influence; and throughout it all Arthur Deakin treated the London busmen sympathetically, but without discrimination and certainly with no departure from his set pattern of loyalties.

THE BREAKAWAY

The National Passenger Workers' Union, in its endeavour to expand and gain recognition, was restricted by war conditions and war-time legislation regulating strike action. It would certainly have aroused the opposition of the public and the Government if it had added to the war-time dislocation of London transport by causing internecine troubles in the garages through its recruiting activities. But the union was protected by the same factors which restricted it, for the Transport and General Workers' Union, too, was restrained by the war.

The main source of activity sprang from the endeavour of the break-away union to gain recognition from the London Passenger Transport Board through litigation. The relationship between the Board and the Transport and General Workers' Union was governed by Section 6 of the 1927 Trade Disputes and Trade Unions Act which made it unlawful for the Board to impose any condition 'whereby employees who are or who are not members of a trade union are liable to be placed in any respect either directly or indirectly under any disability or disadvantage as compared with other employees'. The breakaway union claimed that the Board was failing to fulfil the terms of the Act by not according to it the same rights as were given to the Transport and General Workers' Union, so it took the issue to Court.

The incident upon which its case was based occurred on 6 February 1939, when the London Passenger Transport Board disciplined a driver called Mr. Archibald Moscrop, who was a member of the National Passenger Workers' Union. Moscrop was cautioned by his Depot Superintendent, so he appealed first to the Divisional Superintendent, and then to the Disciplinary Board which was the last stage of the appeals procedure. When he went before the Disciplinary Board he was accompanied by the general secretary of his union, but he was told that there was no provision for this; that only members of the Transport and General Workers' Union could be accompanied at appeals by a union official. The basis for this decision was a clause in the terms of the settlement of the 1937 bus strike. Moscrop withdrew his appeal.

He then claimed that the Board had violated Section 6 of the 1927 Act and took the case to the High Court. The claim was disallowed on the ground that the right to be represented before a Disciplinary Board was not a condition of service but a privilege conferred upon members of the union which had made the agreement with the London Passenger Transport Board. The judgment was a blow to the National Passenger Workers' Union, so Moscrop appealed to the Court of Appeal. On 4 November 1940 the Court of Appeal issued a written judgment in his favour. Lord Justice Scott in the course of the judgment stated:

> When in 1938 the new National Union was formed the Board were faced directly with the problem of inequality and ought to have realized that members of the new union would be 'liable to be placed directly or indirectly under a disability or disadvantage' in respect of appeals as compared with members of the Transport Union. The defendant Board should have made a general amendment of the representation clause in respect of appeals so as to extend equality of advantage to men of each union and to non-union men. The whole question of section 6 had probably escaped notice.[1]

Victory was acclaimed and W. J. Brown, the honorary president of the breakaway, wrote a leaflet called *Moscrop Wins*. Under the judgment of the Court of Appeal any breakaway union formed in a field covered by a 'Public Authority' could claim the same rights as the parent union. It was a frightening thought to the large trade unions.

The National Passenger Workers' Union case in law was against the London Passenger Transport Board, which in this matter was as intransigent as the Transport and General Workers' Union. Victory for the breakaway was short-lived. The Board appealed to the House of Lords and in March 1942 the Court of Appeal judgment

[1] *The Times*, 5 November 1940.

was reversed. The House of Lords contended, as did the High Court beforehand, that the members of the Transport Union had been given a privilege which did not involve a condition of service.

This final legal decision was virtually the end of the hopes the National Passenger Workers' Union harboured of establishing itself in London Transport. All that remained was the right to represent its members in a number of relatively minor ways, such as in connection with the Workmen's Compensation Act and in handling cases brought before the Law Courts for breaches of the traffic law by busmen.

Without the support of the law, the National Passenger Workers' Union could only obtain recognition in respect of wages and conditions of service by organizing the majority of road passenger transport workers in London. For the breakaway there was a vicious circle: it could not recruit enough members to force the London Passenger Transport Board to concede recognition until it could show busmen that it was able to represent them fully, i.e., that it had obtained recognition. The London Passenger Transport Board consistently refused to recognize the breakaway and the Transport and General Workers' Union equally consistently declined to take part in any discussions in association with it.

The war period on the whole favoured the Transport and General Workers' Union in this inter-union dispute. The initial glow of attraction for the breakaway dimmed considerably in the cold reality of war. And those who returned to London transport at the end of the war, or who joined it fresh from the armed forces, entered an industrial scene that bore little resemblance to the pre-war one.

While the justification for creating a breakaway was obscure or unknown to most of the busmen, the attack on unity which the creation and continuance of the breakaway union embodied was neither forgotten nor forgiven by the hard core of loyal Transport and General Workers' Union members on London Transport, and as soon as circumstances permitted they pressed for action against those London road passenger transport workers who were not members of their Union.

The Closed Shop

The first act of any significance taken against members of the National Passenger Workers' Union occurred in the early summer of 1946. Then the London Passenger Transport Board suspended with pay thirteen members of that union because workers in the New Cross, Wandsworth, and Clapham depots, where they were employed, refused to work with them.[1] All along, the Board had

[1] Ten of the thirteen were from the New Cross depot.

viewed with disfavour the activities of the breakaway and it was not prepared to have its services disrupted by a strike for the sake of perpetuating the breakaway. It could not dismiss the thirteen tramwaymen, because that would undoubtedly have been a violation of the Trade Disputes and Trade Unions Act, 1927, and in any case the Board was still covered by the Essential Work Order. The first obstacle was removed when the 1927 Act was repealed in May 1946. When news that the Essential Work Order was to be withdrawn on 1 September 1946 became known, more positive action against the breakaway union was planned by members of the Transport and General Workers' Union.

The initiative came from the ordinary members in their depots and garages. On 20 June 1946 representatives of the bus, tram, and trolleybus sections in the Central London Area and of the County Services Trade sections, met in a joint conference and asked the Executive for plenary powers 'to deal with the question of non-unionists within the Area No. 1 Passenger Trade Group as and from September 1st 1946, it being our opinion that all who share in the present arrangements between the Transport and General Workers' Union and the L.P.T.B. shall be Members of the T. & G.W.U.'. They asked for a plan of action to be drawn up to achieve 100 per cent. Transport and General Workers' Union membership and suggested that information on the subject should be circulated to the branches. The General Executive Council was not directly involved. Meanwhile Deakin had been having informal discussions with the Chairman of the Board about the likely developments after the withdrawal of the Essential Work Order.

It is not possible to say when a 'closed shop' agreement was envisaged but clearly, until the middle of August 1946, a concerted effort was made in the garages to recruit members of the National Passenger Workers' Union back to the parent Union and it was relatively successful. It was estimated from reports from the garages and depots that during the month preceding 19 August the number of non-unionists (including members of the National Passenger Workers' Union) had been reduced from 3,264 to approximately 1,000 and that by 1 September only a hard core of about 500 workers would be remaining out of the Union. The National Passenger Workers' Union had claimed 8,000 members in 1945.[1]

A meeting of the section committees concerned and the Finance and General Purposes Committee, took place on 19 August 1946. Here, reports on the attitude of the ordinary members were received and discussed, and in the light of them the main lines of policy in relation to the breakaway union were determined. They

[1] *Strikes*, by K. G. J. C. Knowles, p. 44.

agreed to try to prevent any unauthorized stoppages of work. Between 19 August and the date of the next conference on 27 August the whole matter was formally discussed by the Union, represented by Deakin, and the Board, and on 26 August the Board issued a statement of policy in relation to non-members of the Transport and General Workers' Union.

It stated that the Executive of the Union had informed the Board that 'their members in the employ of the Board have decided that they will not work with employees in the grades concerned who are not members of the Transport and General Workers' Union'. In response the Board

> after careful consideration, have decided that the existing unsatisfactory situation, by seriously hampering the Board in its efforts to provide an efficient transport service, is prejudicial to the public and must be brought to an end. It is recognized by the General Executive Council of the Transport and General Workers' Union that it is essential to the fulfilment of the Board's duties to the public that the Board should be able to rely upon the observance of collective agreements and the full co-operation of the staff. Upon this basis, and on the understanding that an opportunity will be given to all non-members of the Transport and General Workers' Union to join that Union, the Board have decided not to continue in their service any employee in the grades concerned who is unwilling to join the Transport and General Workers' Union.

The statement was accepted by the members and the policy contained in it was implemented from 31 August 1946.

The end of the activities of the breakaway was in sight. Altogether 176 London busmen were discharged. To test the legality of the matter the breakaway tried to secure an injunction restraining the Board from dismissing twelve of the men who would not join the Transport and General Workers' Union, on the ground that according to an existing Union/Board agreement employees could only be dismissed for misconduct, ill-health, old age, or redundancy, but the injunction was not granted. In the following June, the National Passenger Workers' Union had, it was reported, only six regularly paying members and £4 13s. in the bank.[1]

Although the negotiations with the Board were conducted by Deakin himself, the impulse for action came throughout from the lay members and he followed the instructions they laid down through their delegates. And though on many other occasions he deplored compulsory trade unionism, he vigorously defended it in London transport.[2] In the first place, the alternative to an agreement

[1] Ibid.
[2] For the writer's views see *Power in Trade Unions*, Ch. IV.

enforcing compulsion, given the mood of the ordinary members in London transport, was unregulated action by garages and depots such as was taken by the New Cross tram depot. This would have disrupted a public service, perhaps for a long period, and the way would have been open for the members of the breakaway union equally to have refused to work with members of the Transport and General Workers' Union. Such are the mood and confusion of strikes that no matter which side struck work there was a possibility that the breakaway union would benefit.

This issue, then, as far as Deakin was concerned, was about the need to preserve the London transport section of his Union with the least discomfort to the travelling public. It was not about the liberty of the individual. His views were clearly expressed in a speech he made to his Scottish members on 13 September 1946:

> Just a word [he said] about the allegations that the Trade Unions are interfering with the liberty of the individual. The Trade Unions are just as anxious as anyone else to maintain the fullest personal liberty of the individual. This, however, does not mean licence to those people who for some selfish motive or for disruptive purposes seek to destroy organization already in existence and, above all, that joint negotiating machinery which has served this country so well during the war years. . . . This question of personal liberty is very closely associated with the question of breakaway unions whose technique it is to allege that trade union officers are hirelings of the employing classes, betraying the interests of their members—and whose endeavour it is to sow dissension and discord, making the claim that they could do so much better for the worker if only he would transfer his allegiance. It is no wonder therefore that the loyal trade union member takes the challenge thrown down by these disruptive elements and determines to end this attempt to destroy our strength and unity. Liberty cannot be one-sided. . . .[1]

POST-WAR GRIEVANCES

The conditions on London Transport changed after the war for reasons which were beyond the control of the Union and the London Passenger Transport Board. The post-war period was characterized by full employment and expanding manufacturing and export industries. Workers had little need to value the security of a particular job and therefore they were able to place their emphasis on wages and conditions of work and to search for these by moving from job to job. Naturally, men tended to move to the manufacturing industries, where the highest wages were to be found, and away from the servicing industries. This was a reversal of the pre-war situation when workers left the manufacturing industries for the relatively high wage rates, the security in employment, and the

[1] Scottish Delegate Conference of the T. & G.W.U.

higher status which work in the road passenger transport industry and similar servicing industries offered.

A significant change was the relative decline in the earning capacity of workers in the servicing industries which started during the war. For instance, between October 1938 and October 1946 the average weekly earnings of transport and storage workers, etc. (excluding railways), had increased by 68 per cent. while the earnings of all workers had increased by 90 per cent.[1] London road passenger transport workers had fared worse than transport workers generally, for between 30 June 1938 and 31 December 1946 their average weekly earnings had increased by only 45 per cent. Central London bus drivers had an increase of a mere 35 per cent. in the same period.[2] The earnings of London busmen in 1946 were still relatively high. Central bus drivers were getting an average of 127s. 6d. per week in the year ending 31 December 1946, compared with an average of 115s. 2d. for all male workers for the last pay week in October 1946. But they were being rapidly overhauled and were already less than the earnings of male workers in miscellaneous manufacturing industries.[3] The earnings of the London road passenger transport workers lagged behind those of workers in manufacturing industries, not only because the percentage increases in wage rates were less but, more important, because the basic wage rates could not be supplemented by production bonuses and incentive payments. In many industries after the war the basic rate of wages was meaningful only as a fall-back rate; it was not so in road passenger transport, where supplementary payments were slight.

In consequence the London Passenger Transport Board was faced throughout the post-war period with staff shortages and a high labour turnover. These, together with a shortage of vehicles and an increase in the demand for public transport due to the Government decision to release restrictions on entertainment shortly after the war, caused the Board to seek an extension of the war-time relaxation of union and road traffic regulations. It was not possible for the labour problem to be resolved by offering competitive wages to workers on the buses, trams, and trolleybuses, for the Board's sole source of revenue was the fares it charged and the Board was faced with continual pressure from the Government and the public to keep them down. Moreover, fares were regulated by a statutory authority.

[1] *Ministry of Labour Gazette*, April 1947, p. 106.
[2] *Labour Relations in London Transport*, by H. A. Clegg, p. 95. The figures are not strictly comparable. The Ministry of Labour figures for transport and storage workers, etc., and all workers relate to the average weekly earnings in the last pay week of October in 1938 and 1946 whereas Clegg's figures for London road passenger transport workers relate to the average weekly earnings in the years ending 30 June 1938 and 31 December 1946.
[3] Cf. *Ministry of Labour Gazette*, April 1947, p. 106.

Road passenger transport workers in London experienced a deterioration in working conditions as well as relatively low earnings.

In addition to grievances over wages, the principal sources of friction on London transport during the post-war years until Arthur Deakin's death were schedules, standing passengers, and payment for overtime. Occasionally, dissatisfaction over one or other of these was expressed through strike action but, on the whole, London transport was relatively strike-free during the period. There were only six recorded strikes: three were over complaints about schedules; two about overtime payments; and one about a claim for higher wages. No strike was officially recognized by the Union. Never more than half of the 56,000 Union members on London transport went on strike at one time. The two largest post-war strikes involved 22,780 and 18,740 members on 1 January and 6 July 1949 respectively; each was of one day's duration only and both concerned overtime payments. The longest strike was for six days in October 1954 over revised service schedules, but it involved only 16,600 members. This strike record compares most favourably with that of the other strike-prone groups, the miners and the dockers.

The introduction of new service schedules is always a potential source of dissatisfaction to busmen. Indeed, in the provinces most of the strikes were caused by this factor. In the main, however, the need to implement unpopular schedules arises from the need to cut costs or from labour shortages, which in turn can be traced to the prosperity of the industry in relation to other industries. The relative prosperity of the road passenger transport industry is determined in part by the productivity of its workers. Therein lay the reason for speeding up the scheduled pace of buses and, given the size of buses, adding to the permitted number of standing passengers, for these were virtually the only means of increasing productivity in the industry.

It can be seen, then, that all the factors which gave rise to friction between the workers and the London Passenger Transport Board were facets of the same problem; a problem which the Board would have liked to have solved just as much as the workers and the Union. Under such conditions it was largely incidental as to whether one factor or another caused a grievance. Only the permitted number of standing passengers ceased to cause friction while Deakin held office.

The Interventions of Arthur Deakin

In some ways the problem of integrating the activities of the London busmen into the Union eased during the post-war period.[1]

[1] Outside London there were some relatively minor, short-lived disturbances. The only strike of note involved 13,580 busmen from various districts in England and

By not supporting the National Passenger Workers' Union and then by pressing for its elimination, the members showed that they were not really interested in forming a separate union for busmen. Then the changing composition of the London bus labour force under conditions of full employment reduced the effectiveness of aggressive 'ginger' groups by dissipating their propaganda. Moreover, the existence of alternative occupations enabled individual workers to take unilateral action to improve their respective living standards. It became much more difficult to organize collective unofficial action as a consequence.

Arthur Deakin only handled the affairs of the Central London Bus Section when important issues arose concerning either the wages and conditions of the busmen or constitutional practice. He gave them no special treatment nor, in order to placate them, did he exempt them from observing principles which he considered to be of prime importance. After negotiating the 'closed shop' agreement his principal interventions occurred in 1949 and 1950.

1. The first was about the need to honour industrial agreements. On 1 January 1949 almost 23,000 bus, tram, and trolleybus workers went on strike for one day for a better overtime payment on Saturday afternoons. The strike was not recognized by the Union and was contrary to the Union's agreement with the London Transport Executive, as the Board was then called. It seemed likely that a similar strike would occur the following week, so both the Chairman of the London Transport Executive and the Chief Conciliation Officer of the Ministry of Labour communicated with Deakin to discover the Union's attitude towards its contractual obligations. On 5 January Deakin met the elected delegates of the London road passenger transport workers and successfully induced them to take their grievance through the negotiating procedure.

During the meeting Arthur Deakin lectured the delegates about the sanctity of agreements. His attitude was uncompromising. He told them what they expected of employers they should do themselves and that they could not complain if in their so-called militancy the employers became as militant. He said: 'Trade Union organization can only function effectively provided there is observance by all parties concerned of the obligations we have entered into. If that fails then you have got to devise some other method of dealing with

Wales and lasted from 19 June to 13 July 1947. Early in June 1948 a breakaway union called the National Union of Public Vehicle Drivers and Operators was formed in Salford. At one stage it claimed 3,000 members but the T. & G.W.U. stated that it had never had so many members (stated by the secretary of Region 6 at a National and Regional Secretaries' Conference 1948). By March 1949 it was virtually without any membership and was not heard of more. Also in 1948 there was an attempt to form a National Association of Passenger Transport Inspectors, but little was heard about it. The provincial busmen had their grievances, of course, but they were not reflected in secessionist movements.

questions that . . . affect the working lives of the people employed in industry.

2. The second issue was a variation of the first. It involved Union constitutional rights as well as the sanctity of agreements. In May 1948 an agreement was reached which allowed a maximum of eight standing passengers to be carried during peak hours instead of five. The agreement was negotiated by Deakin and the London Transport Executive and it was endorsed by the Executive of the Union. It allowed for a review of the matter to take place after twelve months. In April 1949 a joint delegate conference of London bus, tram, and trolleybus workers took precipitate action and notified the London Transport Executive that as from 18 May 1949 they would revert to five standing passengers between the hours of 12 midnight and 9.30 a.m. and 4.0 p.m. and 6.30 p.m., except on Saturdays when the latter period would be between 12 noon and 2.0 p.m. and on Sundays when no standing passengers would be carried.

The Deputy Chairman of the London Transport Executive wrote to Deakin complaining about the action. Deakin agreed with his protest and arranged to recall the joint conference to get the matter cleared up. He repeated his argument about honouring agreements, then added bluntly:

> This resolution cannot stand, it cannot be implemented, and until the Conference decides that it cannot be operated, that this question can only be dealt with in the ordinary course of negotiations, then nothing can be done. . . . I want to make it clear that I will not move one finger to seek a discussion with the London Transport Executive so long as you have taken your decision, which is in flat contradiction to the policy of the Union and the agreement that your Executive has appended its name to on your behalf. . . .

Before the April 1949 Conference Deakin had persuaded the members of London Transport to submit an issue of overtime payment to an independent arbitration tribunal. They had been dissatisfied with the award. 'I am putting it to you', he said, '. . . that you passed this resolution in a spirit of vindictiveness . . . in fact, you are seeking to punish the travelling public by reason of your inability to get from the London Transport Executive that to which you think you are entitled. Your attitude is wrong.' This statement did not antagonize the delegates; it drew from one an admission that Deakin's interpretation was correct; then the conference proceeded to pass a motion to satisfy Deakin's wishes.

3. A strike of 14,420 London transport members took place on 13 September 1950 and lasted for four days. The members had two complaints: they were dissatisfied with the refusal of the General

6*

Executive Council of the Union to submit a claim for an increase of
£1 per week on their behalf, and they objected to the recruitment of
additional women conductors on the ground that their employment
would prejudice a demand for higher pay. A joint delegate conference was held during the strike at which the Assistant General
Secretary, Arthur Tiffin, submitted a report and the delegates
recommended a resumption of normal working. The recommendation was accepted. Then on 19 September, the delegate conference
met Deakin and the Finance and General Purposes Committee to
receive a full statement of the Executive views. Deakin made the
statement in his usual forthright manner. Where criticisms were
justified, they were made; in this he was consistent. He made no
false or empty promises, nor did he in any way endeavour to win
support by misrepresentation or the use of half-truths; but support
he was given.

He said: 'If the Executive disregard these considerations to which
it is their duty to pay attention, if they proceed to act merely as a
clearing-house for any claim put forward, or in pursuit of any policy
which a particular Section may advocate, then I suggest they are no
longer worthy of the name of Executive.' He told the delegates of
the privileged position of London transport members compared with
similar workers in the provinces, both in relation to the Union
constitution and to the level of wages, and he said that the claim
would widen the wages differential between London and the provinces.
He pointed out that the increase in wages was only one claim amongst
a number which needed to be settled. Ought it to be submitted if
it prejudiced the chances of obtaining the important Sick Pay Claim
they had submitted? Or if it prevented the Union from obtaining
a pension scheme?

About the merits of the wages claim itself, he said:

. . . the Executive were bound to measure the cost involved. . . . when
we have regard to the fact that 56,000 members are concerned in the
claim, and the effect on the plus payments over and above the basic
rates, it could not possibly cost less than four million pounds a year.
It is not suggested for one moment that the London Transport Executive
have no surplus, but we do say very definitely that it is not possible to
get four million pounds out of their present profits, particularly on top
of the cost of the concessions recently negotiated. This could only be
done by increasing fares, and in this respect you will understand me
when I say that we cannot blow hot and cold. We cannot at one
moment oppose an increase in fares and the next moment strive to create
a condition whereby it would be necessary to increase fares. . . . I have
heard it said in this room that it does not matter what happens to the
claim, that should not be for us to decide. In other words, we should

let some one else turn the claim down. If that is leadership, then I do not want to lead under such conditions.

The second complaint was based on the assumption that they could increase their bargaining power by restricting their labour supply. Deakin said to the delegates:

> If we are to take the line that . . . we are not prepared to consider the employment of women even though it is quite clear that men are not available, then we must see where we go from there. . . . There was a time when we had insufficient vehicles at our disposal to operate the services required by the public. That time has gone; the vehicles are there, but there are not sufficient crews to run them. The London Transport Executive . . . cannot refuse to give the public the necessary services. . . . Therefore . . . we must face up to this particular issue in a realistic way.

Deakin reminded the delegates of the Union's responsibilities to its 150,000 women members and of the fact that it was committed to the principle of equal pay and equal opportunities for women.

The events described above revealed Deakin in his various moods: dominating yet reasonable; persuasive and understanding; outspoken, sometimes to the point of rudeness, but then this was a feature of the relationship between himself and his members which was taken for granted. It could not be said that he completely dominated the men in conference, for London busmen are not men who succumb readily to control. Yet on each occasion his arguments and opinions were accepted as valid. Each settlement was, however, an *ad hoc* settlement; industrial troubles on London transport recurred and doubtless will continue to do so. The inclination to take unofficial action in support of their claims has remained. In 1954 a ban on overtime was imposed to expedite a claim for higher wages, and when in October 1954 revised service schedules were introduced to overcome the effects of the ban, about 16,600 members struck work for six days. An unofficial strike occurred during the week of Deakin's death, in protest against new summer service schedules, but it lasted for only one day.

Yet the troubles on London transport in the post-war years were only minor irritants to the normal running of the Union. It is difficult to see how they could have been avoided without an Executive policy which gave recognition to unregulated and spontaneous strikes—a policy that had never been pursued by the Union—or without a willingness by Deakin and the Executive to press for all claims made by the men regardless of their merit.

Chapter Eleven

DOCKWORKERS IN THE UNION[1]

(1) DECASUALIZATION

THE dock membership of the Transport and General Workers' Union undoubtedly presented Arthur Deakin with his most difficult problem of integration. The problem proved to be as intractable to him as it had been to Ernest Bevin. Its importance in both internal and external affairs of the Union is reflected in its treatment here. Its relatively lengthy treatment is justified by another factor. Arthur Deakin was much maligned for his handling of the dock problem as if he were solely responsible for it and as if, in any case, the problem were easy to solve. A detailed examination shows the accusations against Deakin as half-truths and it reveals a problem, complex and bewildering.

This chapter is concerned with the attempts to end the employment of casual labour in the dock industry. It deals with the pre-war pressure for decasualization, the establishment of war-time dock labour schemes, the difficulties associated with the permanent decasualization of dock labour, and the obligations for dock workers which decasualization carried with it. Arthur Deakin was involved personally or through his immediate subordinate, the National Docks Officer of the Union, in the war and post-war decasualization schemes. The purpose of the chapter is to act as a basis for a better understanding of the post-war situation on the docks as well as to show the emergence of Arthur Deakin in the affairs of dock labour.

PRE-WAR PRESSURE FOR DECASUALIZATION

From the moment Ernest Bevin succeeded in getting a national award for dockers at the Shaw Inquiry, 1920, he made it his business to work for the decasualization of dock labour. Other people

---

[1] In 1938 the Transport and General Workers' Union had a docks membership of 87,500. This compared with the approximate membership of 7,000 in the National Amalgamated Stevedores and Dockers (London); 4,000 in the Watermen, Lightermen, Tugmen and Bargemen's Union (London); 3,000 in the Scottish Transport and General Workers' Union (Glasgow); 9,000 in the National Union of General and Municipal Workers (N.E. Coast); and 1,000 in the Cardiff, Penarth and Barry Coal Trimmers' Union. In 1954 the Transport and General Workers' Union had about 83,000 dock members and until then the distribution of dockers amongst the other unions remained roughly the same. About three-quarters of the dock membership of the Transport and General Workers' Union are registered dockers employed on a half-daily basis and it is with the activities of these that this and the following chapter are concerned. The remaining quarter are mainly maintenance workers.

before him had stated the need for a form of guaranteed employment on the docks, but in the main they had been independent persons unsupported by organized labour.[1] Bevin's support meant the pressure of a Union. In speeches, discussions, and negotiations he condemned the situation where a pool of labour was required in each port which was large enough to meet peak demands; where labour was employed by the day and had to be in continual attendance for work even though no work might be available, and to be ready to answer any call made by the employers without warning; and where employers were not liable for any payment to the men during periods of unemployment.

The only progress which was made before 1940 was through the establishment of registration schemes, 'the initial objects of which were to regulate the pool of workers who, while adequate in number and qualifications to meet all likely demands, could have a preference . . . over general unemployed and thereby secure greater certainty of livelihood'.[2] The first scheme to be inaugurated was at Liverpool in 1912; then schemes were started at Bristol, Preston, and Southampton in 1916, at Newport in 1917, Manchester in 1919, and London in 1920. By 1931 more than two-thirds of all port transport workers in the country were directly covered by registration schemes.[3] The Maclean Committee which reported on Port Labour in 1931 was not able to reach agreement on measures 'which would by themselves constitute a solution of the problem of decasualization of labour'.[4] It did agree, however, that registration schemes were a vital means to the end in view and recommended the main administrative principles upon which they should be operated. In a separate memorandum Bevin and his union colleagues on the Committee emphasized the limitations of registration schemes and proposed the establishment of a 'comprehensive Scheme' which provided for 'a minimum weekly income, pensions, registration and distribution of employment under one statutory authority . . .'. The employers rejected the Scheme because, they stated, it 'would involve a rigid statutory system of registration and control applying to employers and workers alike, which would destroy the initiative and goodwill necessary for working the machinery created'.[5]

The difficulties which caused the impasse on the Maclean Committee continued to prevent agreement on the solution to decasualization. Then from the middle of 1938 the docks trade group of the Union began to exert concerted pressure on employers. A National Docks Delegate Conference on 17 June 1938 adjourned

[1] Cf. *The Dock Worker*, University of Liverpool (1954), pp. 1–11.
[2] Report of Port Labour Inquiry, 1931, Ministry of Labour, p. 13.
[3] Ibid, p. 16.
[4] Ibid., p. 61.
[5] Ibid., p. 68.

'to enable further negotiations to be carried forward on the question of Decasualization. . . . Consideration . . . to be given to the possibility of introducing forthwith, schemes of Decasualization in separate ports or groups of ports, pending completion of negotiations on the full question.' Under the threat of war the employers became more responsive and four days later the National Joint Council for Dock Labour agreed 'that both sides should communicate with their representatives in the ports, emphasizing the desirability of co-operation with a view to more progress being made in devising schemes of decasualization'.[1] But the obstacles were still too great to be overcome through negotiation and nothing more was done until after Bevin had become the Minister of Labour in the Coalition Government.

WAR-TIME SCHEMES

By this time Arthur Deakin, as the Acting General Secretary of the Union, was in a position to intervene in docks' negotiations at points of importance. Like Bevin he interested himself closely in the affairs of the docks trade group. Unlike Bevin he had no background of experience with dockers to draw him to improve their welfare in particular; his interest was partly handed down by Bevin, partly a realization of the significance of the behaviour of dockers on the Union, and partly a reaction to the deplorable conditions of employment on the docks. In the matter of decasualization of dock labour the Union had developed its own momentum with the motive force coming from the rank-and-file dockers. The quickening of the pace at the outbreak of war as concessions were being asked of the dockers by the Government, and the transference of Bevin to a position where he could influence the power of the Government in favour of statutory decasualization, meant that, in any case, Deakin would be involved in negotiating decasualization schemes.

The war-time need was to get the ports working at full capacity with a labour force which was less than that required to meet the peak demands. The first step was to arrange for the transference of dockers from port to port to satisfy needs arising from the diversion of port traffic. A suggestion was made late in 1938, presumably by the War Office, that a khaki battalion of dockers should be formed to perform emergency work, but the dockers rejected the suggestion. They agreed, however, to co-operate in forming a civilian scheme and on 6 October 1939 a Voluntary Docks Transfer Scheme was established. In June 1940 Bevin made it compulsory for all dockers to be available for transfer. It was a

[1] T. & G.W.U., G.E.C. Minutes, 6 July 1938.

logical and equitable step then to ensure that dockers under statutory
control should receive guarantees concerning their wages and conditions of work.   The next statutory regulation for dock workers
dealt with decasualization.

From Monday 10 March 1941 all registered dockers employed
on the North Western Approaches[1] became employees of the
Minister of War Transport on a guaranteed weekly basis, combined
where possible with payment by results.   The simplicity of this
statement belies the difficulties which Deakin and the employers
encountered before agreement was reached.   Then in May 1941 the
National Joint Council for Dock Labour was informed that the
Minister of Labour proposed to bring all dockers within the Essential Work Order and it was suggested that the industry should
draw up a special decasualization scheme.   The National Joint
Council subsequently reported to the Minister that agreement had
been reached on new conditions of employment for the dockers concerned, and that a company was to be established to finance and
administer port schemes which embodied the new conditions.   Thus
came into being the National Dock Labour Corporation Ltd.[2]

Briefly the new scheme was as follows.   In the ports not covered
by the Ministry of War Transport schemes, Local Boards equally
representative of unions and port employers were established by the
Corporation to be responsible for matters of local policy and administration and to co-operate with Regional Port Directors and
Port Emergency Committees in arranging a quick turn-round of
ships.   The Local Boards decided the number of workers to be put
on the register and whether they were to be classified as able-bodied
workers or workers who qualified for light work, according to the
provision of a national agreement drawn up in July 1941.   All men
on the register ceased to be casual workers and became permanently
employed.

The Local Boards, therefore, controlled the arrangements for
engaging labour.   Each registered dock worker in a port was
allocated to a port employer by the Port Labour Manager on behalf
of the Local Board and was paid the appropriate rate for the job.
As soon as he finished his job he automatically came into the employment of the Corporation.   Thus all men waiting for work were
officially employed by the Corporation.   They were paid attendance
money for each half-day they were not working for port transport

[1] Liverpool, Birkenhead, Manchester, Preston, Garston, Bromborough, Ellesmere
Port, Partington, Widnes, Runcorn, and Western Point.   The dockers on the Clydeside were included later.
[2] It consisted of twenty-four members (with equal numbers nominated by the two
sides of the National Joint Council), who in turn appointed a Board of Directors
consisting of three trade union and three employer representatives.   The chairman
of the Board and a financial director were appointed by the Minister of Labour.

employers, up to a maximum of eleven half-days each week. It was a condition of the docker's employment that he should report regularly for work as required and be prepared to take any suitable work offered in his own or any other port. If he failed to comply with these conditions he either lost pay or was disciplined, which could mean suspension or dismissal from the scheme.[1] The men's wages were paid by the Port Labour Manager, who received each week from employers the amount of wages earned by the men allocated to them. The employers, too, had to register for port transport work and could be removed from the register for failing to comply with the conditions.[2] They had to inform the Port Labour Manager of their labour requirements and were allowed to employ only their own permanent workers or men allocated to them by the Port Labour Manager. The cost of the scheme was met from a National Management Fund maintained by the Corporation and financed by contributions from registered employers, which were not to exceed 25 per cent. of their gross wages bill.

The first local scheme was introduced in Bristol in December 1941. By February 1943 all except about 1,000 dockers scattered amongst the small ports were covered either by the Ministry of War Transport Schemes or the dock labour schemes established by the National Dock Labour Corporation. About 60 per cent. of the dock labour force was covered by the latter type of scheme.

The obstacles which had been insuperable in peace were overcome in war. The reason undoubtedly was to assist in the war effort. 'Every docker must know', Arthur Deakin wrote, 'of ships which he helped to load or discharge, but which are now lying at the bottom of the sea. The tonnage available to carry our increasing requirements of essential food supplies and munitions of war is getting less . . . it is therefore urgently necessary that we make the best possible use of every ship coming into port, securing the quickest possible turn-round and discharging or loading. . . .'[3] But one is equally sure that both Bevin and Deakin were fully aware of the social implications of their actions. For Bevin the National Dock Labour Corporation was the realization of an ambition; for Deakin it was the beginning of a social experiment. He wrote that the 'scheme in its present form may go on only for the duration of the war, but setting up as it does a form of workers' control, expressed through the trade union organizations acting jointly with representative

---

[1] In the case of dismissal, except where it resulted from serious misconduct, dockers were entitled to seven days' notice and were given the right of appeal to an Appeal Panel set up by the local Joint Committee which was part of the voluntary negotiating machinery responsible for determining wages and conditions of work.
[2] Employers had a right of appeal to the Minister of Labour.
[3] *The Record*, October 1941, p. 91.

employers, it may be regarded as a great experiment—the principle of which we may desire to retain . . .'.[1]

The Union pressed long before the end of the war to have the post-war fate of the decasualization schemes determined. The Union Dock Trade Group report for 1943 and 1944 stated:

> The dock labour schemes were introduced as a war-time measure, but the dockers are seriously concerned about what is to happen after the war. This problem has been the subject of serious consideration at the Centre, as the result of which we requested the Government to state its intentions. We have been informed that a decision has been taken by the Government to the effect that the dock industry must not revert to the pre-war casual conditions of employment. Negotiations are now proceeding in an endeavour to agree on one common scheme for the port industry under peace-time conditions.

The negotiations were not successful. No scheme for decasualization was formulated before the end of the war, much to the concern of the National Committee of the Dock Trade Group of the Union.[2] When the matter was discussed by the Executive in June 1945 Deakin stated that the principle of decasualization had been accepted and the

> indications were that an Enabling Bill would be introduced by the Government of the day which would provide for the continuance of the present Dock Labour Schemes until the end of the war and for a period of two years thereafter, the Ministry of War Transport Scheme being brought within the control of the National Dock Labour Corporation, Ltd., if necessary. Further, that in the event of failure on the part of the industry to produce a scheme through the appropriate machinery, within the period stated, provision would be made for the Ministry of Labour and National Service to prepare and apply a suitable scheme.[3]

That is what actually happened. The Dock Workers (Regulation of Employment) Act was implemented in February 1946 providing for the war-time schemes to continue up till 30 June 1947. The unions and the employers were given until 30 September 1946 to prepare a scheme of their own, failing which the Minister of Labour was to have a scheme prepared to operate from 1 July 1947. No scheme was to become effective unless it had been endorsed by the Minister and until it had been embodied in an Order and laid before Parliament.

DIFFICULTIES IN POST-WAR NEGOTIATIONS

In two important respects the post-war attempts of employers and trade union representatives to decasualize the dock industry

[1] Ibid.
[2] T. & G.W.U., G.E.C. Minutes, 8 June 1945.
[3] Ibid.

differed from any previous attempts.   Firstly, both sides were negotiating with the experience of the war-time schemes behind them.
The men and the port employers had had ample time to weigh up
the advantages in terms of security and efficiency against the irk-
someness of regulation and discipline which were inherent in any
centrally administered scheme or indeed, as far as the men were
concerned, in any scheme.   Their representatives in various capacities had had experience as administrators of schemes.[1]   Secondly,
they knew that whatever the result of their deliberations a decasualization scheme would be introduced.

It was in the interests of both sides to settle the outstanding points
of difference between them.   This they failed to do and on 23
August 1946 a joint letter from employers and trade unions was
addressed to the Minister of Labour informing him of the unsettled
issues.   Then Sir John Forster, K.C., was appointed by the Minister
to hold an inquiry into the proposals for the preparation of decasualization schemes.   His recommendations formed the basis of
the Scheme submitted by the Minister under the terms of the Dock
Workers (Regulation of Employment) Act, 1946.   Still outstanding
issues were examined in two further inquiries established by the
Minister.[2]   The result was The Dock Workers (Regulation of
Employment) Order, 1947, which laid down the form of decasualization in the post-war years.   Before proceeding to discuss the relevant
features of the Scheme it is necessary to describe the differences
that emerged during the initial negotiations.

Effective negotiations with the employers could not take place
until the dock workers had resolved their own differences.   There
were regional differences within the Transport and General Workers'
Union and differences between unions which, because of their local
character, were also in effect regional differences.   The dockers who
had been employed by the Ministry of War Transport under
separate schemes were not at first in favour of a national scheme.
The Transport and General Workers' Union held conferences of
delegates and officials in Liverpool and Manchester to explain the
nature of a proposed scheme and the value of its national scope.
Then they held meetings with representatives of the Executive of
the Scottish Transport and General Workers' Union, who at first
wanted to be treated separately.   Eventually all the provincial
dockers agreed on the principle of a national scheme.

[1] Arthur Deakin and the National Secretary of the Dock Trade Group had been on
the Board of Directors of the National Dock Labour Corporation.   Sir Robert
Letch, who was the Chairman of the National Association of Port Employers at the
time, had been the Port Regional Director at Liverpool; other employers had had
comparable experience.
[2] Conducted by Mr. John Cameron, K.C., and Sir Hector Hetherington, respectively.

The Workers' side of the National Joint Council for the Dock Industry then submitted the following proposals to the Employers' side of the Council:

SCOPE OF THE SCHEME. There shall be a permanent scheme of decasualization, which shall include: (*i*) All workers directly connected with the handling of cargo in or on ship, quay, warehouse or craft. . . .

LOCAL SCHEMES. There shall be local schemes for a port, or group of ports, details of which shall be determined locally within the framework of the national scheme. . . . The schemes shall be under the control of a body consisting of equal representatives of trade unions and employers, both nationally and locally. . . .

BASIS OF GUARANTEE. Each port transport worker under the scheme shall be entitled to an attendance payment for each half-day he is available for work, but in addition shall be entitled to a basic guarantee which shall be calculated by taking into consideration attendance payments and all earnings during normal working hours, Monday a.m. to Saturday noon.[1]

The employers' objections were levied particularly at the form of control and the basis of guarantee. These are examined below.[2]

(*i*) *Problem of Control.* In the first place the employers were averse to a national administration of decasualization and felt that it should be linked to the separate administrations of ports and confined to those ports which had a considerable volume of overseas and coastal trade, but which accounted for about 90 per cent. of all the dockers. This was contrary to the trade union suggestion of a nationally administered scheme covering the majority of the approximate number of 319 ports in Britain.[3]

Secondly, the employers wanted the port schemes to be financed and administered by the Port Authorities. This was an attack at the very heart of the problem. The Port Authority, the employers stated, 'gives the dock workers a good legal Employer and provides a satisfactory solution to the problem of disciplinary control'.[4] At no time did the employers envisage a decasualization scheme under joint trade union and employer control. In support of their contention they pointed to the effectiveness of the Ministry of War Transport schemes in ports which accounted for almost half of the trade in the country and which had been controlled, not jointly, but by Regional Port Directors. They stated that, in contrast,

---

[1] T. & G.W.U. Finance and General Purposes Committee minutes, 11 April 1946. For a full week without work the unions wanted a higher rate than the multiple of the number of half-days in a working week and the rate per half-day.

[2] The arguments of the trade unions and the employers have been drawn from the Minutes of Proceedings of the three Inquiries mentioned above.

[3] Estimated by J. Donovan, National Secretary of the Dock Trade Group of the T. & G.W.U., and principal spokesman for the unions at the Inquiries.

[4] Minutes of Proceedings of the Forster Inquiry, October 1946.

important and substantial differences existed between the two sides of the National Dock Labour Corporation, with the result that often no effective action was taken. They could not understand why port employers should be treated differently, in terms of the exercise of authority, from private enterprise or public utilities.

The Port Authorities varied in composition and constitution.[1] They had been established at various times dating from the 1840s and they undertook different functions. The common features were that they had no provision for trade union representation and that they represented, in the main, the interests of employers. Such bodies, the unions maintained, were entirely unsuitable for administering a social experiment under modern port transport conditions. To hand over to them the administration of decasualization would be tantamount to giving the employers unilateral control.

The unions were not prepared to enter any scheme administered solely by employers. They gave two main reasons in support of joint control. Their first related to the need to take decisions disliked by the men. 'We will take our responsibility equally with you', Donovan stated for the unions, 'and we will fight our men if they are not playing the game, but if you try to put trade union officers in a position that they are in an advisory position by your goodwill and consent and you take decisions which hurt our people and we have to stand the rap for that, we are not prepared to do it.'[2] Donovan spoke of the difficulty of cutting down the size of the register in any port. If this had to be done the dockers, undoubtedly, would raise objections and might possibly strike over it. The unions felt that their association with decisions of that kind would assist in their implementation. More than this, if there were joint control, Donovan stated, and 'the circumstances in a port were such as to justify a reduction in the register and we were satisfied, there would be a reduction in the register'.[3] Given the difficulty of handling dockers in any case, this point weighed heavily in the deliberations. Secondly, the unions submitted as evidence the Port Labour Inquiry Report of 1931, which, though referring mainly to registration schemes, stated: 'We find that there is general commendation of the system of registration when jointly administered by Committees representative of the port employers and the workpeople.'[4] If

[1] Those at Bristol and Preston were administered by the respective Local Government Authorities; in south Wales, Southampton, Plymouth, and Weymouth they were under railway control; at London and Liverpool they represented the interests of people and bodies with a direct concern in port transport, such as the Local Authorities, Wharfingers, owners of craft, and those payers of rates whose principal business was connected with vessels or goods; the remainder ranged from resembling public trusts such as at Manchester, to being controlled by private industry, as at Workington.
[2] Minutes of Proceedings of the Forster Inquiry, October 1946.
[3] Ibid.
[4] p. 17.

registration schemes could work effectively under joint control, why then not decasualization schemes?

The recommendations submitted by Sir John Forster included a provision for joint control but the employers remained opposed to it. So when a further Inquiry was held before Mr. John Cameron, K.C., to hear objections to the Minister of Labour's draft scheme, the matter was raised again. The employers proposed two amendments: First, that the Minister of Labour should determine the conditions on which members of the joint body should be appointed. Donovan replied that he was worried about the Minister's having so much control, whoever he might be. The competent industrial body for the industry should continue to be the National Joint Council.[1] Secondly, the employers proposed that the acceptance of majority decisions should be a condition of appointment to the National Dock Labour Board. If such were the case, trade union representatives on the Board would be bound by decisions even if they were in violent conflict with trade union principles. 'I am not prepared', Donovan said, 'to give such an undertaking for a thousand boards. I am prepared to give an undertaking to act honourably, and do the very best for the industry. . . .'[2] This amendment raised the cardinal issue in joint control but it was one which could not be pre-determined or determined *a priori*; it depended so much on industrial circumstances, on the types of men selected to serve on the Board, and on the responsibility of trade union demands and actions.

Neither of the employers' amendments was accepted and joint control was embodied in the scheme.[3] The Minister determined only the period for which each appointment should last and not the condition under which each appointment was made.

(*ii*) *The Basis of Guarantee*. A docker under pre-war conditions was paid only for work performed; he received no compensation for attending his work-place nor for travelling expenses incurred in getting there. When he was not required for work he signed on at the Labour Exchange to qualify for unemployment benefit. Under the Unemployment Insurance Acts a man qualified for benefit provided he had three days unemployment within six consecutive days, regardless of the amount of his earnings during his days of employment. Consequently in port transport the paradoxical

[1] Notes of Proceedings, 14 May 1947.
[2] Ibid.
[3] The final form of the relevant section of the scheme stated that 'The chairman, vice-chairman and other members of the Board shall be appointed by the Minister after consultation with the National Joint Council for the Port Transport Industry and of the members (other than the chairman and vice-chairman) eight shall be so appointed on the nomination or renomination of the said Council, four being appointed to represent dock employers and four to represent dock workers.' Dock Workers (Regulation of Employment) 1947, Order No. 1189, Clause 4 (3).

situation existed of some dockers being able to earn relatively high wages through intensive piece-work or excessive overtime and still obtain unemployment benefit.

State unemployment insurance, however, was not a satisfactory alternative to a guaranteed wage for a variety of reasons; the defects of casual employment remained untouched.[1] The war-time schemes gave dockers a guarantee of a reasonable weekly wage and, because it was based on half-daily attendances for work and not on earnings, compensated them for making themselves regularly available for work.

The employers had protested, without effect, against the form and amount of the war-time wage guarantee and when negotiations over a post-war scheme began this became one of the obstacles to agreement. The unions, naturally, wanted to retain the principle of the war-time schemes; the employers did not, and proposed instead that the guarantee should be a fixed sum per four weeks and that the total earnings of a docker, including piece-work and overtime, should be reckoned before the guarantee was met. They suggested a lunar monthly guarantee of £16, which was equivalent to 34 hours per week at the existing rate of wages. The disadvantage of the employers' proposal, as was pointed out at the Forster Inquiry, was that a docker could conceivably earn more than the £16 during the first three weeks of the month, yet he would have to be available for work for the remaining week even though there might be no work and the employers would pay him nothing; or his earnings could exceed £16 per month in spite of frequent days of unemployment spread throughout the month, during which the docker would be required to attend for work without any compensatory payment from his employers. At the Forster Inquiry the employers conceded a point to the unions and agreed to give a weekly lump sum guarantee subject to certain conditions. Sir John Forster, however, accepted the Union's proposal and recommended that dockers should be paid for each half-day they proved attendance at the docks but were given no work. So the employers, continuing their resistance, pressed the issue at a separate Inquiry under the chairmanship of Sir Hector Hetherington on 19 May 1947, but again without avail.

The employers and trade unions were separated on this issue by a different conception of purpose. To the employers the guarantee payment formed a part of an employment scheme which was necessary for port efficiency. They wanted a labour force which would adequately meet port requirements under conditions that were neither restrictive nor costly. At the same time they had no desire to obtain their labour on the terms of the pre-war casual labour

[1] Cf. the Port Labour Inquiry Report, 1931, pp. 45–61.

system. The trade unions, on the other hand, were primarily concerned about welfare. It was assumed, rightly or wrongly, that greater efficiency would follow if their conditions were satisfied. The guaranteed attendance payments were a protection against under-employment; they compensated dockers for the expense and trouble of attending work and they placed the charge of providing dockers with a reasonable wage, which they claimed as a right, squarely on the shoulders of the industry.

THE OBLIGATIONS OF THE NATIONAL DOCK LABOUR SCHEME

The Scheme as implemented by the Minister of Labour from the end of June 1947 contained the principles which had been advocated by the unions. Arthur Deakin, the National Dock Secretary, and the representatives of other unions involved were justifiably pleased with the result. It resembled the war-time schemes but this was not a detriment, for, as was stated earlier, they were Bevin's creation and he had thought on the problem of decasualization for many years. Deakin treated the Scheme in a large part as his own handiwork. Many factors, of course, contributed to its achievement: there was the presence of the Labour Government and of the politically powerful Bevin, of rank-and-file dockers who had known what decasualization of the dock industry meant, and of sympathetic port employers. Even so, peace-time decasualization could have been delayed, perhaps gone by default, had not the official pressure of the Union been constantly exerted to bring it about. Moreover, the issues over which the employers had protested had been vital in trade union eyes, and the trade union view had prevailed before independent persons.

Only over discipline were the unions dissatisfied. They would have preferred less definitive measures which did not stipulate how and when men should be disciplined, for they knew how easily dockers went on strike over such matters.[1] Whether or not there was substance in their objections is not easy to determine. One can list the disciplinary issues over which dockers have struck work, but one does not know if strikes would have been any less frequent if there had been no disciplinary measures, or even regulations. What is sure is that the dockers could have had no decasualization scheme without some regulations and penalties for breaches of regulations, and dockers were aware of this. Decasualization had its cost as well as its income aspect for dockers. This can best be illustrated by a description of the Scheme.

The overall administration of the National Dock Labour Scheme

[1] Notes of Proceedings of the Cameron Inquiry, 14 May 1947.

was in the control of a National Dock Labour Board and in each port it was administered by a Local Dock Labour Board. The Boards, both national and local, were under joint control. They regulated the recruitment and discharge of dock workers and effected their allocation to employers, who were also registered under the Scheme. The National Board laid down the labour requirements for each port twice yearly, but the actual size of each port register was determined by the Local Boards and depended upon port and local labour conditions. It was stipulated that the Local Boards should be delegated as many other functions as the National Board considered to be practicable in order to stimulate local interest in the successful administration of the Scheme.[1] The Scheme was to be uniformly applied in eighty-four ports where most of the dockers were employed; no flexibility was permitted to meet variations between ports in matters such as the number and types of port employers.

In the allocation of labour within ports, the Local Boards were required to 'use every endeavour to supply men accustomed to the employer and his operations and cargoes' or to arrange for employers to select their own workers.[2] Those who were not allocated to employers on any particular day formed the reserve pool of port labour and were considered to be in the employment of the Board; they were paid an attendance allowance on a half-daily basis, with a maximum of eleven such periods in a week.

It was the intention of the Scheme to provide dock workers with a security which was consistent with 'the full and proper utilization of dock labour for the purpose of facilitating the rapid and economic turnround of vessels and the speedy transit of goods through the port'.[3] This could only be fulfilled by providing dockers with continuity of employment in the sense that they always had work to do. The payment of a guaranteed wage by a constant legal employer, for which the Scheme provided, was a necessary provision, but if the ports were to run efficiently it could be no more than a buffer in the last resort. Given a fluctuating demand for labour between ports and between employers within ports, the effectiveness of the Scheme depended upon its provisions for regulating the supply and distribution of dock labour. As the supply of dock labour could not be treated as a short-term variable without militating against the purpose of the Scheme, the economic success of the Scheme depended on the mobility of dock labour. Thus, regulations concerning the distribution of labour were written into the statutory order. It was made an obligation for every registered docker under

1 Dock Workers (Regulation of Employment) 1947, Order No. 1189, p. 4.
2 Ibid., pp. 6–7.
5 Ibid., p. 3.

the Scheme to 'report at such call stands or control points and at such times as required but subject to any agreement come to with the appropriate joint industrial organization'; to 'accept any employment in connection with dock work, or any other work agreed by the local board for which he is considered by the local board to be suitable . . .'. He was required to 'travel to any other port or place within daily travelling distance of his home as required by the local board' and, in the sentence which achieved notoriety in 1954, to 'work for such periods as are reasonable in his particular case'.[1] Failure to meet these obligations was penalized by measures which ranged from 'disentitlement to payment' to 'termination of employment' and in order to provide a means of redressing grievances an appeals procedure was instituted.

In 1947, when the Decasualization Scheme was presented to the dock members of the Transport and General Workers' Union through their branches and through Dock Delegate Conferences, the regulation of dock work in one form or another had existed for longer than many dockers could remember. From the inception of Registration Schemes dockers had had to undergo restrictions as a condition of registration. The Port Labour Inquiry Report of 1931 stated that 'the rules of most schemes give power to the Joint Committees to take disciplinary action on ordinary breaches of the rules, while in many cases this power covers all forms of misdemeanour, such as pilferage, misconduct, and breaches of working rules, etc.'[2] Occasionally the dockers protested by striking against the application of regulations, as they did at Middlesbrough in 1925, or against the penalties imposed for infringement of regulations, as at Salford in 1934.[3] Such strong protests, however, were relatively uncommon, for dockers in the main knew the value of the regulations they were required to obey.

Then during the Second World War dock work regulations became much more stringent to satisfy the conditions of the Essential Work Order and to enable the decasualization schemes to operate. These were not accepted so readily by the men. During the period of the war-time decasualization schemes there were thirty-three dock strikes recorded by the Ministry of Labour. Many of these were in protest against the exercise of regulations, some of which, such as the method of allocating labour in a port, the transfer of labour between ports, and the powers of a Port Labour Inspector, were obviously products of the war-time schemes. The strike of 10,770 dockers in London and Tilbury for a week from 1 March

[1] Ibid., pp. 7–8.
[2] p. 31.
[3] 900 men struck work for two days at Middlesbrough, 11–12 February 1925; at Salford 1,800 men were on strike from 21 to 24 November 1934.

1945 'originated in the men's feelings of resentment against the alleged harsh exercise of discipline under the Port of London Dock Labour Scheme'.[1]   The Committee of Inquiry which investigated the strike concluded in its report 'that the experience of working the Scheme for the past three years in London shows that there is need to review some of the disciplinary and other related arrangements . . .'.[2] This strike indicated that the war-time schemes in certain instances might have been operating at the margin of the men's tolerance; that the cost of decasualization to dockers in terms of liberty of action could outweigh the social and economic advantages. The dockers knew through practical experience what sort of obligations decasualization involved when they accepted the National Dock Labour Scheme in 1947.

[1] London Dock Dispute, March 1945, Report of Committee of Inquiry, H.M.S.O., p. 4.
[2] Ibid., p. 7.

Chapter Twelve

DOCKWORKERS IN THE UNION
(2) UNION LEADERSHIP IN THE DOCKS

ALONG with decasualization, dock workers achieved a substantial increase in their relative earnings during and shortly after the war. Though their basic wage rate compared favourably with that of workers in many other industries before 1940, their earnings were relatively low.[1]   Then, through higher basic rates, better piece-rates, less under-employment, and more overtime, their earnings rose, absolutely and relatively.   The average weekly earnings of dockers for the last three months of 1942 were 12·2 per cent. higher than the national average weekly earnings for all adult males.   By 1943 this figure had increased to 22·0 per cent. and by 1944 to 33·3 per cent. Thereafter it varied around 19 per cent. until 1952 when, due to under-employment, it fell to 3 per cent.   The average weekly earnings of dockers recovered in 1953 and 1954 when they were 13·4 and 14·4 per cent. higher than the national average.[2]

In their enhanced social and economic state and from a powerful bargaining position the dockers engaged after the war in strike action on an unprecedented scale.   Their strikes, in every case, were in defiance of trade union advice; they were in contravention of agreements and negotiating procedures, and they stood in marked contrast to the conciliatory attitude of the trade union movement during this period of national economic crises.   This is not the reaction one would expect of a group when its main grievances are removed.

An examination of the dockers' behaviour and some of the problems it created for the General Secretary of the Transport and General Workers' Union is the subject of this chapter.   But first it is necessary to examine the allocation of responsibility within the Union for dockers' affairs, so that Deakin's own role can be seen more clearly.

[1] Cf. *The Dock Worker*, University of Liverpool, pp. 146–147.
[2] Calculated from estimates of earnings in the *Ministry of Labour Gazette*, April 1947 and March 1955.   The dockers' figures are average weekly earnings for the months October to December in each year.   The average weekly earnings for all adult males apply to the last pay week in January in the year following, up till 1946, then to the last pay week in October of the same year.   Because of the casual nature of dock labour it is justifiable to compare a three-monthly average with a single week's earnings in other and more stable industries.

RESPONSIBILITY IN THE UNION FOR DOCKS' AFFAIRS

Since 1920 matters of principle and material factors such as basic wage rates which applied to all ports have been determined at national level by the National Joint Council for the industry. But the scope of national determination has been limited because of the wide local variations in the industry. It was reckoned in 1952 that probably more than 80 per cent. of all daily dock workers were paid piece-rates which were determined between employers' and dockers' representatives in each particular port.[1] Local negotiations were retained because of the wide disparity in docking facilities, in the mechanization of similar processes, and in the cargoes handled, between one port and another and even between one employer and another. The ships themselves lacked uniformity.[2] It follows that there was also a disparity between speeds of stowing and discharging cargo. Overtime and compulsory trade unionism has in every case been decided on a local basis.[3] There has, then, been a diffusion of responsibility throughout the Union for negotiating wages and working conditions, and lay members as well as full-time officials have helped to carry it.

A characteristic of trade unionism on the docks is the relatively high proportion of full-time officials in relation to lay members. In 1951 in the Transport and General Workers' Union there were ninety full-time officials dealing with a registered dock membership of about 65,000.[4] The proportion varied between ports; for instance in London fifteen officials catered for 17,000 dockers, whereas in Liverpool there were twenty-one officials for about 15,000 dockers.[5] Most of these officials were full-time dock delegates who were available to deal with the many disputes which arose concerning piece-rates, size of gangs, overtime, and the like. 'Rarely does a ship enter or leave my port', a member from Bristol said, 'without some matter arising which calls for a ruling by the Docks Officers, or joint consideration. . . .'[6] The same could be said of other ports. The settlement of the varied and wide range of problems which were caused by the different occupations, cargoes, and construction of

---

[1] 'Dockworkers' Earnings', by K. G. J. C. Knowles and Ann Romanis, *Bulletin of the Oxford University Institute of Statistics*, September and October 1952, p. 334.

[2] Cf. *Working Party Report on the Turn-round of Shipping in the United Kingdom Ports*, H.M.S.O., 1948, p. 9.

[3] When the subject of overtime was discussed at the Cameron Inquiry in 1947 the unions objected to having it included in the National Dock Labour Scheme because they preferred it to be arranged by local agreements.

[4] The other 20,000 members of the Docks Group were also served by the 90 officials but they were assisted by 34 additional officials who undertook dock work along with other jobs.

[5] These figures are not strictly comparable, for in London there are full-time branch secretaries who are not included in this figure, whereas in Liverpool there are no such people.

[6] T. &. G.W.U., B.D.C., 1951.

vessels demanded the services of men with specialist knowledge; and the need for speed of settlement to enable vessels to work to schedules demanded men on the spot—hence so many full-time officials. When a dispute has occurred the practice has been for it to be referred to a full-time official who has taken the matter up with the employer; failing a settlement it has been referred to the local joint conciliation machinery and only when all local procedures have been used has the matter been submitted to the National Joint Council. Much patience and trouble have been used to effect settlements at local level.[1]

Arthur Deakin's responsibility in the handling of the docks membership was a broad administrative one except over issues which had become of vital national importance. Like the head of any other organization the efficiency of his subordinate officials was his concern, but it was equally his concern to see that they were given scope to tackle their problems in the best way possible without continual or frequent interference from the head office. This was not always appreciated by the members. When disputes arose they wanted to see their General Secretary on the spot and he was criticized for his non-attendance. But not only was it physically impossible for him to be on call to the dockers because of his many other commitments, it was also undesirable, for it could have undermined the morale of the local officials. What Deakin did was to offer to the local officials all the assistance they required whenever a dispute flared up. He intervened primarily at the request of the constitutional docks committees and through the internal committees of inquiry which were established to investigate the causes of unofficial action on the docks.

In the face of the customary spate of criticisms levelled against the Union during strikes, Deakin gave his officials his ardent support, which was a natural and reasonable thing to do. His loyalty towards them, always strong, hardened considerably on these occasions.[2] It may have happened that this loyalty sometimes prejudiced his interpretation of the case of the members in dispute; that is, he may have accepted the version of officials too readily and without seeking to corroborate their statements. But it was

---

[1] Pages 35–37 of Cmd. 8236, *Report of a Committee of Inquiry into Unofficial Stoppages in the London Docks*, May 1951 (Leggett Report), give a good example of the use of local procedures.

[2] He mentioned that sometimes the dockers refused to give the officials a hearing. 'They shout them down', he said; 'immediately there is a stoppage they regard the officers as being their deadly enemies because they have the responsibility . . . to get them back to work. I defend our officers. We are entitled to a square deal. We are not going on to wasteland or any bombed site to be jeered at, spat at and physically threatened. We don't mind; I don't care a damn, I will go anywhere with anybody, but it doesn't do us a bit of good; unless you can get reasoned consideration of those factors which are material to a situation of this character, you can't do anything. . . .' (T. & G.W.U., B.D.C., 1951.)

important that he should accept the evidence of his officials, for once it became public that one or other of his officials was untrustworthy it would cast doubt on the integrity of others. It was unreasonable to accuse Deakin of 'dictatorial intolerance of criticism'[1] in view of his responsibility to preserve the unity of his organization. He undoubtedly disliked criticism from outside quarters, but his was not an unusual attitude. Many specialists have reacted in much the same way when outsiders have attempted to tell them how best to do their work.

THE DOCKERS' USE OF THE STRIKE WEAPON

Whenever the dockers went on strike both during and after the war they did so in disregard of the established procedures for settling disputes and for negotiating claims; and by creating *ad hoc* port workers' committees they flouted their Union constitution. Either they failed to submit their grievances for settlement through the established machinery, or they grew impatient with its operation, or they rejected its findings.[2] There was an element of spontaneity in their actions which was incompatible with the use of voluntary negotiating machinery. As has been stated before, constitutional machinery must be used fully by both sides and its findings must be honoured if it is to be effective; and because the basis of the machinery is compromise it sometimes entails accepting findings which are unfavourable. Spontaneous docks disputes have appeared as intra-Union disputes because Union officials have honoured their obligations under the agreements they have signed.

One can submit several reasons for the dockers' preference for strike action, though, as will become clear, the state of knowledge about the causes of strikes is very incomplete. A meaningful answer to the simple question 'Why do workers strike?' cannot yet be given. Most explanations have been the product of deductive reasoning, but of all things dockers have not been logical in their actions, with the result that the explanations have often gone awry. The problem that this raised for the Union can easily be seen. A planned policy necessarily had to be based on certain assumptions about the behaviour of dockers. If, due to erratic behaviour, the assumptions were invalid from one dispute to another, then there could be no constant policy. Indeed, such has been the unpredictable behaviour of dockers that by the time it became known what action the Union ought to take, it was often too late to take it and the event has had to drag out its weary course.

[1] Cf. *New Statesman and Nation*, 23 October 1954.
[2] Cf. Cmd. 8236, op. cit., p. 6.

(*i*) *The Casual Tradition.*   It has been said that 'the persistence of the casual tradition' has in part contributed to the tendency of dockers to practise opportunism.[1]   For this to be wholly valid there has to be a causal relationship between casual work and the inclination to strike.   Dockers were casual workers who were strike-prone. But this fact alone does not establish the required correlation. Building trade workers, also in casual employment, have not engaged in strike action on anything like the same scale as dockers. Moreover, if casual employment were the dominant cause of strike action then its removal should have resulted in there being fewer strikes.   An examination of strike statistics shows that the reverse has taken place.

Over a period of twenty years from December 1918 till December 1939 there were fifty-eight dock strikes, of which only three involved more than 5,000 workers; two of the three and eleven much smaller strikes lasted for a week or longer.   Only two strikes, in 1923 and 1924, were national ones[2]; most of the remainder were confined to single ports.   A different statistical picture is revealed after the introduction of decasualization schemes.   From July 1941 until July 1955, a period of fourteen years, sixty-four strikes occurred. Few during the war were of any moment: the majority were snap strikes involving relatively small groups of dockers.   The national strike which occurred in September 1945 and lasted for nearly six weeks was the first of its kind since 1924.   After that, large strikes became the rule rather than the exception.   Sixteen strikes, including the September 1945 one, each involved more than 9,000 dockers, and eleven of these lasted for periods ranging from nine to forty-one days. These figures give no comfort to those who are looking for easy explanations, for the improvement in the dockers' social position should have reduced strike action.   But although decasualization eliminated one source of friction it, or post-war conditions, may have introduced others.

(*ii*) *Impatience with Formality.*   Though the connection between casual labour and strike action is dubious, there might be some relationship between impatience with the constitutional settlement of disputes, which dockers have displayed,[3] and the state of mind which casual employment creates.   Dockers were not normally subjected to industrial discipline for longer than it took to unload or load a ship; their security of employment in any case was measured by the day.   So dockers grew accustomed to frequent movements

---

[1] Ibid.

[2] Excluding the General Strike, 1926.

[3] Space does not permit a description of the somewhat intolerant and perplexing use of negotiating procedures by dockers.

from one completed task to another. Even security of employment had its irksome side to men whose habits and even mode of living were geared to insecurity.[1] How wearisome and unreasonable it must have seemed to dockers when they were required to submit their disputes to a treatment which was sometimes protracted over weeks or months.

This apart, there was a material reason for dockers' wanting a quick settlement of their own separate problems. In the words of the Leggett Committee Report: 'it must also be remembered that many dock workers are liable as soon as a job is finished to find themselves working for another employer, perhaps in a different part of the docks, and men in this position often feel that negotiations while they are still doing the job in question are likely to be more satisfactory from their point of view than negotiations after the job is finished'.[2] In this, dockers were encouraged by the attitude of some employers who often agreed to rates to suit their own individual circumstances, regardless of the effects on industry generally, and thus tending to weaken the authority of the negotiating machinery and making it difficult to resist unreasonable demands at other times.[3] 'When for various reasons', the Leggett Report states, 'there is individualistic action among employers, it is to be expected that there will be opportunist action by workers.' But, whatever the reasons for the dockers' impatience with the formal treatment of their industrial grievances, it does seem that their attitude was marked by a lack of understanding of the need for negotiating procedures and often of the issues involved.

(*iii*) *The Absence of Understanding about Procedures or Issues.* This absence of understanding may have resulted from ignorance which could have been removed by more effective Union communications; from an inability to understand, though this is unlikely; or from an unwillingness to understand. The Leggett Committee, when commenting about the unofficial leaders of strikes, stated: 'It is our belief that those who direct the activities of the unofficial group have no interest whatever in strengthening and reforming the organization of their respective Unions. Indeed, many of them do not appear to have taken the trouble to inform themselves about the constitutional working of the Unions . . .'.[4] These strictures did not apply to all unofficial strike leaders.

In the case of the ordinary dockers it is likely that avoidable

---

[1] This phenomenon was by no means confined to dockers. I experienced it personally and saw it reflected in the behaviour of many workers whilst working for a number of years as a casual worker in the building industry.
[2] Op. cit., p. 6.
[3] Ibid.
[4] Ibid., p. 10.

ignorance caused misunderstanding.   When the research group from Liverpool University interviewed dockers in Manchester who were on strike for six weeks in 1951 against the suspension of two men who refused to work overtime, they found 'that the majority of them did not understand the complexities of the Scheme, and were unfamiliar with the negotiating machinery of the industry'.[1]   Yet, Arthur Deakin remarked on another occasion, 'every registered port worker under the scheme has been given a copy of the scheme at the time of registration which sets out the obligations of the individual and the procedure in disciplinary cases is well known'.[2]   In the case of the Manchester strike it was the lack of information about the proceedings of the negotiating machinery and not the procedure which caused much trouble: an agreement had been negotiated which had not been sufficiently and promptly explained to the members.

> It is true [the Leggett Committee reported] that information about Union affairs is supplied to the Branch membership in reports from delegates to higher bodies, by circulation of minutes of the meetings of Branches and other committees, by the issue of leaflets during times of crises and by the Union's journal, *The Record*.   In our view, however, this publicity has tended to be deficient in quantity and quality, and has not been presented in a way calculated to catch the interest of the average member.[3]

The national strike over 'compulsory overtime' in October 1954 was the product of a number of factors, but its central issue provides an example of misunderstanding and misrepresentation which could possibly have been avoided.   The strike had been called by the National Amalgamated Stevedores and Dockers in opposition to 'compulsory overtime' in London and was supported by about 32,000 members of the Transport and General Workers' Union from various parts of the country.   The misunderstanding and misrepresentation occurred over the position of the latter Union.   It opposed the strike because it was contrary to its agreement with employers and not because it agreed with compulsory overtime; yet its opposition to the strike created the impression that it was not in sympathy with the members who were striking and that the smaller union was the champion of the dockers' cause.   A widely publicized recapitulation of the attitude the Union had adopted when the issue of overtime had been raised might have helped to clear away this misrepresentation.

None of the unions concerned with dock workers had ever

[1] *The Dock Worker*, p. 209.
[2] *Court of Inquiry into a Dispute in the London Docks*, 21 October 1954, Minutes of Proceedings.
[3] Op. cit., p. 27.

maintained that overtime should not be worked: such was the nature of the industry that overtime was unavoidable. When the employers submitted their proposals for decasualization in 1946 they contained a stipulation that dockers should 'work . . . such overtime and additional turns (including weekends from Saturday noon to Monday morning and statutory and proclaimed holidays) as the legal employer may prescribe as being reasonable and necessary'.[1] The unions, however, wanted no reference to overtime at all in the Scheme. Arthur Deakin went so far as to say that it was over the issue of overtime that the initial post-war negotiations for a decasualization scheme had broken down.[2] A midway position was adopted in the Minister's draft scheme and a worker was 'required to work for such periods as are reasonable in his particular case'. At the Cameron Inquiry in May 1947 the employers asked for the deletion of this clause and for its substitution by a clause which specifically mentioned overtime. Again Donovan, the Union representative, objected and emphasized that the unions wanted no reference to overtime in the Scheme. He said an important point of principle was involved. As a condition of becoming a decasualized docker should a man, he asked, have to give up his right to use his leisure time as he pleased? When Mr. Cameron asked the general secretary of the National Amalgamated Stevedores and Dockers whether he wanted to say anything on this matter he replied simply that he agreed with all that Donovan had said. The clause from the draft scheme remained unchanged.

It gave rise to much contention, and on various joint committees over a number of years representatives of the Transport and General Workers' Union insisted that overtime was in principle voluntary and not compulsory.[3] Why was the clause accepted at all? For the unions it was preferable to specifically mentioned compulsory overtime and for the employers an implicit mention of overtime was preferable to complete omission. The unions realized that in order to get an agreed and workable Scheme they would have to make concessions. The clause was one concession. A Union committee reported: 'it is to be noted that under the Dock Labour Scheme reasonable overtime working is obligatory and part of a port worker's conditions of employment, this as a *quid pro quo* for the advantages and benefits conferred by the Scheme . . .'[4] These were points of substance which might have assisted in clearing up misunderstandings by the ordinary dockers.

1 *Minutes of Proceedings of the Forster Inquiry*, op. cit.
2 *Court of Inquiry into a Dispute in the London Docks*, 21 October 1954.
3 See Cmd. 9310. *Final Report of a Court of Inquiry into a Dispute in the London Docks*, pp. 8–12.
4 Internal inquiry into the Manchester dispute of 25 April–6 June 1951.

Furthermore the possible consequences of the strike were never really made plain to the provincial dockers who were striking in sympathy with those from London. Overtime was governed by local agreements, and if the contentious clause had been specifically defined for the benefit of the London dockers the definition would have applied to provincial dockers too, and might have upset arrangements to which they had not objected.[1] As the *Manchester Guardian* reported: 'A new agreement . . . could . . . mean that many of Mr. Deakin's members would be worse off than they are at present. In many ports Mr. Deakin's men enjoy advantages in the matter of overtime which they would not like to lose, or risk losing, as a result of fresh negotiations. . . .'[2] In December 1954 when the Union was losing members to the National Amalgamated Stevedores and Dockers, arrangements were made to communicate regularly with the dockers at their homes so that the Union's position could be more fully explained.

(*iv*) *A Reaction Against Restraint.* Some dockers may have felt needlessly constrained by negotiating procedures because they acted as a brake on the power that the dockers had accumulated from the post-war economic conditions. If this was believed, it was a misconception. Whatever power the dockers possessed as an organized labour force over and above what they had possessed before the war, was exercised around the negotiating table and was reflected in their enhanced economic and social position in society. Perhaps it was not the negotiating procedures alone with which the dockers were impatient, but the constitutional treatment of moderate claims, as stipulated by Union policy, at a time when their industry was flourishing, when prices were rising for most of the time, and when employers, in consequence of this and the dockers' increased organized power, were willing to make concessions.

An examination of the recorded causes of dock strikes since the end of the war reveals that wage grievances were a relatively insignificant cause. The first strike after the surrender of Japan on 15 August 1945 was a national one in the autumn of 1945, ostensibly for a wage increase, and long before the Union's declaration of a wage restraint policy.[3] A small one-day strike occurred in London in February 1946 over the retrospective payment of a wage increase. Twenty-six thousand dockers from London, Manchester, the Clydeside and the Merseyside struck work for twenty-six days in February

[1] Manchester dockers were an exception. They had strongly objected to their agreement in 1951.
[2] *Manchester Guardian*, 30 October 1954.
[3] The strike was in support of a Dockers' Charter, the essence of which was contained in demands already made by the Union to the employers. This was a strike which defies analysis; an excellent example of the inscrutability of dockers' behaviour.

1951 over, it is said, their dissatisfaction with a recent national wages award, but it was linked somehow with a protest against the arrest and prosecution of seven dockers accused of conspiracy and inciting dockers to join an illegal strike. Three other strikes had some connection with local piece-rates. But there were thirty-seven strikes altogether between 15 August 1945 and 1 May 1955.

(*v*) *Solidarity or Fear.* Two related factors of considerable but immeasurable importance in all dock strikes have been the tradition of solidarity which dockers have developed and their fear of being ostracized by their mates, both at work and in their social lives, for blacklegging. It is not easy to distinguish between the two. The solidarity in terms of responses to strike calls may have been real in that the majority acted freely and consciously in support of each other, or it may have been in part false and based on the fear of moral oppression. It is doubtful whether a cause and effect relationship could ever be established between the two factors.

It is true, however, that a degree of solidarity exists amongst dockers which far exceeds that found amongst most other industrial groups. The Leggett Report stated:

> It appears to be incredibly easy to bring dock workers out on strike. We were given repeated instances of men stopping work almost automatically, with little or no idea why they were stopping. In the words of one witness, himself a dock worker, 'All that was needed was for a man to go round the docks shouting "All out" and waving the men off the ships, and out they would come.' Many dock workers, themselves firm supporters of constitutional methods and resolutely opposed to the activities of unofficial elements, told us frankly that it was too much to expect of the average dock worker that he should remain at work when his mates were out, irrespective of his opinion of the merits of the dispute. He was quite likely to join a strike without even inquiring about the reasons for it.[1]

Such an instance occurred at Liverpool during a national strike in October 1954. The *Manchester Guardian* reported that

> the thoughtful docker can hardly have been cheered by one revealing statement from one platform speaker, Mr. Ted Lawless, at the daily show of solidarity on the Lord Street bombed site. 'The lads in No. 7 and 8 controls are now complete', he said, which was taken to mean all on strike, 'and they want a full report from me about what they're really out on strike for.' He said he would tell them. No one seems to think it an odd request on the strike's fourth day.[2]

Arthur Deakin thought that dockers had been moved 'to take strike action against their better judgment, often by reason of a fear

1 Op. cit., p. 7.
2 *Manchester Guardian*, 22 October 1954.

complex that they would be classified as scabs'.[1] The Leggett Committee took a similar view.[2] The strikes in 1949 called in support of the Communist-dominated Canadian Seamen's Union provided them with ample illustrations.[3] In March 1949, during a dispute between the Canadian Seamen's Union and the East Coast Canadian Shipowners over wages and conditions, the union ordered a 'sit-in' strike. The men were ordered out by a Court order obtained by the employers, who proceeded to man their vessels with members of a rival union called the Seafarers' International Union. From then onwards the dispute was an inter-union one and formed part of a campaign in Canada to reduce the power of Communist-controlled unions, though the Canadian Seamen's Union persisted that they were only in dispute with the East Coast Shipowners. The dispute moved to Britain when members of the Canadian Seamen's Union in vessels belonging to the East Coast Shipowners went on strike in British ports and requested dockers not to handle the cargoes of their ships or of the Canadian ships from the East Coast manned by members of the Seafarers' International Union, on the ground that the ships were 'black'. At different times between 16 May 1949 and 23 July 1949 a total of almost 28,000 dockers from Avonmouth, Bristol, Portishead, Liverpool, and London refused to handle cargoes from ships which had been declared 'black' by the Canadian Seamen's Union. The dispute was not at any time about the wages and conditions of British dockers.

It may have been that some dockers responded to these particular strike calls because they believed in international solidarity. But the International Transport Workers' Federation had stated that after 'careful consideration of the matter it was unanimously decided that there was no occasion for unions abroad to interfere in the dispute . . .'.[4] And Canadian dockers had ceased to take sympathetic action before the British strikes occurred. It seems more likely, as the following examples show, that the solidarity of British dockers was exploited to assist with organized industrial disruption.

A ship called the *Ivor Rita* from the Canadian East Coast but with a crew under British articles arrived in London on 2 April and was due to have its cargo discharged, when Canadian Seamen's Union strikers 'stigmatised the crew' as 'scabs' and 'blacklegs' and in consequence London stevedores refused to handle her cargo.[5] On 1 May a Seafarers' International Union crew which had been flown over to take a ship back to Canada was denounced in similar terms, so the lockgatemen and tugboatmen refused to handle the ship and the

<hr />

[1] Ibid., 29 November 1954.
[2] Op. cit., p. 7.
[3] For a full description of the strikes see Cmd. 7851, H.M.S.O., December 1949.
[4] Cmd. 7851, p. 7.
[5] Ibid., p. 8.

whole of the dockers in Avonmouth, where the ship was, went on strike for a day. A curious case occurred at Liverpool on 27 May. A British ship was having part of its cargo discharged at Avonmouth when the dockers there went on strike. Rather than wait for the strike to end the owners of the ship moved it to Liverpool where the rest of the cargo was scheduled to be discharged. While on passage the crew moved fifteen tons of the Avonmouth cargo to enable the Liverpool cargo to be handled without obstruction. The Liverpool dockers refused to unload the vessel. 'The reason for refusal is not clear, but has been given as being on the grounds that the Avonmouth part of the cargo should not have been moved by the seamen, and also that as Avonmouth dockers had refused to touch her, Liverpool dockers would be "blacklegging" if they unloaded her.'[1] At Southampton the deck chains on a strike-bound ship which should have been removed by seamen were removed by an outside contractor. Dockers refused to unload the ship because the chains had been removed by blackleg labour. And so one could go on. Throughout the period intensive propaganda was conducted so that the dockers could not forget the moral consequences of blacklegging.

(*vi*) *The Spreading of Strikes*. The exploitation of the loyalty of dockers was a post-war phenomenon which gave dock strikes an enigmatic quality. Dockers have always been noted for their solidarity, but it had rarely before been expressed so illogically and on such a widespread scale. The strikes before the war were in the main confined to single ports or sections of ports where the troubles lay. This was not so afterwards. The phenomenon is stranger because there has always existed a parochial attitude amongst dockers in each separate port. They have been proud of their separate achievements and intent on retaining them. Moreover, there have been undercurrents of hostility between dockers in various ports so that a strike call has not had an automatic response.[2]

Whenever a strike occurred in a port in the post-war period the ephemeral or semi-permanent unofficial port workers' committee which organized it would despatch envoys to other ports to appeal for support. The envoys became accomplished in the art of strike spreading and rarely failed to secure an extension of the strike. Unofficial inter-port communications during disputes became an accepted procedure, and dockers would wait in anticipation of a call

[1] Ibid., p. 13.
[2] Cf. *The Dock Worker*, op. cit., p. 208, for an illustration of the hostility between Manchester and Liverpool dockers; and on page 228 for a similar instance involving Liverpool and Birkenhead dockers. In 1945, 360 Liverpool dockers who had been directed to work at Birkenhead wanted to return to Liverpool so as not to become involved in a Birkenhead dispute.

to strike whenever they heard that men in another port were striking, or even contemplating strike action.

Strike-spreading created a twofold difficulty for the officials of the Transport and General Workers' Union. First, there was the problem of keeping pace with the envoys. Where a strike was localized presumptuous action by the officials of the Union might have precipitated its extension. Even the mention of strike action can start dockers thinking of the issue, of solidarity and of black-legging. So it was often necessary for local officials of the Union to act as if a strike in another port was not their business rather than to exhort their members not to support it. This left the initiative in the hands of the unofficial strike leaders. Speed of action then became important for the Union. Once it became known that unofficial representatives were intent on securing widespread sympathetic action, national Union officials had to try to get to the ports first. Emissaries had to be countered by emissaries.

Secondly, when in the ports what were the national officials to do? In the first place they were advised by local Union officials, for these were in a position to know the facts of the situation and the temper of the men. Were they to hold their own meetings in an endeavour to dissuade the men from striking and thereby compete for attendances with unofficial strike leaders? Or were they to compete more directly with the unofficial leaders and attend the same or closely related meetings? All kinds of difficulties were associated with both methods that were frequently not recognized by those who were waiting impatiently for the Union machine to be geared into action.

It was quite possible that unofficial meetings would be timed to coincide with official Union meetings, so that the Union officials would not necessarily be addressing the members who were con-templating strike action. Or the Union meetings would be packed by men intent on striking, to prevent the officials stating their case. This was a frequent occurrence.[1] Where should the meeting be held? In a hall, usually unfortunately situated away from the docks, or in the open air? Dockers prefer open-air meetings, for these are associated with tension and excitement. But it is difficult to regulate admission to open-air meetings to those who belong to the Union and who are involved in the dispute; particularly is this so where more than one union caters for dockers. On the whole, properly constituted Union meetings held whilst the initial struggle for the allegiance of dockers has been going on have not been successful.

---

[1] A mass meeting in Victoria Park, London, called by the Union to end the 'Zinc Oxide' strike in 1948, broke up in confusion without having heard the officials. Similarly at Newport in May 1949 the Union held a mass meeting to consider the situation but the meeting was so unruly that the official could not make himself heard. (Cf. Cmd. 7851, *Review of the British Docks Strikes* 1949, p. 10.)

They have been held and have produced resolutions against unofficial action or for a return to work which have had little or no effect. More success has been achieved by some well-timed mass-meetings on or near the docks: a factor which lends support to the opinion that prompt tactical Union action could have contained some strikes.[1]

The alternative method of taking part in meetings organized by the unofficial committees has been frowned upon by the constitutional dock committees, for it conceded recognition to the unofficial bodies. It is difficult to assess the advantages or disadvantages to the Union cause of the Union national officials' associating at meetings with unofficial groups advocating strike action. The Leggett Committee, whilst acknowledging the difficulties, believed that in many cases it was only by opposing the unofficial group on their own ground that the men could be adequately forewarned against unofficial tactics.[2] Deakin described such an incident when attempts were being made to spread a strike from London to Southampton in 1948.

> In Southampton [he said] we were advised against holding a meeting but I felt there that it would be right for a meeting to be held and I got hold of Bro. Bird (National Docks Group Secretary) who went down to Southampton. When he got there he found that there were two members of the Unofficial Strike Committee there, and they were given facilities to address the meeting, after which Bro. Bird addressed our members, and a unanimous decision was secured against strike action.[3]

The odds have usually been against the Union official on these occasions. He may have had conclusive arguments against strike action but, whatever the facts, figures, and logic he may have produced, an appeal not to strike is essentially an appeal to reason and reason in the atmosphere of a dock strike is nearly always at a discount. The unofficial leaders without responsibilities or obligations have been able to be free with their promises and loose with their facts. Moreover, the strike envoys have made vital statements which have not always been in accord with the facts but which have been difficult to refute on the spot. There was much of this during the series of strikes in 1949.[4] The Leggett Committee reported that

[1] When the strikes in sympathy with the Canadian Seamen were spreading to Liverpool the officials prevented one from encompassing the whole port and from extending to Birkenhead. The strike that started in Southampton over the removal of deck chains by 'blackleg' labour, mentioned above, was ended the same day by the timely intervention of the Union Regional Secretary. (Cmd. 7851, p. 14.)

[2] Op. cit., p. 28.

[3] National and Regional Secretaries' Conference, 17 August 1948.

[4] In an attempt to get the Newport dockers to strike, a representative of the Canadian Seamen's Union read out a telegram, supposedly from the general secretary of the National Amalgamated Stevedores and Dockers, which stated: 'London stevedores and waterfront workers solid in support of official strike Canadian Seamen's Union. We call upon all waterfront workers throughout the United Kingdom to follow our example. . . .' After an investigation it was shown that the telegram had been sent, not by the general secretary of the Stevedores' Union, but by the headquarters of the Canadian Seamen's Union in London. (Cmd. 7851, p. 10.)

although 'it may be that only a small proportion of the workers concerned may have voted for a stoppage, this has usually been a sufficient nucleus to start the trouble. Indeed, false statements are often made that a stoppage has already commenced'.[1] When representatives from the Merseyside Port Workers' Committee visited Manchester early in February 1951 to induce the Manchester dockers to strike they obtained a unanimous vote in favour of a strike, in part by 'stating untruthfully that no dockers were at work in Liverpool, and claiming that by the end of the day the London dock workers would have joined in also'.[2] The truth is often uninspiring alongside such statements.

Mass meetings may be the most convenient method of communication but they by no means always faithfully record the wishes of the ordinary dockers. Dockers no less than other types of people like to be on the winning side, and this has resulted either in a large number of abstentions or in majorities being inflated once the trend of opinion has been revealed.[3] Most of the decisions which were ignored were those in favour of returning to work. This may have resulted from the dockers' fear of blacklegging. A most revealing instance when decisions to stay on strike did not reflect the wishes of the dockers occurred during the national dock strike in 1945. Details of the cases are given below for they show, perhaps, how strike-spreading could be made more difficult.

The strike had originated on Merseyside and throughout the strike the dockers there held the initiative, for the other ports in dispute had decided to continue the stoppage until the Liverpool workers agreed to resume work. The Union, therefore, had concentrated on persuading the Liverpool dockers to return to work. When the strike was almost a month old a National Docks Delegate Conference was held which advised a general return to work. Its advice was rejected. Two days later, on 25 October, the National Secretary of the Docks Group attended meetings in Liverpool but with negative results. Arthur Deakin was, however, getting reports that the decisions reached at these local meetings were not representative of the actual desires of the members, so it was arranged for postal ballots to be held in Liverpool, Manchester, and Grimsby and Immingham. At the last two ports a decision to return to work had been taken at meetings by a small majority but not acted upon. The ballot in Liverpool was carried out under the supervision of officials

---

[1] Cmd. 8236, op. cit., p. 10.
[2] *The Dock Worker*, op. cit., p. 229.
[3] At a meeting of men from the Royal Docks in London which was convened by the Canadian Seamen's Union in an endeavour to get more complete sympathetic action in London, only about one-third of the 1,200 dockers present voted; of those who did vote there was a majority in favour of striking, so the workers in the Royal Docks joined the strike. (Cmd. 7851, p. 19.)

7*

of the Ministry of Labour. Out of a total of 10,088 Liverpool dockers who voted, 7,177 voted for a resumption of work; at Manchester 1,350 dockers out of the 1,726 who voted were in favour of returning to work; and at Grimsby and Immingham they reversed their previous decision by a majority of two votes—358 were in favour of a resumption and 360 were against it.[1] The conclusiveness of the Liverpool result brought the strike to an end, for even the unofficial port workers' committee had to recognize it.

This is not the only occasion on which a ballot was held to determine the result of a strike. One took place in Avonmouth on 19 May 1949 when the dockers were supporting the Canadian Seamen's Union. Whilst it was in progress the president of the Canadian union appeared in Avonmouth and addressed the men. He may or may not have influenced the result, which was 466 dockers for a full resumption of work and 646 against.[2] When that strike reached Liverpool the local docks officials arranged a secret ballot, but the unofficial strike committee arranged a mass meeting at the same time and disorganized the ballot.[3] A similar fate, but caused by a boycott, was had by a ballot held by the Executive Committee of the National Amalgamated Stevedores and Dockers on 7 July 1949 during the same series of strikes.[4] One can only speculate what would have happened if there had been no intimidation.

DEAKIN'S SUPPORT OF THE NATIONAL DOCK LABOUR SCHEME

Union leadership in the docks has been exercised in two ways: it has been exercised through the Union machinery and through the National Dock Labour Scheme. Full-time trade union officials, as members of the National and twenty-two Local Dock Labour Boards, have jointly administered the Scheme with the representatives of employers. Trade union officials, therefore, have been responsible for enforcing the disciplinary clauses of the Scheme. This aspect of the Scheme has been much criticized, and to it has been attributed some blame for the increased intensity of unofficial action on the docks.

It will be recalled from the previous chapter that the joint control of the Scheme resulted from trade union pressure. Arthur Deakin believed in its effectiveness at the outset and he did not at any time deviate from that opinion. He believed too, just as consistently, that discipline should be enforced through the Local Boards and not

[1] T. & G.W.U., General Executive Council Minutes, 9 November 1945.
[2] Cmd. 7851, op. cit., p. 11.
[3] Ibid., p. 13.
[4] Ibid., p. 22.

by the unilateral action of Area Labour Managers or any other persons in their individual capacities. Given these two main tenets of the Scheme, Deakin was prepared to accept changes in it where it could be shown by members of his Union that they were necessary. For instance, when the first strike over the enforcement of discipline under the Scheme occurred in June 1948 Deakin told the strikers that the operation of the Scheme would be investigated.[1]

The cause of this strike was the penalty meted out to some London dockers for infringing the regulations of the Scheme.[2] They had been suspended from the Scheme for seven days without pay, and had had the right to receive attendance money taken from them for three months. The London dockers thought the penalties were too harsh. So did Deakin. 'I think we must lay down the principle', he said, 'that if there is to be a penalty of suspension from the benefits of the Scheme . . . that no penalty shall exceed 14 days.'[3] But the penalty could have been harsher and Deakin emphasized this as an example of the value to the dockers of having union officials on disciplinary boards. In his words: 'The officers who sat on the local committee to hear the case against the men had to face the position of either seeing the men dismissed from the Scheme or imposing some other penalty. They felt in face of the strong demand of the employers for the dismissal of the men from the Scheme, that it was better to temporize and get some other penalty imposed.'

When the strike had ended, local Union committees sent in suggestions for the amendment of the Scheme which were discussed by the National Dock Group Committee and a National Dock Delegate Conference. No evidence was produced to justify any significant changes in the Scheme, and the only amendment agreed upon by the Delegate Conference was the one submitted by Deakin, namely that the period of suspension from the benefits of the Scheme should not exceed fourteen days. The maximum period of suspension eventually agreed upon with the Board was four weeks.

As the volume of outside criticism of the Scheme grew during strikes, so Deakin, not unnaturally, set his mind against changing it. After the Minister of Labour[4] had announced the establishment of a Committee of Inquiry in May 1950 under the chairmanship of Sir Frederick Leggett to investigate the problem of unofficial stoppages in the London docks, Deakin said he had been asked to attend a preliminary meeting with the Committee. 'I cannot forecast beyond this', he said, 'but one thing is certain, we must offer

---

[1] At a mass meeting at the Royal Albert Hall, Tuesday 22 June 1948.
[2] Called the Zinc Oxide strike. It lasted from 14 to 29 June 1948.
[3] National and Regional Secretaries' Conference, 17 August 1948.
[4] Then Mr. Alfred Robens, M.P.

the most rigid opposition to altering the principles of the Scheme.'[1]

The Report of the Committee criticized the basic principle of joint control.

> We have no doubt [it stated] that the participation of Union officials who are members of the Board in the exercise of the Board's disciplinary powers, and particularly the power of dismissal, has had the effect of damaging the standing of these officials with their Union membership. Certain decisions of the London Dock Labour Board have inevitably been unpopular with the men, and the fact that their own Union officials were participating in such decisions has caused disaffection among elements of the Union's membership. . . . Unless they evade their responsibility as members of the Board by repudiating to the men the Board's decision, Union officials are bound in such circumstances to create a great deal of resentment among the members whom they represent and to offer to dissident elements an opportunity to discredit them in the eyes of the men.[2]

During a meeting of the National Joint Council for the Port Transport Industry the employers contended that the Report demonstrated that the principle of joint control had failed. 'This, however, we cannot accept', Deakin reported; 'neither can we accept the suggestion they have advanced that there should be an alteration of the disciplinary clauses under the Scheme.'[3]   Sir Walter Monckton, as the Minister of Labour from 1951, found Deakin to be willing to compromise on most matters but not over the Dock Labour Scheme, and whenever it was suggested that the Scheme should be investigated Deakin steadfastly refused to co-operate.   As late as 2 March 1955 no official Union comment had been offered in reply to the announced intention of the Port Labour Employers to ask for a revision of the Scheme. Not long before he died, Deakin's attitude softened and he gave the Minister of Labour the impression that an inquiry into the Scheme would not be confronted with his formidable opposition.[4]

Was Arthur Deakin's defence of the principle of joint control a simple illustration of his inborn stubbornness, or was it justifiably defended? He undoubtedly felt he had cause to defend it for the reason that the factual evidence against it was so unreliable. His defence in the first instance was based on a belief that the decasualization of the dock industry made such a substantial improvement in the lives of the dockers that its advantages by far outweighed any disadvantages created by the restrictions which were necessary to make the Scheme work, and that in any case the restrictions

---

[1] T. & G.W.U. Report to G.E.C., 5 June 1950.
[2] Cmd. 8236, pp. 13–14.
[3] T. & G.W.U. Report to G.E.C., September 1951.
[4] In conversation with Deakin I was given the same impression.

were no more onerous than those experienced by many workers in other industries. He believed that workers responded favourably to social and economic improvements. If this were true, the unrest on the docks could only have resulted from the Scheme if its disadvantages to dockers outweighed the advantages. As was stated above, Deakin did not believe this of the Scheme. According to Deakin's mind, whatever factors caused the dockers to act as they did were external to the Scheme.

The objections to joint control came from outside the Union and not from the members themselves, and this weighed heavily with Deakin. A motion on the agenda of the 1953 Biennial Delegate Conference asking 'That no Permanent Officers shall be members of Local Dock Labour Boards' received no support and was not even moved: this was the only occasion on which such a motion appeared on the agenda of a Biennial Delegate Conference. The unofficial strike leaders who gave evidence before internal Union committees of inquiry after each major dock strike did not complain of the presence of Union officials on the Local Dock Labour Boards. In fact many active members saw joint control as a most effective means of enforcing compulsory trade unionism on the docks. If his members raised no objections, then, what did it matter to Deakin if outside bodies diagnosed that joint control created 'confused and divided loyalties'?

The criticisms of the Scheme which came from the members concerned the disciplinary clauses, but they were not made consistently. 'You do not get any criticism', Deakin said in 1948, 'when work is slack and they are securing the advantages of the Scheme, but only when work is plentiful.'[1] The events of the post-war years illustrated his point. The year 1952 was the only post-war year during which there were no strikes of any kind on the docks and no organized protests against the restrictions of decasualization. 1952 was also the year during which the National Dock Labour Board made provision to reduce the size of the register of dock workers because of the excessive number of dockers who were compelled 'to prove attendance' daily. In 1951 the average number of men proving attendance amounted to 6·0 per cent. of an average labour force of 82,359. During 1952 the labour force decreased to 77,867 and the numbers proving attendance increased, so that in the fourth quarter of the year 16,153 dockers comprising 20·7 per cent. of the labour force were receiving the benefits of the Scheme.[2]

The correct assessment of the value of the Scheme could not be

---

[1] National and Regional Secretaries' Conference, 17 August 1948.
[2] *Ministry of Labour Gazette*, December 1952, p. 413.

made during the years of plentiful and regular dock work, for the
security which the Scheme aimed to provide was not cherished and
the freedom of action inherent in casual work, which pre-war
dockers would willingly have relinquished for greater security, took
on a new significance. Although the pre-war years with their high
rates of unemployment do not present an analogous case, because
no decasualization schemes operated then, it is worth noting that
neither the restrictions of the registration schemes nor their joint
operation by trade unions and employers were the subject of criticism
from within or adverse comment from outside the dock industry.
On the contrary the Maclean Committee remarked that the registration committees 'in working towards a common ideal are able to
exert a potent influence upon the maintenance of good relations
between employers and workpeople and the general efficiency of the
ports'.[1]

AN INTERIM ASSESSMENT

The last and most difficult docks problem to confront Arthur
Deakin arose out of a decision on 19 August 1954 of a group of
dockers in Hull to secede from the Transport and General Workers'
Union and join the hitherto local London union, the National
Amalgamated Stevedores and Dockers. The decision, made during
a ten-day strike involving 4,000 Hull dockers,[2] was followed by
similar decisions in Birkenhead, Liverpool, and Manchester, so that
by the end of December 1954 about 10,000 dockers had switched
their allegiance. The act of recruiting the dockers by the National
Amalgamated Stevedores and Dockers was an infringement of the
Bridlington Agreement which regulated inter-union relationships,
and in consequence the union was suspended from the Trades Union
Congress and ordered to return those dockers who had been members
of the Transport and General Workers' Union.

The seceded dockers were recalcitrant. When in March 1955 the
Local Dock Labour Board on Merseyside issued new Record Books
to members of the Transport and General Workers' Union alone,
without which dockers could not get employment on the docks,
there was a two-day strike of members of both unions against the
discriminating act. The strike, covering Liverpool, Birkenhead,
Garston, and Manchester, achieved its purpose and Record Books
were issued to all registered dock workers. Then on 23 May 1955
a strike was started in various ports in England to support the
demand of the National Amalgamated Stevedores and Dockers for

---

[1] Port Labour Inquiry, 1931, op. cit., p. 17.
[2] The strike was in protest against the use of the hand scuttling method for unloading grain.

representation on provincial port joint committees. The strike lasted forty days and ended unsuccessfully for the dockers. The executive of the Stevedores' Union had by now decided to hand back the dockers it had recruited in the provincial ports and on 6 July 1955 it wrote to its Northern branches to this effect; but, having minds of their own, the dockers refused to go. Indeed, they claimed that the National Amalgamated Stevedores and Dockers did not possess the right to exclude them from membership once having accepted them into membership and this right was successfully challenged in the courts.[1]

The events of the few months before he died saddened Arthur Deakin; he was a tired, sick man nearing retirement, and from his point in life the act of secession had a flavour of ungraciousness about it. He had been long enough at the head of affairs in the Union to look upon criticisms of the Union as personal affronts. Deakin felt that his Union was in the right and that eventually the Northern dockers who had joined the Stevedores' Union would realize this and return. It will be long before the correctness of Deakin's assertion can be tested, and before it will be possible to identify the cause of the trouble and state whether the secession was the culmination of the consequences of the Union policy in the post-war years, a spontaneous action, or the result of the efforts of a small group of malcontents.

The dockers were given no preferential treatment in the Union nor were they exempted from following the main lines of the Union policy as laid down by the Executive. No attempt was made by Deakin to steal the initiative from the unofficial leaders by outbidding them in the extravagance of their promises. Just to have kept pace with the unofficial leaders it would have been necessary to have altered the Union policy in several main respects. First it would have been necessary to have pursued a high-wages policy for dockers in contrast to the policy of wage restraint advocated by the Union executive. Deakin advised against following any such course. It might have been necessary on occasions to have authorized the violation of voluntary agreements. For Arthur Deakin that would have amounted to sacrilege. The violation of an agreement is 'not merely a question affecting the docker', he said, '[it] is a question as to whether or not we are people who having signed an agreement and having accepted a procedure for the settlement of disputes are going to carry out our obligations'.[2]

1 Spring *v.* National Amalgamated Stevedores' and Dockers' Society. Judgment was given in the Chancery Court on 14 March 1956 that the Bridlington Agreement did not entitle a union to exclude members and the plaintiff Mr. Francis Spring, who was a Liverpool docker, obtained an injunction to restrain the Stevedores' Union from excluding him from membership.
2 T. & G.W.U., B.D.C., 1949.

Given the mood of the post-war dockers Deakin could possibly have rallied the dockers behind him if he had been willing to lead them out on strike. It was in the atmosphere of strike action that the secessionist movement started and was fostered in 1954 and 1955; it is possible that it could have been crushed in its early stages by the same process backed by official Union support. The only national dock strike led by Bevin was more in the nature of a show of strength than a dispute with employers, so why could not Deakin have used similar tactics?[1] He could have created his own excuses for doing so, such as submitting a wage demand he knew would not be conceded, or his Union, more justifiably than the Stevedores' union, could have embraced the issue of 'compulsory overtime'. The circumstances he worked under were different from those of Bevin's early days with the Union, and Deakin would have considered it gross dishonesty and irresponsibility to cause and lead a strike for the purpose of maintaining the unity of his organization. In addition to this, however, Deakin had deprecated strike action for so long and so frequently that in his later years he was in a position where he could not possibly support it without undergoing an embarrassing *volte face*.

From 1945 Deakin became less tactful in his denunciation of the dockers' unofficial actions. During the national unofficial strike in 1945 he displayed a useful caution in his treatment of the strikers. When he reported to his Finance and General Purposes Committee about the strike he stated

> that he had considered the advisability of convening the General Executive Council in Special Session, and had arrived at the conclusion that such a step would be ill-advised, inasmuch as the Council would be forced to deliver an ultimatum which, at this time, with feeling running high and a refusal to accept constitutional action, would undoubtedly be resented and, in point of fact, contribute nothing towards a solution of the problem.[2]

Such caution became less obvious in later years, though possibly he may have been thwarted by the extensive publicity given in the press to every important dock strike and particularly by the publicity given to the statements of the unofficial strike leaders which often required official Union denials. He became prone to deliver massive denunciations in public which contained little consideration for the legitimate grievances of the dockers and gave the impression that he held no sympathy for them. Consequently, he sometimes became alienated further from the dockers during disputes than was necessary to maintain a constitutional position.

[1] The strike took place in 1924.
[2] Report to the Finance and General Purposes Committee, 25 October 1945.

Though organized unofficial activity threatened to undermine the procedures and negotiating machinery of the Union, in most instances the unofficial strike leaders were treated lightly and the assurances which the majority of them gave to abide by the constitution of the Union in future were accepted in good faith. It was as Deakin said on one occasion: 'We are not out on a punitive expedition against our members. Our only concern is to see that the constitutional machinery of the Union is used.'[1] The activities of each member of an unofficial port workers' committee were investigated carefully by a sub-committee of the Union Executive, and the members themselves had the opportunity of giving evidence and making statements before decisions were reached about any one of them. Altogether seventy-seven members were summoned to appear before Union committees of inquiry to account for their activities in five major strikes between the end of the war and 1954. They had been members of unofficial port workers' committees or had undertaken some of the various duties involved in strike organizing and spreading. Only three were expelled from the Union for their activities; others were cautioned or debarred from holding office in the Union for varying lengths of time.[2]

Where members provided an opportunity for the Executive to exercise leniency, it was done. There was good cause for tolerance, as Deakin pointed out in an interview with the Labour Correspondent of the *Manchester Guardian* in 1947. 'It is true', he said, 'that we have power to expel members, and in extreme cases do so, but I don't think it would help to stop unofficial strikes if we expelled more people. It is much more likely that it would increase unrest. Once men are expelled the union can have no more influence over them. It is much better that we should maintain our influence rather than weaken it by expulsions.'[3] Events bore out Deakin's contention, for over 14,000 dockers struck work for ten days in London over the three expulsions in 1950.[4] More than once the qualities shown by unofficial strike leaders enabled them to become full-time docks officials. In general Arthur Deakin and his Executive trusted to the common sense and loyalty of the dock

[1] Note on a conversation with a journalist, 12 September 1946.
[2] The three expelled members, who were involved in the Canadian Seamen's strike, had been warned over their activities during a previous strike and had given an assurance that they would use the constitutional machinery of the Union. On the second occasion they said that 'if they considered that a particular issue arising was worthy of their participation then they would feel entitled to participate, irrespective of any provision contained within the rules of the Union or any decision recorded by the General Executive Council and/or the Biennial Delegate Conference.' In such a case there was no reasonable alternative to expulsion. (Report of Special Committee of Inquiry, 7 March 1950.)
[3] *Manchester Guardian*, 12 May 1947.
[4] From 19 to 29 April 1950. The strike was complicated and made larger by the endeavour to implicate members of the National Amalgamated Stevedores and Dockers. See Cmd. 8236, op. cit., pp. 38–41.

members and, other things being equal, this seemed to be a wise long-term policy. But prominent amongst the other things was and is the feeling amongst dockers that their interests were and are served best by the Transport and General Workers' Union.

This leads one to the last point in this chapter. Why should the dockers form a part of the Transport and General Workers' Union? Would not their interests have been best served by a single autonomous dockers' union? The answer must in part be speculative but some points can be made. It would be folly to ignore the role of history in an assessment of today's situation. The amalgamation of dockers, road transport workers, and general workers was not an accident; it grew out of the needs of a belligerent industrial situation. The Union grew because of the imperfections of federations and was formed as a fighting organization. 'When in the old days there was a cry for unity', Bevin said in 1939, 'we in this Union . . . tried to give effect to it.' The industrial atmosphere was one in which trade autonomy seemed so much less important than the need for industrial unity. At successive Union Biennial Conferences members expressed their faith in the logic of its creation. Said a delegate in 1927, 'I hold the view as one who went into this amalgamation . . . that we were going to be a band of brothers. That if the carmen were in trouble that was the dockers' business and the busmen's business and the tramwaymen's business.'

There is little doubt that the views of such members were correctly held. There was a need for mutual assistance between relatively small unions. In fact the whole trend towards large unions through amalgamation has been because in all the fields of trade union activity problems have arisen which have not been capable of solution by small unions, even when they have acted in concert through federations. One of the problems was survival. By comparison the difficulties of integration seem insignificant. But after fifteen years of plenty the needs of the lean years tend to be forgotten. It is wrong to assume, however, that mutual assistance is only necessary during lean years or that sympathetic strike action is the only form it can take. The advantages of size, the benefits of specialization, the large common fund and the strength that size gives, all accrue to each of the different sections in a large amalgamation and constitute mutual assistance. And if sympathetic strike action is ever needed, who else are better able to practise it than the constituent parts of an amalgamation?

There is no knowing what form of organization the dockers would have devised if they had not joined the 1922 amalgamation; they might have continued as sectional unions, or they might have evolved into one national organization. But one can pertinently ask whether, without the organized might of the Transport and General Workers' Union in the background, they could have made such an advance as decasualization. The arguments in favour of trade autonomy can be cogently put, but only in good years do they carry any weight, and even then they constitute a reversal of the developments in the trade union movement during the last thirty-six years.

Chapter Thirteen

ADMINISTRATIVE LEADERSHIP

(1) THE EFFICIENCY OF A TRADE UNION ADMINISTRATION

THE presence of this chapter which is neither about Arthur Deakin nor the Transport and General Workers' Union needs some explanation. So far, Part II has been concerned with what can be termed the production side of trade union activity, and with the obvious difficulties of integrating the activities of different groups of workers into one organization, with which Arthur Deakin was confronted. Now we come to an examination of the task of administering such an organization and of the role which Deakin filled as the head of an administration.

It would be possible to examine an administration without assessing its worth. But such an examination would be of little value. Administrations, after all, exist to get things done and one wants to know how efficiently they do them. An attempt to assess the efficiency of a trade union administration and of its administrative head raises, however, certain general questions which need to be answered if the attempt is to be successful. Is there a standard by which efficiency in a trade union can be measured? What factors other than leadership are involved in an assessment of a trade union administration? Brief answers to these questions are given in this chapter.

Any administrator who is aware of the significance of his task is bound to ask himself what criterion or criteria he can use to measure administrative efficiency. He needs to know the extent to which the administration is implementing decisions, and to relate its results to needs and resources, as well as methods. It is not enough simply to show that an administration gets things done quickly and easily. This may indicate efficiency; it is not proof of it, since quick answers can so often be the wrong ones. The main question a trade union administrator should ask himself is: 'Are the members getting the best possible service from their contributions in terms of whatever they decide in their policy deliberations?' The answer is not easily given because there is no readily available cardinal measurement.

A trade union is an organizing and an administrative body. Its organizing function is the production side of trade union activity; it is concerned with all forms of industrial and political action, with the recruitment of members, and with the formulation of policy in all spheres. The management of the production side of trade union activity is the administrative task. It is necessarily a secondary function, and because it has the appearance of being non-productive, even unrelated to production, it is commonly neglected. Union officials usually work with the barest framework of an administrative machine.

Trade unions achieve most things on the basis of their strength *vis-à-vis* employers, the State, and other trade unions. As there is a positive correlation between the power a trade union possesses and its size in relation to its total potential membership, recruitment takes precedence over administration. In other words there is more concern over the size of a trade union than the way in which it is run. Within limits this attitude is justifiable, but unfortunately in some cases it is taken to the extreme and recruitment is regarded as an alternative to administrative efficiency. In no way can an increase in members be a satisfactory substitute for efficiency; indeed, unless the increase is accompanied by administrative improvements the advantages of size are likely to be dissipated. A bigger membership does provide extra income from which administrative improvements may be made, but these are a consequence of increased income only if the chief executive officers of the union are aware in the first instance of the value of efficient administration.

Then it is said that if a union is expanding, its administration must be satisfactory. An expanding or even a stable union membership may indicate membership satisfaction, but neither shows that the union resources are being fully utilized, because trade union members may be satisfied with less than an effective use of their union resources. Moreover, an expansion or contraction of membership may result from factors entirely unrelated to satisfaction, such as the discovery of fresh organizing fields or changes in the state of the labour market. In one way membership changes and administration may be related: other things being equal the level of membership may be determined by the quality of organizing in the field and this can be a product of administration.

A comparative analysis of membership changes between unions has only a limited value as a gauge of relative administrative efficiency. Workers may change unions for a variety of reasons, and even if some left a union because of its inefficiency they would hardly know the effectiveness of alternative union administrations until they had tested them through actual membership.

Hardly ever does one find the conditions for valid efficiency comparisons between unions so that one can say that the differences in the services rendered to the respective memberships result solely or principally from differences in administration. The resources of unions and the demands made on them vary considerably. Some unions have relatively low contributions but memberships with complex and exacting requirements; the opposite is the case with others. Organizing responsibilities vary, too, as well as management responses. In general terms it may be possible to say that one trade union is more efficient than another; but for a detailed assessment each trade union should be examined separately and the following factors should be considered: (1) the constitutional framework of the union; (2) the task confronting the union; (3) the level of its income; (4) the manner in which its income is used; (5) the types and abilities of administrators; and (6) administrative leadership. All of these factors are variables to a greater or lesser extent.

1. Trade union administrations are formed in every case within the framework of written constitutions. In each union the rigidity of the framework varies; here it is inflexible, there it permits latitude. Between unions there are considerable variations. The constitutions have one thing in common: they impose the influence of democratic beliefs on practical affairs and in doing so sacrifice efficiency. The sacrifice is by no means complete. Necessity drives trade unions hard in the opposite direction from which the constitutions would have them go. From certain rules, however, there is no escape except through alterations. These mainly concern finance. Contributions are fixed by rule and therefore, for a static organization, income is fixed too. Unions are committed by rule to certain expenditures; for example, to periodic conferences of given sizes and durations, to methods of electing officials—perhaps to periodic elections—and to branch officers' remuneration. Some union executives are restricted in the total amounts they can spend on administration and can only exceed these by the sanction of their members.

Union constitutions prescribe the decision-making processes which form an essential part of every administration. Here a distinction should be made between decisions on administrative matters and on policy. Union constitutions define the stages of a union hierarchy and set the lines of communication between those stages. Policy decisions can only move up the hierarchy, from the members in their branches to whichever body is entrusted with policy-making powers—the executive council or national delegate conference. Downward decisions are administrative ones. The distinction is not clear cut, however, for branches are administrative units as well as initiators of policy, therefore some upward decisions are administrative ones.

It is easy to get confused about the relative effects of constitutions and administrations on the effectiveness of trade union activity. Not many constitutions are so restrictive as to prevent the development of workable administrations; some of the restrictions imposed are organically healthy ones calculated to ensure that the unions act in the interests of their members. When this does not happen to everyone's satisfaction; when, for example, communications are inadequate and responses sluggish, constitutions are blamed. Often this is bad diagnosis and, instead, men and their administrations are at fault.

2. The task of a union is to provide various kinds of services to its members. The combined effect of the types of services, and the composition and requirements of the members, create in part the administrative problem. In most cases these factors are inter-dependent. It is unlikely that a union will have a legal department unless its members have a particular need for legal protection; similarly with social insurance and industrial injuries. The provision of the ordinary service of negotiations may be made more difficult by the distribution of the members, as in the case of seamen and agricultural workers. On the other hand, a compact homogeneous industrial group may create difficulties because of the services it requires. A heterogeneous membership raises special problems which are by no means confined to the general unions. Even apparently uniform industrial groups have within them fine distinctions of grade which can give rise to intense feeling over relative treatment. The trade union task is rarely unaffected by such complications.

3. The income of a union is determined mainly by the amount of the contributions and the size of the union. The contribution varies only over a long period. In fact unless there are exceptional circumstances a trade union leader must take the amount as given. Ordinary members are quite obdurate over union contribution increases. In order to raise its income, then, a union must usually increase its size. This enables it also to enlarge its surplus of income over basic expenditure, for extra members can often be served by the existing administration. Even where additional administrative costs have to be incurred they are normally less than the increase in income. Most unions receive income from investments, but this forms a small proportion of their total income.

4. Partly by tradition and partly by necessity a limitation is placed on the proportion of a union's income which can be allocated for organization and administration. The first call on a union's income is for the accumulation of a strike or contingency fund to

provide trade protection.   The rules of some unions require them
to maintain their funds at a given *per capita* level.[1]   Those unions
which pay social insurance benefits normally do so from extra
charges levied on the members, and the basic contribution in most
cases entitles a member only to trade protection.   The obligation to
meet benefit payments, however, can be a charge on the general fund,
so that if a union pays sickness benefit and an epidemic occurs
amongst its members it could drain the general fund.   Because of
the legal obligation under the Trade Union Act, 1913, a separate
fund is kept for political purposes, financed by a political levy, and
no part of the ordinary contribution may be used for political
activities.   Like the total income, the amount of the income of a
union devoted to the development of an organization varies in the
main only as the membership varies.

As has already been stated, the development of organization has
been given precedence over administration, though this does not
signify that it has always received serious attention.   With few
exceptions the mechanism of trade union organizations has grown
more through addition than adaptation.

Broadly, two forms of organization are used.   On the one
hand there is the trade union that is run predominantly by lay
members, with a small number of national full-time officials to
give oversight to the work of the lay members and undertake
activities which could not easily be done on a part-time basis.   And
on the other hand there is the trade union which uses full-time
officials extensively in an endeavour to provide its members with
specialist services.   In between the two forms lie many variations.

Underlying the development of the two extreme forms of organization is a difference in the conception of the function of trade unions.
Those who consider that trade unions are training grounds for
Socialism, equipping workers for the task of controlling industry,
believe in the utmost degree of lay participation in trade union
activity.   This attitude is determined by a belief of what *ought* to be
rather than what is.   But trade unions in their day-to-day operations
have to provide services, and it is on this provision that those unions
which use full-time officials concentrate extensively.   They practise
what is called 'Business Unionism'.   It is not suggested that either
type completely neglects the basis of the other.   All unions depend
on lay activity; all unions have an ethical basis for their actions and
they all provide day-to-day services.   The difference lies in emphasis.
One cannot say that all of the trade unions depending preponderantly on lay members do so primarily for ethical reasons.

In practice the theoretical distinction between the two forms loses

[1] For some examples see *Power in Trade Unions*, op. cit., p. 178.

much of its point, for in unions which employ only national officials, lay office-holders in branches and districts are virtually occupied full-time on union business.   These men suffer from the attempted pursuit of dual occupations, for they have neither a continuous and intimate contact with the ordinary members nor the time for developing specialist trade union techniques and few facilities for creating efficient organizations.   They do not carry the status of organizers nor do they possess their freedom of action.   In consequence, decisive action can often only be taken after reference to the appropriate lay committees, involving either delay or the additional cost of summoning meetings.   The use of lay members is not always less expensive than the employment of full-time officials and is almost always less efficient.

5. Trade union administration in all except a few unions has developed in a much cruder fashion than organization and it has lagged considerably behind the complexity and size of the tasks it has faced.   One of the reasons for this can be found in the nature of trade union administrators.   The full-time officials at national and district levels, lay-secretaries and chairmen of district committees, branch officials and, to a limited extent, shop stewards are all involved in carrying out union policy.   They are the administrators. They are assisted in general by clerical staffs and in a few cases by specialists in finance, legal matters, social insurance, education, and research, but these have extended into relatively few unions and, in most cases, do not possess the status of union officials.

Very few officials are wholly administrators; they are primarily organizers and negotiators.   When they first become trade union officials they normally lack any previous training and guidance and they equip themselves as well as they are able for the many administrative tasks they have to undertake. Very few unions arrange training courses for branch officials and potential branch officials.   Full-time officials in almost all unions possess prior experience as branch or district lay officials, but if any of them have administrative ability it is in most cases fortuitous.   Where appointments are made on the basis of interview and examination, questions about administration may be put to candidates, but they take their place behind questions concerning recruitment, handling industrial disputes, negotiating, and the like.   In the case of elective posts the question of ability in any of the operations is likely to be subordinate to personality; where it is not, there is no clear way of distinguishing between ability in one operation and ability in another.

With few exceptions the recruitment of officials is confined, by rule, to those who have worked at a trade covered by the respective union.

The majority of the officials are thus drawn from industrial groups with experience only of manual work. Moreover, they are recruited at an age long after their formal education has ended and much of it has been forgotten. The effect of this is inevitably reflected in trade union administrations. National trade union leaders, except some financial secretaries, go through the same processes as other union officials.

6. The last factor is administrative leadership. How this is exercised and its effect on practical administration depend on many things which vary considerably between unions and which change within a single union over time. Of primary importance is the quality of the leader. This cannot be taken as given, for despite the combined effect of environment, selection processes, and restrictions imposed by union rules, men with administrative ability do emerge as trade union leaders. And when this happens the other factors decrease in importance. It is within the scope of a trade union leader to create limited but nevertheless significant changes in any of the five factors described above. He can do so mainly through his influence as a specialist amongst amateurs; by guidance and advocacy. In straightforward administrative matters he sometimes has authority to make final decisions so that he may employ clerical staff and buy office equipment. He may, thereby, introduce new methods into his administration and perhaps purchase dictaphones and accounting machines instead of employing shorthand typists and clerks.

The type of quality required from a general secretary depends upon the size of the union he leads and its method of organization. The smaller the union is, the more he will be directly responsible for administrative action, but the less opportunity there will be, in general, for administrative leadership. He will do things himself rather than employ people to do them for him. The general secretary of a large highly centralized union may have a more direct effect upon administrative efficiency than the leader of a union of comparable size with effective regional administrative machinery. In the latter case, however, a greater ability to co-ordinate will be required.

Less administrative creativeness is required from a person who becomes general secretary of an established, stable union, than from a leader of a young organization. For instance, administrative creativeness was required from Ernest Bevin but not from Arthur Deakin. Indeed, the administration of the Transport and General Workers' Union would have tackled its day-to-day tasks regardless of the type of person who followed Bevin: it was geared to operate independently of a single leader for short periods, given no sudden change of conditions, but eventually someone would have had to make decisions which no subordinate person was responsible to make; the regional and trade parts of the Union would have had to be co-ordinated; guidance would have had to be given to the Executive Council.   Through these actions the quality of the general secretary would have been impressed upon the administration of the Union.

Chapter Fourteen

ADMINISTRATIVE LEADERSHIP

(2) WAR-TIME TENSIONS

THE administration of the Transport and General Workers' Union was subjected to two main tensions while Arthur Deakin was its General Secretary. The first was caused by the intensity of the war and its impact on institutional activities; the second was the unprecedented growth in the Union membership, which made it far and away the biggest trade union in the country. The increase in the Union membership was in the first instance a consequence of the war but it was continued, though at a reduced rate, after the war.

I. THE IMPACT OF WAR

Just before the outbreak of war Ernest Bevin had drawn up a plan for the 'Organization and Administration of the Union under War Conditions' and had circulated copies to his Regional Secretaries. So when Arthur Deakin became the Acting General Secretary the stage was set. Bevin anticipated the disruption of travelling facilities and normal channels of communication which would throw a greater degree of responsibility upon the regional administrations. As early as December 1938 he had decided to retain the head office of the Union in London, though with a reduced staff so that some of its members could move to offices not so dangerously situated. The plan provided for a radical devolution of the work of the central office to the regions, which were not to call for national assistance unless they were compelled to do so. The Executive was to maintain contact with the members through monthly issues of *The Record* and only circulars containing essential Executive instructions were to be sent to the branches. It was late in September 1939 when the Executive Council discussed the plan and by that time steps had been taken to implement parts of it, though it was never fully invoked. The nearest stage occurred in 1944 when travel facilities and communications were restricted and a greater responsibility for decision-making was thrown upon local administrations. The general effect of the war, however, was to encourage Regional Secretaries to act independently of the head office as far as was practical.

Through the initial impact of the war the constitutional elections for the 1940-1941 electoral period were postponed. The organization was in a state of flux; many members had been called up for service in the armed forces, others were undertaking civil defence duties in addition to their ordinary work, and some had been transferred to work in various parts of the country. A large number of members would have been unable to exercise their right to vote. In addition, not all branches had made satisfactory arrangements under the black-out conditions for holding branch meetings where most of the voting took place.

Immediately the war started some full-time officials applied to the General Executive Council to be released from their Union duties so that they could enlist for the Armed Forces. The Executive gave its permission and agreed that they should 'be treated on leaving the Forces and resuming with the Union, in a similar manner to an Officer who enters Parliament and who loses his seat at a subsequent election, i.e. he will be found employment with the Union at the same salary as he was receiving at the time of his enlistment but not necessarily the same position'. The reason for this provision was that the Executive had to appoint replacements for enlisted officials, and, whether or not the replacements were temporary appointments, they could not easily be removed without arousing resentment among the ordinary members. Each official collects a hard core of personal support from the members he serves, and a wider area of goodwill.

The labour controls which were introduced after the formation of the Coalition Government created a demand for trade union officials in a civilian capacity and many were drawn into Government posts as Labour Officers in one industry or another. This demand was particularly heavy in the dock industry. Between 24 June 1940 and 1 August 1940 twenty-two full-time officials had taken up Government work as Labour Supply Officers or Port Labour Inspectors and seventeen of these were Union docks officials. From 27 June 1940 Arthur Deakin had been given the authority by his Executive to decide all further applications from Union officers for leave of absence. Just over a month later Deakin had to justify to his Executive the release of so many officials from one trade group. He stated that the work of the men was complementary to that of the Union and that the Union would derive advantages from having contacts in the new administrative arrangements for labour.

Such a justification was necessary because the released men, often experienced and efficient officials, were difficult to replace. Even during normal times the Union could not easily undertake to replace so many of its officials. The position was worsened during the war because many Union members who would have been qualified to take full-time posts were either in the Armed Forces or on important war work which they had no desire to leave. In general there were depleted lists of candidates for full-time posts.

The Transport and General Workers' Union had a higher full-time official to membership ratio than any other union and was most concerned about the position of full-time union staffs on the Schedule for Reserved Occupations. To varying extents other unions were concerned with it too. Consequently when proposals were made to change the Schedule in 1941 the General Council of the Trades Union Congress made representations to the Minister of Labour. The Report of the General Council stated that it believed that

> these proposals would completely wreck the Trade Union machine without producing any substantial number of men for the Armed Forces. It was pointed out . . . that the outpouring of Orders and Regulations by Government Departments, the proposals for the concentration of industry, the dispersal of vital industries through enemy action, the recruitment of large numbers of women into industry, all combined to throw an overload on the shoulders of existing full-time officials. The Minister was reminded that the training of full-time officials during normal periods was a difficult matter requiring time and experience, and that during the present conditions it would be a practical impossibility. . . .[1]

This was the problem clearly stated, but the General Council secured only minor alterations to meet its needs.

The transfer of full-time officials to the Armed Forces or to Government work was known in advance by Deakin, and he was therefore able to make arrangements either to distribute their work amongst others or to seek replacements. Much work, however, was undertaken by voluntary branch secretaries, collectors, and shopstewards, and they were liable to be moved to employment in other districts at short notice as well as to be called for service in the Armed Forces. The maintenance of the organization often depended then on the speed with which new lay officials could be obtained; this was a branch responsibility, but in so many cases the secretary was the branch conscience so that when he left branch activities lapsed or deteriorated—unless full-time officials were on the spot.

The war increased the work of trade union officials, as the quotation from the Trades Union Congress Report above indicates. They were responsible for seeing that the multifarious Government Orders were operated in the interests of trade union members; in that they were anxious to have Government labour controls imple-

[1] T.U.C. Report, 1941, p. 146.

mented fairly and effectively they often became unofficial Government representatives. Those who belonged to unions which were 'recognized agencies for placing workers' acted as Labour Exchange officials too. More and not fewer trade union officials were required by trade unions in the interest of all-round efficiency. Many of the members of the Transport and General Workers' Union were on essential work in the dock, road passenger, and commercial transport and general engineering industries and were controlled during and after 1941 by Essential Work Orders. The Union officials were the custodians of the rights of workers subject to control by these and other wartime Government Orders concerning labour. Other war-time functions were the establishment of joint production committees, the supervision of the relaxation of pre-war practices, and the operation of Part III of the Conditions of Employment and National Arbitration Order concerning the obligation upon employers to observe recognized terms and conditions of employment. This increase in the intensity of work, coupled with the rapid extension of the activities of the Union, placed an inordinate strain on the administration of the Union.

2. THE EXPANSION OF THE UNION

From its formation the Transport and General Workers' Union has been a relatively large union, though not until 1937 was it larger than any other union in Great Britain. Its years of expansion and contraction have roughly corresponded with the years of expansion and contraction in the trade union movement as a whole. The changes in the Union membership, however, have been more pronounced, as can be seen in Table I. The figures for the Union do not indicate the true extent of the natural growth or decline in every year, because the Union was involved in so many amalgamations. Had it not been for amalgamations during the inter-war years the loss of membership would have been greater during years of decline and the increases smaller during years of expansion. But except for 1929, when the Union amalgamated with the Workers' Union, these do not grossly distort the comparisons.[1]

After 1933 the Union recovered the membership it lost during the years of high unemployment. For four years, until the end of 1937, the annual percentage increases were 14·5, 13·7, 13·9, and 16·5 for each respective year and were much higher than for the Movement.

---

[1] Occasionally large numbers of 'non-paying members' were crossed off the Union membership books, so that the losses in some years were exaggerated and should, in part, have been attributed to other years. The total loss over a number of years remains unaltered and, of course, the exaggeration enters into the figures for the whole Movement, though with much less effect than for the Union.

TABLE I

CHANGES IN THE MEMBERSHIP OF THE TRANSPORT AND GENERAL WORKERS'
UNION AND THE AGGREGATE MEMBERSHIP OF TRADE UNIONS, 1922–1955[1]

| Year | TRANSPORT AND GENERAL WORKERS' UNION | | | ALL TRADE UNIONS IN G.B. | |
	Total Membership	Annual inc. (+) or dec. (−)	Percentage inc. (+) or dec. (−) on membership of previous year	Total Membership	Percentage inc. (+) or dec. (−) on membership of previous year
(i)	(ii)	(iii)	(iv)	(v)	(vi)
1922	297,460	—	—	5,625,000	−15·2
1923	307,273	+ 9,813	+ 3·3	5,429,000	− 3·5
1924	372,560	+ 65,287	+21·2	5,544,000	+ 2·1
1925	376,251	+ 3,691	+ 1·0	5,506,000	− 0·7
1926	335,791	− 40,460	−10·8	5,219,000	− 5·2
1927	319,533	− 16,258	− 4·8	4,919,000	− 5·7
1928	315,819	− 3,714	− 1·2	4,806,000	− 2·3
1929	422,836	+107,017	+33·9[2]	4,858,000	+ 1·1
1930	422,048	− 788	− 0·2	4,842,000	− 0·3
1931	408,374	− 13,674	− 3·2	4,624,000	− 4·5
1932	372,992	− 35,382	− 8·7	4,444,000	− 3·9
1933	378,869	+ 5,877	+ 1·6	4,392,000	− 1·2
1934	433,816	+ 54,947	+14·5	4,590,000	+ 4·5
1935	493,266	+ 59,450	+13·7	4,867,000	+ 6·0
1936	561,908	+ 68,642	+13·9	5,295,000	+ 8·8
1937	645,510	+ 92,602	+16·5	5,843,000	+10·3
1938	679,360	+ 24,850	+ 3·8	6,054,000	+ 3·6
1939	694,474	+ 15,114	+ 2·2	6,298,000	+ 4·0
1940	743,349	+ 48,875	+ 7·0	6,613,000	+ 5·0
1941	948,079	+204,730	+27·5	7,165,000	+ 8·5
1942	1,133,165	+185,086	+19·5	7,867,000	+ 9·8
1943	1,122,480	− 10,685	− 0·9	8,174,000	+ 3·9
1944	1,070,470	− 52,010	− 4·6	8,087,000	− 1·1
1945	1,019,069	− 51,401	− 4·8	7,875,000	− 2·6
1946	1,273,920	+254,851	+25·0	8,803,000	+11·8
1947	1,317,842	+ 43,922	+ 3·4	9,145,000	+ 3·9
1948	1,323,679	+ 5,873	+ 0·4	9,320,000	+ 1·9
1949	1,305,056	− 18,623	− 1·4	9,267,000	− 0·5
1950	1,293,403	− 11,653	− 0·9	9,243,000	− 0·3
1951	1,337,060	+ 43,657	+ 3·4	9,481,000	+ 2·6
1952	1,329,057	− 8,003	− 0·6	9,524,000	+ 0·5
1953	1,309,583	− 19,474	− 1·5	9,461,000	− 0·7
1954	1,289,989	− 19,594	− 1·5	9,495,000	+ 0·4
1955	1,305,456[3]				

[1] Sources: Annual Reports of the General Executive Council of the Transport and General Workers' Union and the *Ministry of Labour Gazette*, September 1939, November 1951, and November 1954.
[2] In this year the Union amalgamated with the Workers' Union.
[3] Total membership at the end of March 1955.

Then the membership increased at a much slower rate until, after May 1940, it received a boost from the effects of the war. Between December 1939 and March 1955 the membership of the Union increased by 87·96 per cent. Almost all of this increase was obtained in the four years 1940, 1941, 1942, and 1946. In the first three years 438,691 members, amounting to 63·2 per cent of the 1939 membership, were enrolled and retained. The reasons for such a high percentage increase are to be found in the conditions of the Second World War.

The incidence of the increase amongst the trades covered by the Union was very uneven and was greatest in the groups catering for general workers and metal, engineering and chemical workers: i.e. in those industries which expanded to meet the needs of the war. Table II shows, however, that the membership increased in all groups except the docks group between 1938 and 1943. Dock workers were highly organized and the decline was caused by a decrease in the dock labour force. The factors which were mainly responsible for the membership increase are given below. They operated for the whole of the Movement but, as will be seen, were often of greater consequence in those unions with existing extensive organizations.

Reasons for the Expansion

There was a change both in the attitudes and the behaviour of workers and employers towards trade unions during the Second World War. It is not possible to assess the exact importance of the change in attitudes, but one gathers from talks with trade union

TABLE II

COMPARATIVE MEMBERSHIP CHANGES IN THE TRADE GROUPS OF THE
TRANSPORT AND GENERAL WORKERS' UNION, 1938 AND 1942[1]

Trade Group	Total Membership		Increase (+) or Decrease (−)	Percentage Increase (+) or Decrease (−) in 1942 over Membership in 1938
	1938	1942		
(i)	(ii)	(iii)	(iv)	(v)
Docks	87,509	80,154	− 7,355	− 8·4
Waterways	8,000	8,473	+ 473	+ 5·9
Road Passenger Transport	150,836	169,960	+ 19,124	+ 12·7
Road Commercial Transport	79,991	97,554	+ 17,563	+ 22·0
General Workers	171,000	276,604	+105,604	+ 61·8
Building Trades	32,422	39,869	+ 7,447	+ 23·0
Metal, Engineering and Chemical	96,037	400,268	+304,231	+316·7
Admin., Clerical and Supervisory	9,214	17,020	+ 7,806	+ 84·7
Power Workers	28,709	38,450	+ 9,741	+ 33·9

[1] Excluding the North Wales Quarrymen's Group. The slate quarrying industry in north Wales employed only about 10 per cent. of its pre-war labour force during the first year of the war. This increased to about 60 per cent. during 1941 and 1942. Most of the slate quarry workers were organized by the Group.

8+T.U.L.

officials that its effect was relatively small.   There is no doubt that
the temper of industrial relations was influenced by the need for a
united war effort, by the vital role of labour in pursuit of this effort,
and by the willingness of trade unions to co-operate with the Coalition Government.   As far as workers were concerned, trade unions
were ready-made organizations for giving expression to their
dissatisfaction with past social and economic conditions which was
unleashed by the war.

The behaviour of workers and employers was primarily determined
by two factors.   First, there was from 1940 a state of full employment.   Under full employment workers are able to afford union
subscriptions and can indulge in union activity without fear of unfair
discrimination from employers.   Those who were conscious of the
value of trade union activity belonged to trade unions during the bad
as well as the good years and were unaffected by the change in the
state of the labour market.   In the main the workers who were
brought into trade unions by full employment were those who,
whilst they were not prepared to join unions on their own initiative,
offered no resistance to being recruited.   Some of the new entrants
to industry, particularly women, had an exaggerated conception of
the extensiveness and importance of trade unions and believed that
joining a trade union was a condition attached to taking up work in
industry.   They were thus psychologically conditioned towards
becoming trade unionists.   Moreover, a large part of the influx
of new workers went into trades and sections of industries which
were already organized and possessed active shop-stewards' organizations.   Non-unionists were virtually powerless when confronted
by determined shop-stewards.

Secondly, a material change in industrial relations was created by
the application of the Essential Work Orders, the Conditions of
Employment and National Arbitration Order, 1940, and the Undertakings (Restriction on Engagement) Order, 1940.   Any firm could
apply to be scheduled under an Essential Work Order.   A scheduled
firm was classified as being engaged in essential work if the work was
'expedient for securing the defence of the realm or the efficient
prosecution of the war or for maintaining supplies or services
essential to the life of the community so to do'.[1]   Such a firm had its
labour supply protected, and as there was an ever increasing demand
for a contracting civilian labour force this protection was important.

Under the Orders the permission of a National Service Officer was
required before a worker could leave his employment or be discharged, and not in any circumstances could a worker be dismissed
for legitimate trade union activity.   It was an administrative

[1] Essential Work (General Provisions) Order, 1941, No. 302.

practice of the Ministry of Labour, not specified in the Orders, to consult unions about firms before scheduling them. If the working conditions in a firm were bad or if the firm paid less than trade union rates the union could object to the scheduling. Firms which had their applications refused often approached the union or unions concerned and thus provided trade union officials with the opportunity to enter factories and to organize workers. There were many relatively small organized groups within factories which possessed no negotiating rights. Firms wishing to be scheduled often found it advantageous to grant these rights, and by doing so they enhanced the factory status of the union or unions concerned. In consequence recruitment became easier.

There was no provision in the Orders granting trade union recognition and no regulation to prevent a non-union firm from being scheduled if it complied with the conditions of the Orders.[1] But the Orders accorded a status to unions and thus implied recognition. For example, National Service Officers in dealing with applications from workers to leave employment, applications by employers to dismiss workmen, etc., were instructed to advise workmen to raise their grievances through their trade union and to accept absence on official trade union business as being within the definition of 'leave for public duty'.[2] The effect of the Orders on recruitment was indirect and was largely determined by the existence and initiative of trade union officials. The full-time officials of the Transport and General Workers' Union were urged to take advantage of the opportunities the Orders presented and to get their lay members to act under their protection.

Under the terms of the Conditions of Employment and National Arbitration Order a unilateral application could be made to have a dispute referred to arbitration. A group of workers in a firm which did not grant union recognition were able (under the guidance of trade union officials) to make such an application if they failed to secure satisfaction from their employer. Some firms retained a prejudice against unions, but they did not like having it made public that they were using a relatively expensive arbitration process because of their anti-trade union prejudices, and they grudgingly conceded

[1] No Government Order during the war gave the trade unions a legal right to claim recognition from employers. Ernest Bevin was pressed to include in the Conditions of Employment and National Arbitration Order, 1940, a clause making recognition a matter for arbitration. He refused because he said he would have to put over to a judge the question as to whether or not a breakaway union should be recognized. He said: 'It is a principle of law that everybody must bear in mind: the law will not discriminate between citizens. So the judge would almost have to decide in the High Court that that union must be represented, even if it had only half a dozen members. That is a very dangerous principle, and once the courts have decided you are done. . . .' (Biennial Delegate Conference of the Transport and General Workers' Union, 1945.)

[2] Annual Report, Trades Union Congress, 1941, p. 144.

full trade union recognition. Workers also became aware of the fact that legal redress existed against those firms which did not observe recognized conditions and rates of pay, and they were quick to call in union officials to negotiate with managements. Once in the factories the officials were able to recruit new members.

During the war there was an extension of night and shift working for women and young persons. The extension could be sanctioned by the Factory Inspectorate who issued permits, but before doing so they normally consulted unions which had, or were likely to have, memberships in the factories concerned. This meant that officials of the Transport and General Workers' Union often had advance notice that an employer was seeking a permit, and if they acted quickly the intended introduction or extension of night or shift working gave them a good talking point on which to base a recruiting appeal. It can readily be seen that the Transport and General Workers' Union was in a position to take advantage of the opportunities for expansion created by the war.

Facilities for the extension of trade union membership were created by the establishment in various industries of joint production committees.[1] Though the workers on these committees were often the properly elected representatives of trade unionists and non-trade unionists alike, they were invariably active trade union members themselves. Members of the Employers' Federation in the Engineering Industry agreed that the workers' side of Joint Production Consultative and Advisory Committees should consist solely of trade unionists.[2] In a few cases, such as in the Royal Dockyards, the worker members of the committees were nominated by trade unions; in other cases the ballots were conducted by the unions or by the unions and management jointly.[3] During the first three years of the war, more than ever before, non-trade unionists were a consequence of trade union inactivity rather than social and economic conditions.

Table I shows that during the years 1943, 1944, and 1945 the Transport and General Workers' Union lost members. The losses were small compared with the gains of the previous years but they were large by the standards of other unions and caused Arthur Deakin some concern. In a report to the General Executive Council

[1] Yard committees in the Shipbuilding and Ship-repairing Industry were formed in most shipyards and existing ones were strengthened with widened functions. An Agreement was reached between the Ministry of Supply and the unions concerned, in February 1942, for the establishment in each Ordnance Factory of a Consultative and Advisory Committee 'for the regular exchange of views between the management and the workers on matters relating to the improvement of production'. (*Industrial Relations Handbook*, H.M.S.O., 1944, p. 114.)
[2] In an agreement with the engineering trade unions on 8 March 1942.
[3] *Industrial Relations Handbook*, H.M.S.O., 1944, p. 115.

he outlined the factors that he thought were responsible for the decline. He wrote:

> I find that it arises from a number of causes, not the least being the closure of certain factories, with a transference of members to other employment and a consequent loss of contacts. A further factor is the outlook arising from the attitude to wage claims related to the temporary stabilization that is at present operating in certain industries. On top of this is the growing feeling that we are nearing the end of the war, with the result that the workers will return to their ordinary way of life. This has the effect of creating an apathy and indifference to trade union organization; in other words, there is no permanency to a great number of people in their present employment.[1]

A possible further reason is that the expansion during 1941 and 1942 was too great for the administration to carry. Many people found themselves enrolled into branches which could not possibly cater for their needs but which happened to be the only ones available to distribute cards and collect contributions. Factory workers on one occasion were known to have been enrolled by a busmen's branch.

At the end of the war Deakin was prepared for a bigger loss of members. 'Having regard', he said, 'to the experience following the 1914–1918 war, when the Trade Union Movement in this country had to face a serious setback, we should not have been surprised if our Union, during the period of the switch-over, had lost a fairly substantial number of members. We regarded the rock-bottom position as possibly leaving us with 750,000 members.'[2] That is, with a loss of more than 260,000 members. As it happened, almost that number were gained in 1946 alone, giving the Union the biggest increase in its history to date.

The main reasons for this last increase seem to be that the demobilized service men and women returned to a state of full employment and quickly found jobs, and they became employed in occupations, trades, and industries which in many cases had been organized in their absence. Consequently many who had been non-unionists before the war found in 1946 and 1947 that they were expected to join a trade union, which, with the optimism of returning soldiers, they were prepared to do. Since 1947 there have been only slight fluctuations in the membership of the Union.

[1] 6 December 1943.
[2] Scottish Delegate Conference, 6 September 1946.

Chapter Fifteen

ADMINISTRATIVE LEADERSHIP

3. DEAKIN AS AN ADMINISTRATOR

THE administrative actions of Arthur Deakin fell into two phases, though it is difficult to indicate where the division between them lay. The first phase started when he was appointed as Acting General Secretary on Ernest Bevin's recommendation; it ended and the second phase began when Deakin felt sufficiently confident and independent of Bevin's influence to act solely on his own judgment. He became the elected General Secretary of the Union in March 1946 but before then he felt he was the leader of the Union.

There is no positive evidence that Bevin directly interfered in the affairs of the Union during the war. He attended the three Biennial Delegate Conferences held during the war, and out of nine meetings that Deakin held with National and Regional Secretaries of the Union between May 1940 and August 1945 Bevin was present at five of them, but he did not attend Executive meetings until the end of 1944. In later years Arthur Deakin insisted that he had suffered no interference from Bevin in the course of his work. This may well have been the case. Ever since he had entered Transport House as a National Secretary in 1932, Deakin had been much under Bevin's influence. He admired Bevin and accepted his decisions because he thought they were correct. He did not construe an interest in the affairs of the Union by Bevin as interference nor did he see anything wrong in seeking Bevin's advice.

There were no constitutional restraints imposed on Arthur Deakin other than those imposed on a properly elected general secretary. When Bevin approached his Executive Council about the question of the executive administration of the Union in his absence, he stated that the Assistant General Secretary (Arthur Deakin), the Financial Secretary (Stanley Hirst), and the Senior National Trade Group Secretary (Harold Clay) understood and accepted that Deakin should act as the chief executive officer. He had made suggestions, he said, to Deakin and Clay with regard to the allocation of responsibilities, 'although . . . this would be a matter to be decided by the Acting General Secretary following the Council Session, in consultation with the Acting Assistant General Secretary (Harold Clay)'. When

Bevin again met the Executive Council in December 1944 to explain that the National Executive of the Labour Party had decided that on the dissolution of the existing Parliament they would break with the Coalition and go to the country free and independent of all other parties, he stated that his leave of absence would come to an end on the dissolution and that he would return to the Union as its General Secretary to complete his term of office until March 1946. This raised an issue for the Council to determine, but his own view was that even on his return he should not interfere with the administrative arrangements then operating, and that neither Deakin nor Clay should be demoted. He did not state in what way he was going to function as General Secretary but he confirmed that he regarded Deakin as the chief administrator.

Regardless of the constitutional position of Deakin during the war and of the admiration he possessed for Bevin, it was not possible for him to act independently of Bevin's policies and methods. He was operating an administrative machine which had been largely created by Bevin and which was staffed in the main by people who had an intense admiration for him. Already a legend was beginning to grow around Bevin and Deakin had to live and work with it. It is hard to envisage a more difficult assignment of trade union leadership than that which Arthur Deakin undertook in 1940. It was inevitable that frequent comparisons should be made between Bevin and Deakin and that, in the early stages at least, they should not be favourable towards Deakin. The comparisons were unfair, for they were being made between a man whose leadership qualities had been fully developed and tested over many years, and a man who had been thrown into a position of leadership without warning and who had not shown evidence of great ability in his previous positions. At points of departure from Bevin's policy Deakin was reminded of it, but he insisted on pursuing the policy he thought best.[1] His position was invidious, for he might have had to work under Bevin again, perhaps in quite a short time.

Nevertheless, Deakin gradually emerged as a leader in his own right. He set himself diligently to master the details of his job, which fortunately was not interrupted by any large-scale industrial troubles for his first four years of office. The influences set up by the job slowly created changes in him and revealed latent ability. The outward manifestations were not immediate reflections of inward changes and, in consequence, there was no stage when one could

[1] At the 1943 B.D.C. Deakin was drawn to say: 'I do not want anyone to set the declared expression of opinion of Brother Bevin in previous years against mine. I have never given anyone any reason to suppose that I doubted the wisdom, sagacity and policy pursued by Brother Bevin over a number of years, but I do say that as far as the present time is concerned I am in a position to judge whether or not the organization is capable of being developed in a particular direction.'

have said that he emerged as the leader of the Union. The difficulty of demarcating the phases was increased by his confident manner and self-assertiveness during the whole period. He gave those who worked with him no cause to doubt, in appearance at any rate, the authority of the position he held. But he attempted no bold or sweeping changes in the organization of the Union. At all times he proceeded with caution, as the remainder of this chapter shows.

I. FINANCE

As the chief administrator it was Arthur Deakin's function to keep a check on the financial position of the Union. From the Regional Secretaries he received fortnightly reports and more detailed quarterly reports containing comparative statistics relating to the membership and financial returns of each branch. The percentages of contribution income used by each region for administration, benefits, and for remission to the Central Office were calculated for him, thus enabling him to obtain a fairly complete picture of the financial state of the Union.

In the Transport and General Workers' Union the Regional Secretaries are responsible for the level of membership and the collection of contributions. From the contribution income collected each Regional Office pays out all the benefits except dispute and victimization benefit which the Central Office distributes; it also pays for its own and branch administration expenses. The residue is remitted to the Central Fund. During Arthur Deakin's term of office approximately 52 per cent. of the contribution income was spent by regions in the ways described above. The most important item of expenditure in any of the regions is the salary bill for officials and staff, and this is subjected to stringent central control. The General Executive Council directly controls the number and salaries of officials, but in so far as other employees of the Union are concerned it has delegated its authority to the General Secretary. Other items on the expenditure account of the regions which are financed out of contribution income are the responsibility of the Regional Secretaries and their committees under the general supervision of the Executive. The General Secretary's influence concerning these items is an indirect one. In 1954 the percentages of the contribution incomes that were expended by the Regional Offices on administrative expenses varied between 21·5 and 57·6. The differences were in some measure due to variations in the concentration and types of workers and therefore in the difficulties of organizing workers. But they were also due in part to the use of different administrative methods which were determined to varying extents by Executive decisions, by tradition, and by the initiative of Regional Secretaries. Regions are able to accumulate their own funds from sources other than contribution income and from these funds the Regional Committees can purchase equipment for specific regional purposes.

If Deakin wished to increase the income of the Union he had either to increase the Union membership or raise contributions or both. The methods used to increase the membership were the direct concern of Regional Secretaries and were only indirectly affected by the General Secretary. The decision to increase contributions lay in the hands of the Rules Revision Conference of the Union,[1] though in this matter Deakin carried much influence.

From the outset Arthur Deakin was concerned about the financial position of the Union for three main reasons. First, because of the temporary nature of his post, he wished to conserve the General Fund so that its *per capita* value was not less than it was when he became Acting General Secretary. Secondly, he believed that the bigger the accumulated reserves of the Union the more effective the Union would be in its negotiations with employers. He said in 1942 that 'money does talk, in dealing with employers; they are always much more ready to fight when the workers have nothing to fight with'.[2] Lastly, he anticipated large-scale industrial unrest after the war and a need for a large strike fund. This last point appeared prominently in Deakin's reports and speeches up till the end of 1945. He believed that there would be a repetition of the post-First World War conditions.

Contributions

The first increase in the Union contributions resulted from pressure by Deakin. A proposal for a 1*d*. per week increase on all contribution scales was examined by the General Executive Council in May 1941, and was turned down for the time being 'having regard to the present stable financial position of the Union'. Tables III and IV show the financial state of the Union during the early war years. The surplus of income over expenditure shown in Table III fell from £222,086 in 1939 to £205,273 in 1940 and then rose substantially; in 1942 it was almost double what it was in 1940. There had been no drain on the General Fund since the 1937 Coronation strike of London busmen, and it was rapidly approaching the high level of £2 million. Nor did the expenditure account give cause for concern. The total administration costs as a proportion of contribution income rose from 1938 until 1940 and then fell, so that in 1942 it was back to its 1937 level, despite rising prices.[3]

[1] Before 1950 this authority lay with the Biennial Delegate Conference.
[2] Recalled Biennial Delegate Conference, October 1942.
[3] Shown in Table IV and in Figure I, p. 262.

8*

In May 1942 the General Executive Council re-examined a proposal by Deakin for an increase in the contributions, but no firm decision was made until July 1942, when the Finance and General Purposes Committee, still of the opinion that administrative costs were not unreasonably high and that the finances of the Union were

TABLE III

CHANGES IN THE TOTAL INCOME AND THE GENERAL FUND OF THE
TRANSPORT AND GENERAL WORKERS' UNION, 1922–1954[1]

Year	Total Income[2]	Annual Deficit (−) or Surplus (+)[3]	Deficit or Surplus as a Percentage of the Total Income	General Fund
(i)	(ii) £	(iii) £	(iv) %	(v) £
1922	367,850	+ 9,312	+ 2·5	388,077
1923	409,566	+ 17,647	+ 4·3	399,686
1924	492,108	− 78,484	−15·9	319,196
1925	507,399	+109,070	+21·5	437,925
1926	520,593	−395,819	−76·0	46,036
1927	458,247	+ 60,961	+13·3	103,104
1928	440,611	+ 73,993	+16·8	170,892
1929	520,111	+ 62,149	+11·9	242,033
1930	616,794	+ 80,020	+13·0	324,549
1931	606,723	+ 55,720	+ 9·2	368,570
1932	566,722	+ 48.638	+ 8·6	407,260
1933	533,685	+ 49,120	+ 9·2	451,089
1934	584,139	+103,997	+17·8	434,881
1935	657,102	+110,712	+16·8	638,141
1936	756,627	+168,381	+22·3	798,237
1937	867,233	+123,262	+14·2	907,962
1938	946,795	+252,583	+26·7	1,163,951
1939	947,030	+222,086	+23·5	1,356,574
1940	934,356	+205,273	+21·9	1,537,464
1941	1,017,620	+253,370	+24·9	1,761,292
1942	1,263,613	+409,499	+32·4	2,139,374
1943	1,493,049	+512,238	+34·3	2,619,276
1944	1,553,487	+512,738	+33·0	3,098,861
1945	1,487,471	+402,001	+27·0	3,472,572
1946	1,808,574	+623,439	+34·5	4,073,499
1947	2,114,482	+676,146	+32·0	4,762,971
1948	2,200,137	+746,665	+34·0	5,476,813
1949	2,259,778	+696,971	+30·9	6,140,212
1950	2,219,276	+643,199	+29·0	6,746,114
1951	2,298,187	+576,225	+25·1	7,284,554
1952	2,362,986	+587,484	+24·9	7,832,269
1953	2,557,351	+694,475	+27·2	8,486,795
1954	2,590,756	+612,007	+23·6	9,055,363

[1] *Sources*: Annual Reports and Balance Sheets. The figures relate to December in each year.
[2] Total income consists of income from members, derived mainly from contributions, and of income from property and investment.
[3] Deficits are met from the General Fund. Surpluses given here are of income over expenditure; a few small allocations to funds are made from a surplus before it is added to the General Fund.

TABLE IV

THE ALLOCATION OF CONTRIBUTION INCOME FOR THE ADMINISTRATION OF
THE TRANSPORT AND GENERAL WORKERS' UNION, 1922–1954[1]

Year	Income from Contributions	Branch and Regional Administration Costs		Central Office Administration Costs	Total Admin. Costs as a Percentage of Contribution Income
		All Branches	All Regional Offices		
	£	£	£	£	%
1922	284,184	77,672	129,613	78,627	100·6[2]
1923	363,446	82,383	126,205	73,138	77·5
1924	437,387	88,726	133,103	106,350	74·8
1925	455,832	83,787	152,049	81,096	69·5
1926	439,243	86,296	161,392	91,314	77·1
1927	408,254	87,180	148,496	75,501	76·3
1928	395,740	85,733	136,601	87,139	78·2
1929	445,629	94,827	163,364	88,294	77·8
1930	500,457	100,253	201,215	98,724	79·9
1931	499,837	105,790	203,824	87,664	77·5
1932	470,074	100,561	202,024	90,415	81·6
1933	489,148	95,657	201,263	66,115	74·3
1934	536,000	98,171	197,796	65,818	67·5
1935	609,851	109,500	208,282	71,414	63·9
1936	692,598	123,186	228,691	69,605	60·8
1937	797,786	140,353	252,165	79,594	59·2
1938	883,034	156,753	279,731	86,365	59·2
1939	866,366	153,223	285,697	87,895	60·8
1940	845,810	148,434	303,464	94,834	64·6
1941	942,400	152,257	340,450	101,846	63·1
1942	1,148,649	185,752	390,117	96,428	59·2
1943	1,370,155	217,578	425,617	110,891	55·1
1944	1,411,961	224,922	461,342	119,691	57·1
1945	1,337,555	218,636	477,651	139,761	62·4
1946	1,620,080	255,504	546,737	140,894	58·2
1947	1,909,157	302,812	622,973	192,541	58·5
1948	1,988,656	322,120	678,821	165,204	58·6
1949	2,031,244	352,721	702,823	175,733	60·6
1950	1,971,447	348,895	718,605	179,388	63·3
1951	2,027,520	357,966	782,620	219,917	67·0
1952	2,071,803	337,375	837,557	261,345	69·3
1953	2,248,611	394,209	861,304	270,422	65·8
1954	2,254,786	395,292	879,219	259,420	68·0

[1] *Sources*: Reports and Balance Sheets.
[2] In this year administration costs were in excess of contribution income by £1,726, though, as can be seen in Table III, out of its total income the Union had a surplus of 2·5 per cent.

sound, decided 'that the time was opportune to consider the advisability of consulting the membership on the question of an increase
in contributions'. The reason they gave was an apprehension about
post-war conditions. The General Executive Council accepted this
decision and in October 1942 a specially recalled Biennial Delegate

Conference agreed to increase all contribution scales by 1*d.* per week, thus making the basic contribution 7*d.* per week.

Ten years elapsed before the Executive again approached the membership for an increase in contributions. This was not because Arthur Deakin thought that an increase during the interim period was not necessary or could not be justified. He thought that trade unionism was cheap but that the members did not realize what good value they were getting for their money, and consequently begrudged paying more.[1]

In 1948 Deakin made the point that 'the only way you can adjust balances is by way of increases in contributions'.[2] During the inter-war years it is doubtful whether contribution increases could ever have been contemplated as a solution to the financial problems of a union. Trade unions were beset with financial problems, through the exhaustion of their funds and declining memberships, which would have been aggravated by any attempt to increase contributions. Arthur Deakin's attitude was a reflection of the times as well as a difference of approach. Throughout the whole of his period of office there was full employment with rising price and wage levels. Consequently, not only were workers much more able to afford union contributions than they had been during the inter-war years, but they were mentally adjusted to accepting price increases.

Yet the Executive of the Union in 1952 was still cautious about asking for an increase in the contribution. Deakin mentioned in March 1952 that it might be necessary to increase contributions, but added, 'It is merely expressed at this time to condition your minds to the possibility.'[3] Then, at its June quarterly meeting, the Executive Council decided to recall the Rules Conference to consider changes in the contribution scales. Two proposals were eventually submitted by the Executive to the Conference on 9 October 1952. One asked for a flat-rate increase of 2*d.* per week on all contribution scales with a 'consequential increase in the Dispute, Lock-out, Victimization and Accident Benefits'; the other for an increase of 1*d.* per week on all contribution scales without any adjustment in benefits. The first proposal was rejected by the Conference by 66 votes to 29; the alternative was carried by 84 votes to 6.

Three points of interest emerge from the second increase in contributions. (*a*) The alternative proposal was based, in Deakin's own words, 'upon the advisability of having two strings to our bow'. 'It may well be', he told his Executive, 'that the Members are not over-concerned to provide additional benefits at this time. On the

1 National and Regional Secretaries' Conference, August 1948.
2 Ibid.
3 T. & G.W.U., Report to G.E.C.

other hand, it is necessary for us to have an increased contribution income. . . .' (*b*) The principal reason for the second increase was completely different from that given in 1942. The Executive case in 1952 was that administrative costs were rising in relation to contribution income. Figure I[1] shows an uninterrupted rise from 1947 till 1953. In his speech to the Conference Deakin described the make-up of administrative costs in detail and made comparisons with 1943 figures. 'A trade union', Deakin said, 'like any other organization must of necessity be run on a business basis. . . .' (*c*) In a Standing Orders Committee report to the Conference it was suggested that the date of the application of any increase should be decided by the Executive. The reason given by Arthur Deakin was that the 'General Workers,[2] the Union most in line with ours, had a proposal at their Annual Conference [for an increase in contributions] which they withdrew for the time being but which they are going to re-submit . . . we must make common cause with the National Union of General and Municipal Workers in this matter. I have undertaken, as an Executive Officer, to consult with the General Secretary of the N.U.G.M.W. and we will make any increase that is agreed upon common as far as the date of its application is concerned.' In trade union relations this action was most unusual.

Control of Costs

The General Executive Council and its chief executive officers kept as tight a control over administrative costs as the circumstances permitted. The most difficult part of their task was to regulate regional expenditure. Ernest Bevin endeavoured to do this by stipulating the maximum proportion of contribution income which should be spent on administration in each region. The effectiveness of this method depended upon the proportion providing a fair indication of the costs at which the regions could operate efficiently. The application of a single figure, however, to a complex cost structure was bound to have a limited use. Operating costs differed so widely between the regions that any attempt to produce uniform costs would have undoubtedly dislocated the Union administration. Moreover, the original proportion was derived from Bevin's intuition and was not based on detailed calculations.

At the 1927 Biennial Delegate Conference, in a Supplementary Report, the General Executive Council stated that the total cost of administering a region should not exceed 40 per cent. of the income from contributions and that administrative costs for the whole

[1] P. 262.
[2] The National Union of General and Municipal Workers.

Union should be restricted to 50 per cent. of contribution income. The figures, Bevin said, were based on the 1925 income. In 1925 the branch and regional office costs amounted to 51·7 per cent. of the contribution income. It can be seen that if Bevin's proposal had been applied in 1925 it would have entailed a severe pruning of Union services. In 1927, when branch and regional office, and total administrative costs were 57·8 per cent. and 76·3 per cent. respectively, damaging restrictions might have been required. There was undoubtedly a real need for economy in 1927 apart from the desirability of improving the efficiency of the administration. Bevin wanted to be able to 'budget for the payment of benefits and administrative changes at a given figure enabling a definite sum to be placed in reserve each year'. The General Strike had virtually wiped out the reserves of the Union and these had to be rebuilt, for 'in view of the monopolistic tendency of industry the Union is at all times faced with the possibility of large sections of its members being involved in disputes quite apart from any consideration of national strikes or movements of that character . . .'.

There was an upward revision of the suggested percentage limit on regional administrative costs in August 1932. Bevin stated to his Executive that 'due to the amalgamation with the Workers' Union and the depression, it had not been possible for Areas to keep their administrative expenditure down to 40 per cent. of their contribution incomes'. As the Union income was falling the Finance and General Purposes Committee proposed that 'there be no increase in expenditure in any Area where the administrative costs already exceed 45 per cent. of the income on any ground whatever, without the special sanction of the Executive Council given for exceptional reasons'. That the Executive proposal was having little effect in the regions was indicated by Bevin's periodic reports. In May 1933 he stated: 'When we have arrived at a more sound position in relation to Staff, it seems to me that it will be absolutely essential to arrive at a definite percentage allowance for the Areas for Administration purposes'. He returned to his theme in May of the following year and added that 'it is fatal to build up overheads which, in the event of a sudden slump, become fixed liabilities very difficult to carry'.

During 1940 only two regions out of thirteen had kept their administrative costs down to 45 per cent. of their incomes; seven regions were well over 50 per cent. and one was as high as 65 per cent. References to the percentage limit by Deakin served only as reminders that administrative costs should be kept to a reasonable level. He did not press for stringent economies; it was not necessary, for the Union income increased in every year of his period of office with the exception of 1945 and 1950. Administrative costs, he told his National and Regional Secretaries in July 1946, are

> repeatedly the subject of examination within the Areas with a view to effecting economies wherever possible, but it is necessary to have regard to the high standard and prestige enjoyed by the Union today which, in the main, has been created on the firm basis of service. To do anything which would have the effect of limiting administration costs unreasonably, would have an adverse effect, both from a membership and income point of view.

He suggested that the regional administrative costs should not exceed 50 per cent. Two years later he told a similar gathering: 'We used to say it was safe to work on 40 per cent.; then we revised our ideas to a figure of 50 per cent. and now, taking in everything, it is 60 per cent.' Towards the end of his career Deakin was not worried particularly by administration costs, but in June and September 1954 he sounded words of warning. He reported in September:

> It is my practice to look at the financial returns of other Unions, which are obtainable through the medium of the Registrar-General. From my examination of these returns and my contacts in the T.U.C. it is clear that many Unions are running into the position where they are only able to balance their budgets by reason of their investment revenue. This, I suggest, is dangerous finance. . . .

So far we have been concerned with what can be termed as control by exhortation. The exhortations Deakin made were always backed by the authority of the General Executive Council but the attention they received depended also on three other factors. One concerned the practical steps taken by the General Secretary to reduce costs by improving the administrative efficiency of the Union: another was the attention given by the General Secretary to the costs which came directly under his and the General Executive Council's control; the third concerned the relationships that existed between the General Secretary and the Regional Secretaries—in the main the manner and extent to which the General Secretary confided in and trusted the Regional Secretaries. This factor belongs to another section and is discussed later.

2. ADMINISTRATIVE METHODS

Arthur Deakin revealed no administrative creativeness and he was not particularly concerned about administrative methods. His behaviour in these matters was no doubt in part determined by the conditions under which he worked. His Union was an established institution and its membership and income were increasing, so there were no urgent administrative problems for him to solve. Regional administration, moreover, was primarily the responsibility of the Regional Secretaries and their lay committees. He did not stand in the way of improvements which were initiated by others, nor did he consciously tolerate inefficiency. Where inefficiency was indicated through the dissatisfaction of the members with the services they were receiving he would support an inquiry into the matter. But he did not initiate inquiries to discover better administrative methods, nor did he attempt to put into practice any ideas he may have had concerning administration.

There had always been scope for improvement in the Union administration: in the collection of subscriptions, in the submission and tabulation of branch returns, in the distribution of arrears notices and the collection of arrears, in the payment of benefits by branches, and in maintaining contact with mobile members. It was not a case only of pressing for general improvement but of seeking also to raise the level of efficiency in the least efficient branches and regions.

It had been Bevin's intention to centralize the Union administration, and as a first step he pressed for uniformity between branch practices in each region. When he mentioned this in 1927 there were three main types of branch administration. There were branches where the branch secretary collected the contributions and performed no other financial transaction; he did not even record the contributions in a ledger but passed the job on to the Regional Office. In other branches lay secretaries collected contributions and recorded them; they interviewed members in need of assistance and paid out benefits. Lastly, there were permanent branch secretaries who had their wages paid out of branch income; these undertook all the secretarial functions in their branches. When the problem of administration, with particular reference to the collection of arrears in subscriptions, was discussed in 1938[1] it was revealed that the differences in methods which had once been characteristic of branches had to some extent become characteristic of the regions. It was discovered, for instance, that the responsibility for collecting arrears varied considerably between the regions: in London and the Home Counties it was centralized; in the south-west of England it was devolved to districts; and in Liverpool it was completely in the hands of the branches. Some regions had no system for collecting arrears, and not all regional secretaries thought it necessary to have a complete list of the addresses of their members.

Membership Turnover

Many of the problems with which Ernest Bevin was faced in the middle and late 1930s also confronted Arthur Deakin. Accumu-

[1] At a Conference of National and Regional Secretaries, December 1938.

lated arrears, though less after 1940 than before, were still high.[1]   A related problem, the high turnover of members each year, was perpetually with the Union, but it became more important after 1940 simply because it was numerically much larger.   In two ways it imposed a greater strain on the Union administration than any other single factor.   Firstly, a loss of membership meant an equivalent loss of income; and, secondly, in order to retain a membership of a certain size, the Union had to be capable of organizing considerably more.   Thus to make a net gain of 43,922 members in 1947 as many as 480,628 new members had to be recruited.

Membership turnover figures show the lapsed membership in a year as a percentage of the previous year's total membership.   The gravity of the administrative problem they reveal depends on the extent to which they show the proportion of preventable losses in a year; i.e. the losses that are the direct responsibility of the union administration.   As the gross losses are the result of a number of factors, some of which are beyond the control of a union administration, and as the recorded figures show gross losses only, the figures should be handled with much caution.   Moreover, since only a rough and ready attempt can be made at isolating the preventable losses, precise conclusions about them should be avoided.

Some proportion of the gross losses must be rated as normal wastage.   These are caused mainly by death or retirement from work for health reasons, or on reaching the age limit, or, as in the case of most women, on getting married or having a child.   It can be seen that the normal wastage will depend very much on the sex and age composition of a union, and in some unions the normal wastage may be relatively high.   Other losses are caused through the labour turnover in industry.   Where a worker changes his job by moving to another district, industry, or occupation he may break his contact with his union in such a way as either to make it impossible for him to remain in membership—for example, if he moves into the recognized territory of another union—or to make it too costly for the union to keep a check on him as would be the case if he moved frequently, like builders' labourers.   Many of these losses are as inevitable as the normal wastage.   If in a trade union a high normal wastage is combined with high proportionate losses through industrial labour turnover, the number of reasonably preventable lapses of membership may be quite small.   One should, therefore, always look closely at the types of workers a union organizes before reaching conclusions about its membership turnover.   The figures might be inflated, moreover, by the inveterate casual worker who is just as casual about his union membership.   By joining a union, lapsing,

[1] *The Government of British Trade Unions*, by Joseph Goldstein, ch. 6.

then rejoining, and so on, it is possible, in some unions, for him to appear two or three times in the annual figures.

The Transport and General Workers' Union has a high gross loss of members each year, coupled with a high annual intake; its average annual rate of membership turnover for the years 1936–1947 inclusive has been calculated at 33 per cent.[1] The reasoning in the paragraph above indicates that a high membership turnover rate is not likely to be confined to the Transport and General Workers' Union. What evidence there is supports this contention and shows that high rates predominate in the general unions; that is, in those unions which cater for transient female workers and the occupationally mobile sections of the working population.[2]

A further factor which has to be considered is that there is usually an absence of trade union consciousness amongst workers in industries with a rapidly changing general labour force. In these cases there is no impulse to keep a worker in a union except that which comes from the union administration; indeed, many such workers would lapse their membership before changing their jobs if they were permitted to do so. Deakin referred to the importance of this factor during the war, but it was not a war-time phenomenon. It was a continual source of anxiety to Bevin, who believed that the great task confronting the Union was not the making of new members but consolidating them once they were organized. Doubtless after the war, too, many workers took the first opportunity to cease paying contributions because they had no feeling for trade unionism.

The administration of the Transport and General Workers' Union was therefore only in part responsible for the high membership turnover from which the Union suffered. The effects on the Union are such, however, that it would be unwise for the Union at any time to under-estimate its share in the responsibility. Although the constitution has placed the onus of remaining in membership on the individual member, in practice it has been undertaken by the union administration, and the extent to which subscription arrears have been collected and members have been pursued in their occupations has been reflected in the membership turnover figures and has been a measure of the success of the administration.

The ease with which members were recruited in the war and postwar years softened, almost hid, the effects of membership lapses on the Union. It was easy to be philosophical about it under those

[1] Cf. ibid., Table II, p. 74.
[2] The Workers' Union had an average membership turnover rate for the years 1916–1927 of 38·5 per cent. It ranged, though not in sequence, between 22·0 per cent. and 70·6 per cent. (Annual Reports, 1916–1927.) The membership turnover in the National Union of General and Municipal Workers is high (*General Union*, by H. A. Clegg, pp. 27–31); as it is also in the Union of Shop, Distributive and Allied Workers, which is becoming more general in character and which caters for a large number of young female shop assistants.

conditions; even to regard it as being in the nature of things. It was the latter attitude that Arthur Deakin adopted during the post-war years. He showed some concern about lapsed members during his early years in office but he never said, nor seemed inclined to say, as Bevin did, 'I am at my wits' end as to how to bring about an improvement.' He stated in December 1954 that it was not a worrying problem, even though during that year there had been 349,430 lapsed members compared with 329,836 new members. When discussing the matter with the writer he said some people suggested that it was too easy to get into the Union and Union membership was not valued as it ought to be and that, therefore, new members ought to be initiated into the branches as is done in craft unions. But, he added, difficulties in the way of joining a trade union are inconsistent with mass membership. How could a union organize new large factories in this way, he asked, particularly if they were situated away from the homes of the workers? It was difficult enough getting existing Union members to branch meetings. He said nothing about introducing administrative changes to reduce the number of members who lapsed each year.

The Quality of Branch Officials

In one important respect Arthur Deakin displayed administrative leadership ability. He encouraged and gave practical support to the provision of educational services in the Union in a manner and on a scale calculated to improve the administrative efficiency of branch officials and to raise the quality of candidates for official Union positions.

When he became Acting General Secretary the Education Department of the Union was small and of little consequence. Educational services of a non-vocational kind had been provided by the Union since its formation, but until 1938 they had depended in the main upon the efforts of men who were principally trade union negotiators and not educationalists. From 1938 there was a full-time secretary of the department that included education amongst its functions. The Union gave financial assistance to two adult educational bodies, the Workers' Educational Association and, to a lesser extent, the National Council of Labour Colleges, and left them to provide courses according to their own standards. During the second half of 1939 the Union started its own postal study course called 'The Union, its Work and Problems', in order to help to equip members to become better officials.[1]

Deakin came on the scene before the scheme had recovered from the setback it received at the declaration of war. The idea belonged

[1] Stated by Bevin at the T. & G.W.U., B.D.C., 1939.

to Bevin, not Deakin, but the fulfilment of the idea was Deakin's achievement. Deakin had had an early interest in educational activities. He had been a prominent member of the Local Education Authority in Flintshire when he was an Assistant District Secretary in the Union. But his support for the development of the Education department was not immediately wholehearted. It had to be won over. His interest for some years after 1940 was, in general, for non-vocational subjects. Then slowly he changed his approach until he came to look upon trade union education as a means of training trade unionists to become full-time officials. He was motivated, he said, by the poor quality of candidates for official jobs in the Union whom he had interviewed over many years.[1]

An expanding Education department was a double charge upon the revenue of the Union without showing any immediate tangible returns. The cost of the administration of the department was an increasing item of expenditure, and the expansion of the work of the department entailed the allocation of a bigger sum of money each year for the provision of courses and for scholarships. In 1942 the sum of £10 was distributed as educational grants; this had increased to £7,544 for the year ending 31 December 1947 and to £34,764 for the year ending 31 December 1954. Given the rapid increase in costs and the absence of immediate returns it would have been understandable if Deakin had preferred to use the Union money in a different manner. He could have advised his Executive to spend the money on Union propaganda to justify his own and Executive actions to the rank and file and to prepare the rank and file to accept future Executive decisions. Alternatively, but with less justification, he could have advised the use of Union funds for a form of indoctrination—of his own brand of Socialism, for example. Both methods have been used in other unions.

Instead, Deakin supported a liberal approach to education which eventually became blended with vocational training. The first residential Union Summer School was arranged by the Workers' Educational Association in 1950. The tutors were selected by the W.E.A. and they drafted their own syllabuses under an agreed general heading. This was a traditional W.E.A. and University type Summer School. Changes occurred in the organization of later schools and in the teaching methods used. The courses involved more intensive study and combined a theoretical examination of trade union subjects with practical training in trade union methods and techniques. Separate training provisions were made for shop-stewards, branch secretaries, branch chairmen, and branch

[1] Speech to the Educational and Social Council of Region 6 (centred on Manchester), April 1948.

committeemen. Exercises in branch administration formed an important part of these courses, and such matters as letter-writing, note-taking, the preparation of minutes and agendas, and the handling of branch accounts were examined and discussed.

The courses continued to be run in conjunction with the W.E.A. which supplied the tutors, mainly from its own staff and from Universities. Much planning for the courses was involved and the compilation of syllabuses was co-ordinated at the centre, but neither Deakin nor any other leading official of the Union attempted in any way to control the manner in which the individual tutor tackled his syllabus or what he taught. The spirit of liberal education remained unimpaired.

Deakin's desire, which he expressed in 1948, to improve the quality of officials showed signs of fulfilment by 1955. In 1950 only 51 students attended the Summer School, whereas over the two-year period 1954–1955 there were 1,036 students. In absolute terms the number was still small, but it was high in relation to the active membership of the Union and one could see, in 1955, many former Union students in Union administrative and policy-making posts and figuring prominently amongst the successful applicants for full-time Union jobs.

It is always difficult to assign credit to individuals for the achievements of an organization. The pioneering work was led by the Secretary of the Education Department but it could not have been done at all without Deakin's support. The Education Department has now become the largest department in the Central Office and its services have penetrated every section of the Union. This contribution by Arthur Deakin towards administrative efficiency may have far-reaching effects in the Union.

Central Office Costs

In the control of the expenditure within his direct sphere of influence, Deakin exercised the utmost care for, he said, 'we have got to have regard to the fact that we are spending every time the hard-earned . . . 7*d*.s of the people who are our membership of this Union. That is a responsibility we must never ignore.'[1] By virtue of his post, he was in charge of the Central Office, assisted by his administrative assistant and the Financial Secretary. Day-to-day matters had been delegated by Bevin to his assistant and only matters which could not be settled by a subordinate ever reached Bevin. Arthur Deakin, however, was much more concerned about the exercise of his constitutional power in the office than was his predecessor, and slowly though not altogether obviously he collected

[1] T. & G.W.U., B.D.C., 1944.

under his immediate supervision some of the delegated jobs. As he did not make clear the distinction between those matters he wished to control and those he did not, and because he always showed an interest in small matters, his administrative assistant found it prudent to pass many things on to Deakin which he could have settled himself. This meant, of course, that Deakin controlled large and small items of expenditure to a much greater extent than did Ernest Bevin. The net effect of the control remained unchanged. Central Office costs, as Figure I shows, started to decline in the mid-1930s and levelled off at approximately 10 per cent. of the contribution income; thereafter they roughly followed the same course as total costs.

Union Salaries

For each year of Arthur Deakin's period of office the largest single item of expenditure by the Union was the salaries bill for officials and staff. The bill increased both in amount and as a proportion of the contribution income throughout the years. In 1940 it amounted to 23·2 per cent. of contribution income; in 1945 and 1954 the percentages were 23·7 and 27·0. These percentages do not include payments to branch officials or collectors' commission. From a cost aspect it is clear that the total salaries bill needed to be scrutinized carefully.

The negotiating procedure for determining salary levels changed between 1940 and 1955, but in each procedure Arthur Deakin played a prominent, perhaps dominant, part. From 1940 until 1947 there was no national negotiating machinery for Union salaries; consequently Deakin's control over salary adjustments was considerable. His position was made clear by a General Executive Council statement in 1941. The staff of Region I had sent a deputation to the Region I Committee to have their wages reviewed. This was stated by Deakin, and later ruled by the Executive, to be unconstitutional on the ground that salary adjustments in a region could not be made without affecting the entire staff of the Union and were, therefore, the responsibility of the Executive. If the staff in any region wanted a salary increase, it should, the Executive stated, approach the Regional Secretary concerned, 'who shall in turn make representations to the General Secretary of the Union to whom authority is delegated by this Council to deal with all questions affecting the salaries and conditions of employment of the Union Staff'. A Staff Representation Scheme was approved by the Executive in March 1947 which provided for national negotiation; Deakin still negotiated on behalf of the Executive but his decisions had to be ratified by the Executive.

Arthur Deakin's views about changes in the level of the salaries of the officials and staff of his Union altered with his general attitude towards wage increases. In 1942, when he was not an advocate of wage restraint, he used the need to give officials equitable salary increases as a part of his case for an increase in contributions. After the war his views changed. He spoke more frequently of salary increases as increases in administrative costs and he set an example in his own Union of the restraint he was advocating for workers as a whole. As evidence of this, when the Regional Secretaries sought wage parity with National Officers in 1951, Deakin said: 'there could be no reasonable argument against parity . . . when due regard was paid to the relative duties and responsibilities; in fact, but for the policy which had applied of *rigid wage restraint* [1] a proposal designed to establish parity would, in all probability, have been submitted at an earlier date'. By constantly refusing increases in his own salary he set a standard which he thought other officials ought to adopt. He may not have realized fully the implications of his action. In part it resulted in officials in his Union getting less than officials in some other unions, particularly the comparable National Union of General and Municipal Workers, and in their salaries lagging behind the wages of the workers for whom they negotiated. This in turn adversely affected the recruitment of officials in certain sections of the Union.

Full-time Officials and Staff

A part of the increases in the salary bill for the Union was caused by the employment of more officials and staff. Regardless of whether the Union was expanding or contracting there were requests from the regions for more organizers, who were required either to cope with an increased membership or to organize a potential membership. Sometimes more full-time officials had to be taken on to cope with changes such as the establishment of a new trade group. The control of this form of expenditure was vested in the General Executive Council.

Each Regional Committee wanted sufficient full-time officials and staff to tackle its own problems, and it was Deakin's task to relate these demands to the needs of the Union as a whole and to concede them only in so far as they would make a positive contribution to efficiency in the Union. This is not to say that he did not consider the needs of particular regions or trades. He did. Some rural areas, for example, were given more officials than their actual memberships justified; and the building trade was treated likewise because of its vast potential membership.

[1] My italics.

It was some time after 1940 before Arthur Deakin felt that an expansion of the organization was necessary. In a report to his Executive in March 1942 he stated:

> The Areas must of necessity recognise the need to go cautiously in the creation of additional machinery, and especially in the appointment of additional officers, which would, if overdone, saddle the Union with a responsibility which it would be difficult to carry at the conclusion of hostilities with the possibility of a dislocation of trade and a consequent loss of membership.

He had analysed regional administration costs in that report and warned the Executive 'as to the necessity for exercising close control over future commitments in relation to any considerable extension'. He returned to the theme in his next report and added that for 'a number of years we have proceeded on the premise that the Officers and Staff were capable of carrying on the administration for a very much greater membership . . .'.

When motions for extending the trade group system were discussed in the 1943 Biennial Delegate Conference Deakin objected on the grounds of cost.

> At the moment [he said] there are 1,000 people employed by this Union, in round figures—500 officers, and a staff of 500; our salary costs in respect of that staff amount to 25 per cent. of our income. I ask you whether you can go on indefinitely developing an arrangement of that character. I have to keep my eye on the future. I know that at the present moment we are officered up to the full extent. You cannot have one officer for every few hundred members; to be on a safe level you must not have more than one officer at least for every $2\frac{1}{2}$ thousand members. . . .

It had been calculated that approximately 2,000 members could maintain a full-time official from their contributions and make appropriate allocations to other costs. At his last appearance at a Biennial Delegate Conference as a General Secretary in 1945, Ernest Bevin also spoke of the cost of extending the trade group system. He told delegates:

> You are very proud of the accumulation of funds, but what has helped you to accumulate them? Arbitration for five years and no strikes. Although you may have £3,500,000 of money to date, if the tide turns and you have to pay strike pay . . . your surplus will vanish into thin air. If you are not very careful the members will turn and rend you if you overload the machinery with officers and committees, and the money is eaten up with administration. They don't take any notice when nothing happens, but if you fail to foot the bill when it does, then the trouble commences.

The number of officials and staff employed by the Union grew even when its membership did not and, occasionally, Arthur Deakin doubted whether the Union was wise in permitting this. Between October 1952 and September 1954 the total number employed by the Union increased from 1,335 to 1,434. The doubts were not created solely by the rising costs of administration, as his words to delegates in 1952 illustrate. 'I wonder sometimes', he said, 'whether we have not gone astray in this respect, whether we have not provided too much service and sapped the vitality of our people to such an extent that they are not ready to help themselves as much as they once were . . .'.[1] But he knew well that a cut in the services would be a false economy. The Union service in the main was a source of its strength; the weaknesses it tended to create, such as reducing the activities of lay members, needed to be tackled by something more positive than economy measures.

3. THE EXERCISE OF AUTHORITY

It was stated earlier that the success of control by exhortation as practised by Arthur Deakin depended upon his relationship with his Regional Secretaries. This statement can be enlarged in two directions. Arthur Deakin's relationships with the General Executive Council and all of his officials were important, particularly those who were nearest to him in the hierarchy of the Union; and the importance of the relationships extended beyond control by exhortation to the exercise of authority in general in the Union, with a consequent effect upon administrative efficiency.

General Executive Council

The allocation of authority in the first place was, and is, prescribed by the rules of the Union. The ultimate responsibility for the administration of the Union lay with the Biennial Delegate Conference but the practical operation of the Union was entrusted to the General Executive Council.

'The General Executive Council shall set up the necessary departments for the proper administration of the business of the Union; allocate Officers and prescribe their powers and duties and terms of employment.' (Rule 6.13.) 'In addition to any express powers in these rules provided, the General Executive Council shall have power generally to carry on the business of the Union, and may delegate such of their powers to the general secretary as they may deem necessary, and do such things and authorize such acts, including the payment of moneys, on behalf of the Union as they, in the general interests of the Union, may deem expedient. . . .' (Rule 6.15). 'It shall be the duty of the General Executive Council to keep themselves informed as to the general administration

[1] Recalled Rules Conference, 1952.

of the Union; to exercise a general supervision over the keeping of
the accounts; and to verify, from time to time, any cash balances in the
hands of the secretary and other officers.' (Rule 6.18) etc.

Arthur Deakin was an *ex-officio* member of the Executive with
the right to speak but not to vote.   He was undoubtedly its most
influential member and his relationship with its lay members was a
crucial one.   According to the rules he was required to 'act generally
under the orders of the General Executive Council' and to 'perform
all the duties laid down by the General Executive Council and . . .
generally supervise the work of the Union in all departments'.   His
own interpretation of his role was that of 'defining Executive policy
in the ordinary way of things'.[1]   Thus the Biennial Delegate Conference propounded on major matters, the Executive interpreted the
Conference decisions, and the General Secretary defined the Executive interpretations.   This is more than the rules stated but less than
the true position.

Three main factors placed Arthur Deakin in a strong relative
position on the General Executive Council.

1. The Executive and the Finance and General Purposes Committee
of the Executive met quarterly and monthly respectively, whereas
Deakin, as the chief executive officer, was in continual contact with
the national affairs of the Union and consequently was required to
act in between the meetings of those committees.   He worked within
the confines of Executive decisions.   On new matters which arose
when neither the Executive nor the Finance and General Purposes
Committee were meeting, he often took immediate unilateral action
in the manner of a business executive, choosing to justify his actions
to his Executive rather than seek a decision from them before acting,
as Bevin did.   He did not usurp Executive authority for it was,
after all, within its right to compel him to retract statements
he had made or to alter decisions he had taken.   The need for
'collective responsibility' to preserve the unity of the organization
made it extremely unlikely that the Executive would exercise this
right and in practice Deakin's actions were endorsed.

To some extent he changed the character of Executive meetings;
they became more concerned with receiving reports than with formulating lines of future action, and consequently had less to say than
they had had in Bevin's day.   It is not implied that Deakin did not
have to argue with his Executive to accept his point of view, or that
his actions were not moderated by Executive deliberations.   Changes
in the details of policy rather than in courses of action resulted from
the intervention of the Executive.   And until 1950 Deakin was
harangued bitterly by the Communist members of the Executive.

[1] T. & G.W.U., Report to G.E.C., 5 March 1951.

They presented a formidable disciplined group who stimulated opposition to Deakin from others. In those days Deakin could never be absolutely sure that he could carry his Executive with him on controversial matters.

A danger inherent in Arthur Deakin's approach to his Executive was that sometimes the members may have felt that they were not determining policy, and this may have weakened morale during difficult periods. The success of the approach depended partly on the results that Deakin could show his Executive, but more, perhaps, on his ability to persuade them that his actions were the right ones in the circumstances.

2. The second factor lay in his position as a permanent official on a lay committee with a changing composition. In the six biennial elections held from 1942 the percentage changes in the membership of the General Executive Council were 61, 44, 44, 51, 54, and 46. Few members possessed Deakin's length and continuity of service and those who did were in no sense comparable to him as Union officials. His intimate contact with the affairs of the Union, with the trade union movement at home and abroad, and with political events generally, gave him a depth of knowledge and an understanding of problems that the Executive members could hardly have hoped to possess. The skills that he had developed in committee and conference work, in negotiating and in representing the Union, combined with the specialist services of different departments of the Union that he had at his disposal, gave him an undoubted position of superiority.

3. The two factors already considered would have acted in favour of any General Secretary of the Union. The third factor lay in his personal qualities. Though he could present factual and reasoned cases, much of his power in Committee was derived from his force of presentation, his determination to get his own way, and his ability to overawe his opponents. These applied on whichever committee he sat, whether with employers, trade union leaders, or his own members, and they were almost always equally successful. He had the faculty of making his presence felt simply by being present, and when he intervened it was at his own discretion, regardless of procedure or the wishes of other members of the committee. That such methods could be successful with employers and other union leaders gives some indication of the authority he commanded with his own members.

The relationship between Deakin and his Executive was frequently a subject of criticism. He was aware of this and resented it as he resented any form of criticism which was based on half-truths. 'It has been said', Deakin remarked, 'that I dominate the Executive.

That is entirely untrue . . . is it conceivable that I, as one individual, can dominate thirty-nine Members of an Executive? . . . if I can reason with the Executive, if I can give them that leadership which I am paid to give, then surely no one can fairly criticize.'[1] At no stage did he deny that he virtually controlled the Executive, he only disputed the way in which it was said that he did it. He defended himself by saying: '. . . it is not to be held against me if, by logic and reason, I am able to convince the Executive that certain policies are best for our Union. When I have done and said that, they make their decision and you have no right to cavil at what your Executive representatives decide to do, and seek to attribute the decision to me.'[2] He was a powerful person on the Executive but did he really dictate its deliberations? He gave his own characteristic answer in 1952. 'There is', he said, '. . . a disposition to mistake leadership for dictatorship. It is said sometimes that I am too forceful a personality, that I exercise too much persuasion over the constitutional bodies of the Union. I reject that statement with contempt.'[3]

Other Union Officials

The duties of the Financial Secretary are prescribed by rule and concern only the finances of the Union. The rules make no mention of the duties of the Assistant General Secretary, the National Trade Group Secretaries, the Administrative Officer, National Officers, heads of departments, and Regional Secretaries.[4] The functions of the National Trade Group Committees and the Regional Committees are expressly laid down and it can be assumed that their respective secretaries work under their direction and possess a similar relationship to the General Secretary as those Committees possess to the General Executive Council. The duties of the Assistant General Secretary were stipulated in the terms of the appointment in 1948 when a vacancy occurred, and required him to 'work under the direction of the General Secretary and the General Executive Council' and, in addition to undertaking industrial negotiations, 'to supervise and control staff and deal generally with the administrative work of the Union under the direction of the General Secretary, or in his absence'.

A point of some importance is that the General Secretary is the only National Official (excluding the Financial Secretary who has specialist duties) with constitutional recognition, and therefore

1 London Transport Three Section Committee's Conference, September 1950.
2 T. & G.W.U., B.D.C., 1953.
3 Scottish Delegate Conference of the T. & G.W.U., November 1952.
4 Except to say that the 'regional secretary shall have control of the regional office' (Rule 14, Section 2).

whilst others may acquire authority he is the only one who can claim it constitutionally. In the event of any dispute between the General Secretary and a National Officer or Officers over the allocation of responsibilities this could be the determining factor. The General Secretary exists in his own right whilst the remainder exist by the will of the General Executive Council. In addition, one should note, the General Secretary is the only National Official who is elected by the votes of the membership, and from this he derives a status and moral authority which is denied to others.[1] Thus the constitution only indirectly laid down the limits within which the first officers of the Union had to work. Once the organization became established a division of work took place between individuals which in effect distributed the authority. As changes occurred in the personnel of the Union so authority was redistributed. One needs to consider now the impact of Deakin's behaviour on the distribution of authority.

Ernest Bevin had, within the terms of the constitution, set around him his own pattern of duties and responsibilities and Deakin succeeded to them. Arthur Deakin, however, was a man with different qualities confronting problems that Bevin did not have to face, so it was not surprising that changes in the pattern should occur. The alterations resulted from a combination of four main factors: (*a*) Arthur Deakin had a problem of succession; (*b*) he possessed an innate concern for minor matters; (*c*) he did not find it easy to delegate authority; and (*d*) he enjoyed the exercise of power.

In most circumstances it takes a man of courage and ability to devolve responsibility effectively, and in any case he must possess an absolute confidence in the security of his position as a leader. Deakin lacked this confidence at first. This is not surprising considering that he followed immediately after a man of Bevin's calibre in an organization which was Bevin's creation. He had to assert his independence of Bevin and gain confidence in the loyalty as well as the ability of his colleagues. In the meantime he avoided measures which might have weakened his position. In small ways he collected power around him and to that extent made subordinate officials more dependent on him. He interested himself in minor matters such as the details of central office administration mentioned earlier. From the beginning he displayed a characteristic which marked his behaviour until the end. He liked to deal with affairs and problems that could have been dealt with effectively by others whose tasks were less exacting than his own. This preference was a natural one for him and was not primarily caused by the desire to

[1] The National Secretary of the Power Group holds an elective post but he is elected only by members of his Group.

exercise power, though undoubtedly it added to the impression that he liked power.

The General Secretary is a man who is expected to make the decisions which no one else can or is in a position to make in the Union. His time ought therefore to be conserved for these high-level and—because the General Secretary is the highest paid official —high-cost decisions. If he devotes much time to minor matters he has less time for the important aspects of his work and presumably does them less effectively. He is also expending his own high-cost time on matters which could be done more cheaply. From the subordinates' angle, he is wasting their resources and, not the least important, he is not showing the confidence between them and himself that is necessary for efficient administration. These effects were not all apparent in Deakin's case. He made his job much more onerous than it should have been, but it did not seem to have impaired his ability to handle the major affairs of the Union.

Arthur Deakin assumed the role of leader obtrusively. Biennial Delegate Conferences, for example, were characterized by his high degree of participation in the debates. Though he had National Trade Group Secretaries with him on the platform he would deal with motions and questions relating to their special fields of operation. On every aspect of Union work he was able to give satisfactory information and on very few occasions was his point of view not carried. As well as being the chief, sometimes only, spokesman for the General Executive Council, he virtually controlled the Conferences. He showed a wide range of ability and a facility to handle men which constituted an undoubted leadership quality and which in other aspects of his work brought him considerable success. But the Conferences were part of the activities of his own organization in which the national officials should have had positive functions to perform.

The manner in which Arthur Deakin handled his officials at the Trades Union Congresses and Labour Party Conferences was similar. He maintained a relatively strict control over delegation speakers and played a dominant part himself in the conference proceedings. These conferences, however, were not comparable to those of his Union. Firstly, it was a matter of prestige that he should in appearance and in fact lead his organization delegation at conferences in the Labour Movement; in this he never failed. Secondly, the composition of the officials in the delegations was not related to the subjects for debate as it was in his own Conferences. National Trade Group Secretaries attended the Trades Union Congress and the Labour Party Conference on a rota system.

Before 1940, a few of the delegates from the Union had established the practice of speaking to motions on subjects in which they were particularly interested, and they continued with the practice when Deakin became General Secretary. The Secretary of the Legal Department of the Union, Frank Stillwell, frequently spoke on matters relating to his Department and Harold Clay intervened whenever transport or education were being debated. The reputations of these men gave them an independence of action which no other officials enjoyed. No doubt the control that Deakin wielded over his delegations would have been weakened had they contained more such men, or persons with the prestige and independence of Ben Tillett, James Sexton, and Harry Gosling, who intervened in debates at their discretion. In 1930 James Sexton actually opposed a motion moved by Ernest Bevin at the Trades Union Congress, but it is inconceivable that any delegate would have done this when Deakin was General Secretary. Deakin's reluctance to spread delegation duties to his specialist officials gives a more definite example of his attitude towards officials than one can get from his relations with them in other aspects of his work. It provides, too, a good indication of his attitude towards the devolution of responsibility.

The position of Assistant General Secretary, though it has certain duties ascribed to it, is basically determined by the relationship between the incumbent and the General Secretary. The holder of the office from 1948 till 1955, Arthur E. Tiffin, made it clear at the outset that he did not regard himself as an assistant to the General Secretary but as the Assistant General Secretary; that is, as a person with his own duties, responsibilities, and rights. Nevertheless, the extent to which he held these was determined by the General Secretary. Arthur Deakin, in his full capacity as a trade union leader, always had more work to do than he could undertake himself and he was compelled to pass jobs down. He made his own choice in this matter, but he was subject at any time to pressure from the Assistant General Secretary. Because the attitudes and personalities of the persons concerned were so important, a new Assistant General Secretary did not automatically inherit all the jobs his predecessor undertook. When Bevin moved to the Ministry of Labour it was understood that the gap he left in the administration was to be filled jointly, but not equally, by Deakin and Harold Clay, who became Acting General Secretary and Acting Assistant General Secretary respectively. This placed Clay in a stronger position than if he had been appointed under an established General Secretary, and the functions he performed were more extensive and responsible than those Deakin himself had undertaken when he was the Assistant General Secretary. The resignation of Clay in 1947 permitted Deakin to rearrange the duties of the Assistant General Secretary to suit his own requirements.

The National Trade Group Secretaries were in a different position from the Assistant General Secretary. They had more readily defined tasks to do and their contact with Deakin was determined by their need for assistance in the solution of their problems and by his interest in the work they were doing. Thus the working relationships between Deakin and the National Secretaries varied from trade group to trade group. Deakin had his own special interests. He retained an interest in the galvanizing trade because of his early association with it, and with docks and the London bus section partly because they were trouble spots and partly because they formed important sections of the Union in which Bevin had played an active role. The Secretaries handling these trades saw more of Deakin than did other Secretaries and sometimes he conducted negotiations for them. Within the limits imposed by the job each National Secretary had as much responsibility as he wished to carry, and provided that he met with no important industrial disputes he had relatively little need to consult Deakin. The initiative for contact, however, also lay with Deakin.

The demarcation between showing an interest in the work of a trade group and interfering in that work is vague and uncertain. The difference may lie only in approach. When Deakin showed an interest it often appeared as interference. He did not possess the faculty of handling individuals easily. He was clumsy, over-sensitive, and, surprisingly, shy. His shyness was obscured by an assertiveness which sometimes became almost aggressive; frequently, instead of revealing his true feelings he displayed irritability. This explained why he could appear to be enraged by an official and then, when the official had left his room, warmly comment that he was one of the best officials the Union had.

Because of Deakin's difficulty in communicating effectively with individuals, his officials did not confide in him; and he did not engage in those personal relationships in which members of an organization at different spheres or levels mix socially and exchange advice and information. In a way this was an advantage, for in an organization such as a large trade union where there is much manoeuvring for positions of relative power, it is often advisable for the chief official to remain aloof. Once he becomes intimate with a few of his subordinates he loses his authority as an arbiter by becoming personally associated with internal issues. He is less able to assist in the solution of problems, by being unable to bring a third and independent mind to bear on them. The fact that information was not always transmitted upwards to Deakin because there were few informal channels between himself and his officials was offset, to some extent, by another aspect of the activities of an organization. Jurisdictional disputes in an organization, or disputes between officials on other grounds, as Herbert Simon has pointed out,[1] can be an important means of bringing to the top administrator significant issues of policy; they prevent issues from being decided at lower levels without his knowledge and they inform him of the characteristics and viewpoints of his subordinates. Simon wrote:

> Particularly when policy in the organization is in its formative stages, there may be important advantages . . . to the top administrator in a somewhat indefinite allocation of authority that would permit such disputes to arise. Certainly, the technique of 'playing one against the other' is used by top administrators so often that it cannot be casually dismissed as poor administration.

In Deakin, perhaps more than in any other trade union leader of his generation, could be seen the incompatibility of some of the qualities required for leadership in a large modern union. His position as an administrator required him to be able to handle individuals, to trust them, and to extract the best from them; but his natural facility, hence his main qualification for leadership in general, was in the way he handled masses of men. These he could understand and interpret and he could communicate with them more effectively than with individuals. He was required to exercise authority, and so long as this necessitated only obtaining the acquiescence of subordinates he was successful. But in a trade union the exercise of authority should also be based on persuasion and suggestion, and these Deakin was less capable of using. Perhaps this was a consequence of his origin. He felt that basically his members were his equals and that only his position of authority distinguished him from them; perhaps he tended to make the distinction clear by being authoritarian.[2]

It is more likely that Deakin was authoritarian by nature. He was capable of making quick, firm decisions and he had the utmost faith in his own simple, straightforward opinions and ideas. He was intolerant of people who were long-winded and indecisive. He exercised authority naturally and easily. In contrast, it should be mentioned here that in his relations with employers in negotiations he practised persuasion and suggestion and accepted compromise solutions. But this is only a further illustration of the complexity of the qualities required by a modern trade union leader.

Though Arthur Deakin's inability to devolve responsibility to his subordinates may be interpreted as absence of loyalty to them, it

[1] *Administrative Behaviour*, by H. A. Simon, p. 145.
[2] Cf. *Political Parties*, by Maurice Duverger, p. 171 (Methuen, 1954). See above, pp. 111–112.

9+T.U.L.

was not so. He possessed an undeviating loyalty to his officials, which comprised part of the structure of loyalties he had created and which had such an important place in his life. Persons outside the Union who were prominently concerned in industrial disputes with Arthur Deakin have expressed the view that his allegiance to his officials sometimes hindered the settlement of disputes. He neither admitted that his officials had acted wrongly nor that they could possibly be inefficient. There was some justification for this attitude. A top administrator who refused to stand behind his subordinates would seriously weaken morale and would tend to stifle initiative within the organization. All organizations must guard against the feeling of insecurity which could result from the application of excessive zeal for efficiency by senior executives. Moreover, in a trade union dismissals could result in defections from the organization. There are always some lay members who are willing to stand by an official threatened with dismissal, regardless of his inefficiency, and in some cases other officials are prepared to act likewise because they can imagine the same thing happening to themselves. Nevertheless, a trade union leader should possess discriminating loyalty and this Deakin did not have. He stood just as solidly behind those who were dilatory as those who were enterprising. When disputes occurred between officials and lay members, on most occasions he supported the officials, sometimes with adverse repercussions upon his own relations with the ordinary members.

One quality which Arthur Deakin demanded from his officials was absolute loyalty to the Union, and the cause for which it stood. He was critical of officials who left the Union to take up other occupations, as some did when the Government nationalization measures were implemented after 1945, though he staunchly supported their right to go. In his opinion they should have refused to leave the Union, as he had done on three occasions in 1948. Loyalty to the Union Deakin valued for its own sake, and, regardless of their efficiency, he gave credit and support to men who possessed it. Although Deakin was leading an organization which, on his own admission, was dependent for its existence upon the service it rendered to its members, he was never so concerned with efficiency as to allow it to take precedence over loyalty. He could not accept the standards of business organizations, because he rejected the yardstick they used. 'I hope,' he said, 'that we shall never get to that position where we have got to compensate people on a market basis for the service that they give to this movement. When we get into that position . . . we have lost the soul of this movement and very speedily we shall come to disaster.'[1]

[1] T. & G.W.U., B.D.C., 1945.

Though one ought not to expect a trade union leader to fulfil all the canons of administrative behaviour, it could be said that Deakin did less as an administrator than could have been expected; he had little interest in administrative efficiency, could not successfully delegate authority, and was inept at handling subordinates. But to admit this without any qualification would be doing less than justice to him. One knows that administrative inefficiency unchecked can result in chaos; this did not happen in the Transport and General Workers' Union. It remained, as far as one can tell, a relatively efficient organization during a period when its size was approximately doubled. At all times Deakin remained firmly in control of the organization, which in itself is some measure of administrative ability, particularly when one considers the multifarious other jobs he did. He made mistakes and faulty decisions, of course, but it was possible to check some of them near the source because the responsibility for implementing many of the administrative decisions made by Deakin lay with his Administrative Assistant, an able man, with a profound knowledge of union administration. On the whole, Deakin did only those things that the job required him to do under post-war conditions. For this he can be criticized, yet it was no mean achievement when one looks at the complete man and his activities.

Chapter Sixteen

ADMINISTRATIVE LEADERSHIP

(4) CHARGES OF CENTRAL BUREAUCRACY

THIS chapter closes the examination of administrative leadership in the Transport and General Workers' Union. It is concerned with the charge, made often and from various quarters, that the Union is bureaucratic; it shows the extent of central control and the manner in which it was exercised by Arthur Deakin.

First, the charge itself. Bureaucracy has become a catchword with a derogatory meaning, which, though rarely clearly stated, is that the Union has become over-centralized and is slow moving with a sluggish reflex action; that its system of communications has become inadequate through the rigid use of rules, regulations and procedure by officials in offices, and that the officials, particularly the top administrators, have become divorced from their original sense of purpose through an excessive preoccupation with institutional factors. These, some say, result from the growth of the Union.

> This growth [wrote social scientists from Liverpool University] . . . has forced them to set up an elaborate institutional framework divorced from the private lives of their members, to develop a complicated system of regulation and control, to impose sanctions in support of the subordination of individual to group interests, and to accept a number of responsibilities and obligations incompatible with their original functions.[1]

The writers, more reasonable than many Union critics, added, 'Slowness is an inevitable result of the size and complicated structure of the union.'[2] The second quotation is a hypothesis, not proven, from which the charge of bureaucracy usually springs. The Union is big, it is said, therefore it must be bureaucratic.

Secondly, the formal meaning of the word. A bureaucracy is a specific type of administration which is indispensable for large-scale organizations. It involves an elaborate institutional framework, for continuous administrative work cannot be carried out in any field except by means of officials working in offices. It is organized on

1 *The Dock Worker* (University of Liverpool), p. 117.
2 Ibid., p. 135.

the basis of knowledge; that is, it is undertaken by experts, who are not elected but are appointed either by superiors or by examination. And it is conducted within a hierarchy of levels of authority so that the actions of each individual are disciplined and fitted into a pre-determined pattern of activity.[1] This is a simple and valid inter-pretation of bureaucracy.

In fact it is a description of an extremely successful form of ad-ministration most common amongst business organizations, less common amongst trade unions. Trade unions are essentially representative organizations and can, therefore, never develop into formal bureaucracies. But for the benefit of increased adminis-trative efficiency a trade union can approximate towards one. It can appoint its officials by examination; it can use full-time officials extensively in offices with clerical staffs; it can use experts; and for the purposes of administration it can institute a hierarchy of control. And it can do these things without changing its representative form. It is true that the Transport and General Workers' Union is bureau-cratic in this sense. But to attach the above meaning to bureaucracy does not dispose of the complaints about the Union administration; it simply evades them.

Thirdly, the possible causes of the complaints. Bureaucracy in its popular derogatory sense is a relative term; particularly is it so when its cause is said to be the growth of a union. If one takes the inverse, the smaller a union gets the less bureaucratic it should be-come. But over-centralization, sluggish reactions, and bad com-munications are not necessarily related to size. Other factors, notably the service provided, change with size, and it is these which may be the real cause of the complaints. The functions, and con-sequently the services, which were undertaken by most small unions when they possessed only one office and very few officials were restricted, uncomplicated ones. As unions got bigger they extended their services and widened the range they provided. The Transport and General Workers' Union has done this. Consequently, the Union touches the members at many more points of their lives than hitherto and increases the opportunities for complaint. A union nowadays may be accused of bureaucracy because of the way in which it has handled a member's application for a University scholarship. To those who assert 'we did not have such bureau-cracy when the union was smaller' might be retorted 'neither did you expect such service'. Complaints may also arise whenever a union, whatever its size, complicates its task without making cor-responding improvements in its administrative machinery; for then the services may not be efficiently run.

[1] *The Theory of Social and Economic Organization*, by Max Weber, pp. 309–310.

Another possible cause may be the inefficiency of officials. This is something which a bureaucracy, almost by definition, ought to avoid, but it is found in large and small unions alike. It has a connection with the previous point, for it is easier to feel the impact of inefficiency when the services the officials are required to provide are extensive and complicated.

It could be that the factors giving rise to the complaints lie on the demand side and not the supply side. Trade union members have been known to be unreasonable in their expectations. This point is supported by the fact that charges of bureaucracy, with all its critical implications, have always been levied against the Transport and General Workers' Union regardless of its size.

Lastly, is there substance in the complaints themselves? They are related complaints, for they all basically concern the responsive-

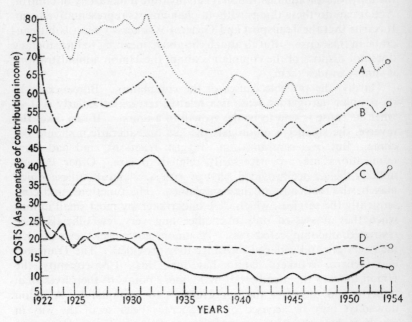

Figure showing the proportion of contribution income spent on administration in the Transport and General Workers' Union, 1922–1954.

A. TOTAL COSTS
(Source: Table IV)

C. REGIONAL COSTS
(Source: Table V, Col. iv)

B. BRANCH AND REGIONAL COSTS
(Source: Table V, Col. v)

D. BRANCH COSTS
(Source: Table V, Col. iii)

E. CENTRAL OFFICE COSTS
(Source: Table V, Col. vi)

TABLE V

THE TOTAL INCOME FROM CONTRIBUTIONS AND THE PERCENTAGES OF IT SPENT
ON ADMINISTRATION BY BRANCHES, REGIONAL OFFICES AND THE CENTRAL OFFICE
OF THE TRANSPORT AND GENERAL WORKERS' UNION, 1922–1954[1]

Year	Income from Contributions £	Branch and Regional Administration Costs			Central Office Admin. Costs as a percentage of Contribution Income[2]
		Admin. Costs of all the Branches as % of Contribution Income	Admin. Costs of all Regions as % of Contribution Income	Total %	
(i)	(ii)	(iii)	(iv)	(v)	(vi)
1922	284,184	27·3	45·6	72·9	27·7
1923	363,446	22·7	34·7	57·4	20·1
1924	437,387	20·1	30·4	50·5	24·3
1925	455,832	18·4	33·3	51·7	17·8
1926	439,243	19·6	36·7	56·3	20·8
1927	408,254	21·4	36·4	57·8	18·5
1928	395,740	21·7	34·5	56·2	22·0
1929	445,629	21·3	36·7	58·0	19·8
1930	500,457	20·0	40·2	60·2	19·7
1931	499,837	21·2	40·8	62·0	17·5
1932	470,074	21·4	43·0	64·4	19·2
1933	489,148	19·6	41·2	60·8	13·5
1934	536,000	18·3	36·9	55·2	12·3
1935	609,851	18·0	34·2	52·2	11·7
1936	692,598	17·8	33·0	50·8	10·0
1937	797,786	17·6	31·6	49·2	10·0
1938	883,034	17·7	31·7	49·4	9·8
1939	866,366	17·7	33·0	50·7	10·1
1940	845,810	17·5	35·9	53·4	11·2
1941	942,400	16·2	36·1	52·3	10·8
1942	1,148,649	16·2	34·0	50·2	8·4
1943	1,370,155	15·9	31·1	47·0	8·1
1944	1,411,961	15·9	32·7	48·6	8·5
1945	1,337,555	16·3	35·7	52·0	10·4
1946	1,620,080	15·8	33·7	49·5	8·7
1947	1,909,157	15·9	32·6	48·5	10·0
1948	1,988,656	16·2	34·1	50·3	8·3
1949	2,031,244	17·4	34·6	52·0	8·6
1950	1,971,447	17·7	36·5	54·2	9·1
1951	2,027,520	17·6	38·6	56·2	10·8
1952	2,071,813	16·3	40·4	56·7	12·6
1953	2,248,611	17·5	36·3	53·8	12·0
1954	2,254,786	17·5	39·0	56·5	11·5

[1] *Sources*: Transport and General Workers' Union Reports and Balance Sheets for each year ending December.

[2] Central Office administrative costs are not given separately in the Balance Sheets. The figures for column (*vi*) have been obtained by subtracting from the total expenditure for the Union, benefits and branch regional costs. Affiliation fees are included in the administration costs of both the regional offices and the central office, but they form only a small part of the total and enter consistently into the costs. The expense incurred in organizing the Biennial Delegate Conference has not been included in central office costs because it is not an annual expenditure.

ness of the administrative machine to the wishes of the ordinary members and they pivot around the main charge of over-centralization. One might say that a union is over-centralized when there is such a concentration of control at the centre that the decision-making process becomes jammed, misdirected, and too far removed from the members.

The starting point for the process of decision-making in the Transport and General Workers' Union is the constitution. Branch practices, which are not prescribed by the constitution, vary between regions and between trades. The administrative bodies to which the branches are responsible are the Regional Committees. About these the rules are more definite. Rule 8 (1) states that the functions of each Regional Committee 'shall include the organization of groups within the region, the co-ordination of the work of the various regional trade groups and sections, the conduct of necessary propaganda, the administration of such business of the Union as affects all sections of the membership in the region such as general industrial movements, educational work, political administration, etc. . . .'. The rules relating to the General Executive Council and the General Secretary were quoted in the previous chapter.[1]

Since the formation of the Union there have been very few changes in the rules, and, as the Union practices can and do deviate from them, the extent of changes in control from the centre can only be shown by an extensive empirical examination. Here only a few general, but significant, points can be made. Table V shows the percentages of the contribution income used for administration by the Branches, Regional Offices, and the Central Office for the years 1922–1954, and Figure I illustrates the figures graphically. The expenditure of income by the different sections of the Union hierarchy gives some indication of the allocation of functions between them and the measure of centralization practised. It does not show the precise control exercised from the centre, but it can be taken that by far the greater part of income expended by branches and regions is expended without reference to the centre.

Branch costs have decreased in relation to other regional costs, though only slightly. For the first five years of the Union the branch and regional administrative costs averaged 21·6 per cent. and 38·2 per cent. of the contribution income respectively, whereas the averages for the five years after 1949 were 17·3 per cent. and 36·1 per cent. The decrease in branch costs has been caused partly by the rationalization of branch organization and partly by the transference of some branch functions to the Regional Offices. There is no indication here of an appreciable move towards centralization

[1] See pp. 249–250.

within the regions, although this was consciously attempted by Bevin.

The most significant comparison, however, is between total regional and branch costs on the one hand and central office costs on the other. The former costs were high in 1922, then for the rest of the period they fluctuated around 54·0 per cent. of contribution income. The highest percentage was reached in 1932 when the difficulties of amalgamating with the Workers' Union were combined with the effects of a high level of unemployment. The lowest percentage was in 1943—a year in which the combined effects of a rapid rise in membership and an increase in individual contributions were felt. The proportion of the contribution income used for central office administration fell considerably during the period. Until 1933 it remained at a relatively high level and averaged 20·7 per cent from 1922 to 1932 (inclusive). Then the percentage fell quickly and was 12·3 in 1934; it fell again and rose to 12·3 per cent. only once during the remaining years. The low level of central office costs reached in the mid-1930s, at a time when the Union had regained its lost membership and was beginning to increase substantially in size, was roughly maintained until 1955.

There is no evidence from these figures to support the contention that more and more functions have been vested in Transport House. The absolute amounts spent on central office administration shown in Table IV reveal that for many years there was no expansion at all in the central office. The amount spent in 1924, £106,350, was not exceeded until 1943. Afterwards most of the increases in costs were due to price rises. The most important newly acquired expenditure was on education, and this, because it tended to bring the necessary competence into the lowest levels of the hierarchy, was in effect a movement towards decentralization.

CENTRALIZATION AND DECENTRALIZATION

Argument is sometimes conducted as if centralization and decentralization were distinct and independent forms of organization. In practice, of course, there are desirable qualities in both, and those which are mutually incompatible must be weighed against each other.[1] It was shown in Chapter III that Regional Secretaries were left with much freedom of action because the task of welding so many unions into one under disturbed industrial conditions was too big a task for a few men in the central office. The practices the Regional Secretaries inherited and perpetuated and those they were able to institute themselves became accepted Union practices.

[1] Cf. *Administrative Behaviour*, by H. A. Simon, pp. 35–36.

9*

Through its form of regional administration the Union gained the most important benefit to be had from decentralization, for it allowed the administrators in the field (branch officials) to be near the point at which decisions were made, and in some cases to participate in the decision-making process. It shortened, too, the lines of communication, so that the chances of distorting information from the ordinary members were less and the responses of the administrators were quicker. With the advantages of decentralization came some of its disadvantages, such as a variety of administrative systems, duplication, and an absence of an adequate demand for specialist services.

The constitution, the flexibility of which permitted such decentralized action, also set its limits, and to these the top administrators worked. They prevented unwarranted extensions of regional administrative action; indeed, where there were weaknesses they endeavoured, not always successfully, to move in to provide the benefits of centralized control. The shifts either way have been slight, but gradually they are removing the more obvious disadvantages of decentralization and centralization. It should not be imagined that the process is anywhere near completion; a glance at some of the problems of financial administration mentioned in the previous chapter shows that there are still many benefits to be gained from greater centralization; as does one's own observation of the organizing of educational and training courses in the Union. It is clear that the Union is not over-centralized in its administration.

In this process Deakin did not present a consistent pattern of behaviour. Though he enjoyed handling power and exercising control, he set in motion what was more a resistance to extension of decentralized action than a movement towards greater central control. With him, centralization really took place within Transport House and not within the Union itself. He showed little desire to interfere with regional practices; indeed, he did what he could to preserve them. On a number of occasions when someone in the Union had demanded more uniformity of practice, Deakin pressed to have the impetus for change remain with the Regional Offices. The variety of practices in the Union were a factor which Deakin did not at any time desire to change. 'When you are dealing with a Union of this character', he said, 'you cannot create uniformity.'[1]

COMMUNICATIONS

Even with the charge of over-centralization disposed of, there could still be grounds for complaint by members that control from the centre was badly exercised. This would be tantamount to over-

[1] T. & G.W.U., B.D.C., 1947.

centralization and could result from causes which involve the Union system of internal communications. Arthur Deakin could have received incorrect information or no information at all. A practical problem of administration is to 'secure an organization of the decision-making process such that relevant knowledge will be brought to bear at the point where the decision is made'.[1] Arthur Deakin obtained his information from four main sources: from the Union research department, from official reports from National and Regional Secretaries, from constitutional committees, and from formal and informal contact with members. The research department provided him with technical information; he got to know about situations, incidents, and the wishes of the members from the remaining sources.

In addition to the fortnightly and quarterly reports from the Regional Secretaries he received quarterly trade reports from the National Trade Group Secretaries which were presented to the General Executive Council. From officials in Transport House he was able to receive information through the medium of minutes and personal contact. He received much information, very often at first hand, from the trade group and regional representatives on the Executive, in addition to that transmitted to the Executive through formal constitutional channels; occasionally he would attend National Trade Group Committee meetings to elicit information about specific matters.

His contact with the members was made in various ways. The most frequent formal contact was made at the Union delegation meetings at the Trades Union Congresses and Labour Party Conferences and at delegate meetings of the Union and trade sections of the Union, notably those held for dockers and London busmen. Sometimes he would meet deputations, though on the whole he was reluctant to do so for fear of undermining the constitutional committees of the Union. Rank-and-file members and lay officials sent many letters to him, sometimes abusive and ill-tempered, but they provided him with details and opinions which he might not have obtained otherwise. During his period of office Deakin attended many branch meetings—to make commemorative presentations to members, or simply to address them, or to placate them—and he was always willing to devote time to questions and discussion and to listen to complaints in conversation; though sometimes he tended to place too much emphasis on rumour. At times the formal and informal channels of communication to Deakin may have been inadequate or inaccurate but on the whole he was well informed about the activities of the Union.

[1] *Administrative Behaviour*, by H. A. Simon, p. 82.

Many of the matters which went to Deakin for his decision had features in common. They involved the same people, or arose out of comparable circumstances, or concerned common principles, so that an important factor when some particular matter was referred to Deakin was his knowledge of previous problems. And he possessed a remarkably good memory for detail.

The movement of information up to Deakin enabled him to establish some measure of rationality in his decision-making. He could never have been completely rational, however, for he was often presented with courses of action which were contrary to his subjective trade union standards. This dilemma was a possible source of conflict with his members. For example, sometimes he gave his own values, which may have differed from those of his members, precedence over facts; at other times he allowed the facts of a situation to determine his behaviour, whereas his members might have acted differently. Such conflicts, and they formed the majority of those incurred, had nothing at all to do with the size of his Union or the extent of Deakin's physical remoteness from the rank and file.

When the decisions had been made they had to be transmitted to those they concerned. This involved communications down the hierarchy of the Union. When they were ineffective by being slow or incomplete, or when the decisions were distorted from their original sense, they provided a cause for complaint. Most of the media for transmitting information upwards were used in reverse. Additional media which were used were branch circulars, press notices, and the monthly Union Journal, *The Record*. The drawback of all except the press notices was that the decisions could not be communicated immediately. Even when special meetings of committees and conferences were held there was inevitably some delay. Decisions which concerned individual members could be sent by letter or delivered individually, and speed and accuracy in these cases depended upon administrative efficiency. But so many Union decisions were the concern of groups of members who elected their own representatives and in these cases there were no satisfactory alternatives to holding meetings of one kind or another. To aggravate matters, the press, radio, and television provided their own interpretations of major matters long before they were able to be communicated through the Union to the members.

Finally, an aspect of central control not yet mentioned is the use of methods by the top administrators to influence the decisions of the members in their branches and low-level constitutional committees. All the downward lines of communication were used for this task. Exhortations, explanations, arguments, and plain facts proceeded through the normal union channels by the written and the spoken word and formed an important element in the acceptance of decisions.

Deakin's own activities supplemented this process. In his forthright and forceful manner he used every opportunity through public speeches, articles in the press, broadcasts, and television appearances to convince his members of the rightness of the actions and policies he advocated. When he was addressing his members Deakin could do no more than offer advice; but with him, as with experts in other fields, advice often became indistinguishable from decision. He practised thereby a form of central control which was none the less important because a few groups rejected it.

Chapter Seventeen

A CAMPAIGN AGAINST COMMUNIST
TRADE UNIONISTS

ARTHUR DEAKIN was most probably best known to the general public
for his campaign against Communists in trade unions. He, more
than any other British trade union leader, led the drive against them
after the Second World War. Openly and on every conceivable
occasion he attacked them for their activities and motives in the
British and international spheres of trade unionism.

This chapter concerns his campaign against Communists in his
own Union: it describes the extent of the influence of Communists
in the Transport and General Workers' Union, Deakin's reasons
for opposing them, and the manner in which he used his authority
to do so.

The Transport and General Workers' Union was one of those
unions which refused to accede to the request of the General Council
of the Trades Union Congress in 1934 to alter its rules so as to
prevent Communists from holding Union offices. The request,
which was made to the executives of affiliated unions through
Circular 17,[1] received the following reply:

> That the Union cannot, under its rules, declare a Communist ineligible
> to serve in any capacity in the Union, and the Council doubts the wisdom
> of introducing such a rule because of its repercussions. . . . The Council
> takes the view that having accepted a person into membership, the Union
> cannot deny the full rights of association so long as that person does not
> violate the constitution and policy of the Union.[2]

Bevin was nevertheless aware of the dangers of Communist
activity, as he revealed during a debate on the Circular, when
he called Communist activities 'the most nefarious practices that
this Movement has ever had to face'.[3]

The trouble spot for Bevin was in the Road Passenger Transport
Group of the Union and it was that Group, particularly the London
section after 1935, which provided Arthur Deakin with his first
substantial contact with Communist methods.[4] He was then the
Assistant General Secretary, and at Bevin's request he conducted the

[1] The text of the Circular can be seen in the T.U.C. Report, 1935, pp. 110–111.
[2] T. & G.W.U., G.E.C. Minutes, December 1934.
[3] T.U.C. Report, 1935, p. 275.
[4] A description of the participation of the Rank-and-File Movement in the 1937
Coronation strike is contained in chapter IV.

Union inquiry into unofficial activities in the road passenger transport industry. He saw Communists at work in the lower reaches of the Union in what might be called their gestation period. Union members who were Communists or were later to become Communists were receiving publicity for their identification with the demands of the ordinary members and were preparing the way for later important electoral successes.

THE COMMUNISTS' WAR-TIME STRENGTH IN THE UNION

The position of the Communist trade unionists was undoubtedly strengthened by the entry of Russia into the Second World War and by that country's subsequent war victories. It is more than a coincidence that the major Communist gains in trade unions occurred either during the war or in the flush of victory afterwards. For one relatively short period the prestige of Communist trade unionists was enhanced by their political allegiance to Russia. They made gains in some unions, most notably the Electrical Trades Union and the National Union of Foundry Workers, which they have retained since. In the Transport and General Workers' Union their achievements were less striking but were nevertheless important.[1]

The presence of Communists in Union positions was only occasionally reflected in the policy of the Union. A few innocuous motions with a Communist origin were passed by Biennial Delegate Conferences of the Union, but over important matters such as the affiliation of the Communist Party to the Labour Party, the Union was consistently unsympathetic towards the Communists.[2] The decisions of the General Executive Council which possessed a Communist Party bias were usually those which appeared under the item of 'Any other Competent Business' and which in no way affected the main policy of the Union. When Russia was in the war, however, there were very few industrial issues over which Communists and non-Communists on the Executive fundamentally disagreed.

Even after Deakin had decided to publicize the number of known Communists on the Executive, it was difficult to estimate their strength because it lay not only in the number of Party members but also in those who were prepared to follow Communist leads. Two war-time incidents occurred, however, which pointed to their strength.

[1] The members in Region No. 1 elected two Communists as their representatives on the General Executive Council who became, in effect, the leaders of Communist activity in the Union, and around whom a strong Communist faction on the Executive formed.

[2] A determined effort was made at the 1945 B.D.C. to get Union support for the affiliation of the Communist Party to the Labour Party, but it was defeated by 352 to 208 votes. Bevin was present on that occasion and used all his influence to oppose the motion, so the figures give a fair indication of the support which Communists had among the delegates.

In March 1942 A. F. Papworth, who had been expelled from the Union for his activities in the 1937 London bus strike and later re-admitted and who had become a member of the Communist Party, was elected to the General Executive Council by the members of Region No. 1. He was immediately chosen by the Executive to serve on its foremost sub-committee, the Finance and General Purposes Committee. Papworth was already a well-known figure in the Union and a former member of the Executive, but his stature alone was hardly sufficient to get him such a prompt election to the sub-committee. The second incident also concerned Papworth. The Union each year nominated two persons to serve on the General Council of the Trades Union Congress. Just before the war the Executive had decided that one of the persons should be the General Secretary and the other a lay member of the Executive. In 1944 the Executive decided to nominate Deakin and Papworth for the two seats on the General Council; these were elected so the Union then provided the General Council with its only Communist member. Given the value of the General Council seat to the Union in terms of prestige it showed clearly how powerful the Communists were on the Union Executive.

In the meantime Arthur Deakin's personal experiences with Communists were widening. He was learning how intransigent Communists could be on committees and what a remarkable facility many of them possessed in making their political views relevant no matter what topics were under discussion. The differences which Deakin had with the Communists during the war years were hidden by a façade of unity. His criticisms of them were vague; often only implied; and he showed no signs of the tirades he was to make against them in later years.

It is difficult to say what impression Deakin's war-time contacts with Communists made on him, but there is no doubt that his expressed concern about the influence of Communists on his Executive and about the threat to the unity of his organization which they created, dates from the end of the war. From then, he ceased to consider the presence of Communists solely as a matter of personal inconvenience to himself; it took on much wider implications. But he did not immediately express his thoughts in public nor did he feel inclined to name his adversaries. For instance, he looked back on the national dock strike in 1945 as the result of changed tactics of the Communist Party due to its having been heavily defeated at the polls in the General Election.[1]   At the time he spoke only of 'disruptive influences' and 'certain vested interests'.[2]

[1] In conversation with the writer, 13 April 1954.
[2] T. & G.W.U., G.E.C. Minutes, 3 December 1945.

THE COMMUNISTS' POST-WAR STRENGTH IN THE UNION

It is hard to establish exactly how many Communist Party members were on the Union Executive from 1945 onwards. Deakin's estimates were based on claims made by the *Daily Worker*, but it is not certain that the *Daily Worker* claimed its full complement. All that can be said with certainty is that there were not fewer than the figures given by Deakin, and that the Communists received much support from non-Communist members of the Executive. On an Executive of thirty-four members, nine were claimed to be Communists in the 1946–1948 electoral period, and three were members of the small select Finance and General Purposes Committee. On the complete Executive the Communists were defeated on a number of vital matters by small majorities, sometimes by a single vote; and when in 1947 the chairman of the Executive retired, the Communists' nominee for the post was defeated but the distribution of the votes was in the approximate ratio of 3:2. Such were the reports and rumours of the Communist strength on the Executive in the immediate post-war years that when the Executive election results for the 1948–1950 period were known Deakin issued a press statement with the intention of disclaiming false notions. That the statement was issued at all was indicative of Deakin's mood. It is reproduced here in full:

> The elections for the current Electoral Period for the General Executive Council and Constitutional Committees of the Transport and General Workers' Union have now been completed and show a very definite set-back for the Communist Party.
>
> Out of twenty-seven Territorial contests only four members who are claimed by the *Daily Worker* to be members of the Communist Party have been returned, as follows:
>
> | | |
> |---|---|
> | Area No. 1 (London and Home Counties) | 2 |
> | Area No. 7 (Scotland) | 1 |
> | Area No. 11 (Ireland) | 1 |

In Area No. 9 (Yorkshire) the Communist Executive Member who was standing for re-election was defeated, receiving only 4,759 votes.

> In addition to the foregoing, four members of the Communist Party have been elected by National Trade Group Committees, as follows:
>
> Passenger Services Group
> Metal, Engineering and Chemical Group
> Building Trades Group
> Commercial Services Group.

The Passenger, Metal and Building Trades Group Representatives were only elected by a majority of one vote in each case.

The claim made in the *Daily Worker* today that the two Territorial

Executive Representatives elected for the London Area shows a re-
sounding success for the Communist Party, is not borne out by the facts.
Actually, there was a diffusion of forces on the part of the non-
Communist membership and a carefully planned campaign in the case
of the Communist candidates. In fact, whilst it is true that the two
successful candidates secured an increased vote compared with the
last election, the votes cast against them are in the proportion of two to
one.

The total vote cast for the successful Communist Party candidates
in the Territorial elections (bearing in mind the fact that in each of the
Areas concerned the members had two votes) was 53,114 out of an
over-all Union membership of approximately 1,300,000.

The position now revealed shows that on the old Executive Council
there were nine members of the Communist Party out of 34, whereas
on the new Council they have only eight members out of 38.

The Territorial elections, where the whole of the membership in an
Area votes as opposed to elections by and from the National Trade
Group Committees, accurately reflect the views of our members through
the process of a secret ballot, and show that on this basis the Communist
Party have only been able to secure the election of four of their candi-
dates.[1]

The election results may have revealed the weakness of the
Communists in territorial elections, but they also showed their
strength on the National Trade Group Committees where voting
was done on a show of hands; four National Committees had Communist majorities even though they may have been frail ones.
Amongst the full-time officials there was only a sprinkling of Communists.

Though Deakin endeavoured to give the public the impression
that he did not consider the Communist problem to be serious, he
was in fact worried to the extent of wanting to proscribe Communists
from holding official Union positions. What factors, then, determined his attitude?

REASONS FOR DEAKIN'S ANTI-COMMUNIST ATTITUDE

Arthur Deakin was opposed to the Communists in his Union for
four main reasons. (1) They endeavoured to use the Union for
their own political ends; (2) in doing this they employed methods
which conflicted with the established practices and agreed policy of
the Union; (3) their primary allegiance was to the Communist Party
and not to the Union; and (4) he was personally antagonised by
Communists on his Executive. Each reason is examined briefly
below.

[1] Issued on Monday, 2 February 1948.

1. It has always been an accepted feature of the Communist ideology that trade unions should be used for a Communist end. In one of the few references Karl Marx made to trade unions he wrote: 'In addition to their original tasks, the trade unions must now learn how to act consciously as focal points for organizing the working class in the greater interests of its complete emancipation.'[1] The Communist Party has claimed to be the custodian of the interests of the working class and has given itself the task of determining policy in pursuit of those interests. Trade unions have therefore been regarded as subordinates in the class struggle, working under the leadership of the Communist Party and following the policies it decreed. The intrusion of the Communist Party into trade union affairs, then, has been regarded by Communists as a legitimate and necessary activity.

In Deakin's opinion this intrusion was an unforgivable sin. It formed the main theme in his speeches about Communists. 'I would also refer', he said on one occasion, 'to the tendency of the Communist Party in Great Britain to project industrial programmes . . . and I ask myself how long has it been the prerogative or duty of any political party to devise charters relating to the wages and conditions of employment of workpeople who are well organized within their own trade unions?'[2] Such interference, he said, was never undertaken by the Labour Party.[3] He frequently warned his members against using the Union for political ends. 'The prime purpose of this Union', he said, 'is to serve the industrial interests of its members. It must never become a forum for the Communist Party or for any other Party. . . .'[4]

2. In Communist eyes, the subordination of the unions to the Communist Party gave it the right to correct trade union activities whenever they deviated from its projected policies. This it endeavoured to do in two main ways: (*i*) by operating Communist factions as determined minorities on constitutional committees or at conferences, and (*ii*) by competing for the allegiance of the ordinary members through encouraging mass unofficial action. In both cases the Communist Party has submitted its policies as alternative lines of action to those being followed by unions. Arthur Deakin strongly deprecated the use of the two methods and considered that they threatened the unity of his Union.

(*i*) The policy of infiltration which Communists have used to get on to constitutional committees has been well-worn in the trade union

---

[1] In a resolution for the First International Workingmen's Association, quoted in *Marx and the Trade Unions*, by A. Lozovsky, p. 11.
[2] Eighth Scottish Delegate Conference, T. & G.W.U., 1948.
[3] T. & G.W.U., B.D.C., 1949.
[4] Ibid., 1947.

movement, but their highly disciplined group activities have introduced a new and potentially disruptive factor. They have acted as closely-knit groups, pursuing the same policy, supporting the same candidates, consistently exploiting loopholes in union constitutions and weaknesses in union electoral systems. They have arrived at union committee meetings with their policies decided and their plans for getting them accepted drawn up.

In order to secure acceptance of their motions the Communists have not always needed a majority representation; in many instances, provided the other members have acted in a random fashion, it has only been necessary for a relatively small number of Communist members to act as a determined minority. The correlation between minority activity and its chances of success has been illustrated in statistical terms.[1]   For example, in a committee of three people, one member will obtain the decision of his choice in 75 per cent. of the votings if the other two members vote in a random manner; similarly a resolute block of three votes has a 75 per cent. chance of imposing its decisions in a committee of twenty-three if the twenty vote in a random manner. The bigger the relative size of the block the greater are its chances of imposing its will over the majority. Uniform Communist voting behaviour in union elections for selected candidates (they never submit more than one candidate for each vacancy) when the votes for other candidates have been diffused, has often resulted in Communist election successes.

In the Transport and General Workers' Union the Communists were assisted by its electoral system. The Union has always used the relative majority method for electing its representative committees and delegates; that is, the candidate with the highest number of votes secured election regardless of the proportion his votes bore to the total votes cast. It was possible, therefore, for candidates representing minorities to secure election.

A condition for the success of Communist group activities is that non-Communists should either act and vote in a random fashion or be so indifferent about union affairs as not to attend branch meetings or participate in union elections. It is common knowledge that in most unions this last condition has been fulfilled, despite the pleas of trade union leaders to their members to vote, and the publicity given to the consequences of mass inactivity in trade union affairs.

It would be wrong to assume that Communist trade unionists have always needed determined minority tactics to secure election to constitutional committees. There are many trade unionists who see

[1] 'The Elementary Statistics of Majority Voting', by L. S. Penrose, *Journal of the Royal Statistical Society*, Vol. CIX, p. 56, 1946. See also *Power in Trade Unions*, op. cit., Appendix C, pp. 295–296.

Communists in a different light from their general secretaries, and to whom the exhortations not to elect Communists to union offices create a dilemma. Communists at all levels of trade union activity are assiduous workers. In the branches and in the workshop organizations they undertake onerous and time-consuming duties; they support the men's demands no matter how extreme they are, and exert perpetual pressure on the union organizations through their succession of resolutions, continual haranguing, and usually well-documented cases. During disputes they emerge on almost all occasions as local leaders representing the interests of the men against employer or union. Frequently the ordinary members can only distinguish Communists by the extremity of their opinions and by their persistence in pressing them in the branches and workshops. The constant, unceasing repetition of argument by Communists has a nuisance value in branch activity; it wearies active non-Communist branch members and tends to drive the marginal branch attenders away from meetings. But the willingness of Communists to work in branches often outweighs their nuisance value. So, sitting solidly on their reputations as trade union workers, many Communists get elected to branch offices; whence some move on to other trade union posts of varying responsibilities.

(*ii*) Communists appear to be indigenous to industrial unrest. Whenever there are unofficial strikes they emerge as strike leaders, stipulating their own terms for settlements and criticizing the official leaders for their unwillingness to support the men's demands. Arthur Deakin saw much of this among the dock membership of his Union. During the 'Zinc Oxide' strike on the London docks in June 1948, Deakin claimed that out 'of an Unofficial Strike Committee of 48 members, 36 were either members of, or fellow travellers with, the Communist Party'.[1] The Government review of the dock strikes over the Canadian Seamen in the following year, concluded that their salient feature was 'The way in which the campaign in this country was founded upon the support mainly of members of the Communist Party and their sympathizers'.[2] The same could be said of other strikes in the Transport and General Workers' Union and in other unions.

The danger to the constitutional practices of trade unions from unofficial strikes does not need to be repeated here. It need only be said that the responsibility for the danger lay fully with the Communists if they caused the strikes. If they acted so as to prolong or extend the strikes some, but not all, of the responsibility was theirs. If Communists neither caused nor extended the strikes then their

[1] T. & G.W.U., Eighth Scottish Delegate Conference, 1948.
[2] Cmd. 7851, op. cit., p. 27.

emergence as unofficial leaders was not a justifiable contributory reason for discriminating against them.

Did Communists cause strikes? At first Arthur Deakin thought not and he said so in 1947. He said, however, 'that immediately there has been a manifestation of unrest the Communist Party have been in, and have been trying to shape a policy'.[1] What evidence there is of the causes of strike action supports Deakin's contention. It shows that they are deep-rooted and that strikes are not manufactured by men on the spot. In that case if the Communists had not taken over the leadership of unofficial strikes, others would have done so. But it did appear that the Communist Party was involved in influencing the course of unofficial strikes, although it was always difficult to see the hand of the Communist Party *per se*; in most cases it was implicated by inference. What Deakin disliked about Communist unofficial strike leaders was not only their disregard of agreements but also their disciplined thoroughness; and as this often resulted in longer, bigger, and more successful unofficial strikes, to this extent his reason for disapproving of their methods was justified.

3. This point concerns the allegiance of Communists to their trade unions. It follows from what has been said about the Communists' conception of the relationship between the Communist Party and trade unions, that a Communist trade unionist's first allegiance is to his Party; that in his capacity as a trade unionist he acts under the instructions of Communist Party policy-makers; and that he is bound by constitutionally determined decisions in trade unions only when these do not conflict with Communist policy. The machinery by which the Communist Party in Britain sought to direct the policies and activities of trade unions has been described by the General Council of the Trades Union Congress in the following terms:

> For instance, it is known that there are industrial committees set up by the Communist Party which exist in many industries and trades—e.g. railways, transport, seamen, cotton, mining, etc., etc. The membership of these committees consists of representatives drawn from the trades and industries in which they function. From these industrial subcommittees the Communist Party secures information on which the officials of the Communist Party, who have no connection with the industry concerned, frame industrial policy and tactics which are used as the basis of instructions and propaganda directed at all levels inside the Unions. . . . [2]

Arthur Deakin believed that the Communist members of the

[1] T. & G.W.U., B.D.C., 1947.
[2] *The Trade Union Movement and Communism*, issued 24 November 1948.

General Executive Council of his Union arrived at meetings with briefs prepared by the Communist Party and that they passed important Union information and decisions back to the Communist Party headquarters; though, as was to be expected, he was able to produce no material evidence to substantiate his belief.[1] The awareness that men whom he was called upon to trust were being disloyal to the Union tested Deakin's patience and interfered with the effectiveness of Executive deliberations, for he became cautious in the manner in which he examined certain problems with his Executive.

4. Lastly, the antagonism which existed between Deakin and the Communist members of his Executive. Arguing with Communists involves a test in patience for which the Communists are better equipped, for they argue from dogmas and have ready-made answers to complex problems. If the Communists are not willing to forsake their dogmas and the other side is equally unwilling to embrace them, no progress can be made towards reaching agreement. What often happens when Communists and non-Communists have to meet relatively frequently, and by the nature of their contact are compelled to discuss problems and reach decisions, is that the non-Communists tend to forsake reasonable argument because of its ineffectiveness. Issues are then decided by votes and not by agreement. Arguments which do not have to be logically derived from assumptions which bear some relation to fact, can be based on anything, legitimate or illegitimate, which can give them force. A handy but illegitimate weapon is personal invective. Here again the Communists hold the advantage, for they have invective to suit all occasions; they simply accuse their opponents of treason against working-class unity.

The ability and the willingness to argue were part of Arthur Deakin's tools of trade but, like others in comparable positions of leadership, he liked to argue successfully. Thus the experience of arguing with Communists was doubly frustrating for him; neither did reason prevail nor was he successful except that the anti-Communists could command more votes than the Communists. Inevitably both he and the Communists went through the stages described above and reached and settled at the level of recrimination and invective. At this Deakin was an able exponent; he had a good command of words and a lively imagination. But he was sometimes goaded into losing his temper—which he did relatively easily—and occasionally he said things which he regretted later. Even so, some members of his Executive at the time have said that they wondered at his patience and tolerance in the face of such abuse.

The relationship between Arthur Deakin and Communist trade

[1] At the 1949 B.D.C. he said: 'Do not make any mistake, there are members of the Communist Party holding office in this Union who are using their positions within the Union for the purpose of furthering the Communist policy.'

280 *A Campaign Against Communist Trade Unionists*

unionists outside of his Union grew as strained and antagonistic as with those within. The years 1947, 1948, and 1949 were noted for the voluble and frequent speeches by Deakin on the activities of Communists in trade unions. He attacked them vigorously, gaining support on the way from other trade union leaders, from his members, and from the Labour Government. 'The Communist Party', he said in 1948, 'stands indicted as the declared enemy of the British working class.'[1] Equally, Deakin was condemned and castigated by the Communists. In the sphere of international trade unionism, Deakin and the Communists were likewise at daggers drawn, but this is the subject of the last chapter of this book.

THE SETTING FOR POLITICAL DISCRIMINATION

The feeling in Britain about Communists in trade unions in 1947, 1948, and 1949 was not entirely the result of their trade union activities whether within national unions or abroad. It formed a part of the increasing general repugnance of the British people towards Communism, created by numerous international incidents. Through the press and radio the ordinary trade unionists were learning with depressing regularity of the wide area of disagreement in principle, methods, and aims between Communists and non-Communists. The offer of American aid to Europe by Mr. George Marshall in June 1947 and its prompt acceptance by Britain and certain European countries brought out the Communist and non-Communist policies in marked contrast. The Communists rejected Marshall Aid and in September 1947 established the Cominform. From that time the Communist Party of Great Britain, which had hitherto supported the Government drive for increased production, opposed the major economic and industrial policies supported by the trade union movement. The Communist *coup d'état* in Czechoslovakia the following February gave a crude example of their tactics and *The Economist* was not alone in thinking that the 'leading part played in the Czechoslovak revolution by the trade unions and works councils is an ominous example of the very precise aims and methods pursued by the Communists in these bodies'.[2] People in Britain were asking 'can it happen here?' More seriously than previously, they were beginning to examine the implications of Communist activity.

The fall of Prague prompted the Prime Minister to make a 'Statement on the employment in State Service of members of the

---

[1] T. & G.W.U., Eighth Scottish Delegate Conference, 1948.
[2] *The Economist*, 6 March 1948, p. 369.

Communist Party' in the House of Commons on 15 March 1948. He said

> that from experience, in this country and elsewhere, membership of the Communist Party might well involve the acceptance by the individual of a loyalty which, in certain circumstances, would prove inimical to the State. The Government had reached the conclusion that the only prudent course to adopt was to ensure that no one, known to be a member of the Communist Party, was engaged on work the nature of which affected the security of the State. . . .[1]

Then, in April, there was tension over the Italian elections in the fear that the experience of Czechoslovakia would be repeated. And in case there was a tendency during the summer months of 1948 to forget about international crises over Communist methods, the blockade of Berlin and the Allied air-lift existed as grim reminders.

In this setting political discrimination did not have such an illiberal ring about it as it would have had in more sober circumstances, and there was talk of the need to use it to protect the larger liberties which the British people enjoyed. The British, whilst deploring heresy hunts, were prepared to accept the restriction of Communist activities in certain fields. The trade union movement was not excepted from the general feeling; indeed, through its intimate experience of Communists, it had long been prepared to consider proscription more as a matter of practical significance than as an issue involving individual liberties. It was not surprising, then, that the proscription of Communists from trade union offices should have been discussed with serious intent in 1948 and 1949.

POLITICAL DISCRIMINATION IN THE TRANSPORT AND GENERAL WORKERS' UNION

The constitutional position of Communists in trade unions was raised by a published statement of the Trades Union Congress General Council on 24 November 1948. Each affiliated union was asked to consider whether it was consistent with the obligations and loyalty to the policy of a trade union and to the Movement as a whole that any of its members should serve on a committee of the Communist Party. Copies of the statement had been circulated to members of the General Executive Council of the Transport and General Workers' Union, and at the December meeting of the Executive it was debated and endorsed but no action was agreed upon other than that the membership should be informed of the endorsement.[2] After this decision had been circulated a few protests

---

[1] Labour Party Report, 1949, p. 61.
[2] T. & G.W.U., G.E.C. Minutes, 2 December 1948.

were received from constitutional committees, mainly in the Passenger Transport Group and the Scottish region, but most members tacitly accepted the strictures on Communist activity which the endorsement implied.

Arthur Deakin was one of the members of the General Council of the Trades Union Congress on whose initiative the General Council policy statement had been compiled, and no doubt he had his own Union in mind as one suitable for the kind of action suggested in the statement. No steps could be taken in the Transport and General Workers' Union to exclude Communists from office, or to discriminate against them in any way, under the Union constitution as it stood. A Communist who refused to accept the terms of the constitution could be excluded from office or even from membership, but so could any other member who acted similarly. There was nothing in the constitution which permitted political discrimination. When a delegate at the 1947 Biennial Delegate Conference asked whether Deakin was going 'to clear out of the Executive all the avowed Communists, of which it has a big percentage at the moment', the Chairman replied, 'He can't. You elect them.' That was precisely the position.

The rules of the Union could only be changed by decisions of the Biennial Delegate Conference on motions from branches and specified constitutional committees of the Union, including the General Executive Council. The most straightforward course for Deakin to have taken would have been to get an Executive recommendation for a change in the rules. But such an act would have been tactically unwise. This was fully realized by the Communist members of the Executive, who pressed him hard to agree that an Executive recommendation be made to the 1949 Biennial Delegate Conference; but they were unsuccessful. It was a matter, he said, for the rank-and-file members to decide; the initiative for a change of rule as well as the sanction had to come from them. So often had the Communists caustically reminded him about the rights of the rank and file that he gained much satisfaction from being able to retaliate. Altogether, Deakin said very little on the Executive about the proscription of Communists.

The issue was raised in the manner desired by Deakin. When the Biennial Delegate Conference met on 11 July 1949 at Scarborough there were thirty-two motions on the agenda relating to the activities of Communists in the Union; eighteen of them were in favour of excluding Communists from office and fourteen were against any such action. In some of the latter group Arthur Deakin was criticized and attacked for his anti-Communist views.

The attitude of those of the 634 delegates at the Conference who were Communists was plain; they would put up strenuous vocal resistance to any form of discrimination against themselves. But what of the others? They all had plenary powers and, therefore, the right to make up their minds in the way they thought best. What factors were likely to influence their reasoning? Few, if any, of the delegates would have been subjected to the influences which had made Arthur Deakin such a rabid anti-Communist. None was a member of the General Executive Council, though some were undoubtedly members of the National Trade Group Committees or Regional Committees on which they may have had experiences of Communist tactics.[1] In most of these cases, however, their experience of disruption would have been relatively superficial. Many of the delegates would have met Communists in their branches and, because of the tendency for delegates to be re-elected to attend successive conferences, some in 1949 would have witnessed the noisy and recalcitrant behaviour of Communists at the 1947 Biennial Delegate Conference.

It was clear that the attitudes of many delegates towards Communists were determined less by actual experience than by their interpretation of the images created by the popular press, by politicians and trade union leaders, and by the factual accounts of Communist behaviour in national and international spheres. But just because events appeared to favour the promoters of anti-Communism it would have been wrong to conclude that the delegates with little or no personal experience of Communist activity would favour political discrimination: some people recoil from accepting ready-made images. The issue appeared as a fairly open question, but with a much more solid core of support against discrimination than for it.

Arthur Deakin was active in the formation of anti-Communist opinion until the item on the agenda of the Conference concerning Communists in the Union was reached. A week or so before the Conference he had written an article in the Union Journal entitled 'Trade Unionism versus Communism: The Gloves are Off', in which he stated that Communists worked

> by carrying on whispering campaigns, encouraging people to believe that they can only make progress by being in a constant state of conflict with the employers. . . . by carrying on constant agitation against a disciplined approach to the solution of these problems with which we are faced, and bringing a barrage of misrepresentation in regard to the intentions of those responsible for leadership either in the industrial or political field. In addition strong-arm methods are used—intimidation and even violence is threatened. . . . In the meantime, our members

[1] General Executive Council members are prevented by rule from attending as delegates.

themselves must take an active part in cutting out the canker. Those people who assume unofficial leadership, who are constantly to the forefront in every dispute which arises, must be dealt with and given their marching orders. . . .[1]

Some of the delegates carried this advice with them to the Conference. He had publicly declaimed against the activities of the Communists in the dock strikes supporting the Canadian Seamen's Union, one of which was taking place whilst the Conference was sitting. To add emphasis to the Communist issue, on the same day as it was discussed by the Conference the Government declared a State of Emergency under the 1920 Emergency Powers Act to enable it to cope with the London dock strike.

The Conference met on the morning of 11 July 1949 and that day dealt with the items relating to Communists. The Chairman focused attention on them in his address; after which the Conference approved the Executive's endorsement of the Trades Union Congress General Council policy statement, 'Defend Democracy', by 508 votes to 123. This debate provided Deakin with the opportunity of discussing the Communist problem without having to speak of their proscription; and it indicated how the delegates were thinking. The points which Deakin made were couched in terms of trade union morality: he said that once a decision had been reached by democratic means it should be loyally observed; that it was naïve to suggest that Communists were good trade unionists—they were not free agents; and that the Union's properly elected representatives and constitutional procedure should always be used.

The motions in favour of discrimination were combined into the composite motion 'That no member of the Communist Party shall be eligible to hold any office within the Union, either as a lay member or as a permanent or full-time officer, this rule to take effect as and from the beginning of the 1950–1951 electoral period.' By the time it came up for discussion most of the relevant points had been made. The tenor of the debate was against discrimination, for the Communists were the most vocal and most eloquent of the delegates and on this occasion Deakin intervened only to make a short statement. The arguments of the Communists, particularly the one concerning political liberty, were left virtually unanswered; and, because the Executive had not determined its attitude towards the motion, there was no Executive spokesman. An impression of an observer at the Conference was that the motion would be defeated despite the large majority in favour of the previous motion on Communist activity. Yet it was accepted by 426 votes to 208.[2]

[1] T. & G.W.U., *The Record*, July 1949.
[2] An amendment to include members of the Fascist Party was accepted afterwards.

Discrimination in Practice

The first tasks were administrative ones. The new rule had to be registered and then applied. Lay officers were classified under five headings,[1] and all nominees for these offices were required to sign a revised declaration form. Already they had to sign a declaration that they possessed the prescribed membership qualification and that the essential conditions governing the holding of office in the Union had been brought to their notice. To this declaration was added:

> That I conform to the requirement set out in Schedule I, Section 2, of the Rules, that is to say, I am not a Member of the Communist or Fascist Parties. . . . That I understand and accept that should I be elected to hold office within the Union and subsequently become a Member of the Communist or Fascist Parties, it will be necessary for me to automatically relinquish office in accordance with the foregoing requirement.

Existing full-time officials and applicants for full-time posts were required to sign a similar declaration.

Then the Executive had to deal with the protests which came from the constitutional committees with strong Communist factions. It should be noted that the Communists continued to hold lay offices in the Union until January 1950 when the offices for the new electoral period were filled; and they made what use they could of their period of grace. Resolutions of protest were received from the National Committees of the Road Passenger Transport Group and the Chemical and Allied Trades Section, from the Scottish Regional Committee, and from 104 out of 4,759 branches of the Union. The resolutions were rejected by the Executive.

An unofficial body called the 'Committee for Trade Union Democracy' was established to aim for the suspension of the operation of the new rule and for the convening of the Rules Conference. This body organized a national deputation of forty-five members, purportedly representative of branches and committees of the Union, to meet the Executive during its session on 14 December 1949. The Executive refused to meet it, but raised no objection to the General Secretary explaining the constitutional position to the deputation and other members who had joined them, at the end of the Executive session.[2] The deputation received this decision with dissatisfaction, and in an endeavour to make their objections known and felt some of the members attempted to force their way into the Council Chamber. Whereupon the Chairman declared the session at an end and the Executive dispersed. Two days later at the

---

[1] (a) Branch Offices and Committees; (b) Constitutional Committees; (c) General Executive Council; (d) Biennial Delegate Conference, and (e) Rules Conference.
[2] T. & G.W.U., G.E.C. Minute 1102, 14 December 1949.

renewed Executive meeting the Communist members made their last attempt whilst still on the Executive to persuade the majority 'That a Special Rule Conference be called by this Council with the object of dealing with the question of Communists holding office inside the Union.'[1] There was no disposition, however, for the majority to make any concessions to Communist requests.

When it became clear to the Communists that they could muster insufficient support for their demand to have the rule changed, they concentrated their attention on the terms of its application. Nine full-time officials of the Union returned the declaration unsigned and these were given a month's notice of dismissal. First, it was maintained that, as some of the dismissed officials would exercise their right of appeal against dismissal, no action should be taken to replace them until the appeals had been heard. This suggestion was rejected on the ground that the rules of the Union specifically provided that a decision of the Executive which was the subject of appeal was binding until the appeal was heard. Then it was contended that the decision of the Biennial Delegate Conference did not apply to existing full-time officials but only to new appointments. The contention was first made at the Executive meeting on 15 December 1949; later it formed the basis of the appeals of the dismissed officials.

The Union appeals procedure states: 'The General Executive Council . . . shall have power to suspend and/or dismiss any officer, but any officer who is dismissed shall, by giving notice in writing to the General Secretary within seven days, have a right of appeal to the Appeals Committee, or at his option to the next Biennial Delegate Conference.'[2] The dismissed Communists opted for the Biennial Delegate Conference which next met in 1951. Before the appeals were heard at the Conference the Chairman emphasized that they were not against the rule itself but against the manner in which the Executive had applied the rule in the appellants' own particular cases.

The gist of the cases submitted by the men was that the rule had been wrongfully applied and that this amounted to victimization. In the trade union movement the word 'victimization' has a strong emotional appeal, and in normal circumstances anyone who had been victimized would be sure of powerful support from his fellow trade unionists. Yet the delegates at the Conference had relatively little sympathy for the dismissed officials and rejected the appeals. This was not because the members of the Transport and General Workers' Union were different from other trade unionists. Indeed, at the 1949 Biennial Delegate Conference, shortly after the decision to ban Communists from holding office had been made, the delegates

---

[1] The right to make and amend rules had been entrusted to a Rules Conference by the 1949 Biennial Delegate Conference.
[2] T. & G.W.U. Rule 6, Section 10.

had resolved 'That this Conference demands that the present purge of workers from their jobs because of their Communist Party membership or sympathy is absolutely undemocratic and demands actions by the full force of the Union machinery in support of any Member purged from his or her job for this reason.' Although it may be thought that the members were insincere on that occasion or were guilty of paradoxical behaviour, it was not so, as is explained below.

The rejection of the appeals was a logical consequence of the application of trade union standards to the cases. This was made clear by the speeches of delegates and by Deakin's own contribution. The dismissal of a worker who refuses to join a trade union is not considered to be victimization; it is treated as an action necessary to maintain trade union unity. The dismissal of the Communists was considered analogous. One delegate compared them with the many busmen he had helped to get dismissed because they would not join the Transport and General Workers' Union. He said, 'there is a time in our lives when we must in some degree surrender our personal liberty if we are actively interested in something much greater than ourselves'. Arthur Deakin made a similar point. 'It has been said', he remarked, 'that we have deprived these people of their jobs. My answer to that is short and simple. They deprived themselves of their jobs by reason of their inability to signify their undivided allegiance to this Union.'

But, it could be maintained, these were not ordinary members but legal employees of the Union and therefore the Union had a special responsibility to them. Neither the Union constitution nor trade union practice has created a distinction between full-time officials and lay officials in terms of rights.[1] The feeling of the delegates was revealed when one of them said that the dismissed officials wanted different treatment from the ordinary members who had had the rule applied against them—'Well, they just cannot have it', he stated amid applause from the Conference. This point was emphasized by Deakin who said, 'obviously the officers of this Union are not a privileged class; the rules of the Union must apply in precisely the same way to the officers as they do to the ordinary members'.

The 'no Communist' rule operated for the remainder of Deakin's tenure as General Secretary. He thought that democratic processes needed protection and saw nothing undemocratic in taking away the political liberty of those who did not believe in political liberty; nor did he think that the problem of Communists could be solved in his Union without, what he called, a 'constitutional device'. The ease with which the 'device' was introduced and implemented suggests that the strength of the Communists in the Union may have been

---

[1] For a brief discussion of this point see Ch. V, pp. 81–82.

over-rated. But one should not ignore the general tension about Communists when their strength was reputedly high and when particular perspectives may have been distorted.

In what material way the rule has affected the Union is difficult to judge. It removed some assiduous officials from office but still left them in the branches eager to press their points of view and to get them accepted as resolutions. In a less material way it influenced opinion in the Union. Officials who gave vent to dissident expression drew attention to themselves and sometimes cast a reflection on their own integrity. They might, it was thought, be Communists who had signed the declaration. All told, the Union went into a phase of orthodoxy in the opinions expressed in it and in the decisions it recorded.

After 1949 Deakin's direct and formal contact with Communist trade unionists ceased. But his campaign against them was intensified. He went so far as to state in 1954 that the Communists not only exploited the grievances which gave rise to unofficial strikes but created them.[1] In public he attacked Communists in a less discriminating manner than before. The public picture emerged of Deakin as a man with an anti-Communist phobia which prevented his seeing real grievances when they existed. And for this he was treated less seriously. But the picture was distorted. In private and in his handling of specific issues he was much less inclined to see the hand of Communism as the cause of all his troubles.

[1] Speech at the Midland Festival of the T. & G.W.U., at Birmingham, Saturday, 16 October 1954.

Chapter Eighteen

THE WORLD FEDERATION OF TRADE UNIONS:

AN EXPERIENCE OF DISINTEGRATION

FROM September 1946 until January 1949 Arthur Deakin was president of the World Federation of Trade Unions. This was a position of unparalleled prominence in the world of trade unions at that time, yet it was a position with responsibility but little power. Admittedly, in relation to other trade union leaders Deakin exercised great influence, but it was influence over pace and not direction. The World Federation of Trade Unions became divided by political forces which had already rent the world. Arthur Deakin and his fellow international trade union leaders had no control over these forces, nor, therefore, over the ultimate fate of the World Federation; for them it was a question of how soon or late the forces should take command.

This chapter is mainly concerned with the deliberations of the Executive Bureau of the World Federation, for it was that organ which decided policy and took decisions and which was, to all intents and purposes, the World Federation.[1] The chapter shows how interests on the Executive Bureau were aligned and the factors which revealed their antagonism, the state of British trade union opinion, and the secession of the British from the World Federation. Throughout it all one can see Deakin and his fellow members on the Executive Bureau arguing out the destiny of the World Federation of Trade Unions within the narrowly prescribed limits set by the raging post-war political forces.

Arthur Deakin was thrust as quickly and more prominently on to the world stage of trade unionism in 1946 than he had been thrust on to the British stage in 1940. Throughout the delicate operation of forming the Anglo-Soviet Trade Union Committee in 1942 and the complicated negotiations which followed it, leading up to the establishment of the World Federation of Trade Unions in 1945, Arthur Deakin was little more than a bystander. The negotiations

---

[1] The constitutional organs of the World Federation were the World Trade Union Congress, the General Council, the Executive Committee, and the Executive Bureau, with degrees of authority in that order. During Deakin's tenure the Congress did not meet, the General Council met once, and the Executive Committee twice. Each of the first three organs discussed the recommendations of the Executive Bureau, and endorsed them, throughout the existence of the World Federation.

were directed by Sir Walter Citrine and it was he who became the first president of the World Federation. Deakin began with a minor job as auditor.

The dominant members of the Executive Bureau in its early stages were Sir Walter Citrine, Sydney Hillman (who was president of the Amalgamated Clothing Workers of America),[1] V. V. Kuznetsov, the Russian trade union leader, and Louis Saillant, General Secretary of the French Confederation of Labour and General Secretary of the World Federation. The first three in particular developed a close working relationship which was prematurely ended by Hillman's death in July 1946 and Citrine's resignation in September the same year. The replacements of these two were men of different types who had to learn to work together under changing, strained conditions. No doubt Citrine, Hillman, and Kuznetsov would have reached a stage of fundamental disagreement under the conditions of 1947 and the years following; but on a few occasions when an impasse was reached in the Executive Bureau deliberations, Kuznetsov referred nostalgically to the days when he had worked with Citrine and Hillman.

When Citrine resigned to take up a post on the National Coal Board, Arthur Deakin was pressed by the General Council of the Trades Union Congress to accept nomination for the vacant position of president of the World Federation. Before the final decision to accept was made, Ernest Bevin, at that time the Foreign Secretary, advised Deakin not to take on the presidency because, suspicious of Russian motives, he felt that an international trade union organization would gradually move over into the Russian sphere of influence and that a non-Communist president would be used to give an appearance of unity which in fact would be non-existent. The advice was rejected by Deakin because he believed he could prevent such a situation. On 20 September 1946, at Washington, Deakin was provisionally elected to the presidency by the Executive Bureau and on 7 June 1947 his election was ratified by the Executive Committee. The Soviet Delegates were foremost in supporting Deakin's nomination and were eulogistic in their description of him.

The Executive Bureau was a strange body. Arthur Deakin and Louis Saillant, the general secretary, were present at all the Executive Bureau meetings described in this chapter. The other members had substitutes who were allowed to attend at any time and to take part in the discussions. Only the actual members or, in their absence, the substitutes were allowed to vote. A variety of trade union leaders

[1] Hillman was a vice-president of the Congress of Industrial Organizations which affiliated to the World Federation of Trade Unions. The other national trade union body in America, the American Federation of Labour, consistently and strenuously opposed the W.F.T.U.

also attended as assistants to voting members or as observers, and they too were permitted to join in the discussions. It was in the capacity as assistant or observer that Vincent Tewson, the general secretary of the Trades Union Congress, attended many of the meetings and expressed the view of the Trades Union Congress in the place of Deakin, who was restricted as a spokesman by his duties as president.

The members during Deakin's tenure of office were: Frank Rosenblum, vice-president of both the American Congress of Industrial Organizations and the Amalgamated Clothing Workers, with James Carey, Secretary Treasurer of the Congress of Industrial Organizations, as his substitute; V. V. Kuznetsov, the Russian trade union leader, who had different substitutes on each of the three occasions he was absent; Leon Jouhaux of the French General Confederation of Labour[1]; V. Lombardo Toledano of the Confederation of Workers of Latin America[2]; Chu-Hsu-Fan of the Chinese Association of Labour, who was eventually replaced by his substitute Liu-Ning I; Evert Kupers, president of the Trade Union Federation of the Netherlands; and G. Di Vittorio of the Italian General Confederation of Labour.

The Executive Bureau contained a ready-made ideological division, fairly evenly balanced, potentially disruptive. On the one side with reputations for adopting an anti-Communist attitude, were Deakin, Rosenblum, Jouhaux, Kupers, and the Chinese delegate, Chu.[3] On the other side, Kuznetsov, Toledano, and Di Vittorio supported Communist policies. The General Secretary, Saillant, denied that he was a member of the Communist Party,[4] though he pressed its point of view sometimes more vociferously than the Communists did themselves.

THE ALIGNMENT OF INTERESTS[5]

Until late in 1947 controversial matters which came before the Executive Bureau were in their preliminary stages and major

[1] Jouhaux relinquished his position when he led an anti-Communist French breakaway organization, 'Force Ouvrière', in November 1947. France lost its representation on the Executive Bureau after this until 1949; and the non-Communists lost an ally.

[2] Toledano was expelled from his union, the Workers' Confederation of Mexico, in 1948 and consequently lost his seat on the Executive Bureau.

[3] Chu had had a long association with the British Labour Movement. As the Red Army in China gained increasing successes he became more and more non-committal, until eventually he ceased to attend the meetings and Liu, his substitute and a Communist, replaced him.

[4] W.F.T.U. Executive Bureau Minutes, 2 May 1948, p. 45.

[5] The minutes of Executive Bureau and Executive Committee meetings, which have provided much of the information for this section of the chapter, contain relatively full reports of the statements made by each speaker, unlike minutes of British meetings.

differences had not been revealed. On some matters, such as the problem of trade union rights in Spain, a real unanimity was shown over the action to be taken as well as the ends to be pursued. On other matters there was a wider divergence of opinion between the British and American delegates than between Communists and non-Communists. From the outside the Executive Bureau presented an appearance of absolute unity. Rarely were issues decided by votes; instead, the content of expressions and resolutions was changed until unanimity could be shown. This resulted in decisions which were vague and indecisive and which became the subject of disputed interpretations by the Secretariat. The result was often delay and confusion.[1] Final decisions were deferred from meeting to meeting —for further information, for conditions to improve, for a report from the Secretariat, and so on.

Beneath the veneer of unity each side was suspicious of the motives of the other. Anything which savoured of propaganda or politics was suspect. It may have been that ulterior motives were seen where none existed, but under conditions of mounting international tension it grew increasingly difficult to make distinctions between political and trade union acts. Deakin was suspicious of the desire of some members of the Executive Bureau to hold meetings of the Bureau in various parts of the world. When it was suggested that they should meet in Havana Deakin objected because he considered the Communists only wanted to go there to establish contacts and propagate their policy. The Executive Bureau, instead, met in Prague.[2] During its session there the members addressed a mass demonstration which was used to display and test the solidarity of Czechoslovakian trade unionists under Communist leaders and, Deakin believed afterwards, to hold a full-scale dress-rehearsal for the Communist *coup d'état* in February 1948. The presence of Deakin and other non-Communist trade union leaders at the demonstration helped to give credulous masses the impression the Communists wanted to convey to them—that their cause was an internationally supported one. To this extent Bevin's warning to Deakin was correct.

When the Executive Bureau met in Rome in May 1948 the Bureau members were invited by Di Vittorio to participate in a May Day demonstration of the strength of Italian trade unions. This time there was not such a ready response from Deakin and other non-Communists. They asked for details about the demonstration and agreed to go only on the fulfilment of specific conditions. This was

---

[1] So vague were some decisions that the Secretariat had to wait for the publication of the transcription of the Bureau proceedings to help it discover what was intended.
[2] In June 1947.

the last time the members of the Executive Bureau were invited to speak at a mass trade union demonstration in the town which was their meeting place.

A related matter was that of sending delegations to backward areas. 'One of the purposes of the W.F.T.U.', Deakin said, 'has been to send delegations to Asiatic countries, to African countries, to anywhere there is a possibility of establishing Communist contacts for the purpose of furthering the Soviet Communist philosophy.'[1] For almost three years negotiations were held in an endeavour to convene an Asiatic trade unions' conference. When the subject was discussed by the Executive Bureau on 24 November 1947 in Paris, Sidorenko, the Soviet Russian substitute delegate, suggested that the trade union organizations of Soviet Asia and Transcaucasia should be invited to the proposed conference. Immediately Sidorenko had stopped talking Deakin intervened in the debate and said that 'If the Executive Bureau were to accept such a proposal, it would only increase the fears, already existing in many Centres, that the purpose of this Conference was not to increase the trade union influence of the W.F.T.U. but to utilize this organization for political purposes. Such a measure would go far towards digging the grave of the W.F.T.U.'[2] Rostovsky, the Soviet assistant to Sidorenko, expressing surprise at the unexpected turn which the debate had taken, asked whether it was 'intended to draw a sanitary cordon of a political nature around the Soviet organizations'?[3] Both Deakin and Rostovsky were showing signs of strain and they hastened to cover what were obviously their true feelings. Deakin objected to the remark and asked Rostovsky to withdraw it, which he did.[4] The Asiatic conference never met.

Even where delegations were formed they functioned ineffectively because the members who composed them were unable to agree amongst themselves. This resulted, the General Council of the Trades Union Congress reported, 'because of the efforts of the Communist delegates to present the acts and policies of the Soviet authorities and of the Communist Parties as being of a purely democratic character, while seeking to represent everything done or said by the democratic nations of the West and by the Movements which supported them as being the desire of vile reactionaries'.[5] Because ideological differences permeated the Secretariat it became unsafe to entrust the compilation of a report to any one of its

[1] T.U.C. Report, 1948, p. 449.
[2] W.F.T.U. Executive Bureau Minutes, 24 November 1947, p. 86.
[3] Ibid., p. 88.
[4] This exchange plainly resulted from an error in translation. Rostovsky was referring to a 'cordon sanitaire'—a policy of insulation. Other difficulties were created by errors in translation.
[5] Supplement to Section G of the T.U.C. Report, 1954, p. 511.

members: it was likely to be inaccurate or incomplete and in any case was bound to create disagreement on the Executive Bureau.

The criticisms did not all emanate from the non-Communists. For example, Kuznetsov regarded delegations to various countries as disguised interventions in the affairs of those countries by the British Trades Union Congress. He said 'that the Soviet trade unions had always been opposed to interventions such as those which the T.U.C. had carried out under various forms'.[1] This drew Deakin to reply: 'It was not true that the T.U.C. had interfered in the affairs of any National Centre, but such a criticism could be made against it if it employed the same methods as the Soviet trade unions.' Annoyed by Kuznetsov's assertion, Deakin said that he would report it 'to his National Centre which would reconsider the question of its affiliation to the W.F.T.U.' At this point Kuznetsov interjected, 'Do not frighten us. Where did the U.S.S.R. interfere?' Deakin claimed that it was in Germany, but Kuznetsov said it was the British who had interfered in Germany, and in Greece and Japan. There was no end to this kind of argument.

Nor for that matter was there a satisfactory conclusion to the verbal exchanges on the Executive Bureau concerning matters involving Government action. Comparisons between countries were as black and white as far as the Communists were concerned. No Communist, whatever his nationality, criticized the actions or the motives of Communist-controlled Governments. The alignment of interests was unmistakably revealed by this and by the consequent defensive position in which non-Communists found themselves. The non-Communists on the Executive Bureau were a mixed group who were given a common identity and a common interest by the Communists. If any one of them found cause to criticize his Government, as sometimes one did, he was driven by the Communists' attitude to withhold his criticism and sometimes to veer round to defend those things which he had intended to criticize.

The Marshall Plan

The World Federation of Trade Unions became officially involved in the controversy surrounding the Marshall Plan through the activities of one of its affiliates, the Congress of Industrial Organizations. Mr. George Marshall's offer of substantial economic aid to Europe, made in June 1947, was regarded by the Congress of Industrial Organizations as a means of fulfilling one of the declared purposes of the Federation, namely the rehabilitation and reconstruction of war-ravaged countries, so it brought the matter to the notice of the Executive Bureau at a meeting on 20 November

[1] W.F.T.U. Executive Bureau Minutes, 17–21 September 1948, p. 58.

1947, and requested that James Carey should be allowed to make a statement on the Marshall Plan. This marked the beginning of a long political harangue.

From then onwards the restraint which had been used by Communists and non-Communists alike in their dealings with each other on the Executive Bureau gave way to a deeper reflection of their feelings and revealed the wide political schism which existed between them. It showed, too, the strength of the allegiance that the members of the Bureau held to the foreign policies of their respective Governments and how the troubles in the World Federation of Trade Unions were a small-scale version of international affairs.

The dispute at first was as to whether or not Carey should speak about American aid to Europe at the November session. Saillant wanted the matter deferred in view of the international situation and because national trade union centres were only at that moment defining their attitude towards the American offer. He said that Kupers had written to him in August, asking for the question to be inserted on the agenda of the Bureau, that he had given Kupers his personal opinion, and had then circulated the correspondence to the members of the Bureau who were asked to state their attitudes. Arthur Deakin had answered 'that he did not consider that any useful purpose would be served by inserting the question on the Agenda of the Bureau'.[1] But he had since changed his mind. He said at the meeting that 'he had long foreseen that, sooner or later, the W.F.T.U. would have to define its attitude towards this question'.[2] After consideration he had decided that it should be sooner rather than later. The matter was temporarily resolved by a vote of four to three in favour of hearing Carey's statement.

The Communists were implacably opposed to American aid to Europe. Having failed to prevent Carey making his statement, they resisted a discussion on its content on the ground that it was a matter for a more representative body than the Executive Bureau. They added later that the endeavour to discuss the Marshall Plan on the Executive Bureau was an attempt to turn the World Federation from its declared purpose into an agency of the American State Department.[3] The November session ended without taking a formal decision about the discussion of the Marshall Plan.

The General Council of the Trades Union Congress stated that if the Marshall Plan were not discussed by the middle of February, it would consider itself free to meet the national trade union centres of the sixteen countries which accepted the principle of the Marshall Plan

[1] W.F.T.U. Executive Bureau Minutes, 22 November 1947, p. 52.
[2] Ibid., p. 51.
[3] *Free Trade Unions Remain in the W.F.T.U.*, p. 36 (a pamphlet prepared by Saillant).

and to discuss it with them. Saillant said that the earliest date on which the Executive Bureau could meet was 1 April. This date was considered to be too late by the British General Council because it expected the American aid legislation to pass through the United States Congress during the first week in April and thought it important that the trade union movements in Europe should express an opinion on the proposed legislation before it became law. So a conference of national trade union organizations which approved of the Marshall Plan was held in London on 9 and 10 March 1948 and was attended by twenty-six organizations from fourteen countries. The restiveness of the non-Communists had shown the first signs of developing from verbal exchanges into a secessionist movement.

Administrative Difficulties

The difference in purpose between the two sides on the Executive Bureau was illustrated clearly by their attitudes to the administration of the World Federation. The British wanted an efficient and stable organization even if this entailed a contraction of its activities. The Communists on the other hand wanted a widely diffused organization which could be used for disseminating propaganda and for making contacts. In the first instance the Communists were more concerned about the spread of ideas than about fulfilling trade union needs. So the greater its affiliated membership, the more frequent its delegations to under-developed areas, and the more effective its publicity as an organ of propaganda, the more the World Federation suited Communist needs. It was to meet these needs rather than those of the British, or other non-Communists, that the administration of the World Federation developed under the influence of Louis Saillant.

The Communists' endeavour to use the World Federation for propaganda purposes in underdeveloped territories did not surprise the British, but they found it difficult to understand the purpose of the constant propaganda levelled against the non-Communist members of the Executive Bureau with whom the Communists were supposedly working in a common cause. In between meetings of the Bureau they were accused of various crimes against the working class. There was little difference in phraseology, or in intensity, between national and international abuse of Deakin and his colleagues. The British General Council stated that

confidence and goodwill . . . has been undermined by the way in which matters put forward for consideration are the subject of propaganda, if not before, then certainly after, any major questions are discussed. The stream of vilification and abuse which has been poured on the British T.U.C., American Labour and the leaders of those national centres who are not prepared to become subservient to Communist doctrine and dictation is not restrained by any desire to overcome inherent difficulties. . . .[1]

The British and the American trade union leaders were not, of course, uncritical of the Communists. The national and international policies they supported were, by nature and often by design, anti-Communist. If criticisms of the Marshall Plan by members of the Executive Bureau could be construed as propaganda, so could speeches and articles in its favour by Deakin and other non-Communists. The Americans engaged in anti-Communist propaganda and activities more openly than the British. Indeed, the anti-Communism of the British trade union movement was less sustained, less organized, and more determined by the needs of the organization of the World Federation than was that of most other non-Communist trade union centres; and it was certainly less intense than the pro-Communism of the Communist trade union centres.

As a critic of Communism, Arthur Deakin endeavoured to distinguish between his national and his international activities. He said that the 'Soviet Press had accused him of being anti-communist. It was quite true that in his own country he was connected with the anti-communist movement, but that was no concern of the W.F.T.U. He personally would never dream of reproaching other members of the Bureau with the attitude they might adopt in their own countries.'[2] He added that 'ideological or political differences were not considered an insurmountable obstacle to the smooth working of the organization when the W.F.T.U. was founded, and there was no reason why they should be considered so at this stage.' There were such reasons, of course. The whole temper of international relations had changed so much that it was possible to confuse who had been ally and who had been foe during the war. Deakin himself was involved in the change because he was emotionally tied to the foreign policy decisions of the Labour Government. Moreover, the fact that the Communists used the Federation as a political instrument could not easily be ignored during times of political crisis, for it meant that non-Communist resources were being used to assist in the fulfilment of Communist aspirations.

Arthur Deakin's position in the Federation was complicated by the dual responsibilities he carried. As president he was required to act with impartiality, and as the sole British representative on the Executive Bureau he was obliged to press what he considered to be the British point of view no matter how partial it was. In general Deakin was successful as a president. During meetings and conferences with Communist members of the Federation, over which

[1] *The T.U.C. and the W.F.T.U.* A Statement of Policy on the World Federation of Trade Unions by the General Council of the T.U.C., October 1948.
[2] W.F.T.U. Executive Bureau Minutes, 30 April–2 May 1948, p. 17.

10*

he had to preside, he acted with remarkable restraint and understanding.[1] There were no standing orders governing the procedure in meetings of the Executive Bureau, so the president had the responsibility of giving rulings in cases of procedural disputes, sometimes after prolonged arguments between the delegates.

The task of controlling the Executive Bureau, making sense of its deliberations, and implementing its decisions was made more difficult because there was no person on it who held the confidence of all the remaining members. Deakin was far from being considered an independent person. At the May 1948 meeting of the Executive Bureau he recited some of the accusations made against him. He had been accused in *Trud* on 11 February 1948 of collaborating with the Foreign Office to undermine the World Federation; he had been accused by the *New Times* of plotting with the American Federation of Labour to achieve the same end; and when in the previous November Kuznetsov had recommended the expulsion 'of all reformist or opportunist elements from the W.F.T.U.', in a statement to the All Union Central Council of Soviet Trade Unions, Deakin considered that Kuznetsov was referring to him.

To make matters more difficult for Deakin the balance of opinion, and therefore of voting strength, in the Executive Bureau was changing. After November 1947 both Jouhaux and Chu ceased to attend meetings of the Bureau. Jouhaux led the 'Force Ouvrière' and was no longer, therefore, a member of an affiliated organization, and Chu was replaced by the Communist Liu who was more extreme and colourful in his denunciation of American capitalism than any other Communist on the Executive Bureau. So although the voting strength of the Communists was reduced by the absence of Toledano, who was not replaced, they still possessed a majority of one in the Bureau. Issues were not normally voted on, though the British General Council reported, 'We have constantly found that the British and other representatives have prevented the adoption of proposals dictated solely by Communist political policy only by a flat refusal to continue discussions and by making it clear that if the political manœuvring went on the Federation would break.'[2]

For all this, Deakin refused to state in public that the World Federation was Communist-dominated until it was obvious that the Trades Union Congress could stay in it no longer. As late as 20 July 1948 he refuted the accusation that the World Federation

---

[1] This was stated by his colleagues and admitted by others not so friendly. One of the latter said: 'I do not often hand bouquets to Arthur Deakin. Sometimes I would much sooner throw a brick. But on the question of the World Federation it is a fact and it will go down in history that there would be no World Federation had it not been for the tolerance and the patience of Arthur Deakin.' (R. Edwards, General Secretary of the Chemical Workers' Union, T.U.C. Report 1948, p. 445.)
[2] *The T.U.C. and the W.F.T.U.* A Statement of Policy, op. cit.

was a Soviet tool.[1] But when he was compelled to report on his stewardship to the Trades Union Congress in September 1948, he admitted 'that the World Federation of Trade Unions is rapidly becoming nothing more than another platform and instrument for the furthering of Soviet policy'.[2] In the relative privacy of the Executive Bureau meetings he was candid at an earlier date.

Once the façade of unity had been rent by the dispute over the Marshall Plan and with little semblance of unity outside the meetings of the Executive Bureau, the British, American, and Dutch trade union centres no longer felt that they had to tolerate a misuse of resources simply to preserve appearances. So at the May 1948 meeting of the Executive Bureau they submitted a detailed criticism of the administration of the World Federation. The meeting was unlike any other meeting of the Executive Bureau, for it was the first at which the administration of the Federation was openly criticized and the last to be conducted without the general feeling that a split in the organization was inevitable.

The main points of criticism were made by Tewson. He deprecated the method of public polemics which had been used by members of the Bureau to express their views. 'The unity which the W.F.T.U. sought to establish in the world trade union movement should find its roots within its own executive', he counselled. The General Secretary was criticized for his lack of independence, for his tendency to roam about the world, and for his neglect of simple but important matters of administration. Much money had been spent, and wasted in Tewson's opinion, on delegations which had not functioned properly, as in Iran where the delegation waited three months for the arrival of its chairman; or which had failed to report, as in the case of the delegation to Japan; or which, like the delegation for Palestine, had not even set out. Tewson stated that whereas delegations gave the members of the World Federation an opportunity of making fresh contacts they also provided the trade unionists in the countries they visited with a means of measuring the effectiveness of the World Federation. Lastly, Tewson drew attention to the bias in the publications of the Federation. It should not, Tewson stated, be a function of a trade union centre to criticize its affiliated members, least of all to discriminate consistently against a group of them. The Trades Union Congress had often been the object of criticism but Tewson 'had searched in vain for a single article criticizing the organizations in certain other countries'.

The statement by Tewson was endorsed and in a few places amplified by Deakin. He said, for instance, that he and Rosenblum

[1] At the International Transport Workers' Federation Congress in Oslo, 19–24 July 1948.
[2] T.U.C. Report, 1948, p. 448.

had given Saillant advice in June 1947 about how to improve the administration. But it was still the case that when the General Secretary was absent 'there was no one in the W.F.T.U. who was fully conversant with the activities of the organization, and still less was there anyone capable of assuming the duties and responsibilities of the General Secretary. This applied even to the Assistant General Secretaries. It applied also to the Heads of Departments, who did not seem to have any clear idea of their duties and responsibilities.' Both Kupers and Carey confined their remarks to the political bias of Saillant. The only threat made during the meeting came from Carey, who declared that 'the W.F.T.U. was dead' and added in an intervention that 'the C.I.O. was sufficiently dissatisfied with the administration of the W.F.T.U. to withdraw from the organization'.

Most of the charges were either denied or answered by Saillant, Kuznetsov, and Di Vittorio. Some factors which related to the administrative efficiency of the Federation, Saillant pointed out, were beyond his control, and depended upon co-operation from members of the Executive Bureau and from national trade union centres. This had not always been given. The broader issues involved and the allocation of responsibility to other members of the Secretariat were dealt with by Kuznetsov. He thought it was unjust to condemn the work of the Secretariat so fully when it had received nothing but praise for three years. Kuznetsov then proceeded to deflect attention from the general secretary to Deakin and to two of the general secretary's assistants who were not Communists, W. Schevenels and E. Cope, and accused them of hindering the work of the administration.[1]

As was stated above, only Carey threatened to withdraw from the World Federation. Deakin, Tewson, Saillant, and Kuznetsov either absolved themselves from the accusation that they wished to divide the Federation or stated that they desired to preserve its unity. Both Tewson and Kuznetsov intervened a second time in the discussion to clear up misconceptions they might have caused and showed a desire to be conciliatory. Eventually, after a protracted session, agreement was reached over the contentious points. The friction was eased. The members congratulated each other on the way in which they had reduced 'the sphere of disagreement'. Even Carey, despite his earlier remarks, 'noted with particular satisfaction the unanimity which the members of the Commission had obtained' and said that a 'new era was now opening for the W.F.T.U'.[2] But once the non-Communist delegates were back in their respective

[1] Schevenels and Cope were responsible for the formation of the Trade Departments and the Colonial Department respectively.
[2] W.F.T.U. Executive Committee Minutes, 5–10 May 1948, p. 18.

trade union jobs where they could relate more objectively their own roles as international trade unionists to the situation of international tension, they realized that the unanimity was not durable and that the fundamental differences of approach to trade union questions taken by Communists and non-Communists remained untouched.

International Trade Secretariats

It was a condition of the British participation in the World Federation of Trade Unions that the International Trade Secretariats, each of which represented a distinct group of workers, such as the miners, transport workers, printers, and so on, should become Trade Departments in the World Federation of Trade Unions. This was stated by Citrine at the World Trade Union Congress in October 1945[1] and was emphasized on a number of occasions afterwards by Deakin or Tewson whenever the Executive Bureau discussed the formation of Trade Departments.

The importance of the British condition was clear. The International Trade Secretariats were independent bodies with clearly defined trade union functions, so that if they were not absorbed into the World Federation of Trade Unions there would be two distinct types of organizations catering for the international interests of workers.[2] Just as important was the fact that without the functions of the International Trade Secretariats the Federation would have no specific industrial tasks to perform and might, thereby, tend to indulge more easily in those controversial political activities which could only lead to disruption. It was Saillant's opinion in 1946 that without integration 'the World Federation of Trade Unions would be paralysed and impotent'.[3]

The obstacles in the way of fulfilling the condition were equally clear. Before the Second World War negotiations had been carried on between the International Federation of Trade Unions and the International Trade Secretariats in an attempt to secure the coordination of international trade union activities, but no solution had been reached. At that time no political divisions complicated the issue, for the Russian trade unions belonged neither to the International Federation nor to the International Trade Secretariats. The negotiations failed mainly because the Secretariats desired to retain their autonomy. The position was made more difficult by

---

[1] Cf. the World Trade Union Conference Congress Report, p. 33.

[2] The danger of this was expressed by Citrine when he said, 'If those organizations are not brought within the World Federation within the next twelve months or so they will inevitably be driven to foregather together, and form policies together, and before you know where you are you will have two internationals in fact if not in name.' (T.U.C. Report, 1946, p. 272.)

[3] T.U.C. Report, 1946, p. 399.

302 The World Federation of Trade Unions

the great disparity between the range of activities of the Secretariats. For most of them integration with the International Federation of Trade Unions would have entailed no material loss; indeed they had little to lose. But for the International Transport Workers' Federation the position was different. Its income was sufficient to allow it to undertake a full range of international work which was often greater than that of the International Federation of Trade Unions. For it, integration carried no gains, except the intangible benefits of increased unity. It did not remain aloof from the negotiations but its demands were always such that they could not be met. It remained the most influential of the Secretariats after the war and although its Congress in Zürich, 1946, accepted 'the principle of incorporation of the I.T.F. in the W.F.T.U.' and instructed its Executive Committee 'to continue negotiations with the Executive Bureau of the W.F.T.U. with a view to securing acceptable terms',[1] its terms remained of a highly individualistic nature.

The Article governing the formation of Trade Departments[2] was accepted at the Paris Congress in 1945 in the face of opposition from some of the delegates of the nineteen International Trade Secretariats represented there and from M. Oldenbroek, the Acting General Secretary of the International Transport Workers' Federation in particular. Oldenbroek represented the Trade Secretariats on the Administrative Committee which compiled the Draft Constitution for the World Federation and he opposed the Article at all its stages. He said that there was very little willingness on the part of the Administrative Committee to grant any freedom to the Trade Departments at all.

The intermittent meetings between representatives of the World Federation and the Trade Secretariats which were held between the Paris Congress and September 1948 followed a chequered course. For one thing the Executive Bureau took a long time to make up its mind. Delays, postponements, and affronts were suffered by the International Trade Secretariat representatives. An affront occurred during the first meeting between the Executive Bureau and representatives of all the Secretariats in December 1947. At the meeting it

[1] Proceedings of the International Transport Workers' Congress 6–12 May 1946, p. 210.
[2] Article 13 of the Constitution of the Federation stated in part: (1)—'It shall be the function of the Trade Departments to deal with technical matters concerning their trades. In this sphere they shall enjoy full autonomy within the World Federation of Trade Unions but they shall have no power to make decisions or carry on activities in connection with matters of general policy. . . . The Trade Departments shall be finally accountable to the General Council and the Executive Committee for their activities. . . . (2)—Subject to the provisions of paragraph 1 the aims, methods of work, duties, rights and finances of the Trade Departments shall be governed by a special regulation to be adopted by the Executive Committee and approved by the General Council. . . .' (Report of the World Trade Union Conference Congress, October 1946, p. 269.)

soon became clear that the overwhelming majority of the I.T.S. held substantially the same position as the representatives of the I.T.F., and as the W.F.T.U. was not in a mood to make any real concessions little headway was made. What little there was was upset on the third day, when the Russian delegates arrived, and Mr. Tarasov, speaking for all of them, informed the conference in no uncertain terms that what had been under discussion for a year was completely unacceptable from the Russian point of view. . . . The remainder of the conference was taken aback, and suggested that the governing bodies of the W.F.T.U. should first agree themselves on the terms to be offered to the I.T.S., after which negotiations could be resumed.[1]

It so happened that the composition of the Executive Bureau ensured that the main points of view concerning the integration of the Secretariats into the Federation would be expressed there. The two extreme positions were occupied by the Russians and the British, with the Americans disagreeing more with the British than with the Russians. Both the Russians and the Americans belonged to the group of trade union centres which had never participated in the work of the Secretariats and had little knowledge of their purposes, functions, or needs and could not appreciate the pride and loyalty with which the Secretariats were considered by their members. In the discussions, Arthur Deakin, representing the views of the British Trades Union Congress, adopted the attitude which was most in accord with that of the Secretariats and insisted that not in any circumstances would the British agree to exercising pressure on the Trade Secretariats.[2]

The main points of difference on the Executive Bureau were (a) the timing of the creation of the Trade Departments; (b) the site of their headquarters; (c) the methods of financing them; and (d) the right of Trade Conferences to elect Trade Department officials. Draft regulations were drawn up as a result of discussions between Saillant and Kuznetsov in Moscow and later between Deakin, Kuznetsov, and Schevenels in London. These were examined by the Executive Bureau in June 1947 and on most points agreement was reached. It was then that Deakin pressed for a speedy settlement because he believed that certain organizations 'sought to create a second international trade union movement based on the I.T.S.s'.[3] The method of financing the Trade Departments over which the Executive Bureau had been unable to reach agreement was resolved by a compromise suggestion from Rosenblum at an Executive

[1] International Transport Workers' Federation. Report on Activities and Financial Report, for the years 1946–1947, pp. 94–95.
[2] Proceedings of the International Transport Workers' Federation, 19–24 July 1948, p. 179.
[3] W.F.T.U. Executive Bureau Minutes, 3 June 1947, p. 20. Deakin did not state to which organizations he was referring, but one of them was probably the American Federation of Labour.

Committee meeting later in June. All the draft regulations were approved by the General Council of the World Federation in the same month and circulated to the affiliated members of the Federation for ratification.

It was assumed by Saillant that although the regulations had not been considered by the International Trade Secretariats, a settlement would automatically follow from the approval of the General Council.[1] This seemed to be a reasonable assumption, for the majority of the trade unions taking part in the International Trade Secretariats were also affiliated to trade union centres which were members of the World Federation. In the Federation they had made their decision; surely they would make the same decision in the Trade Secretariats. This did not happen. It was not because trade unions were speaking with two voices. The International Trade Secretariats had been in existence long enough to create their own impulses so that the decisions they reached could never quite be equated with the sum of the decisions of their affiliated members. Moreover, the individual trade unions which composed the Trade Secretariats did not always agree with the trade union centres which composed the World Federation.

When the regulations for the creation of Trade Departments were submitted to a meeting of Executive Bureau and International Trade Secretariat representatives on 18 and 19 August 1947 it was discovered that there were still many unsettled points, and further amendments were made to the regulations, including one relating to finance. The International Transport Workers' Federation found the situation virtually unchanged from when negotiations had first begun, but it was the most recalcitrant of the Secretariats. Integration, if achieved at all, was going to occur without the International Transport Workers' Federation.

When the further amended regulations came before the Executive Bureau in November 1947 it seemed that a settlement was in sight for a second time. Schevenels, the official responsible for Trade Departments, said that if the regulations were accepted by the Executive Bureau they would also be accepted by the International Trade Secretariats. But it was not to be. The Russians, Sidorenko and Rostovsky, refused to accept the two most important of the amendments and proposed that the decisions reached the previous June should be applied in disregard of the Trade Secretariats. This was an invitation to a breakdown in the negotiations. Saillant and Rosenblum, without going so far as the Russians, also displayed their impatience with the obdurate Trade Secretariats. Even Deakin believed that 'the Bureau had really done everything in its

[1] In a letter to Oldenbroek (cf. I.T.F. Report on Activities, 1946–1947, p. 97).

power to give full guarantees to the International Trade Secretariats
. . . and . . . if certain International Trade Secretariats still disagreed,
they should be disregarded'.[1] The regulations for the establishment
of the Trade Departments, except for one point about which the
Russians held reservations, were accepted by the Bureau as being in
their final form, despite a warning from Schevenels that even the
Trade Secretariats which were favourably disposed towards the
World Federation, such as the Miners' Secretariat, would not accept
the regulations as they stood. It was agreed to call a meeting with
the representatives of the International Trade Secretariats for not
later than 10 January 1948 to inform them of the decisions of the
Bureau, without considering any further amendments, and to consult
them about the manner in which Trade Conferences should be
convened as a first practical step towards the formation of the
Departments.

The International Trade Secretariats were sent copies of the final
regulations and were informed that the meeting between their own
and the Executive Bureau representatives was scheduled to take place
on the 12 and 13 January 1948. This information was contained in
a letter from Saillant on 8 December. On 23 December the meeting
was cancelled by telegram. 'No reason was given for the cancella-
tion', Oldenbroek reported, 'but the Marshall Plan, which the
Secretariat of the W.F.T.U. was attacking, had just come to the fore,
and there is little doubt that it feared that if the meeting was held
just then awkward questions might be asked.'[2] Such was the
growing tension between the Communists and non-Communists that
explanations did not have to accompany actions; everyone concerned had an understanding of the situation. It was recognized
that the integration of the Trade Secretariats could not be pursued
in disregard of the political troubles which beset the World Federation; indeed it was dependent upon their solution.

The political reasons which led to the inactivity of the World
Federation caused the International Trade Secretariats to stir
themselves. Their representatives who had negotiated with the
Executive Bureau met together on 12 March 1948 and decided that
(1) the final regulations were unacceptable; (2) the Trade Secretariats
should be informed of this decision and asked to continue with their
activities and to support one another in their work; (3) no Trade
Secretariat should enter into separate negotiations with the Federation; and (4) they should consult one another on issues wider than
their trade functions, such as on the European Recovery Programme.[3] With the initiative wrested from it and confronted by

[1] W.F.T.U. Executive Bureau Minutes, 20 November 1947, p. 13.
[2] I.T.F. Report on Activities for the years 1948 and 1949, p. 73.
[3] Cf. I.T.F. Report on Activities, 1946–1947, op. cit., p. 101.

these resolves with a sting in their tail, the Executive Bureau when it met in May 1948 was compelled to moderate its approach. It decided to call the meeting which should have met in January, not, as had been intended, to consider the step beyond the ratification of the regulations, but 'to enable . . . further consultations to take place'. As it happened, the International Trade Secretariats were not even in the mood for consultations.

BRITISH TRADE UNION OPINION

Most members of the General Council in 1948 were dissatisfied with the situation concerning the World Federation of Trade Unions; this was to be expected when they were contributing approximately £15,000 a year towards the maintenance of an organization intent on propagating Communist views. Some of the members believed that the Trades Union Congress should withdraw from the World Federation, but they feared that British trade unions would not agree to such drastic action. This view of British trade union opinion was tacitly accepted by the majority on the General Council, so, rather than be rebuffed on such a vital issue, the General Council reached no formal decision about its future relationship with the World Federation. In consequence the General Council had no desire to make a statement about the state of affairs in the World Federation when the Trades Union Congress met early in September 1948. When a motion appeared on the agenda of the Congress stating 'This Congress re-affirms its support of the W.F.T.U. and urges its representatives to resist attempts to destroy unity inside this body' and exhorting 'the delegates of the British Trades Union Congress to make every possible effort for the removal of whatever barriers there may be which are retarding the development of the W.F.T.U.', representatives of the General Council tried to persuade the sponsors of the motion to withdraw it. The General Council could not allow the motion to be debated without an opinion from the platform; nor could it truthfully give an opinion which did not show its impatience and inclination. The sponsors[1] refused to withdraw their motion. During the debate, Arthur Deakin, who was chairman of the International Committee of the General Council, was called upon to make a statement on behalf of the General Council. Only he knew its content. For all the members of the General Council the occasion had dramatic possibilities.

Deakin began with regrets, for this was to be his first public criticism of the World Federation of Trade Unions. Hitherto he

[1] The Amalgamated Union of Operative Bakers, Confectioners and Allied Workers and the Tobacco Workers' Union.

had spoken and written of the dangers of Communism, national and international, without directly implicating the World Federation.

> A fortnight ago [he said] the General Council through the Secretariat sought by correspondence and subsequently by discussions to point out how undesirable it was at this time to raise an issue of this character on the floor of Congress. I say . . . that the onus of responsibility for . . . some of the things that will have to be said, rests entirely with the sponsors and the Unions responsible for the resolution. . . . Who is responsible for this resolution? It stands in the names of two Unions, but . . . if the Communist Party had not decided the policy line we should have been able to persuade those Union representatives responsible to withdraw the resolution. [*Interruptions from the floor.*] I knew you would say it was untrue, but it so happens that some of the people with whom we have been discussing this resolution . . . are members of the Communist Party and are not free agents to depart from the Party line.[1]

Then he put his case. He said: 'there has been little or no agreement within the W.F.T.U. The only thing that we have been directing our energies to has been the preservation of the World Federation as a going concern, and that has not been easy. . . .' This had been caused by the attempted use of the organization by Communists for political ends. He told of the misrepresentation of the views of non-Communists, of abuse, and of other matters he considered relevant to his argument and pleaded with the delegates 'to reject this resolution and leave the whole question of the relationship of the T.U.C. with the W.F.T.U. in the hands of the General Council'. The speech, delivered with intense feeling—*The Economist* called it 'a speech of towering rage'—achieved its purpose. The resolution was overwhelmingly defeated.

The success of Deakin's speech was not so much determined by rhetoric or by its composition as by the manner in which its content tapped the sense of loyalty and self-respect of the delegates. No matter what the members of Congress thought of Deakin and Tewson as individuals, they were the British representatives and they were not being treated fairly by the Communists. Moreover, despite the rage, Deakin was moderate in his request; he asked only for plenary powers to be given to the General Council—a request which any group of trade union delegates would have wished for themselves in similar circumstances.[2]

---

[1] T.U.C. Report, 1948, p. 446. At a meeting of the Executive Bureau in the following January Deakin said: 'that it was precisely the Machiavellian tactics of the British Communist Party which had forced him to make such a speech'. (Executive Bureau Minutes, 17–22 January 1949.)

[2] A year later Deakin stated that he believed Congress would have agreed to disaffiliation if it had been asked to do this. (T.U.C. Report, 1949, p. 337.) But this was a judgment after the event.

SECESSION FROM THE WORLD FEDERATION OF
TRADE UNIONS

The days of the World Federation of Trade Unions as an all-embracing world trade union organization were plainly numbered once the Trades Union Congress had declared its attitude. The long drawn-out controversy (negotiation would be a misnomer) over the creation of Trade Departments was finally closed by a decision of the representatives of the International Trade Secretariats at their belated meeting with the Executive Bureau on 14, 15, and 16 September. Not one of the representatives found the regulations submitted by the Executive Bureau to be acceptable; nor did any of them offer any alternative regulations. The only suggestions they made were that the World Federation should delete from its constitution the Article dealing with Trade Departments or that the matter should be postponed *sine die*.[1]

Kuznetsov lightly dismissed the arguments for not proceeding with the integration of the Trade Secretariats. He asked: 'in a national organization are there not differences of opinion? Can there not be the same in an international organization?'[2] His case was based on an appeal to non-Communists to forget the differences they had with Communists for the sake of the ends they were pursuing. 'Our conference', he said, 'is so important that we must place ourselves above whatever complaints we may have to formulate against one another. . . . Our essential basis must be constituted by that which is useful to the working class. . . . If we had an organization which was stronger and more solid, it would be more advantageous to the working class. . . .' This was an argument of the 'Popular Front' type and many of the trade union leaders present had heard it before. They remained unmoved by it.

During the conference, which had consisted of statements from the Trade Secretariat representatives and occasional interventions from Kuznetsov, Deakin had acted in the mechanical role of chairman, intent on getting a final decision. He neither argued for the Executive Bureau nor acted as a conciliator. After the views of all the International Trade Secretariats represented had been heard the

---

[1] The collective opinion of the representatives was expressed most precisely by M. C. Bolle from the International Federation of Employees in Public and Civil Services when he said: 'I think it would not be facing the facts if we pretended, in view of the circumstances which have arisen since our previous meeting, that it was any longer a question of regulations. . . . What we have witnessed for the past eighteen months, even more than before, is a conflict of ideas within the W.F.T.U. about the very aims and methods of trade unionism, and it has begun to appear to many of us as idle even to try to reconcile those different ideas within the W.F.T.U.' (Report of Joint Meeting of the W.F.T.U. Executive Bureau and the representatives of the I.T.S., Paris, 14, 15, and 16 September 1948, p. 19.)

[2] Ibid., p. 27.

Executive Bureau held a short private session and emerged with three questions which Deakin submitted to the representatives. He asked: (1) 'Are you prepared to submit your suggestions or proposals concerning the present draft general regulations?' (2) 'Are you prepared to maintain contact with a view to arriving, by negotiations, at a satisfactory arrangement?' (3) 'Are you prepared to continue the study of this problem in a determined period of time?'[1] After an adjournment, Oldenbroek, who was the *rapporteur* for the representatives of the Trade Secretariats, said they were prepared to study the problem amongst themselves, otherwise their answer to each question was a negative one.

On the day following the conference the Executive Bureau met to consider a long and complicated agenda. All the matters which had provoked disagreement at previous meetings, such as the trade union situation in Germany, the Pan-Asiatic Trade Union Conference and, of course, the creation of Trade Departments, were listed for examination. There was not even a superficial air of cordiality at this meeting. They began with an argument over the unauthorized presence of a French Communist and they continued in the same vein over almost every item. There was no longer a disposition by the non-Communists to compromise for the sake of outside appearances. Over the question of Trade Departments they refused to accept a complete change in the Russian attitude on the ground that it had come two years late: over the German question they would not accept their own decision taken during the previous May in Rome because the situation in Germany had changed so much in the meantime; and Deakin made the unprecedented request that their disagreement about Germany should even be registered in the minutes. When Kuznetsov asked Deakin whether, over the question of the Trade Departments, the relations between the Trades Union Congress and the World Federation were near breaking point, Deakin replied 'Yes'.

Arthur Deakin reported to the October meeting of the General Council of the Trades Union Congress, and arising out of his recommendations it was decided to propose to the Executive Bureau that (*a*) the World Federation of Trade Unions should suspend its functions; (*b*) the organizations having fulfilled their constitutional financial commitments should reach agreement on the precise conditions of this suspension; and (*c*) trustees should be charged with the administration of the funds of the World Federation of Trade Unions, and should meet in twelve months' time or earlier in order to discuss the conditions in which an attempt to revive an international trade union organization could be made. The letter

[1] Ibid., p. 30.

containing the proposal also stated: 'The General Council have further decided that in the event of the W.F.T.U. refusing to agree to the suspension of its activities, a withdrawal of the T.U.C. must follow.'

The General Council seemed to be taking a roundabout route to get to its destination, for it could not seriously have thought that the Communists would agree to suspend an organization they virtually controlled. Commenting on the General Council proposal in November Deakin wrote: 'It would seem clear that the Communist Trade Union Movements in certain other countries are not prepared to accept this suggestion and it follows, therefore, that the T.U.C. will withdraw its affiliation.'[1] Moreover, Deakin's personal view was that the World Federation should cease its activities completely and that it was inconceivable that even in twelve months the situation could change sufficiently to justify a renewal of its functions. Why then did the General Council not take straightforward unilateral action and disaffiliate? It had the authority to do so and it had circulated the affiliated members of the Trade Union Congress with a policy statement which was, in effect, a case for disaffiliation. There was no doubt in the minds of many of the members of the General Council as to what the British relationship with the World Federation of Trade Unions ought to be, but on this occasion, as before the September Trades Union Congress, they were not prepared to commit themselves to a definite decision. Because the Trades Union Congress had been primarily responsible for creating the World Federation, the General Council was naturally reluctant to take a decision in the relatively sober atmosphere of its own deliberations which, at one stroke, would have caused the World Federation to split. If possible its members would have preferred the initiative to have come from elsewhere. As far as its own actions were concerned it reflected the disposition to appear reasonable even in the face of reality.

The British proposal was raised at the Executive Bureau meeting on 17 January 1949, and for almost two and a half days it was wrangled over. Arguments which were now commonplace were repeated by both sides more vehemently and vindictively than before. Each side saw nothing right in what the other side had done. The meeting began quietly with Tewson outlining the reasons for the proposal in a moderate, even optimistic, manner. It might be possible, he believed, for the Trustees who would operate the suspension to decide to resume activities in a year 'or at an earlier date, perhaps in two or three months—if conditions had become more favourable'.[2] But the conditions for a resumption

---

[1] T. & G.W.U., Report to G.E.C., 29 November 1948.
[2] W.F.T.U. Executive Bureau Minutes, 17–22 January 1949, p. 7.

were stiff ones that belied his optimism.   He said, 'if Governments
and nations could recapture that spirit of co-operation in the
winning of the peace as was evidenced during the war there would be
more fertile ground on which to continue our endeavours'.[1]   Deakin
did not share Tewson's optimism and said so.   But on all other
matters they were in agreement.   On the other side Kuznetsov acted
as an interrogator.   What were the motives of the Trades Union
Congress?   What time lapse was envisaged?   What were the
conditions for a resumption?   Who would be the arbiter to decide
that conditions had changed?   Such were the questions he put to
Tewson and Deakin.   Later in the meeting he gave his own answers.

The discussion warmed up as Carey, Di Vittorio, Kupers, and
Liu declaimed against the Communists or the Capitalists and against
each other, with no one looking for a solution, for events had gone
too far for that.   Indeed, it was revealed by Carey that the Congress
of Industrial Organizations had already taken the decision to disaffiliate from the World Federation of Trade Unions.   There were
a number of interjections from Deakin which he used both to put
his point of view and to chide the Communist speakers.   At no
point was he willing to make concessions and he became impatient
of the pointless continuation of the meeting.   He stated that it 'was
time to put an end to the comedy which was being played on the
Bureau, where they tried to give the appearance of agreeing in order
to avoid the obligation of taking an energetic decision'.[2]   An
amendment from Saillant which asked for the proposal to be transmitted to the deliberative organs of the W.F.T.U., namely to the
Executive Committee and the General Council, was rejected by
Deakin because it constituted another motion and previous notice
of it had not been given.   And he refused to accept the suggestion
put by Kuznetsov that the matter ought to be referred to a World
Congress for its decision, for the reason that the Communists would
be so much in the majority there that it would make a 'mockery of
democracy'.   When at last Deakin managed to press the British
proposal to a vote on 19 January the Communists refused to participate, so, the minutes record, 'The Chairman Deakin, Carey,
Kupers, followed by the other members of the British and American
Delegation, and by the Assistant General Secretary Cope, left the
room where the session was taking place.'[3]   That ended the British
connection with the World Federation of Trade Unions.

The sequel was described by Deakin in his report to his Union
Executive.

[1] Stated also in the memorandum which the General Council circulated to British
trade unions.
[2] W.F.T.U. Executive Bureau Minutes, 17–22 January 1949, p. 57.
[3] Ibid., p. 65.

Following my withdrawal from the Presidency, a Communist President was elected and a new Assistant Secretary of the same tendency has been elected to succeed Mr. Schevenels. In addition, it has been announced that the Secretary-General, Mr. Louis Saillant, has recently been in Prague for the purpose of making arrangements for the removal of certain branches of the W.F.T.U. into Czechoslovakia. And so it is very clear, I suggest, that the organization not only passes under the control of International Communism, but its activities are now to be conducted behind the Iron Curtain.[1]

In the same report to his Executive Deakin stated that the General Council of the Trades Union Congress had 'charged the International Committee with the responsibility of developing contacts with non-Communist Trade Union Centres for the purpose of setting up a new International'. This was an inevitable consequence of the withdrawal, as the Communists would otherwise have been left in sole charge of the field of international trade unionism. A preparatory conference was held on 25 and 26 June 1949 at which there were representatives of almost 43,000,000 workers. A new organization, the International Confederation of Free Trade Unions, was formed at a Constituent Congress in London in December 1949.

On a few occasions Kuznetsov had contemptuously reproached Deakin for being unrepresentative of the British workers. At the Executive Bureau meeting in January 1949 he had said that the liquidation of the World Federation of Trade Unions 'corresponded neither to the desires nor to the will of the workers, who would never forgive those who proposed it and would stigmatize them as splitters'.[2] This assertion was based on wishful thinking. There was no evidence up to that date that Deakin had acted contrary to British trade union opinion and when he reported to the Trades Union Congress in September 1949 on the British withdrawal from the World Federation of Trade Unions his behaviour in the sequence of events was supported by 6,250,000 votes to 1,017,000.

[1] T. & G.W.U., Report to G.E.C., 28 February 1949.
[2] W.F.T.U. Executive Bureau Minutes, 17–22 January 1949, p. 42.

Appendix I

SCHEME OF AMALGAMATION, 1920

1. NAME: The new Union shall be known as the *Transport and General Workers' Union.*

2. It shall provide for all the membership of the Unions becoming parties to the Scheme.

3. OBJECTS: Its objects will include the complete organization of Dock, Waterside, Clerical, Waterways, Road and Aerial Transport Workers, and such General Workers as are now members of the Amalgamating Unions and such others as from time to time may be accepted. The regulation of salaries, wages, hours of work, general conditions of employment, provision of strike, lock-out and victimization pay, legal protection and other benefits; promotion and support of Parliamentary action through the Labour Party, and Labour representation in Parliament, on Local Authorities, etc., educational work, research, publicity, etc.

4. CONSTITUTION: The constitution will take the following form:
   (a) *The General Executive Council* (which shall consist of all lay members). Elected: (1) One representative for each area by ballot vote of the whole area; (2) One representative from each National Group Committee; sixteen in all.

   (b) *National Group Committees as follows:*
   DOCKS, with a special sub-section for Coal Shipping.
   WATERWAYS, including estuaries and canals.
   CLERICAL, ADMINISTRATIVE AND SUPERVISORY.
   ROAD TRANSPORT, with sub-sections for passenger and commercial.
   GENERAL WORKERS, with special sub-section for Metal and
      Chemical Trades.

With further sub-divisions in each group where desirable for trade purposes.

5. LOCAL ORGANIZATION:
   (a) Area Committees.
   (b) Trade Committees.
   (c) Branches.

6. THE BRITISH ISLES will be divided into 11 areas as follows:
   (1) London and Home Counties.
   (2) South of England, including Channel Islands.
   (3) West of England.
   (4) South Wales.
   (5) Midlands.

(6) North-West coast, to include Cumberland, North Wales, Liverpool and Manchester.
(7) Scotland.
(8) North-East Coast.
(9) North Midlands and Yorkshire.
(10) East Coast.
(11) Ireland.

7. OFFICES: The new Union will have:
(a) A Central Office situated in London.
(b) A District Office for covering each area.
(c) Sub-offices within each area.

8. OFFICERS:
President.
Vice-Presidents.
Trustees.
General Secretary.
Financial Secretary.
Parliamentary Officers.
National Secretaries of Groups.
Organizers.
Area Secretaries (viz., Chief Officer in each area).
Assistant Secretaries.
Delegates.
Branch Officers.

9. OFFICERS' POSITIONS AND SALARIES: The new Union shall undertake to retain in employment, at not less than their existing salaries, all officers of the Amalgamating Unions who desire to accept office in the new Union. 'Existing' salaries to be regarded as those obtaining on or prior to October 6th, 1920. Advances granted after October 6th, 1920, and prior to the date of the commencement of the new Union, shall be subject to the approval and endorsement of the new Union.

In the event of any officer not desiring to accept office in the new Union, the Committee shall be empowered to make a compensatory arrangement.

The new Union will honour all obligations for pensions, grants, etc., to retired officers or others now in receipt of payment from the existing Unions, providing such retired officers have enjoyed the same prior to October 6th, 1920.

Any office becoming vacant by death or otherwise, the General Executive Council shall have power to decide whether it is necessary to fill the vacancy or not.

The new Union shall undertake the promotion of a superannuation fund for its officers and staff.

10. FINANCE: All funds, assets and properties (other than local funds, assets and properties which are distinct from the general funds of the Amalgamated Unions, and existing to meet benefits and liabilities apart from the benefits, etc., taken over by the new Union) of the Amalgamating

Unions shall become the property of the new Union, and be under the control of the General Executive Council.

Upon the new Union resulting from the Amalgamation being registered, the Amalgamating Unions will cease to exist.

The RULES will provide for proper methods of collecting subscriptions and forwarding to the area office for transmission to the Centre.

Sufficient sums will be banked in each area to meet current expenditure, immediate benefits, etc.

Local autonomy will be given in the area to incur expenditure (with reference to the Centre for confirmation) of moneys up to a given sum.

The new Union shall, during three months after registration thereof, give an opportunity to every member of the amalgamating Unions to decide either to:

(a) Contribute to the new Union at the same rate as previously to the old Union, in which case (subject to the minimum rate of contribution of 6d. per week and 6d. quarterage for males and a graduating scale for women, girls and youths to be provided for in the new Union rules) such member shall be entitled to his existing rates of benefit; or

(b) Pay the new rates of contribution and accept the new scale of benefits.

11. ALL NEW MEMBERS joining the organization must pay the new rates of contribution and accept the new scale of benefits.

12. INSURANCE: The new Union shall be empowered to create a department to enable it to:

(a) Administer Part I of the National Health Insurance Act;

(b) To arrange for a scale of contributions and benefits to enable it to administer the Unemployment Insurance Act, 1920.

13. CONTRIBUTIONS AND BENEFITS: The minimum contributions and benefits proposed are as follows:

Men's Contributions: 6d. per week, plus 6d. quarterage; in all £1 8s. per annum.

Men's Benefits: Strike, Lock-out and Victimization Benefit, £1 per week and 2s. for each child under the age of 14.

Death: Funeral Benefit £5, graduating to £10, according to length of membership.

Legal Protection.

Women's, Girls' and Youths' Contributions and Benefits: Graduating Scale to be agreed upon by the new Union.

Legal Protection.

14. AFFILIATION: The new Union will pay all affiliation fees to National and International Federations, Local Trades Councils or Labour Parties, as the case may be.

15. PROVISION will be made to provide for relief from contributions during certain periods of illness or incapacity and for payment of a smaller contribution when members are no longer able to work, which smaller contribution will confer the funeral benefit only.

16. THE PROVISIONAL COMMITTEE shall be empowered to provide (subject to the endorsement of the delegate conference):

(a) Higher scales of contributions applicable to the whole of the membership; or

(b) Occupational contributions and benefits.

(c) Provide opportunities to receive other organizations desiring to come into the new Union.

17. STRIKE AND INDUSTRIAL POLICY: The new Union shall, for the promotion of wage applications, working rules, etc., relegate the consideration and preparation of programmes, conduct of negotiations, etc., to the national trade and group committees, but the power to sanction strike action, authorize lock-out pay, and decide policy of the organization shall be vested in the General Executive Council. But in the event of a general strike being demanded, the General Executive Council shall call a National Conference fully representative of all groups in the Union.

18. The new Union shall undertake responsibility for and administration of all existing wage agreements and conditions, and shall honour same.

19. GENERAL CONFERENCE: In the event of the result of the ballot being in favour of amalgamation, there shall be called forthwith a delegate conference of the Amalgamating Unions. Such conference shall appoint:

(a) The necessary Provisional Officers.

(b) Provisional General Executive Council.

(c) Trustees.

(d) Decide date of commencement of the new Union.

(e) Decide method and arrangements for the transference of existing funds, assets and properties to the new trustees.

20. PROVISIONAL EXECUTIVE: The Provisional General Executive Council shall proceed forthwith to embody into definite rules the Scheme herein outlined, and such rules shall be submitted for final endorsement to an adjourned delegate conference, and on being so endorsed the new Union shall be registered, and the Provisional Officers and Provisional General Executive Council and Trustees shall continue to act as Officers, General Executive Council and Trustees of the new Union pending the election of persons to fill such offices in accordance with the rules of the new Union.

Appendix II

THE UNIONS WHICH FORMED THE
TRANSPORT AND GENERAL WORKERS'
UNION, 1922–1955

YEAR   NAME OF UNION

1922 Amalgamated Society of Watermen, Lightermen and Bargemen
1922 Amalgamated Carters, Lorrymen and Motormen's Union
1922 Amalgamated Association of Carters and Motormen
1922 Associated Horsemen's Union
1922 Dock, Wharf, Riverside and General Workers' Union
1922 Labour Protection League
1922 National Amalgamated Labourers' Union
1922 National Union of Docks, Wharves and Shipping Staffs
1922 National Union of Ship's Clerks, Grain Weighers and Coalmeters
1922 National Union of Vehicle Workers
1922 National Amalgamated Coal Workers' Union
1922 National Union of Dock, Riverside and General Workers
1922 National Union of British Fishermen
1922 North of England Trimmers' and Teemers' Association
1922 North of Scotland Horse and Motormen's Association
1922 United Vehicle Workers
1922 Belfast Breadservers' Association
1922 Greenock Sugar Porters' Association

1923 Dundee Jute and Flax Stowers' Association
1923 North Wales Craftsmen and General Workers' Union
1923 North Wales Quarrymen's Union
1923 Scottish Union of Dock Labourers

1924 United Order of General Labourers

1925 Association of Coastwise Masters, Mates and Engineers

1926 Weaver Watermen's Association
1926 Irish Mental Hospital Workers' Union
1926 National Amalgamated Union of Enginemen, Firemen, Motormen,
       Mechanics and Electrical Workers

1928 Cumberland Enginemen, Boilermen and Electrical Workers' Union

1929 Workers' Union

YEAR   NAME OF UNION
1930 Belfast Operative Bakers' Union
1930 Northern Ireland Textile Workers' Union

1933[1] London Co-operative Mutuality Club Collectors' Association
1933   Portadown Textile Workers' Union
1933   Scottish Farm Servants' Union

1934   'Altogether' Builders' Labourers and Constructional Workers' Society
1934   Scottish Busmen's Union

1935   National Winding and General Engineers' Society

1936   Electricity Supply Staff Association (Dublin)
1936   Halifax and District Carters' and Motormen's Association

1937   Power Loom Tenters' Trade Union of Ireland
1937   Belfast Journeymen Butchers' Association
1937   Scottish Seafishers' Union

1938   Humber Amalgamated Steam Trawlers' Engineers and Firemen's Union
1938   Imperial War Graves Commission Staff Association

1939   Port of London Deal Porters' Union
1939   North of England Engineers' and Firemen's Amalgamation

1940   National Glass Workers' Trade Protection Association
1940   Radcliffe and District Enginemen and Boilermen's Provident Society
1940   National Glass Bottle Makers' Society

1942   Liverpool Pilots' Association

1943   Manchester Ship Canal Pilots' Association

1944   Grangemouth Pilots' Association

1945   Leith and Granton Pilots
1945   Dundee Pilots
1945   Methil Pilots

1946   Government Civil Employees' Association

1947   Liverpool and District Carters' and Motormen's Union

[1] In 1933 the National Union of Co-operative Insurance Society Employees affiliated to the Union for benefits. It registered separately and conducted its own internal administration apart from benefits. Previously it had had an agreement with the National Union of Distributive and Allied Workers.

INDEX

Administration, 5; of branches in amalgamation, 44; efficiency of, 212–19; costs of, in T. & G.W.U., 237–9, 262, 263; scope for improvement in, 240 et seq.; bureaucracy a form of, 260–1

Administrative Behaviour (Simon), 56n, 257n, 267n

Administrative Leadership, 212 et seq.

Affiliation (s), 65, 66, 70, 126, 271, 294, 296

Agreement (s), 47, 95, 98, 228n; rejection of, 29–30, 58; with amalgamating unions, 49, 54, 78; and dockers, 58, 60, 175, 187, 188n, 190, 193, 195, 207; London busmen, 66, 164; sanctity of, 93, 168–9, 207; and Parliament, 104, 144, 147, 148; and security of employment, 114–15; sliding scale, 121, 133, 136–7

Agricultural Workers, N.U. of, 51

Aims of Leaders, *see* Objectives.

Allan, William, 14, 40n

Amalgamation, resulting in T. & G.W.U., 40–9; difficulties in way of, 40–1, 42; of transport unions, 42 et seq.; policy of, 49–53; for specific services, 49; special agreements instead of, 50; aftermath of, 56–75; benefits of, 57; threat to, 58; difficulties with Scottish dockers, 60–3; after 1940, 155 et seq.; value of, 210–11; and size of union, 223; increases costs, 238

Amalgamation Scheme for T. & G.W.U., 45, 73, 313–16

American Federation of Labour, 43, 50n, 77, 290n, 298, 303

American trade union leaders, in W.F.T.U., 289 et seq.

Ammon, C. G. (Lord), 24n

Anglo–Soviet Trade Union Committee, 289

Appeals, 161 et seq., 176n, 185, 286 et seq.

Applegarth, Robert, 14, 18, 19, 20, 22, 35

Arbitration, 118, 121, 248

Arbitration tribunals, 42, 118, 119; *see also* National Arbitration Tribunal

Arbitrator, 119

Arnot, R. Page, 21n, 95n, 96n

Arrears, 72, 240, 241, 242

Arthur Henderson (Hamilton), 31n, 34n

Assistant General Secretary, 60, 76, 80, 252, 255–6, 270

Astor (Lord), 99n

Attlee, C. R., 36n, 90, 125 et seq.

Authoritarianism, 111–12, 257

Autonomy, 7, 62, 63; of unions, 41, 42, 49; of trades in T. & G.W.U., 74; of International Trade Secretariats, 301 et seq.

Bakers, Confectioners & Allied Workers, Amal. Union of Operative, 51, 306n

Bakers' Union, Belfast Operative, 318

Baldwin, Stanley, appeals for industrial peace, 99–100

Ballots, 45, 49, 50, 53, 54, 60, 143, 228; for general secretaryship of T. & G.W.U., 77, 109; postal ballot of Executive Committee, 86; in dock strikes, 201–2

Barnes, George, 23

11—T.U.L.

defence of profits, 131; opposed
to national minimum wage, 131;
acted in interest of members,
133–5; and rejection of wage
restraint 138–9; against a re-
allocation of wages, 140; political action of, 141–54; political
background of, 145; political
behaviour of, 146 et seq.; loyalty
to Labour Government, 151–2;
cautious about amalgamation,
155; and London busmen, 167–
171; and the sanctity of agreements, 168–9; and docks' negotiations, 174; and docks decasualization, 176–7, 183, 193;
and dockers, 189, 196; loyalty of
to officials, 189–90; and dock
strikes, 200, 201; supports Dock
Labour Scheme, 202–6; defends
joint control, 204–5; and secession of dockers, 206 et seq.; and
membership changes, 228–9; as
administrator, 230 et seq.; influenced by Bevin, 230–1; keeps
check on finance, 232 et seq;
little interest in administrative
methods, 239–40; and union
education, 243–5; unable to
devolve authority, 245–6, 253–9;
controls union salaries, 246–9;
relationship with G.E.C., 249–52;
attitude to centralization, 266;
and Union communications,
266–9; and Communist trade
unionists, 270–88; early experience with Communists, 270–
271, 272; reasons for anti-
communism of, 274–80; argued
with Communists on G.E.C.,
278–9; and political proscription,
281–4, 287; and World Federation of Trade Unions, 289–312;
President of W.F.T.U., 289–90;
suspicious of Communist motives,
292–4; position complicated on
Executive Bureau, 297–8; Communist accusations against, 298;

in negotiations between I.T.S.s
and W.F.T.U., 301–6; condemns
W.F.T.U. at T.U.C., 306–7; in
secession from W.F.T.U., 308–
312; supported by the T.U.C.,
312
Deal Porters Union, Port of
London, 318
Decision-making, 1, 111, 146, 212;
ethical basis of, 15, 17, 25–6; and
members, 84; in Labour Party,
89; in General Strike, 95 et seq.;
and dockers, 180; prescribed by
constitutions, 214–15; a trade
union leader and, 218–19; Deakin
and, 259, 267, 268; in T. &
G.W.U., 264, 266, 288; influence
of top administrators on, 268–9;
and W.F.T.U., 304
Delegations, 84
Democracy, in a union, 83–6
Denationalization (Act), 149
Devaluation and Wages (T.U.C.),
136
Devenay, W., 46
Dickenson, P., 53n
Differentials, 125, 128, 137, 170
Dilution, 103, 158
Direction of labour, 132
Disciplinary action, 69, 70, 176,
183, 185–6, 202 et seq.
Dispute in London Docks 1954,
Court of Inquiry into, 193n, 194n
Distributive & Allied Workers,
N.U. of, 33n, 318n
Di Vittorio, G., 291, 292, 300, 311
Dockers, 5, 57; troublesome be-
haviour of 58–63, 112, 134; earn-
ings of, 181–2, 187; guaranteed
earnings of, 182–3; and National
Dock Labour Scheme, 183–6,
205; use of strike weapon, 190–
202; impatience with formality,
191–2; lack of understanding of,
192–5; and wage restraint, 195–6;
solidarity of and fear of black-
legging, 196–8; and strike spreading, 198–202; secede from T. &

General Secretaries, *see* Trade Union Leaders

General Executive Council (G.E.C.) of T. & G.W.U., 58, 59, 81, 92, 97, 104, 153, 155, 163, 164, 170, 177, 207, 208, 209, 230, 232, 267, 283n; attitude to expulsions, 71; Bevin secured backing of, 83, 84, 85–6; and wage restraint decision, 135–6; role of in war, 220; releases officials, 221; and control of costs, 237 et seq.; and union salaries, 246–9; relationship with Deakin, 249–52; Communists on, 135, 250–1, 271–4, 279–80, 281; and protests against proscription, 285–6

General Labourers National Council (National Federation of General Workers), 32n, 41

General & Municipal Workers, N.U. of, 33n, 34, 42n, 43n, 50n, 51, 56, 86n, 125n, 156, 172n, 237, 242n, 247

General Labourers, United Order of, 317

General Strike, 49, 51, 52, 54, 86, 90, 103, 191n, 238; to prevent war, 87; role of Bevin in, 94–8; aftermath of, 98–9

General Union (Clegg), 42n, 242n

General unions, 56

General Workers, National Union of, 23n, 43, 51

Glasgow docks branch, 60–3

Glass Bottle Makers' Society, National, 318

Glass Workers Trade Protection Assocn., National, 318

Goldstein, Joseph, 241n

Gosling, Harry, 26, 27n, 43, 44n, 45, 46, 47, 76, 151n, 255; Bevin's attempt to depose, 78-9

Government (State), *see* also under Labour Government and Conservative Government, 6, 7–8, 19, 42, 52, 86, 96, 98, 99, 134, 137, 139, 277; openings for

union leaders, 20 et seq.; union leaders in, 21, 23; collaboration with, 23–4; attitude towards unions in war, 25; and distribution of Honours, 30, 32, 37; Labour, 79, 80n, 114; Coalition, 83n, 174, 226; appeals to unions, 103–5; wages policy in war, 117–121; post-war collaboration with unions, 122; asks for restraint, 125 et seq.; assurance of price control, 129; and union interests, 141, 145; consultation with T.U.C., 150; uses union officials, 221–2; and Communists, 281

Government Civil Employees' Assocn., 318

Government of British Trade Unions, The (Goldstein), 241n, 242n

Gowing, M. M., 120n

Group behaviour, 5, 57, 159; of London busmen, 160 et seq.; of dockers, 190 et seq.; of communists, 276

Guile, Daniel, 14

Hall, Lord, 34n

Hallsworth, John, 33n

Hamilton, Mrs. M. A., 31n, 32, 34

Hammond, R. J., 120

Hansard, 125n, 128n

Hardie, Keir, 22

Hargreaves, E. L., 120n

Henderson, Arthur, 23n, 24, 25, 31, 34, 142n

Henderson, Joseph, 33n

Hetherington, Sir Hector, 178n

Hicks, George, 100

Hillman, Sydney, 290

Hirst, Stanley, 45, 76, 78, 230

History of Trade Unionism (Webb), 21n, 23n

History of the United Society of Boilermakers (Cummings), 21n

Hodge, John, 23n, 24, 98

Hodgson, Mark, 33n